Portrait of an
Early American Family

The Shippens of Pennsylvania
Across Five Generations

RANDOLPH SHIPLEY KLEIN

University of Pennsylvania Press
1975

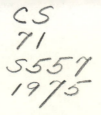

CS
71
S557
1975

*Publication of this book
has been made possible by a grant
from the Haney Foundation
of the University of Pennsylvania*

Library of Congress catalog card number: 75-10128

ISBN: *0-8122-7700-7*

Printed in the United States of America

Table of Contents

Illustrations

Abbreviations

APS   American Philosophical Society
HSP   Historical Society of Pennsylvania
LC   Library of Congress
MHS   Maryland Historical Society

Preface

The generations of the Shippen family which wrestled with life in colonial and revolutionary Pennsylvania, their various activities, successes, and failures, are the subject of this study. The Shippens will be treated as a family rather than as individuals, for that is how they generally functioned. Indeed to treat them solely as individuals would be to lose contact with significant aspects of their reality. Although each member of course had an individual identity, all acknowledged an overriding allegiance to the Shippen family. The structure, functions, style, and meanings of the Shippen family itself changed during the course of the century and a half examined. Despite these changes, the family remained important to its members and influenced their activities. Because the Shippens made a considerable impact upon the society in which they lived, a knowledge of the workings of the family is essential to a better understanding of their society; even those who led obscure lives must be recognized and considered in order to create a thorough understanding of the generations of the Shippen family which flourished before the end of the eighteenth century.

There are many reasons for examining the Shippen family. First, despite the importance of families in colonial society, study of the family in colonial America is a neglected field of inquiry. Second, an analysis of this family provides new insights into many perplexing problems of social history. Other approaches to those questions seem inadequate. Finally, abundant family records exist at the Historical Society of Pennsylvania, the American Philosophical Society, and the Library of Congress. Together they comprise one of the most thorough collections of manuscripts concerning an eighteenth-century family of Pennsylvania. That the records survived attests to the great eminence and power which the Shippens achieved during their first century and a half in America. They were one of the great families not merely of colonial Pennsylvania but of colonial America as a whole. They are on the same level of importance as the Pinckneys and Manigaults of South Carolina, the Byrds, Lees, and Randolphs of Virginia, the Livingstons of New York, and the Hutchinsons and Winthrops of Massachusetts.

It is remarkable that no scholarly study has yet been made of the family which produced so many prominent figures. The founder Edward Shippen was a provincial councillor; his grandson Edward, the dominant figure of Lancaster County; the greatgrandchildren Edward, Jr., and Joseph, Jr., eminent provincial officeholders; and after the War for Independence Edward, Jr., was chief justice of Pennsylvania while his cousin Dr. William Shippen, Jr., who had been director-general of hospitals during the American Revolution, was physician to President Washington. Although the family as a whole merits attention, it is deplorable that not one of these prominent men has received serious biographical treatment in a full-length study.*

The natural beginning of this study is with Edward Shippen, the immigrant, and the sparse information which deals with his English background and early activities in New England. Because a success-

---

*In *Meeting House and Counting House: The Quaker Merchants of Colonial Philadelphia, 1682–1763* (New York, 1963), p. 261, Frederick B. Tolles decries the general lack of full-scale biographies of eighteenth-century Philadelphians. Despite some efforts to eliminate the problem, progress seems slow. For example, not until 1966 was a full-length study of the Shippens' Cousin William Allen, one of the most significant leaders of the Proprietary party completed. Norman S. Cohen's "William Allen, Chief Justice of Pennsylvania, 1704–1780" (Ph.D. dissertation, University of California at Berkeley, 1966), remains unpublished. Betsy Copping Corner's *William Shippen, Jr.: Pioneer in American Medical Education* (Philadelphia, 1951), is only a sketch of certain aspects of the doctor's life. It is not a full-scale biography, and the author makes this clear in her introduction. Not long ago William S. Hanna, in *Benjamin Franklin and Pennsylvania Politics* (Stanford, 1964), p. 225, observed, "The Shippen Papers are a virtually untouched mine of information."

ful family study will analyze the developments which take place over time, it seems several generations require attention. Although the family records make it possible to study the Shippens from their arrival in the New World in the seventeenth century, through their rise to eminence in the eighteenth century, to their relative decline in the nineteenth century, I rejected that alternative. In this case, concentration upon four generations and attention to related and pertinent aspects of the fifth is adequate. Around the close of the eighteenth century, as members of the third and fourth generations died, a particular phase of the history of the Shippen family drew to an end. Reorientations within the family and alterations in the structure began to launch a new chapter in the family's history.

Acknowledgement

I wish to express my gratitude to the librarians and staffs at many institutions. In particular, sincere appreciation goes to my good friends Whitfield J. Bell, Jr., Murphy D. Smith, and William Spawn at the American Philosophical Society; Peter Parker and Vilma Halcombe at the Historical Society of Pennsylvania; Paul Sifton at the Library of Congress; and Hannah Roach at the Genealogical Society of Pennsylvania; thanks also to the helpful people at the Arch Street Meeting House, William L. Clements Library, Friends' Historical Library, Lancaster County Court House, Library Company of Philadelphia, Maryland Historical Society, Pennsylvania Land Record Office, Philadelphia City Hall Archives, and Philadelphia Recorders of Wills and Deeds.

For permission to use and quote the Shippen Family Papers on deposit at the Library of Congress, I am indebted to Edward, William B., and Florence H. B. Shippen.

I extend special thanks for valuable advice, criticism, and encouragement to Whitfield J. Bell, Jr., Richard M. Brown, Henry J. Young, Robert Erwin, Larry Gerlach, Philip J. Greven, Jr., Maryann G. Klein, Maurice Lee, Jr., Richard P. McCormick, and Matilda Riley.

Randolph S. Klein

⟻⟶⟻ I ⟶⟻⟶

The Family Connection

During the past decade the most important new development in the field of American colonial scholarship has been the emergence of a body of studies oriented toward demography, family history, and the process of modernization. Certain historians and sociologists provide particularly useful suggestions on how to proceed. Some family studies offer additional approaches, and in this instance the material on the Shippen family itself helps delineate the area of inquiry. What historians and sociologists urge is study of the family's structure and external relations as well as its economic base, life style, and political activities. Essentially they ask how a family perpetuates itself and transfers position through time. A generational approach is thus required. One must seek to discover patterns and changes in them.[1]

Clear evidence of the need for fresh insights into colonial society and the way it operated appears in the current tendency to rediscover sharp conflicts in the past while rejecting the explanations of simple class cleavages which do not hold up well under careful scrutiny. Close attention to the activities and motivations of merchant and professional families can make many of these conflicts more intelligible. Furthermore, some of the most tantalizing problems in social history involve economic, social, and geographic mobility, demography, and interpersonal relationships. Finally, there are unresolved questions about the nature of the social and political structure of colonial America. This study of the Shippen

1

family comments upon these concerns in significant or suggestive ways.

First, however, there is the pressing matter of a definition of family. Until recently historians have assumed that the colonial family was originally "extended" rather than "nuclear"; that is, many kinsmen such as uncles, grandparents, cousins, and so forth functioned as a family, not simply a couple and their dependent children. Many believe, however, that dislocations accompanying colonization altered the character of the traditional English family and attempts to recreate the essential institution in its usual form miscarried. They conclude that by mid-eighteenth century the family contracted to an isolated nuclear core and fundamental consequences ensued. Among the most important, the individual's view of society changed, for now one "saw it from without rather than from within; from an unfixed position not organically or unalterably secured."[2]

More recently, one authority has claimed that the thrust of studies of the family indicates that it "is almost certainly false that the colonial family was, initially at least, 'extended' rather than 'nuclear.' "[3] He uses a formal definition of family to mean household; however, his article pays no attention to an informal group which may have existed and have had considerable influence over the towns he studies.

Philip J. Greven, Jr., uses a more subtle definition of family, and concludes that the extended family—which was usually composed of conjugal units living separately while also retaining significant economic and emotional ties to one another—existed in Andover, Massachusetts.[4] Greven's definition makes sense when applied to the Shippens; it is the definition used in this study.[5] Within the first generation in America the Shippen family became an extended family, in that more than the parents were closely concerned in the material and emotional well-being of children, various Shippens were engaged in business activities together, and they were generally in close contact with one another. Although particulars varied through time, the Shippen family remained structurally and functionally extended throughout the period; except for the lapse during the second generation, the kinship network was expanding and the family was taking on more significance.

Despite the pleas of Carl Bridenbaugh, Bernard Bailyn, and others, not many historians have explored the colonial family. The field is relatively new, hence, the bibliography, not large. Although useful family studies have appeared, none provides a model which is in all ways satisfactory.

The perplexing problems of social history which receive attention in this study may be comprehended by focus upon three major questions, from which many subsidiaries flow. First, how was the family structured and how did it function? Second, how did the family attain its position in colonial society? Finally, how did the family try to maintain its position and to what degree did it succeed? Edmund Morgan's *Puritan Family* considers at length the first basic question of this study of the Shippen family. For the second two questions, John Waters's *The Otis Family,* Alice Kenney's *The Gansevoorts,* James B. Hedges's *The Browns of Providence,* Richard Dunn's *Puritans and Yankees,* and Aubrey Land's *The Dulanys* are among the more useful historical studies.[6]

Despite the useful suggestions which may be obtained from these authors and the value of their works to an understanding of many aspects of the colonial period, there are weaknesses in them as studies of the family. These authors' primary interest lies in the public careers or activities of the people they study. Personal and family relationships rarely receive close or extended attention, and analysis of family structures is rarely pursued.

In short, although at present we know some things about certain families, we do not yet have a comprehensive account of any. As a result, historians still know very little about either colonial families or how they functioned. Even combinations of the approaches and insights of these historical accounts will not produce an entirely satisfactory account.

The present study of the Shippen family will resemble in some ways these and other studies, yet it seeks to do certain things which they do not attempt. Most of the differences revolve about the approach of dealing with the Shippens as a family. To achieve this, it becomes necessary to draw upon insights derived from sociological studies of the family and kinship. An elaboration of the questions posed in this study of the Shippens reveals the benefits of consulting other branches of the social sciences.

A family's history cannot be comprehended by recounting the deeds of the eminent few. The lives of every member of the family must be reconstructed as fully as possible. So-called failures, insignificant figures, or marginal characters cannot be casually ignored. Frequently the success of certain members of a family is tied to the fate of the lesser members. In any case, a family reconstituted as thoroughly as possible seems the only sensible basis for analysis and the only foundation of any successful family study. By prosopographically weaving together biographies of numerous individuals, it becomes possible to transcend them and provide an overall family-history perspective. Prosopography is an important tool for use in family history.[7]

The study of any family demands answers to questions regarding structure and family patterns. How was the family defined? How did it function? What relationships existed within the family? What roles did members of the family play, especially what was the role of the patriarch? It is evident that relationships between parents and children, among siblings, of uncles and aunts with nephews and nieces, among cousins and other kin existed. It is important to analyze these relationships as closely as possible and to indicate the influence which the family had upon its members. The degree of family cohesion at various times must also be determined. Furthermore, political and economic ties were particularly important in reinforcing bonds of kinship. Careful scrutiny of these bonds is therefore essential.

Beyond this there is the question of what made a Shippen a Shippen. This deals with questions raised by Bernard Bailyn concerning the way in which a family interest or identity, apart from the name itself, transferred itself across generations. Presumably physical monuments such as large town houses, country seats, portraits, and silver plate could reinforce a sense of family continuity through time.

Bernard Farber's concept of the "symbolic estate" is more intriguing.[8] For many modern families, the family history or collective biographies of its members prove the most powerful force for perpetuating family identity. It preserves coherence even when members of the family become physically separated. This "symbolic estate" involves not only a "reference ancestor," an individual whose real or imaginary accomplishments receive attention from all descendants, but also the accomplishments of all that individual's descendants, including the living generations.

Several hints make further efforts to discover a "symbolic estate" worthwhile. With the exception of the second generation, public service, usually in an appointive office, characterized eighteenth-century Shippens. The importance of offices of distinction to the family and also the importance of family in securing these positions is both significant and fascinating.

Furthermore, the Shippens named their children after members of the family. For example, five Edward Shippens, five Joseph Shippens, and three William Shippens lived in Philadelphia before the American Revolution. The Shippens tried to eliminate confusion arising from the redundancy by the use of "Sr.," "Jr.," "3d," or middle names. Although that alternative lessened the confusion, it did not eliminate it. For example, when William Shippen, Jr. [III] went to England, he dropped the "Jr." following his name. When Edward Shippen, Sr. [III] died, his eldest son (Edward Shippen IV) became "Sr.," and Edward 3d [V] became "Jr."; yet at times correspondents failed to make the necessary adaptations. Even before that both Edward III and Edward IV were often addressed or referred to as "Edward Shippen, Esq." In order to avoid most of the inevitable befuddlement, it becomes necessary to reassign ordinal designations affixed to the names. In this study the man usually known as "Edward Shippen, Sr." or "Edward Shippen of Lancaster" will be referred to as "Edward Shippen III"; "William Shippen, Jr." becomes "William Shippen III," and so forth.[9]

Naming children after members of the family is only one pattern in the Shippen family. Throughout this study many family patterns and changes through time will receive careful analysis.

There is the question of how the Shippens attained their position in or near the upper ranks of colonial and revolutionary society. Specifically, it is important to know how the Shippens made their money, the degree of economic mobility they enjoyed, what careers various members of the family followed, and the reasons for their decisions.

Clearly the society in which they functioned helped delineate their course of action. Although Edward Shippen emigrated to

Boston, a society in transition from a Puritan orientation to a Yankee one, the merchant's conversion to the Society of Friends precluded his full participation in benefits he might otherwise have derived from being a successful merchant with some useful connections in England. His move to Pennsylvania greatly enhanced his stature, and as one of the first men of great wealth, who had useful family connections in Philadelphia and had suffered for "the Truth," he benefited from political and economic opportunities in the new Quaker colony.

The Shippens gradually broke with the Society of Friends; yet in time the increasingly heterogeneous nature of the province enabled them to return to power during the third generation. The fourth generation helped lauch the rise of the professions in Philadelphia and Pennsylvania. As highly trained specialists, Edward IV in law and William III in medicine benefited from being among the first capable of meeting an increasing demand for specialized services.

The Shippens however relied on more than special training or simply seizing new opportunities which changing social and economic conditions offered. The family functioned as an important means of educating and motivating its members, and launching them into the world. At crucial times the family's political connections, financial power, and educational talents helped propel upward members of the kinship network. Although hard work and general opportunities for upward mobility often played a significant role, they did not encompass the entire picture.

The functioning of the family in the advancement of the members of this kinship network proved so important that it calls into question traditional methods of measuring social and economic mobility. The traditional approach to historical figures as individuals often turns out to be a misleading preconception. Many figures in the colonial and revolutionary period of Pennsylvania can be understood only if their actions are seen in the larger context of the family. In particular, methods of career-line analysis and analysis of tax lists must begin to take into account the importance of family to some of the individuals being analyzed. With regard to the first method, for example, Joseph Shippen III's rise before the Revolution is instructive. His advancement from an apprentice merchant, to a colonel in the provincial service, to a merchant, to secretary of

Pennsylvania and the Governor's Council substantiates neither the fluidity of Pennsylvania society after mid-century nor the opportunity to rise afforded any individual in that society. Instead, it reflects to a far larger degree the influence of the Shippen family, their politically potent Cousin William Allen, the chief justice, and other family considerations.[10]

In the future, studies of mobility based on tax lists must be augmented and adjusted by knowledge of kinship networks, family size, and other considerations not tabulated by tax assessors.[11] Two examples will indicate why this is essential. In the early 1770s James Burd was a rather luckless ex-merchant, ex-colonel, and not particularly prosperous farmer with genteel pretensions. His large family definitely impeded his ability to realize many of his personal ambitions. Despite this, before the Revolution his daughters married well, and his son quickly obtained several offices in the provincial and imperial structure. The early advances of these children of James Burd resulted essentially from the efforts of their grandfather Edward Shippen III and uncle Edward Shippen IV. Most young women in their economic position would not have married so well, and the advance of most young lawyers would not have been so rapid as the son's. Again, William Shippen III's rather small taxable estate in 1769 does not mean he was near the bottom ranks of Philadelphia society. Career-line analyses and analyses of tax lists are not meaningless exercises in methodology, however; rather they are useful tools which must be improved and refined by analysis of family structures. This is particularly true in Pennsylvania where almost no complete tax lists for the years before 1769 exist.

Finally, it is essential to explore the means by which the Shippens tried to maintain their position. In part this involved inheritance, the most neglected area in social history according to one author.[12] The Shippens possessed considerable real and personal property; hence inheritance often had a significant impact upon their lives. Because neither primogeniture nor entail were utilized, their methods are all the more intriguing, for until recently many assumed those devices of European aristocracies were widely utilized in the colonies. Because the Shippens rejected primogeniture, it becomes important to discover whether all heirs or only certain heirs were expected and encouraged to maintain the family's position.

But more than this, the activities of the Shippens while they were alive figured prominently in efforts to retain their family's position. The means of retaining the family's position often involved strenuous efforts to enable the younger generation to rise. Among the many significant devices used, few rivaled the importance of nepotism. To the Shippens, it proved effective and laudable.

Because the Shippens and their kinsmen maintained or elevated their position so well before the American Revolution, their actions are closely related to the question of whether or not opportunity for advancement generally decreased as the Revolution approached. Those outside the Shippens' kinship network certainly might have cause for complaint.

The American Revolution stands as the most serious threat to the abilities of the Shippens to maintain their position. They were one of the most prominent of the old established families in the colonies when that event began. The course of action they pursued is highly significant. Did all Shippens respond in the same way and with the same sympathies? Did they oppose the rebellion as Tories? Did they welcome it as revolutionaries? Or do other characteristics more accurately describe their response?

The attitudes of their contemporaries toward this old established family and what happened to it during and after the American Revolution has a direct bearing on an understanding of the nature of the revolution in Pennsylvania. In short, was the rebellion revolutionary in either its aims or accomplishments? The degree of continuity and change must be ascertained and explained as carefully as possible.

With a knowledge of what questions other historians and some social scientists have asked and after careful consideration of what else can be done with surviving papers concerning the Shippens, it becomes possible to reconstruct a useful history of the Shippen family. Hopefully this study can illuminate, expand, and refine our understanding of the vital heart of colonial society, the colonial family.

The First Generation:
Uprooting, Transplanting, and Creating

By the mid-seventeenth century it must have seemed to the residents of Hillam, Yorkshire, England, that the Shippen family was permanently rooted in their midst. As far back as anyone could remember there had always been Shippens living in the parish of Monk Fryston and the surrounding area of West Riding. Although a family tradition which claims residence in the parish as early as the thirteenth century cannot be confirmed, church records substantiate habitation there as early as 1538.[1]

William Shippen (1600–1681), father of the founder of the family in North America, continued this tradition of relative immobility. Born in 1600, William Shippen spent at least the next seventy-two years of his life within seven miles of his birthplace. By the time he was twenty-six he had moved to neighboring Methley where in time he married Mary Nunnes or Nuns (1592–1672), the daughter of a local yeoman. Because she was eight years his senior and probably in her thirties when Shippen married her, it is likely that some financial inducement was offered. In any case, William Shippen attained local prominence as an overseer of the poor in 1642 and served as overseer of highways in 1654. Many years later a grandson described him as "William Shippen, of Yorkshire, England, (gentleman)."[2] That he achieved a fair degree of financial success seems apparent from the university education which he provided for his eldest son William (?–1693).

The opportunity of university training drew William, Jr., away from the rolling hills of Yorkshire to Oxford where he received a

9

B.A. in 1656, an A.M. in 1659, and a position as proctor in 1664. With this training William, Jr., became an Anglican rector in Stockport, Cheshire. During the late 1670s he convinced his widowed father to come reside there with him. Of William, Sr.'s three children who survived to maturity, only his daughter Mary, who married William Chapman in 1663, continued to live in close proximity to the family's traditional home.[3]

Edward Shippen (1639–1712), the younger son, shattered the family pattern of geographic immobility most thoroughly. Nothing is known of his life in England other than that his parents, who had him very late in life, provided that he train for mercantile pursuits. By 1668 Edward Shippen had accumulated sufficient resources by his own efforts, and possibly with some assistance from his father, to migrate over three thousand miles to Boston, Massachusetts, a wilderness town of about 3,500 inhabitants. The explanation that he moved to the New World in order to better his fortune, though undocumented, is probably correct. In Boston, he established himself as a merchant. Within three years his fortune was adequate to support a family, and in 1671 at age thirty-two he married Elizabeth Lybrand (?–1688), who bore him eight children during their seventeen years together.[4]

Although Edward Shippen was establishing roots which would keep him in Boston for the next twenty-six years, life was by no means stable and secure. By wrenching himself from family and friends in Yorkshire and settling among Puritans, Shippen had jarred himself loose from his familiar world and traditional values. Although he continued in the familiar role as a merchant and began to move into society by joining the Ancient and Honorable Artillery Company, his mind failed to adjust fully to the new situation. Probably the anxiety created by migration and setting up a new life in unfamiliar surroundings made him particularly receptive to a new mode of religious experience. Within a few years after his marriage, Edward Shippen converted to his wife's faith and became a member of the Society of Friends.[5]

The decision to join the Quakers produced several important consequences. First, it identified Shippen as an outsider in New England and determined to a degree the role which he might play in Massachusetts. He would be persecuted and his achievements

limited to the sphere of business. Positive consequences of this conversion involved the business connections which Shippen made with
other Quakers in Rhode Island, New York, and Philadelphia, and
the stature he later gained in the Quaker colony during the last
eighteen years of his life.

The immediate effect of his conversion was humiliation. Quakers
had been persecuted ever since their arrival in Boston in 1656.
Before 1661, four had been hanged and others whipped or muti-
lated. This overtly hostile attitude toward Quakers abated somewhat during the decade following 1664, but was revived in 1675.
Among the last victims of the policy of harassment was Edward
Shippen who, upon two occasions in August 1677, was arrested and
publicly whipped for attending Quaker meetings. Neither whipping
nor knowing his religious associates had been hanged shook his
faith, for he remained adamant. Years later, when attitudes in Boston had changed, Edward Shippen erected as a monument two posts
at either end of a pit into which the corpses of "martyrs for the
truth" had been tossed.[6]

Despite his religious affiliations, Edward Shippen became a very
wealthy man. Several writers have suggested that he was a very
talented businessman; yet few details survive to indicate the character of his mercantile activities. Like many New England merchants, Edward Shippen utilized family connections in England for
purposes of trade. Early in the eighteenth century Edward's nephew,
John Shippen, invested in several ships trading with Boston. Perhaps he invested in some with his uncle at an earlier date. In any
case, Edward's son Joseph noted in the Shippen family Bible that
John Shippen was "a Spanish merchant."[7] During the 1680s, if not
before, Edward Shippen also traded with merchants in Jamaica.
There are periodic references to Edward Shippen as a merchant in
Boston; however, the suggestion that he amassed a fortune of
£10,000 sterling simply through his own efforts seems implausible.
More likely, the death of Edward's father in 1681 expanded his economic base considerably.[8]

Even before that, however, Edward was busy acquiring real estate
in Boston. In 1671, he and Seth Perry leased for £81, a "warehouse
wharfe & yard" on the east side of "the Great dock."[9] In 1677, Shippen purchased a house and lot for £247. Presumably profits from

trade also helped the merchant acquire another house "on the highway next [to] the sea"; Shippen paid £250 for it in 1680 and sold it "for a good & valuable cause and consideration" after owning it for only three months. At about the same time Edward Shippen purchased for £130 sterling the house on Sudbury Street, with its orchards, yard, and gardens, on about two acres of land which he had previously rented. By 1680, Edward Shippen had expended over £500 New England money and £130 sterling on real estate.[10]

Edward's father died in 1681, and it seems Edward received a substantial inheritance. Between 1681 and 1684 Shippen spent £549 to acquire more property. First, he spent £300 to obtain a lot on Conduit Street, with "the Previledge of a Cart way . . . [to a wharf] for landing and Shipping off any goods wares merchandizes firewood or other things."[11] His other large expenditure was £190 for land on the broad street leading from the Exchange toward the harbor. In 1684, he bought some small adjoining lots. Within thirteen years, Edward Shippen had laid out more than £1,000 to acquire real estate in Boston.[12]

Edward inherited the family's country seat in Hillam, Yorkshire, England, which provided him with an annual income of £15 sterling. Unfortunately further concrete evidence of an inheritance does not survive, but Shippen's activities in the near future strongly suggest that he received additional bequests. For example, in 1686 he purchased a brick tenement and lot in Philadelphia. In the following year he petitioned Sir Edmund Andros setting forth that "for many years past he . . . [had] been possessed of a certain house and ground wherein he now liveth: one other house and ground in the occupation of Thomas Savage: one other house and ground in the occupation of George Dawson: several warehouses and grounds belonging thereto; and about four acres of ground in pasture; all within the town of Boston" and wished the governor to have the properties surveyed so that he might obtain a patent for them.[13] Although this property and Shippen's ownership of several wharves near Faneuil Hall indicate wealth, the petition also indicates he faced economic impediments as a Quaker merchant in Boston.[14]

Given the emerging structure of the merchant community in the little provincial town, it is difficult to imagine Edward Shippen participating fully in the prosperity which many were achieving. When

Shippen arrived in Massachusetts toward the end of the 1660s, he found a society in a state of transition. Social groupings and institutions of the founding generations of Puritans were disintegrating; new men with roots in Restoration England were attempting to make inroads into the society. These merchants strongly opposed Puritan orthodoxy and gradually coalesced into a significant and powerful group by the 1680s. By then their sense of separateness and group identification was unquestionable. They had intermarried extensively among themselves and also with descendants of tradesmen of the founding generation. They had become "what amounted to a single interrelated family; with bonds of marriage . . . [uniting] almost every merchant with every other merchant in the same immediate vicinity."[15] When Shippen, an Anglican immigrant, converted to Quakerism, he destroyed any chance to enter this "family." Although this group lacked social homogeneity and retained variations in attitudes and life styles, its members closed ranks against one group. The rising merchant group agreed with the Puritans that the zealots or Quakers with their "superadded presumptions and incorrigible contempt for authoritie" had no place in Massachusetts.[16]

As an outsider to both the old establishment and the rising merchant community, Edward Shippen must never have been particularly comfortable in Boston. Thoughts of leaving for a more hospitable area were in his mind in 1686 when he bought a house in Philadelphia, capital of William Penn's recently established Quaker colony. Several occurrences during the next few years helped Shippen resolve to remove to Pennsylvania. In 1688 Edward Shippen's family of seven was reduced by the death of his wife and daughters Elizabeth, age twelve, and Mary, age seven. His three surviving children, ranging in age from four to ten years, needed attention which the activities of an industrious merchant precluded. Through his commercial dealings with Quakers in New York and Pennsylvania, Shippen was already in contact with people who would form the new family which he established in Philadelphia in 1694. In New York lived Rebekah (Howard) Richardson, wife of a very wealthy Quaker merchant, Francis Richardson; in Philadelphia, resided Anthony Morris who acted as her husband's agent. During August 1688, Rebekah Richardson informed Anthony Morris that "it hath pleased god to Remove & take to himself my deare husband."[17] Morris took care of Richardson's estate in Philadelphia; Edward Shippen looked after it in Boston.[18]

In September 1689, within a year of the deaths of their spouses, Edward Shippen and Rebekah Richardson married at the house of Walter Newberry in Rhode Island. Doubtless Rebekah had gone there to be with her sister Mary who was the wife of Governor Coddington's son. The couple returned to Shippen's home in Boston where they resided for the next few years. Business and handling the Richardson estate (which greatly increased his wealth) necessitated Shippen's traveling to Pennsylvania in 1690. Shippen must have been favorably impressed by the thriving Quaker community and the opportunities which would be available to a man of his stature were he to settle there.[19]

A number of considerations convinced Edward to move in 1694. The immediate impetus was a personal reason. In Rhode Island, Rebekah Shippen's recently widowed sister, Mary, became the third wife of Anthony Morris (1654–1721), brewer and merchant of Philadelphia and acquaintance of the Shippens. Morris had deserted the Church of England and become a Quaker in London before migrating to New Jersey in 1682. In 1685/6, he moved to Philadelphia and soon acquired local offices of alderman of Philadelphia (1691) and justice of the peace (1692). When Shippen decided to remove to Philadelphia, the thought of establishing family connections was probably in his mind; this belief is based partly upon the rather close relationship in politics and elsewhere which developed between Shippen and Morris during the ensuing years.[20]

Not only would Shippen be at home among a family, but he would be among like-minded religious associates. But Shippen left Boston of his own volition; he did not flee out of desperation to avoid "the persecutions of the Quakers in Boston [which had] reached such a pitch, that Mr. Shippen was driven into taking refuge in Pennsylvania," as one author has suggested.[21] Religious persecution of Quakers had ceased shortly after Edward Shippen was whipped in 1677, and after that Quakers in Boston enjoyed immunity. Furthermore, Shippen's sons, both of whom were Quakers, remained behind in Boston.

Beyond a desire to be among Friends, Edward Shippen was ambitious. Had he not been an outsider in Boston, doubtless his immense fortune would have enabled him to exercise considerably more power than he did, especially power of a political nature. In light of the speed with which he entered politics in Pennsylvania, he ardently wished to expand his activities and had already found Boston too confining.

Edward Shippen left Boston after twenty-six years not simply for one reason, but for a combination of reasons, all of which would have the effect, once realized, of transforming an outsider in Massachusetts into an insider in Pennsylvania. Both family and his religious affiliation instantly would make him an integral part of the small community in the Delaware Valley; his abundant wealth would give him great stature and enable him immediately to enter the world of power and politics which had previously been sealed off. In 1694, the fifty-five-year-old merchant stood on the threshold of a new life.[22]

When Edward Shippen arrived in Philadelphia, the thriving, bustling, young town with its four thousand inhabitants was approximately the same size Boston had been when he arrived there from England. The contrasts between the two towns are more important than the similarities. The most obvious difference to Shippen was the pleasurable knowledge that he would be among Friends, not a stranger among Puritans. Also the newness of this town which had been carved out of the wilderness only a dozen years before contrasted with the relative maturity of Boston which was almost four decades old when he arrived and three-quarters of a century old when he left. With age came social stratification; in Boston of 1687, that meant the "gentry class" or top fifteen percent of the population controlled fifty-eight percent of the town's wealth. Not only was Philadelphia, and Pennsylvania too for that matter, new, but the social structure in which Edward Shippen and his family would operate during the next few decades was very fluid and rather undifferentiated.[23]

Thousands of Englishmen arrived in William Penn's new colony during the twelve months following December 1681. By the end of 1685 when the first heavy influx abated, Pennsylvania contained eight thousand people. Although Penn intended to transplant an ordered, hierarchical society in the new world, he failed. The expectation of creating a haven for Quakers succeeded, but just as artisans, yeomen, shopkeepers, or the "middling sort" predominated among the followers of George Fox, so too did they provide the backbone of Penn's colony.[24] This need not have ruled out a sharply stratified society; however, Penn failed to induce many of the "baronial purchasers" of five thousand acres or more among the first purchasers to migrate. Only about one-third of these weighty Friends became settlers, whereas approximately two-thirds of the small landholders on the list of first purchasers crossed the Atlantic Ocean. As a result eighty to ninety percent of the non-indentured immigrants in the colony were of artisan or yeoman origins.[25] Negro slaves and white indentured servants comprised a third of the early population, and although their number declined in relative terms, it remained sizable. Therefore the nascent elite was too small to exert the influence and control Penn desired. This failure should not obscure the point that "notwithstanding what has been written about Quaker equalitarianism, one searches in vain for evidence that Pennsylvania was ever conceived as an economic or political democracy in nineteenth- or twentieth-century terms."[26]

Just as Pennsylvania's social structure remained for several decades highly fluid, relatively unstratified, rather confused and strife-ridden, so also did Philadelphia's. That town was designed as the political, economic, and cultural capital of the Quaker colony, and it reached these goals during the ensuing century. It achieved prominence not only because of its strategic location on the Delaware River and because Penn established the seat of the colonial government there, but also because it attracted the wealthiest merchant settlers. These men, including Samuel Carpenter, Humphrey Morrey, Anthony Morris, and others, formed the nucleus of an elite which in time became a very important force in the city. During the early years, however, the social and economic distance between the upper and lower ranks of society remained relatively unimpressive. In a tiny wilderness community very few could grasp the opportunity to display consistently a life style which contrasted sharply with that of the shopkeepers and artisans. By and large, merchants lived very much like the general population.[27]

Aside from contemporary descriptions which attest to the relative absence of any great contrasts of wealth or style in Philadelphia or Pennsylvania, more systematic measures may be used. These include analysis of tax lists and inventories of estates of deceased settlers. Neither of these sources is infallible, for only landed property is assessed in the tax lists and only a man's possessions at the time of his decease are evaluated in inventories. In the first instance personal property such as merchandise, silver plate, investments abroad, and the like elude us; in the latter instance, property transferred to heirs before the decease of the testator do. But these records should not be ignored; instead, they should be used with care and with recognition of their limitations.

Unfortunately the only surviving tax list for Pennsylvania before the mid-eighteenth century is for 1693, a year before Edward Shippen arrived. Although the list cannot reveal Shippen's place within the tax structure, it can be utilized not only to suggest Shippen's economic stature relative to others, but also to provide evidence of the degree of stratification in this society. In Pennsylvania, an overwhelming majority of those rated were assessed at less than £50, 694 of 838, to be exact. Only fifty–three were rated at over £200, and no one was rated over £1,000. In Philadelphia, somewhat more stratification existed. More than half (155 of 241) were assessed at less than £50; forty-three were rated at over £200, and the only twelve men in the colony rated at more than £500 resided in Philadelphia. Clearly in contrast to English society, the middling sort appeared in great numbers, and the wealthiest were barely represented.[28]

An analysis of inventories of estates recorded during the first two decades of the colony's existence support the characterization of the society as unstructured. In Chester County seventy percent of the inventories totaled £250 or less. In Bucks County an estate of £250 connoted rather crude living conditions, such as a two- or three-room house, perhaps fifty of two hundred acres under cultivation, and a few farm animals.[29] About twenty percent of the inventories for Bucks and Chester Counties were between £251 and £500. Modest prosperity in seventeenth-century Pennsylvania was enjoyed only by about the ten percent whose estates were valued at more than £500.

Of the ninety-eight Philadelphians whose inventories were re-

corded between 1683 and 1702, about twenty percent were worth
£200 to £500, about twenty percent were worth £500 to £1,000, and
ten over £1,000. The largest estate recorded belonged to James Fox,
baker, grain merchant, and land speculator; its value, £2,746.
Although the extremes in wealth were greater in Philadelphia than
in Pennsylvania, the contrast between rich and poor was slight, and
furthermore, social and economic mobility was more prevalent in
that city than elsewhere in the province.[30]

Philadelphia and Pennsylvania remained pioneer societies during
their first decades. Small subsistence farms were typical and even in
Philadelphia the society, though more complex, remained relatively
undifferentiated. The most recent study of the social and economic
structure of colonial Pennsylvania claims that "even in Philadelphia
clearly defined lines between economic classes were badly blurred
and a distinctive upper class had not yet formed. The top and bottom layers of society, as they existed in England, were still largely
unrepresented. . . . Even those merchants in the city who were later
'Quaker grandees' were still a generation away from that status."[31]

Edward Shippen entered this pioneer society with his wife and
ten-year-old daughter Ann. Both his sons, Edward II, age sixteen,
and Joseph, age fifteen, remained in Boston where they were apprenticed to merchants; the only child of Shippen's second marriage, a daughter named Elizabeth, died in Boston in 1692 within a
year of her birth. The small family was doubtless welcomed to the
community by their "brother and sister," Anthony Morris and his
wife.[32] Unlike most immigrants to Pennsylvania, Edward Shippen
entered at the top of society. His fortune, reputed to be £10,000
sterling, made him one of the wealthiest men in the Delaware Valley; indeed it is doubtful if anyone's economic resources equaled
his.[33] In 1693, only four estates had been valued for tax purposes at
over £1,000, and although property was assessed somewhat below
market value, the economic gap between Shippen and most settlers
was immense. Only ten percent of the estates of those dying in
seventeenth-century Pennsylvania were valued at more than £500,
and few were assessed at over £1,000. Among those few, none exceeded £2,800.[34] With an estate of £10,000 sterling Edward Shippen
was exalted above ordinary men of property, contrary to later
opinions.[35]

A part of Shippen's wealth existed in the form of recent purchases of land in Pennsylvania. In January 1693 Edward Shippen had received from William Penn two hundred acres in Wicacoe, Philadelphia County, and in September 1694 Edward Shippen, merchant, purchased for £100 the adjoining fifty acres from Gunner Swenson, a Swedish husbandman. Shippen owned an additional two hundred and sixty acres as well. This amounts to at least five hundred acres. According to an analysis of 1689 landholders, about eighty-two percent of the people in Philadelphia County owned less than five hundred acres.[36] In Chester County, the other county surveyed, almost the same percentage existed. Shippen was easily within the top twenty percent of the landholders, and furthermore, he owned a landed estate in Yorkshire, England, and presumably still held his property in Boston consisting of three houses and lots, four acres, and wharves.[37]

A man of Shippen's economic stature, who had also suffered physically as a strong witness to "the Truth," exhibited the qualities which William Penn sought in men who should rule the province. Although the statement that the Proprietor invited the weighty merchant to Pennsylvania has no documentation in manuscripts, it is a logical assumption.[38] Shippen also impressed the people of Pennsylvania as a natural leader, doubtless reflecting a certain degree of social deference on their part, and elected him to the Assembly where he served as speaker immediately upon his arrival.

From that time until his death almost two decades later Shippen took full advantage of his power and abilities; thus he figured prominently in local and provincial affairs. He expanded his economic base, rose in political stature, and firmly established his family's position. In the process of serving his self-interest as a merchant and head of a family, he also contributed toward the rise of Pennsylvania, Philadelphia, and a nascent elite.

Edward Shippen remained a merchant throughout his life. Although he left Boston, he retained mercantile contacts there not only with his sons, but with other merchants. He also engaged in trade with merchants in England and the West Indies. A forceful and demanding businessman, Shippen never apologized for "my Sharp writing" to those who failed to settle accounts punctually.[39] The only other details of his merchant activities come from a small

collection of business correspondence with his sons Edward II and
Joseph covering the years 1700 to 1701.[40] A family business seems
to have existed.[41] Both sons ventured to London on business where
their father had commercial connections and then to Philadelphia
to see their father to whom they sent a cargo of linen and cloth. The
Shippens also sent flour from Philadelphia to Barbadoes. Other
letters indicate that the sons sent cargoes to Boston, New York, and
New Castle as well. Beyond these vague hints, the Shippens' merchant ventures remain unknown.

Although the overabundance of goods made market conditions in
Philadelphia unfavorable when Edward's sons visited him, he convinced them of the great opportunities which awaited them in
Philadelphia.[42] This, in addition to the desire to consolidate the
family in one location, caused both sons to move to their father's
city during the first few years of the eighteenth century. Unlike later
generations which saved virtually everything, the first and second
did not; hence, although their merchant activities must have been
extensive, they cannot be described.

Wealth and position, however, were not simply acquired through
trade. Land, particularly land in and around the provincial capital,
attracted the attention of Edward Shippen. As mentioned previously, aside from his residence, Shippen owned 250 acres in the area
adjoining the southern city boundary. Dock Creek flowed through
parts of this and some of the acreage, particularly that closest to
the Delaware River, was swamp land. In 1696 Shippen added a lot
on Second Street (52′ × 300′) to his holdings. A few years later he
acquired another lot on Second Street (irregularly shaped 30′ × 103′
× 92′ × 118′) which bounded his swamp, and one in the city between Second and Third (being 154′ on Second by 195′ by 202′ by
105′), and finally a lot on Second Street (102′ × 396′) granted
to him by William Penn. During the same year in order to better
accommodate his mansion, Shippen traded a city square for a city
tract bounded east and west by Third and Fourth and bounded
north and south by Walnut and Spruce containing four acres. His
holdings in this section were completed in 1703 when he purchased
for £250 a lot 51 feet wide and 243 feet deep on Second Street. It
too bounded the swamp.[43]

Although much of his landholdings remained undeveloped, Edward Shippen made considerable improvements on his mansion house and its immediate surroundings so that, by the end of the seventeenth century, it was the showplace of the province. The large edifice, which served as the governor's house in 1699 when William Penn visited his colony, was situated on a small hill on Second Street, north of Spruce Street. This provided a pleasant view of the city which lay to the north and a beautiful prospect of the Delaware River to the east. Orchards and large gardens of tulips, carnations, and roses graced the estate. In 1698 Gabriel Thomas who had visited Pennsylvania averred that the setting "equalizes, if not exceeds, any I have ever seen."[44] Others have referred to Shippen's deer park; however, because the entire Philadelphia area remained so rural for several decades after the town was founded, deer probably roamed freely almost everywhere.[45]

Shippen's life style perhaps strained a bit at the limitations set by the Quakers who preferred a plain style. He continued to style himself a merchant; yet he resembled a gentleman in more ways than the family seat he built. He rode to town in what many claimed was the largest coach in the province. The very fact that he owned a coach set him apart from most in this pioneer society where coaches and carriages probably numbered fewer than half a dozen. Most people traveled dirt roads on foot, on horseback, or in wagons. Edward Shippen also had his portrait painted.[46] For it he wore a deep brown coat of fine material, white scarf, and ruffled cuffs which reflect the wealthy Quaker's affinity for "the best sort, but plain." His powdered and curled white wig suggests a social station above that of ordinary men. Shippen, however, wished to remain within the Quaker fold and was not criticized by the Society of Friends for extravagant living. As a matter of fact, in 1698 Edward's wife Rebekah and daughter Ann signed the Women's Yearly Meeting's testimony against fashions, speech, and ways of the world.[47] Specifically, they urged mistresses to bring up children and servants to use plain language; they urged women not to wear overlong scarves; they believed that Friends should wear plain apparel rather than striped or gaudy flowered stuffs or silk, that they should not wear their hair piled high on their heads, and finally, that they should not keep superfluous furniture in their houses. Rebekah believed these views important enough to copy in full in her own hand.[48]

Beyond exercising his abilities as a merchant and land speculator and creating a beautiful residence within a short distance of the center of town, Edward Shippen also participated in politics. In 1694, 1700, and 1705 he was elected to the Provincial Assembly; in July 1695 he became speaker of the Assembly. During most of the first two decades of the Provincial Council's existence, that body was also an elective one, and Edward Shippen was chosen a member in 1696 and "was returned every year at the fresh elections."[49] As early as 1697, Shippen seems to have served as president of the Council. The Charter of Liberties of 1701 made no provision for an upper house in Pennsylvania; however, the proprietor created a Governor's Council. In February 1701, William Penn appointed "my Trusty and Wellbeloved Friends" Edward Shippen, Thomas Story, John Guest, Samuel Carpenter, William Clark, Griffith Owen, Phineas Pemberton, and others to the Governor's Council.[50] All these men were " 'of most note for their virtue, wisdom, and ability,' [with] the word *ability* connoting, as it often did in the seventeenth century, wealth or pecuniary power."[51] Shippen served as the Council's first president, and in this capacity acted as chief executive of Pennsylvania from 1703 to 1704 before a new governor was appointed. Another provincial office which indicated William Penn's high opinion of Shippen was that of commissioner of property; Thomas Story, James Logan, and Griffith Owen were the other commissioners appointed in 1701.[52] Shippen retained this office until 1711. Shippen was chief justice of the province in 1699; he served again in 1701 as a provincial judge.[53]

On a local level Edward Shippen was the first mayor of Philadelphia and remained in the Philadelphia city corporation after it was reformed as the governing board of the city in 1704. Philadelphia's Common Council was a closed corporation in that new members were elected by the existing council and served for life. Edward Shippen thus remained an alderman until 1712. From 1705 to 1712 he also served as city treasurer.[54]

Shippen's drive, ambition, and ability as a businessman were utilized by the Philadelphia Monthly Meeting. The Monthly Meeting embodied the "holy community." It sought to nourish the religious life of the settlers, but beyond this, during the early decades of the province, it fulfilled many functions later taken over by civil authorities. For example, it served as a loan office, court of arbitration in economic disputes, advisory board to immigrants, and relief office for the poor or unfortunate. A very pronounced sense of community characterized this Quaker settlement; the entire Quaker community had a stake in the activities of every member. Because even secular behavior might bring "the Truth" into disrepute, it received attention and discipline from all Quakers. An elaborate procedure, "Gospel Order," of negotiations, hearings and arbitration by neutral Friends existed to settle disputes between members of the community. Only if a member were disowned for refusing to abide by the meeting's decisions might his antagonist resort to legal proceedings. The Quakers had adamant aversions to lawyers and courts; hence this informal means of settling problems was "remarkably effective . . . [and] on the whole . . . it is probable that most disputes to which Quakers were parties were settled out of court."[55] So long as Quakers remained a preponderant majority in Pennsylvania, the threat of being read out of meeting and becoming an outsider in the community was a potent force shaping behavior.[56]

Edward Shippen's experience in Philadelphia developed within this Quaker community. Although he appears periodically in the minutes of the Monthly Meeting, this wealthy merchant did not dominate its proceedings; indeed his role was usually peripheral. On occasion, he used its procedures to collect debts. The first mention of Shippen in the minutes was on the third of the Fourth Month, 1695. He was one of nine appointed to meet with Patience and David Lloyd about settling the estate of Thomas Lloyd; in addition, Shippen and Alexander Beardsly were to deal with Joshua Hastins about a complaint brought against him by two merchants. Shippen sometimes loaned money to the meeting and in 1697 he was one of several treasurers of the Yearly Meeting. Aside from infrequent assignments of a similar nature, Shippen's only significant activities were as a member of the building committee which erected the 1696 meetinghouse.[57]

Shippen remained a relatively minor figure in the Monthly Meeting, whereas merchants such as Samuel Preston, Samuel Carpenter,

Pentecost Teague, Isaac Norris, Shippen's brother-in-law Anthony Morris, and numerous Friends of less social stature directed the Society's activity. Either Shippen's religious enthusiasm had waned or his conception of his faith did not include vigorous participation in the business of the meeting.[58] The meeting, however, carefully scrutinized the activities of all its members, even the most wealthy and politically powerful. Wealth and stature provided neither license nor immunity to censure.

Edward Shippen's great status was reflected not only in his own wealth and political offices, but also by the marriage he arranged for his twenty-two-year-old daughter. Ann had several suitors including James Logan and Thomas Story. In 1706, James Logan's humble origins and lack of stature unfavorably impressed Edward Shippen. Young Logan, who had previously lived briefly with the Shippens, was still a relatively obscure clerk for William Penn; hence his insignificance contrasted not only to his later stature but also to the stature of his rival. In any case, Edward Shippen ignored his daughter's inclinations and chose to negotiate a marriage for her with Thomas Story. Ann Shippen was attractive not only for many personal qualities she possessed but also because of her handsome dowry, which included a large house on Second Street in Philadelphia.[59]

Thomas Story, a middle-aged English Quaker who arrived in Pennsylvania in 1699, styled himself a gentleman; his wealth and offices such as keeper of the Great Seal, master of the (Quit Rent) Rolls, and first recorder of Philadelphia indicate the immediate eminence he attained upon his arrival. On 31 May 1706, Thomas Story and Ann Shippen appeared for the first time to declare their intention to marry, first to the Women's Monthly Meeting, then before the Philadelphia Monthly Meeting. A month later they appeared for a second time, and the meeting "left them at liberty to consumate their intentions."[60] The marriage certificate, dated 10 July 1706, was signed by about 130 witnesses, both prominent and obscure, including several kinsmen such as Edward Shippen, his son Edward, Jr., his stepson Francis Richardson, Anthony Morris, Jr., and Sarah Story.[61] Not everyone applauded the union. Ann's brother "Joe appears so disgusted, that no body can reconcile his actions to reason. He went to New Castle to be out of the way."[62]

If Joseph Shippen were displeased by his sister's marriage, he was outraged by his father's third marriage. The latter marriage was viewed in the same light by the entire Quaker community. In 1705, Edward Shippen's second wife died. With almost irreverent haste, the sixty-seven-year-old merchant married in 1706 Esther (Wilcox) James, widow of Philip James, a wine cooper.[63] If his wife's deceased husband's occupation as an artisan was inferior to Shippen's status, at least her brother Joseph was a merchant and mayor of Philadelphia, and Esther owned some valuable property. Charles Jones, "Sopeboyler" of Bristol, England, had conveyed a huge tract of two thousand acres in Pennsylvania with liberty lots in the city to Philip and Esther James, and in 1711 Shippen completed paying £250 still due on the tract. But perhaps considerations of status were not uppermost in Shippen's mind. At the same meeting of 28 June 1706, when his daughter announced for a second time her intention to marry, Edward Shippen and Esther James declared their intentions to do the same. As usual a committee was appointed to establish that both were free to marry; Shippen's brother-in-law Anthony Morris and Nathan Stanbury were appointed. Because Esther had a child by her former husband, David Lloyd was requested to assist in settling matters relating to the child.[64]

The couple did not appear before the meeting a second time as Quaker custom required. Instead what followed was "one of ye darkest weddings that ever" James Logan "knew in the place." Except for Esther's brother the mayor and Alderman Thomas Griffith, a kinsman, "not one person of any credit" attended. According to James Logan, "ye old Lecher" had outraged the Society of Friends because they discovered his intended bride's "apron to rise too fast." The birth of John Shippen early in 1707 confirms the charge that the bride was pregnant. For a time Logan's observation that "ye last departure and Interment of ye small Remains of ye families Reputation" had occurred seemed inevitable.[65]

Until the spring of 1708, the couple suffered humiliation for their behavior. During September and October 1706, Friends labored with Edward Shippen "to bring him to a sense of the reproach he hath brought upon the truth and friends" while representatives of the Women's Meeting visited Esther and laid "open her Deceit and Hypocracy in representing herself, under such Circumstances to the

Meeting."[66] Visitations continued. In November 1706, Friends found Shippen "very tender, and he declared his great sorrow for it, and was willing to do what he could or what friends think fit for him" in order to expiate his error.[67] He was chastised in several ways. On the thirteenth of August, evening meetings which had previously been held at Edward Shippen's house were moved to Ann Parson's " 'till further order.' "[68] Beyond this the Shippens had to condemn publicly their behavior in writing. Esther's condemnation was accepted in February 1707/8, but Edward's was rejected on several occasions as inadequate—all this while Friends dealt with Shippen to help clear "the Truth" by his testimony. The committee included Shippen's son-in-law Thomas Story and brother-in-law Anthony Morris as well as Nicholas Waln, Samuel Carpenter, Griffith Owen, and Richard Hill. Finally, in February 1707/8, the document met the Society's designs, and the final humiliation to the family occurred when Edward Shippen stood before the meeting while his kinsman Thomas Griffith read Shippen's testimony. Copies of Shippen's condemnation were also sent to Friends in New England, Long Island, Burlington (New Jersey), Maryland, Barbados, Antigua, and London where Friends might use it "only as in the Wisdom of God they may be sensible is for the service of Truth."[69]

Although by the end of 1707 Shippen resumed his place on the committee to keep the meeting's property in order, most of his contact with Friends that year was distasteful. For example, while Shippen was already under fire for his marriage Thomas Murray brought "matters in Controversy between my father-in-law Edward Shippen and me" before the meeting for arbitration.[70] The experience failed to embitter Shippen, for he resumed his minor role in the meeting and remained a Friend until his death in 1712, at which time he bequeathed the sum of £50 to the meeting for support of the Friends school and the poor.[71]

The scandal surrounding this marriage proved a passing threat to Shippen's stature. William Penn retained confidence in his strong-willed friend; he not only continued him in office as provincial councillor and commissioner of property, but in 1707 made him a grantee of the Penn Charter School under the new charter. As a gesture of their respect for Shippen, the Common Council of Philadelphia elected him mayor in 1707, a position which he declined. In part this election was possible because more than a third of the members who voted were related to Shippen; they were Edward Shippen, Thomas Story, Anthony Morris, Joseph Wilcox, Thomas Griffith, Samuel Richardson, Joshua Carpenter, Samuel Powel, and Samuel Powel, Jr.[72]

Edward Shippen remained in the center of controversies until his death. Politics in the Quaker community always had been characterized by strife and bitter disputes among factions. Frequently disagreements found expression in the disputes between the Assembly and the Provincial Council. For example, when in 1709 the Assembly complained to the proprietor about "oppressions" which the province labored under during the irregular administration of the late deputy governor, they appended a barb directed at the Governor's Council, for the executive had been "too much influenced by Evill Counsill to whom ye Miserys and Confusions of ye State and Divisions in this Government are principally owing."[73] Shippen joined with the other provincial councillors to defend their position and underscored the point that they received no salary, offices of profit, allowance, or other advantage for their service to the people. The old merchant also become involved in disagreements concerning business and property. In 1711 he complained to the Friends meeting against his stepson Francis Richardson, and in 1712 the meeting asked him to be patient with David Lloyd who owed Shippen debts.[74]

Age certainly took little determination, energy, or spirit from Edward Shippen. By 1712, however, Edward Shippen had wrestled with life for seventy-four years. When he died in October of that year, he left behind a foundation upon which later generations might build. This foundation consisted of several things. First, there was the Shippen family itself. This included not only Shippen's widow and four-year-old son William (named after Edward's father as a symbol of continuity with the family's English past), but also two married sons who had been drawn to Philadelphia by their father. Ann Story, his married daughter, also lived within close proximity of her father. There were at least half a dozen grandchildren and numerous kin, most of whom lived nearby. Second, all the Shippens and their kin were Quakers in a community still largely Quaker in composition; hence they enjoyed status as insiders. Third, Shippen left a very strong economic base, much of which was in the form of landed property. This family fortune was not simply accumulated by Shippen's skill as a merchant, but also received considerable increments from a substantial inheritance from his father and two marriages. The landed property, of course, would increase in value as time passed; it helped anchor the family in Pennsylvania, and because much of the land remained in the family for decades, it served as a concrete form of family identity during ensuing years. Whenever Edward Shippen's descendants leased parts of this property, the documents which they signed referred to Edward Shippen's acquisition and distribution of his landed estate.

Certain laws existed in Pennsylvania which limited what a testator might do with his estate. Primogeniture was limited by a law of 1683 which provided that, unless the estate were divided equally, one-third must go to the widow, one-third to the children equally, and one-third as the decedent wished. The limitation on the use of wills ended in 1693 when it was declared that, except for the eldest son, heirs equal in affinity should receive equal shares. An Act of 12 January 1705/6 required that children share land equally; the widow's share was to equal that of a child.[75]

During the first week of August 1712, Edward Shippen, "being under some present indisposition of body," wrote a will and died.[76] He appointed his sons Edward II and Joseph executors and Thomas Story and Samuel Preston trustees. "Unto my dear wife," Edward Shippen bequeathed £800, all household goods in the front rooms of his house, additional household goods valued at £150 (including "my Negro woman black betty or Bess who was my wife's"), £72 worth of plate, a horse and a cow. Edward set aside the mansion he lived in, with its orchard and garden on a lot 150 feet wide on Second Street extending to Third Street, his warehouse on a lot extending from Dock to Second Street, and fifty acres of his plantation as security for the bequests to his wife and youngest son, William. Edward ordered the trustees of his estate to use the profits from this property to maintain his son William until they turned it over to him when he reached age twenty-one. Rents derived from the house and lot on the west side of Front Street, "now in possession of my son Edward," were to support William until age fourteen. At that time, "in case my said son William shall be bound apprentice to any suitable trade," Edward's wife was to receive £50 to accomplish this. When William attained his majority, he was to receive £800; the house on Front Street with its 260 acres and two wooden buildings were conveyed in trust to Esther to secure the bequest.

The use of trustees and deeds in trust to secure bequests to Edward's wife and youngest son implies that tensions within the family regarding Edward's third marriage had not fully dissipated. In this regard, Edward also specified that, "to avoid controversy," the legacies to his wife were in lieu of the widow's right to a third of her husband's estate. Although Quakers supposedly made no distinction between affinity and consanguinity," Edward scarcely provided for "my said wife's son Philip James. That heir received a silver tankard "that was his father's," a Negro boy, another tankard, two silver porrigers, and six silver spoons. Even legacies of £75 to each of Edward's grandchildren (children of Edward II and Joseph Shippen) dwarfed the bequest to Edward's "wife's son."

Edward's two sons by his first marriage became his primary heirs. Although Edward rejected the concept of primogeniture, he bequeathed to his eldest son "all my messuages, lands, tenements and hereditaments with the appurtenances, lying and being in the town of Hillam in the County of York," in Great Britain. His strong aversion to the practice of entail ruled out that device.[77] Aside from £150 to the trustees of his estate, "one full moi[e]ty or half" of the rest and residue of Edward Shippen's real and personal property went to his sons Edward II and Joseph. Unfortunately no inventory or account of the estate survived. Because of this deficiency in the records, valuable details about Shippen's life style are lost, and one cannot estimate how much he enlarged the value of his estate over the £10,000 sterling it was worth more than two decades earlier.

Clearly Edward Shippen left a very large fortune; even after it was divided among his heirs, the influence of inheritance upon his descendants remained substantial. The inheritance involved more than the material estate described in Shippen's will. Edward Shippen also left an impressive "symbolic estate" as well. The scandal involving Shippen's third marriage dissipated; the death of John, the infant involved, meant that no living symbol continued the memory of Edward Shippen's fall. Because of this Edward Shippen's success as a merchant, political officeholder, and man of great prominence in the affairs of the province and city made him an example which later generations might admire and try to emulate.

III

Second Generation: Contraction of the Family

Children of an aggressive and successful father often find it difficult to emerge from the shadow of his achievements and command
recognition on their own.[1] Several possibilities face such children.
For example, they may wish to emulate their father or even surpass
his accomplishments; success or failure will rest partially upon the
soundness of the inherited foundation and partially upon the
child's initiative and abilities. Another alternative is to reject the
example of the parent and forge off in a different direction. In
doing this one may use or ignore inherited advantages of wealth,
prestige, power, or connections. A third possibility is more passive;
it consists of enjoying the material inheritance and basking in the
merits of one's forebearers while not exerting significant efforts to
improve upon them or to cultivate new interests.

Only four of the eleven children of Edward Shippen I reached
maturity and had an opportunity to make a decision. The story of
the second generation of Shippens therefore involves Edward, Jr.
(1678–1714), Joseph (1679–1741), Ann (1684–1712), and their half-
brother William (1708–1731). Their activities and the relationships
which they established with their families and others in society
indicate which choice each made.

The family's future depended upon the three brothers, for they
bore the Shippen name, and besides, their sister Ann died at the
young age of twenty-eight. Ann's life had been controlled to a considerable degree by her parents, who even decided whom she would
marry. Although she had the inclination to resist their decision, she

31

lacked power, a weakness which the sympathy and encouragement of her brothers could not overcome. She therefore deferred to her parents' wishes and in 1706 married Thomas Story, a Quaker gentleman of wealth and political position. Six years later she died without issue.[2]

William Shippen played an equally minor role in shaping the family's style and fate. Born when his father was sixty-nine, William had only a child's memory of an old man, for he was but four years old when his father died. His mother raised him until he was fifteen. In 1723 she apprenticed the lad for six years to the successful Quaker merchant Israel Pemberton (1684–1754). William lived with the Pembertons in their mansion at Front and Market Streets in the heart of the waterfront and merchant district. Like the life of any apprentice, William's was not his own, for he was forbidden to marry and "without license from his master he shall neither buy nor sell."[3] Even playing cards, dice, or other games of chance were prohibited.

An education in the affairs of merchandising and bookkeeping "after the best manner his master now useth" more than compensated for these restrictions; besides, it is possible that the Quaker youth scarcely looked upon the regulations as restrictions.[4] Furthermore, association with Israel Pemberton could be a useful asset in the future. Israel Pemberton was the only surviving son of Phineas Pemberton (1650–1701/2), a Quaker who immigrated from Lancashire, England to Bucks County, Pennsylvania in 1682 with his wife and three children, father, and father-in-law. Phineas, a man of considerable wealth, served in the Provincial Council with William Shippen's father. Pemberton also served in the Assembly and in several political capacities in Bucks County, such as clerk of the county court, deputy master of the rolls, deputy register general, and receiver general of proprietary quit rents. After Phineas's death, his son Israel moved to Philadelphia where he not only prospered as a merchant, but excelled in politics. He entered the Common Council of Philadelphia in 1718 and became an alderman two years later; he was elected to the General Assembly in 1718 and played a dominant role there as he served thirty-nine of the next forty-two years; he was active in the Society of Friends as clerk of the meeting, overseer, and elder. Although Pemberton had no eligible

daughter with whom William Shippen might establish a family connection, the happy circumstance that all Pemberton's sons were
very young when Shippen's apprenticeship ended made him a
likely beneficiary of this powerful merchant's connections and influence.[5] William naturally cultivated friendships with his Quaker
kinsmen. Several of them, such as "Uncle Joshua Emblen," "Cozen
Samuel Emblen," and "Cozen" Samuel Powel, Jr., became increasingly important men of affairs as Philadelphia developed. Shippen's
sudden death in 1731 at age twenty-three snuffed out possibilities of
notable influence in Pennsylvania which reliance upon these connections within the Quaker community could easily have produced.
Aside from numerous bequests which he left to his family and
friends, the unmarried youth had little impact on the Shippen family or society.[6]

The future of the Shippens lay with Edward, Jr., and Joseph
Shippen; or more precisely with Joseph. Like their father, both sons
became merchants in Boston. They were in business together with
their father in 1700 and 1701 when they ventured to London, New
York, Philadelphia, and Barbados. Joseph, a year younger, appears
a bit more independent and venturesome, for in 1703, while still in
Boston, he married Abigail Grosse. He married at age twenty-four,
eight years sooner than his father had and several years sooner than
his older brother. His bride was of Huguenot descent. This was a
break not only with his national background, but also in defiance
of the Quaker dictum that Friends marry exclusively within the
faith. At this point, however, Joseph did not wish to break completely with his father or with the example his father provided. He
named the child born within a year of the marriage Edward (1703–
1781) after his father. In 1704 Joseph removed his young family to
Philadelphia.[7]

Joseph's brother, Edward, Jr., also took up residence in Philadelphia at about this time. Sometime after his arrival among Friends,
Edward, Jr., married at Newtown, Maryland. His bride, Anna
Francina, was a daughter of Mathias and Anna Margaret Vanderheyden of Bohemia River in Maryland. Presumably Edward, Jr.,
met her during one of his merchant trips. Although there is no
record of the Philadelphia Monthly Meeting condemning Edward,
Jr., for "marrying out of meeting," it seems likely that his wife was

Anglican.[8] Francina Shippen never joined the Philadelphia Monthly Meeting; in 1714 when Edward Shippen, Jr., wrote his will, he specifically desired that his daughter, Margaret, "be Carefully and Religiously Educated and Brought up in ye Doctrine and worship of the Church of England." Margaret Shippen, who was probably named after her maternal grandmother, was to live with her mother during Francina's widowhood. Edward, Jr., left the Society of Friends between 1706 and 1714; yet this contrasted in important ways with his brother's similar action. Joseph acted first while his father enjoyed stature as one who had "suffered for the Truth"; Edward, Jr., left only after his father's humiliation by the Friends. Although Edward I remained a Quaker until his death, doubtless he found his namesake's deflection from the Society less upsetting than Joseph's.[9]

The sparse additional information of Edward, Jr.'s life suggests that he attempted to emulate his father's example. Like his father, he remained a merchant until his death. He also began the familiar pattern of acquiring land in the southern end of the city in the vicinity of his father's extensive holdings. In 1707, Edward Shippen, Jr., and Samuel Powel, another Quaker merchant, purchased from Shippen's stepbrother Francis Richardson, Jr., silversmith, a tract of land in Philadelphia (51 feet by 132 feet) extending from Second Street to the swamp. The property had been granted originally to Francis Richardson, Sr., in 1684 by William Penn, and Edward Shippen, Sr., held it in trust for several years after he married the widow Rebekah Richardson.[10]

Edward, Jr., was a more dutiful son than his brother Joseph. That his father favored his namesake somewhat is indicated by Edward, Jr.'s inheritance of the Shippen family seat in Yorkshire, England. Beyond this, Edward, Jr., had not openly defied his father's decision regarding Ann's marriage to Thomas Story. It seems likely that in time Edward, Jr., might have benefited from this family connection. Story might exert his influence to get Edward, Jr., admitted to the Common Council and probably to other appointive offices. These possibilities evaporated in 1714 when the relatively young merchant died at age thirty-six. Death prevented Edward, Jr., from exceeding his father's achievements. Whether or not in time he might have chosen a different course from his father remains mere speculation.

When Edward Shippen, Jr., died, his personal estate was valued at £279; no assessment of his real estate in Pennsylvania and Boston survived. The merchant left one-third of his total estate to his wife. Another third was devised to Margaret, his only surviving child. If she died childless, the children of Edward, Jr.'s brother Joseph were to divide her share equally. Most of the remainder of the estate went to Joseph Shippen. A Shippen was to retain the family seat in England; hence, Edward, Jr., devised "all my Lands and Messuages in William [Hillam] in ye County of York in Great Britain" to Joseph. Finally, in addition to providing for his daughter's maintenance and education, Edward, Jr., bequeathed £20 to his sister-in-law Augustina, £5 to his sister-in-law, "Ssariana ffibby," and £10 to two clergymen. Edward, Jr., never mentioned his stepmother or his half-brother, William, in the will; the omission implies that Edward, Jr., paid little attention to them while he was alive.[11]

Although Edward, Jr.'s contribution to the family's development and success seems faint in comparison to his father's, his death had important consequences for the Shippen family. It shattered the extended family network which had been developing and sharply impaired the potentials which the Shippens might realize during the second generation. The assistance, material or otherwise, which brother might give brother would not occur, nor would any uncle-nephew or uncle-niece relationships develop to any large degree. Beyond this, Edward, Jr.'s death removed one of the last ties which bound his brother-in-law Thomas Story to the Quaker colony. In 1715 the widower returned permanently to England. Although his contact with the Shippens did not cease, no evidence suggests that during his lifetime he attempted to use his stature to foster the prestige, power, or position of any Shippens.[12] Had Edward, Jr., lived, Story might have aided or assisted him; the antipathy between Story and Joseph Shippen precluded Story's patronage of the surviving family.

Edward, Jr., left no male heirs, and only one daughter, who could not perpetuate the family name, reached maturity. His half-brother, William, died unmarried. The fortunes and the very survival of the Shippen family in the second generation, therefore, rested solely with Joseph Shippen. Joseph had no problem producing heirs, but his ability to promote their advancement diminished appreciably.

The extended-family structure had collapsed; hence, there would not be several significant Shippens in Philadelphia assisting each other in economic and political affairs. Furthermore, Joseph became an outsider and in a sense alienated from the Quakers who still dominated society.

For about a decade after Joseph Shippen arrived in Philadelphia, he followed his father's example by pursuing mercantile activities and acquiring land. In 1706, he invested profits from trade in half a city square (about two acres) on Fourth Street between Walnut and Spruce. This property in the southern end of town adjoined an entire city square lying to the east which Joseph's father acquired in 1701. In 1709 Joseph purchased fifty acres in Germantown, thus making his holdings there about one hundred acres.[13] The death of his father in 1712 greatly enhanced Joseph's fortune with substantial bequests in land; family traditions stemming from the third generation argue that he received additional wealth upon the death of his brother Edward, Jr., in 1714, including the family seat in Yorkshire, England.[14]

An abundant fortune, acquired more by inheritances from his father and brother than his own efforts, enabled Joseph Shippen to contemplate a change in his life style. The example of his father strenuously pursuing profits as a merchant until his death seemed unappealing. Why continue to pursue wealth in business when he was already among the richest men in Philadelphia? Joseph decided to launch out in a new direction. He wished to become a country gentleman.

Upon the death of his wife in 1716, Joseph Shippen retired at age thirty-seven from his mercantile business and moved his family to Germantown. The Shippen country seat on the corner of Germantown Road and Manheim Street impressed travelers with its size rather than its ornateness. The three-story brick building had two entrances, one of which was covered by a porch roof which extended across about a third of the front. Seven shuttered windows graced the second story; three dormers provided light for the attic rooms and also made a pleasing appearance. Chimneys at either end of the house and one in the center suggest the large number of fireplaces required to heat the structure. The mansion on Germantown Main Street sat on the crest of a long rising hill, about eight miles from the bustle of Philadelphia.[15] Although it lay only four blocks south of the market square, the area remained very rural in appearance. Only about one hundred houses existed in Germantown in 1745, and that was fifteen years after the great German migration to the area began. In 1716 the pastoral character of the area was far more pronounced.[16]

Because Joseph Shippen left almost no evidence of his thoughts, the origins of his decision to become a gentleman are not clear. Perhaps they stem in part from his voyage to England in 1700–1701, when he encountered the upper ranks of English society. Years later, one of his sons alluded to a second trip to England about 1704 on which Joseph met the Shippens of England. Joseph's knowledge of the family in England and its stature cannot be denied. In the family Bible he made the following entries: "My relations in England are my uncle William Shippen's children: 1. Robert Shippen, Doctor of Divinity, 2. William Shippen, Doctor of Law, and a parliament man, 3. Edward Shippen, a physician, 4. John Shippen, a Spanish merchant."[17] He knew that his English kin were elevated above the rank of the middling sort (elevation easily inflated because of infrequent and superficial contact with the reality of their station) and more particularly that a Shippen served as a M.P. This knowledge, coupled with firsthand experience of his father's prestige and position in provincial Pennsylvania, doubtless removed much of the anxiety and self-doubt which might plague someone who decided to elevate himself above his peers. Whether or not this background and Shippen's wealth justified to others his pretensions as a country gentleman cannot be determined. No one seems to have recorded comments upon the gentleman of Germantown. Observations must have been made, however, for Joseph Shippen was among the first to display a life style which several decades later characterized many successful Philadelphia merchants.[18]

Several things often distinguish the activities of a member of the aristocracy or a country gentleman in England; first, public service either on a local or national level; second, careful control over one's estate and grooming of an heir to perpetuate the family's position in the upper ranks of society. In regard to perpetuation of the family and indirectly of an aristocracy, primogeniture was often used. Although the father remained the dominant figure, he expended

considerable efforts and money on the education and training of his
first son, who would someday become the new head of the family.
In order to benefit the chosen son most fully and also continue his
own aristocratic life style, an English gentleman often forced
younger sons to shift for themselves. Although exceptions qualify
any generalization, at least through the beginning of the eighteenth
century, the pattern that the first son entered the aristocracy, the
second son, the ministry, and the third son, the army seems to hold.[19]
As a self-proclaimed gentleman, Joseph Shippen indicates by his
actions how closely one of the most important colonial families at
the time resembled the English model.[20] His own activities, his relationships with his sons, and also his sons' early careers may either
confirm or cause serious questioning of generalizations about colonial families and colonial aristocracies which frequently pass unchal-
lenged.[21]

As far as public service was concerned, Joseph Shippen had largely
disqualified himself by actions which alienated him from the tight-
knit Quaker community. Although the homogeneous character of
Pennsylvania fell victim to heavy immigrations of Germans and
Scotch-Irish after the Treaty of Utrecht ending Queen Anne's War,
the Quaker community survived and retained control of Philadelphia and Pennsylvania during the early decades of the eighteenth
century. Joseph's marriage in 1703 to Abigail Grosse, who was not a
Friend, indicates that Shippen's ties with the Society were weak;
indeed, he probably severed them before arriving in Philadelphia.
His name never appears in the minutes of the Philadelphia Monthly
Meeting, although this does not eliminate entirely the possibility of
his attending meetings. Were he still a Quaker when he moved to
his farm, he would have been under the jurisdiction of the Germantown meeting. No records of that group meeting survive; however,
Shippen's actions within about seven years of the move indicate
clearly that he was not a member of the Society of Friends.[22]

Joseph Shippen and his first wife had seven children during their
thirteen years of marriage. Two children died in 1714 (the same
year as their uncle Edward Shippen, Jr.) and an eight-year-old son
died in 1716, when his mother also died. In contrast to the experience of Edward I, the pressure on Joseph to remarry was slight.
Although William, Ann, and Joseph, Jr., were only four, six, and

ten years old respectively, Edward III was thirteen and old enough
to help care for his brothers and sister. By the time Joseph remarried, the youngest child was eleven; hence the decision rested not
on considerations of the need of the children for a mother but rather
Joseph's personal desires.

The personality Joseph Shippen displays over the years suggests
that monetary considerations played more than an incidental role
in this decision. Joseph's new spouse was the twice-widowed forty-
three-year-old Rose (Budd) McWilliams (1680–?). Her father, an
early Quaker settler of West Jersey, had been a yeoman; her first
husband, Charles Plumley, was a joiner in Philadelphia; a close
kinsman, Humphrey Morrey, was a wealthy distiller in Philadelphia.
Although these social origins and connections appear rather inferior
to Shippen's, the wealth accompanying the union would be compensation.[23]

A precise valuation of the material benefits accompanying this
marriage does not exist. A few hints survive. For example, along
with a new wife, Joseph Shippen also added a stepdaughter to his
family. She was fifteen-year-old Sarah Plumley. As part of his marriage obligations, Joseph Shippen, gentleman of Philadelphia, gave
a bond for £600 to Humphrey Morrey. By it, he secured a dowry of
£300 for Sarah and also Flora, a Negro woman, and her daughter
Hannah who were to become Sarah's property upon coming of age
or marrying with her mother's consent. The bond also mentions
"money and effect[s]" which Joseph received by the union; it does
not indicate how much.[24] Part of this was land in Salem, West Jersey, for Joseph Shippen soon paid ditchers and workmen for finish-
ing a bank on his thirty-two-acre marsh. Clearly the monetary value
of this union was well in excess of £300, perhaps two or three times
that figure. This is merely an educated guess, however. Usually a
widow received at least one-third of her husband's estate, a figure
usually larger than that received by a single child if the child were
a daughter. Suffice it to say, the money involved was not inconsider-
able.[25]

Although Shippen's wife was born a Friend, she could not have
been one in 1725 when her daughter married. Joseph's role in the
marriage indicates clearly that he was not a Quaker and also that
he cared little about the success of his eldest son. Edward III was

eighteen years old when his father married Rose (Budd) McWilliams. He found his new stepsister attractive and in time decided to marry her. Such a marriage union was absolutely forbidden by the Society of Friends. As Quakers interpreted the Bible, relatives acquired by marriage were the same as consanguineous kin; thus what Edward III proposed was incest in the eyes of the Society of Friends.[26]

Because Sarah's mother presumably gave her consent, she could not have been a Quaker very recently. It is all but certain that Joseph gave his consent, for his twenty-two-year-old son could scarcely have afforded to marry so young if there were no dowry. Besides, Joseph probably approved the marriage because it meant the money he held in trust for Sarah would not go out of the family. But Joseph probably did not transfer much wealth to his son at this time; that would impair his own position. This reluctance explains why Edward III visited his friends and family in Boston in August 1725. He was seeking financial backing from his kin in order to set himself up in life and found "my relations were overjoyed to see me."[27] His grandmother asked whether she heard correctly that her grandson "was going to have my [Edward III's] Mother in law's daughter"; when the young man answered affirmatively, she exclaimed, "Make haste and marry, and bring her to live in Boston."[28] But as far as receiving financial assistance from her or other kinsmen, Edward III was largely disappointed. He wrote to Sarah, "My grandmother lives handsomely, but has nothing to spare except good will and kindness, until she dies."[29] A maiden aunt lived with his grandmother, but she could not help financially. Perhaps Edward III shows a trace of envy as he records, "All my aunt's and uncle's daughters are extraordinarily well married."[30]

Ironically, a bequest from Edward III's grandmother, Esther Shippen, provided a sizable amount of land which gave the young man some sense of security when he married. Esther divided two thousand acres in Pennsylvania among Edward III, Joseph II, and Margaret Shippen. Although Esther was Edward III's father's stepmother, and Joseph had urged his father to distribute his property before any children came of his third marriage, she evidently bore no malice toward Joseph's sons. Esther died a Quaker and would have been offended by Edward III's courtship of his "sister," if she knew about it. Because she disliked her "son-in-law" Joseph Shippen, she probably had only infrequent contact with him and his children and was unaware of Edward III's intentions.[31]

Because the landed inheritance was only potentially valuable, it seems Edward III received little financial assistance from his father and kindred when he set out as head of his own household. Joseph Shippen not only gave meager financial support to start his son off in life; he also permitted, if not actively contributed to, a stigma of incest which could have marked his eldest son. But Joseph's eldest son was not a member of the Quaker community, which perhaps considered him doubly an outsider.

During Joseph Shippen's lifetime, none of his children rivaled their father's position. Indeed, Joseph's decisions as patriarch of the Shippen family caused all his children to remain rather obscure while he lived. To Joseph, promotion of the family or its members mattered little. His sense of obligation to his children, much less his kinsmen, appeared slight. In short, by the 1720s, Joseph's view of the family contrasted with that of the generation preceding him and those following him.

Joseph preferred to devote most of his energy toward the maintenance of his own life style as a gentleman. Although he succeeded in the attempt to style himself a gentleman, economic conditions in Philadelphia and Pennsylvania at least through 1730 made it difficult.

By 1730 Philadelphia's population was about 8,000; Pennsylvania's was about 80,000, yet this growth had not been accompanied by great prosperity. Although some fortunes accumulated from successful foreign trade with London, Bristol, the Caribbean Islands, Madeira, Lisbon, most colonists advanced only a little beyond the status of pioneers in a wilderness settlement. Most enjoyed at best only modest profits. Philadelphia and Pennsylvania experienced a marked rise in their fortunes and stature after 1740. As a general pattern in population and economics, in both the city and province, rapid expansion during the first two decades after their settlement was followed by a period of relative stagnation which lasted about three decades. For example, Philadelphia already had 6,000 inhabitants by 1690, 7,000 by 1700, yet after that it took three decades to increase the population by 1,000. Indeed its population remained rather static from 1710 to 1730. In part, the reason for this was the growth of population in rural areas. Pennsylvania, which rapidly acquired 30,000 inhabitants by 1700, doubled in the next three decades, yet the sharp increase in immigration occurred after 1725. As far as the growth of towns was concerned, this too remained at a standstill from 1701 to 1729. These population figures suggest relative economic stagnation from about 1700 to 1730.[32]

Philadelphia's success in trade and commerce during its first decade enabled it to join "Boston and New York as a major organizing center, as its Quaker merchants moved quickly to create their own patterns of trade within the British mercantile system."[33] By 1696 Governor Fletcher could inform the Board of Trade that "Philadelphia . . . is become equal to the City of New York in trade and riches."[34] Statistics for the following period from 1700 to 1715 indicate very slow economic growth. Joseph Shippen and his brother had commented upon this on their first trip to Philadelphia in 1700–1701. The 1720s were characterized by a depression. By the end of the decade conditions scarcely had improved; in 1728 the *Pennsylvania Gazette* lamented, "Money here seems very scarce. *Trade* has been long in a deep Consumption, her nerves relax'd, her spirits languid, her Joints have grown so feeble, that she has had of late so terrible a Fall that she now lies bleeding in a very deplorable Condition. . . ."[35] Economic conditions improved remarkably only after 1740.[36]

These economic conditions in Philadelphia and Pennsylvania directly concerned Joseph Shippen. He arrived in Philadelphia just as the initial period of growth and prosperity came to an end; during most of his life he operated in a rather stagnant economy. Ironically, and significantly, he died just as the great upturn in fortunes began. All this suggests that Joseph Shippen lived during a period which did not foster many dazzling successes. True, there were notable exceptions such as James Logan and Samuel Powel, yet most great fortunes came particularly after 1740. Most merchants and artisans found the first three decades of the eighteenth century somewhat discouraging.

Because Joseph Shippen retired in 1716, the pressures on him during the years he dominated the Shippen family were all the more powerful. To maintain his station as a gentleman would be no easy task. Shippen's success rested upon his careful management of properties under his control and also upon his refusal to disperse the family fortune in order to advance the careers of his sons.

As far as properties under his care were concerned, Joseph Shippen was well endowed. As a successful merchant he had accumulated profits during about a decade and a half. By far the greatest portion of his property was inherited from his father. Unfortunately the bulk of this inheritance was in the form of landed wealth. That served well for purposes of status in an age when status was often measured by the acres one owned. But to live as a gentleman income is vital. Because Philadelphia's population did not increase much between 1700 and 1730 the large amounts of city property were frozen assets which yielded little if any income. There is only one deed in the Shippen papers and none at all recorded in Philadelphia to indicate that Joseph Shippen derived income from renting or selling his city lots. In later years the Shippens frequently neglected to have deeds recorded, yet there is reason to believe that this was not the case with Joseph Shippen. The Shippen lands lay south of the city limit or adjoined the southern boundary. Because the city developed for decades in the area several blocks north of this, from about Walnut Street to Mulberry (Arch) Street, it is unlikely that any demand existed for the undeveloped Shippen properties during Joseph's lifetime. The development of Dock Ward and Southwark benefited the third and fourth generations of Shippens.[37]

Joseph had other properties under his care. Both marriages brought dowries. For four years, 1721 to 1725, Joseph had the use of his stepdaughter's dowry. The administration of the estate of his kinsman Humphrey Morrey was in his hands during the 1720s and 1730s. Although this money was not his but simply held in trust, as executor he presumably received financial compensation. Beyond this, Joseph evidently felt no qualms about using legacies which he held in trust for his children as his own. This caused bitter complaints, especially from his ambitious son Edward III, yet Joseph managed to delay payment of some legacies which he held in trust until his death. For example, not until within a year or so of his death did he finally turn over to his children certain legacies from their grandfather, Edward Shippen I.[38]

Because Joseph Shippen left few records of his activities, it is difficult to explain where his income came from other than from profits gathered as a merchant and the inheritances which he utilized. One other source was the Perkiomen Copper Mine in Limerick township, Philadelphia County. It had existed since at least 1723; by the 1730s, when Joseph Shippen and his son Edward III owned about one-sixteenth share each, James Logan, Samuel Preston, and Andrew Hamilton were among the other prominent owners. The mine seems to have been profitable for some time, but the amount of dividends which the Shippens received are unknown. One source of income which was especially important to later generations of Shippens came from officeholding; however, Joseph Shippen, like all Shippens of the second generation, never held an office.[39]

Regardless of the source of his income, several circumstances modified Joseph's expenses as a gentleman. His inheritance included not only land and a mansion in town, but presumably also furniture and other costly objects which would not have to come out of his operating budget. Beyond this, Shippen cut his expenses greatly simply by living in the country. At this time, however, urban living was not the expensive burden it became for gentlemen later in the century. Social life remained relatively plain and simple; signs of luxury were few. As one observer lamented, "Here are no Masquerades, Plays, Balls, Midnight Revellings, or Assemblies to Debauch the Mind, or promote Intrigue," and a young woman who "ventures a Mile out of Town for the Benefit of Air, or [admits] Pleasure of Retu'd Conversation, is sure to suffer her Character, by a Censorious Brood of Ditractors, and Calumniating Preciants."[40]

In Shippen's case, entertaining and other expenses accompanying urban life were diminished. Furthermore, Joseph raised his own food on the Germantown farm. He hired men to reap his hay and wheat which may indicate that he sold the grain and crops raised. Then again, because his sons all lived in town, the gentleman actually had no choice but to hire men to help run the farm.[41]

In addition to the income which sustained Joseph Shippen's station in society, his reluctance to part with possessions during his lifetime explains his success. It also explains why his eldest son resented him; it may have alienated his other children too, for that conclusion seems implicit at least in the life of his youngest son

William. Joseph Shippen paid only minimal attention to the fortunes of his children. Although he contributed in several ways to
their success, he did not try to keep the family tightly bound together. During his lifetime he did not use the family or family ties
as an engine to propel his offspring to success. The father's role
was not one which either his eldest or youngest son wished to
duplicate; nevertheless, Joseph's role was not as negative as his
angry sons suggest.[42]

For example, Joseph arranged a very attractive marriage for his
daughter Ann to the wealthy Anglican merchant, Charles Willing.
In August 1730 Joseph sold at public vendue a lot on Second Street
for £250. Presumably this served as Ann's dowry, and it was a rather
large amount of money. Because the vendue notice indicates that
the property was "part of the estate of Edward Shippen, Dec'ed," it
is probable that this is a legacy from Ann's grandfather rather than
money coming from her own father's purse.[43] Whether or not
Joseph augmented the £250 is not recorded. In any case, the dowry
was sufficient to achieve a well-placed marriage for his twenty-year-
old daughter.[44]

Although he could have done much more, Joseph did make some
provisions for his eldest son's success in the world. Around 1720,
probably a year or two before, Joseph apprenticed Edward III to
to James Logan, a rich and prominent Quaker merchant. At first
this seems peculiar in light of the rough treatment Logan had received at the hands of the Shippens little over a decade before. Yet
it was Edward I who rejected Logan; Joseph had tried to convince
his father to approve Logan's courtship of Ann I, and James Logan
and Joseph Shippen were good friends. Although Joseph had probably deserted the Society of Friends by this time, that scarcely
troubled Logan, who was never particularly vigorous in his religious
faith.[45]

The connection became an important ingredient in the success
of Edward Shippen III. Although this belongs to the story of the
third generation, some hints might be given regarding Joseph's
valuable arrangement for his son. James Logan, the obscure Irish
immigrant who arrived in Pennsylvania in 1699 as William Penn's
clerk, enjoyed a fifty-two-year career "of increasing responsibility
and honor" in the colony. He became secretary of Pennsylvania and

clerk of the Provincial Council in 1701, and he served as a full member of the Council from 1703/4 to 1747. After failure in two courtships, in 1714 he married Sarah Read, the daughter of a very rich merchant. By this time Logan had emerged as the leading political figure in the Proprietary party and thereafter exercised great influence in Pennsylvania politics. His fortune stemmed from shrewd land investments and extensive fur trading enterprises.[46]

Other than securing Edward III a good position as Logan's apprentice, Joseph did little more to forward his son's career. Indeed, Edward III began his adult life as a very minor merchant in Philadelphia. He might have remained rather obscure had not Logan slipped on the ice in his yard in January 1727/28. Logan remained in bed for about three months. After about a year he finally learned his broken hip would relegate him to crutches for the rest of his life. Logan needed help to run his fur business. His own sons were barely teenagers; hence, in 1730 Logan gave Edward III his power of attorney. By 1731 Shippen, "who lived in my [Logan's] house in town Since I have remov'd into the Country," was conducting business for Logan.[47] By 1732 Logan informed a business correspondent that "E. Shippen and I are in partnership . . . on a very limited manner. The Stock all to a trifle is mine and he has a part only of the Profits for his management. . . ."[48] Joseph Shippen might have turned over part of his fortune to his son to advance the young man's career at this point and enable him to become an equal partner with Logan. If Joseph considered such action, he decided against it. Although ascent was thus slower than it might have been, Edward III now had a powerful and influential ally who could serve him well. A simple example of what this might mean is apparent as early as Edward III's 1732 election to the Common Council of Philadelphia at age twenty-nine. Logan became an alderman in 1717 and served as mayor in 1722; it was probably his influence which helped convince the city corporation to admit Shippen, for the young man was a rather insignificant merchant at the time. Shippen continued as Logan's business partner for many years, and even before Joseph's death in 1741 Edward III had begun to grasp his way toward prominence.[49]

Joseph's namesake Joseph, Jr., also became a merchant. The name of the man who trained him is unknown, but at the age of twenty-two he was already on a merchant voyage in partnership with his brother. The slump in trade conditions in the 1720s made it difficult to accumulate resources and his father dallied about turning over any funds to his son so that he might set up his own family. Indeed, it is possible that he gave him none since no record exists. In any case, Joseph Shippen, Jr., did not marry until his late twenties, probably at about age twenty-seven or twenty-eight. His wife, Mary Kearney, was the daughter of a Philadelphia merchant.[50]

At age twenty-three William Shippen II, the youngest son, married Susannah Harrison. William was not only the youngest male Shippen to be married thus far, he was also the first Shippen in America not to become a merchant. Seven before him had. The career which William II chose indicates either an independent spirit coupled with different interests from the others or else a rather thorough lack of concern on the part of his father. William II became an apothecary or chemist. Although the vocation required skill, it indicated that at least one branch of the Shippen family appeared to be heading for the artisan ranks of society.[51]

With the exception of Sarah Plumley's and Ann Shippen's dowries, surviving records give no clear indication that Joseph Shippen gave away any property to his heirs until about a year or so before his death. William II received fifty acres in Wicacoe from his father in 1738, but he paid £50 for it. In the same year five acres and twenty-seven perches in Wicacoe (thirty-one lots in Society Hill) went to Edward III and Joseph Shippen, Jr., for £270. In 1740 Joseph still wished to retain control over his property. Although son William received a house and small lot on Walnut Street bounded by property at the corner of Front and Walnut Streets lately conveyed "for natural love and affection" to his brother Edward III, both sons paid £40 annual rent to their father.[52] Furthermore, the standard clause giving Joseph the right to enter the house and seize William III's goods if the rent were not paid punctually was not omitted from the indenture.

Not until February 1740/41, the year he died, did the sixty-two-year-old Joseph Shippen of Germantown, "Gentleman," decide to begin to distribute parts of his estate. By a deed of 27 February 1740/41, Joseph Shippen "for and in Consideration of the Natural Love and Affection which he hath for and towards his said son . . .

for their better Advancement and preferment in the World" turned over his Germantown properties to his sons.[53] This property, including the messuage "formerly known as Roe Buck Tavern" (the country mansion) was given to all three sons "each son to have one full equal and undivided third Part of the whole."[54]

In 1741 the dying man wrote a brief will. He provided for all four children, but the bulk of his estate went to his sons. He requested that legacies of £75 be paid to each of his four children from their grandfather. No part of them had yet been paid; hence, they were all at least a decade or two overdue. His daughter Ann received an additional £300 from her father's estate with the provision that she and her husband, Charles Willing, sign a release relinquishing any claim on the residue of the estate. The residue of the estate was to be equally divided among his three sons. The testator appointed all three sons executors of the estate. No other bequests were made either to family, friends, servants (if he had any), or philanthropic projects. That he mentioned no other kinsmen such as his brother-in-law, sister-in-law, niece, or cousins suggests that meaningful relationships did not exist with any kin other than his own children. No inventory of Joseph Shippen's estate survives. Once again valuable details about life style elude us; again, the possibility of determining if Joseph significantly increased his fortune above his inheritance cannot be determined.[55]

At the end of the second generation the Shippen family had been in British North America for almost three-quarters of a century and in Philadelphia for almost fifty years. The structure and life style of the family had changed appreciably. The nascent extended family network withered before 1720. Except for Joseph Shippen, the second generation died rather young. The religious unity of the family and its attachment to the Society of Friends also ceased. That it was Joseph rather than his brothers who continued the family through time is significant. The Shippens became outsiders in the Quaker community as they had been earlier in Boston. Joseph exerted no efforts to thrust his way into power even after the homogeniety of Pennsylvania began to crumble. Rather difficult economic conditions in the colony during Joseph's lifetime made it all the more difficult for him to uphold his pretensions as a gentleman. Although he succeeded in enjoying a life style which contrasted with the first generation, the contrast was not always an advancement in terms of prestige. Unlike the first generation, the second cut a small figure in colonial life. No one held a public office and Joseph refrained from philanthropic or other services to the community.

Although Joseph Shippen called himself a gentleman, he was not really part of an aristocracy, if indeed an aristocracy existed as early as the 1730s. Not only was he an outsider, but he displayed no sense of dynastic ambitions for the Shippen family. He produced heirs; hence there would be Shippens in Pennsylvania, but their entry into the upper ranks of society would rest to a considerable degree on their own ambitions and efforts. True Joseph left a large inheritance, yet he not only provided for his daughter, but also insisted that the residue be divided equally among his sons. Although the Shippen fortune had been large, one-third of it would not guarantee any son a place among the elite.

Although his sons resented the apparent lack of interest which their father displayed for their advancement while he lived, their view must be modified. His influence on their success was considerable. Because he forced them to be on their own, the third generation displayed a marked degree of aggressiveness and desire to succeed. Furthermore, his decision to retire to the country as a gentleman is reflected in the third and fourth generations of Shippens. By retaining until his last years almost the entire Shippen landed estate which he inherited from his father, Edward I, Joseph kept the family together. No son moved away to create a new life in another colony. The landed estate was a visible symbol of family continuity which extended into the past and was destined to continue as a binding force and symbol of family identity well into the future. Finally, in numerous ways Joseph's life served as a negative model which his sons, especially the eldest and youngest, sought to repudiate.

IV

Third Generation:
The Formative Period

Unlike the story of the second generation, that of the third is complex, for all four surviving heirs of Joseph Shippen became octogenarians. More than this, however, their varied activities, outlooks on life, and degree of success made them a fascinating group of people. Clearly they did not all fit into the same pattern, and for good reasons. A crucial period for Edward III (1703–1781), Joseph II (1706–1793), Anne (1710–1791), and William II (1712–1801) occurred during the years from about 1720 to 1750. It was during this formative period that determinative decisions and events took place. To a large degree the future role, structure, and strength of the Shippen family and its particular branches were decided at this time.

Although family exerted a significant influence on the lives of the Shippens during this period, the impact and structure of the family stand in sharp contrast with that of the opening decade of the century as well as the last half of the eighteenth century. During those three decades before 1750, the Shippen family remained a loosely associated group of people bearing the same last name. On occasion they acted in concert, but more frequently individuals pursued their own careers and interests independently. For this reason the Shippen family between 1720 and 1750 is more the story of three branches than of a tightly knit unit. In general family associations among Shippens were of personal convenience rather than of economic and political necessity. Although during the 1730s and 1740s Edward III utilized kinship ties for his political advancement, only once were the kinsmen involved named Shippen. For the most part, the use of family remained rather casual instead of closely cultivated. As a result, there was a considerable degree of diversity among the branches in terms of economic, religious, social, and political interests, styles, and success.

Although all three sons were aggressive in economic pursuits, intensity varied with birth position, a circumstance not wholly coincidental. Similarly, all three began to move toward a status of insider as Philadelphia and Pennsylvania became increasingly heterogeneous, yet again differences in degree seem more important than the similarities. Ironically, however, by the end of the period, when geographical dispersion occurred, instead of family disintegration, a new era began in which the Shippens made extensive use of an elaborate kinship network and reached the most impressive pinnacle in their history.

Of Joseph Shippen's three sons, Edward III, the eldest, made the most impressive advances. He achieved the greatest economic and political stature; he became the most significant Shippen of the third generation. Far more than his brothers he displayed a drive to achieve and a very serious nature. He was methodical and careful; in time he developed greater scholarly interests than his brothers and a more pronounced tendency toward paternalism. By contrast his brother, Joseph II, displayed more social ease. William II, the youngest, was perhaps the most relaxed and uncomplicated of the three, a personable individual who showed the most rebelliousness or independence.[1]

Independent life began for Edward III in 1725 when at age twenty-two he married his stepsister. It was an anxious time, and the young man felt unsure about the future. Only after groping for several years did he define the main thrust of his early economic career. At first he seemed about to establish himself in trade using a wide range of relations as commercial connections. His trip to see his Boston kin that year had been enjoyable, and he had been "able to lay out all the money to advantage."[2] Although he declined his grandmother's offer to reside with her in Boston, he continued to look in that direction for a while. Soon Cousin James Halsey desired him "to remit the next proceed in good flower [*sic*] by the first opportunity."[3] In the meantime he and Cousin Murray (Morrey) of Philadelphia entered into a temporary partnership in 1728. Edward III's brother, Joseph II, associated with them on their venture destined for Barbados. As factor on the voyage, Joseph II decided greater profits could be obtained by selling his brother's cargo of port in South Carolina; he then purchased a cargo of rice which he sent to Philadelphia. Despite the profits thus acquired, Joseph II vowed he would not take another "for three times the commission."[4]

About the same time, 1729, another kinsman offered to become part of a budding family trading network. Francis Richardson, Jr., of Kent on the Delaware informed "Coz Shippen" that he needed English goods which he hoped his kinsman could supply. In particular, he wanted some cloth and hats. He further proposed to buy only from Shippen and hoped in return to consign goods to Shippen. Were he to buy elsewhere, Richardson promised to allow Shippen a commission for those goods.[5]

Despite these activities Edward III remained insecure and not at all prosperous. His brothers encountered the same problems in raising a fortune, an experience many Philadelphians shared during this period of economic doldrums. Because he was making little progress on his own, Edward III readily accepted a more secure route toward prominence. When in 1730 his ex-master, James Logan, requested assistance in his flourishing fur-trading enterprise, Edward III gladly accepted power of attorney and immersed himself in the business. This decision gained not only a greater degree of economic security for him, but an immediate improvement in his standard of living, for Logan, who had retired to his country seat at Stenton, allowed Shippen and his family to live in his town house. Previously Edward III had taken another step toward removing anxiety from his life. Uncomfortable with his father's lack of religious affiliation, he joined the Presbyterian church and by 1730 was serving as an elder.[6]

Although Edward III began simply as Logan's manager, by 1731 he became a partner. His lack of capital made him very much the junior partner; this and Logan's crippled condition meant the most onerous tasks invariably fell upon Shippen. During the ensuing years he wrestled with account books and tried to keep track of transactions with fur traders on the one hand and English merchants on the other. Often he traveled about the colony to such places as the Susquehanna, Lancaster, Tulpehocken, and Conestoga

EDWARD SHIPPEN I, 1639–1712

Lithographed by unknown artist after original by Gustavus Hes-
selius *(Historical Society of Pennsylvania)*

JOSEPH SHIPPEN I, 1679–1741

By David McNeeley Stauffer after original by an unknown artist
(Historical Society of Pennsylvania)

ROEBUCK TAVERN

Once a Shippen country house, located on what became Germantown Avenue in Philadelphia. Newspaper copy of a 19th-century
illustration (*Historical Society of Pennsylvania*)

MARY (GRAY) NOWLAND SHIPPEN, 1706–1778

Attributed to Robert Feke *(Collection of the Newark Museum)*

pursuing Indian traders who owed debts to the firm of Logan and Shippen. It was he who threatened men with law suits.[7]

Logan and Shippen were middlemen. They purchased furs such as deer, raccoon, bear, fox, otter, marten, and mink from Indian traders and consigned them to English merchants in London and Bristol. The London firms were those of Nehemiah Champion and also Samuel Storke; in Bristol, Logan relied on contacts which his brother, Dr. William Logan, made for him. From England these Philadelphia merchants received a variety of goods. Articles such as lead, bullet molds, flints, knives, axes, kettles, beads, rings, blankets, and the like were sold to the fur traders. Although both men profited from the enterprise, the risks involved were considerable because the business operated on a credit basis in which substantial sums of money (in the form of goods) were advanced to a large network of traders. Logan requested and expected Shippen's "Care & Diligence in this particular & whatever else may concern my Interest."[8] The ever anxious and often irascible Logan frequently prodded Shippen to make certain that debts did not remain too long on the books. For example, on one occasion in 1730, he urged Shippen to contact a Henry Baily and "press him to his Duty," which was a debt of £500; to discover the whereabouts of James La Fort who owned £300, to find out why Jonah Davenport had not delivered the skins which he had promised, and to speak to Edward Coollidge who went increasingly into debt yet sent nothing of value in return.[9] Although the names changed over the next decade, the responsibilities and problems remained similar while they grew in magnitude.[10]

Logan never shrank from litigation, and if his partner failed to recover debts through verbal exhortations, lawsuits often ensued. Troublesome though they were, they bore results, and only rarely did Logan have to lament philosophically that from "some people I doubt there is but little good to be expected."[11] Other anxious moments in business for both partners often involved physical danger to Shippen. Any incident which threatened to arouse the Indians could impair the fur trade. On one occasion when three Indians were murdered Logan dispatched Shippen to inquire into the matter and determine whether whites or Indians were responsible. If whites were involved, Logan asserted, it would be absolutely necessary that the guilty be apprehended and brought to justice, for "it will most deeply affect the Public Peace & Security of all the Inhabitants."[12] In this and similar incidents involving Indian affairs, the fact that Logan called upon his business partner indicates that he spoke not only as secretary of the province, but also as a concerned merchant.

Because Logan had succeeded so well, he had little patience with inefficiencies within his business. Shrewdness, accuracy, and rigorous energy had enabled him to rise quickly in a fluid society. By the 1730s, however, economic opportunities had lessened; thus greater efforts had to be exerted if one were to continue to prosper. Unfortunately Logan became physically handicapped at this time and unable to remain as deeply involved and in control of his affairs. To a man used to expending great energy and enjoying the profits of his undertakings, the period after 1728 became one of considerable frustration. Edward Shippen often became the victim of Logan's barbs of bitterness and frustration. For example, early in 1731 when Shippen failed to balance accounts during the winter lull in trade, Logan became upset about "considerable quantities" of goods which could not be accounted for. Incompetency rather than dishonesty explained the problem, and Logan rebuked his young partner; "Indeed you have . . . exceedingly disappointed me. The Acco^t of Powder I find has been so confusedly kept I can make nothing of it." To prevent recurrences of such difficulties, Logan urged, "Thou shouldst really step hither [to Stenton] once a week at least."[13]

Time and again during the ensuing years these complaints echoed in Shippen's mind. For example, late in 1731 Logan became very uneasy about a particular outstanding debt and roared, "I think thou hast been inexcusably negligent in it[;] if thou couldst not goe thyself [to collect it], some other methods might have been taken, & thus not let a whole year pass without knowing the least little about it."[14] On rare occasions Logan admitted complicity in the problems, as when he begged Shippen "remember how far all our Accts are behind in which we have both (I am sure I have) been inexcusably negligent."[15] Usually the onus of blame fell on Shippen. Although frequent visits to Stenton might have facilitated business transactions, Shippen found that he was required in town.

The need stemmed not only from business concerns, but also from a desire to be with his family. As a consequence of this decision, a constant refrain of Logan's became "Thou knows I cannot travel without a good deal of trouble, and I very much want to speak to thee, therefore [I] desire to see thee here [at Stenton] as soon as thou canst with any convenience."[16]

But Shippen generally tried to please his partner. Frequently he ran errands for the older man which were wholly unrelated to their enterprise. He delivered books which Logan borrowed, mailed letters, sent newspapers, and purchased rum and implements which Logan required for farming. Later in life Shippen's activities and role in his children's advancement indicate his appreciation for the role Logan played.[17]

In spite of, or perhaps because of, Logan's exhorting, chiding, supervising, and concern, Edward Shippen III soon began to advance his position. Some evidence of this advancement appears in the 1730's; considerably more, in the following decade. Land seemed a sound investment; like his forebearers Shippen embarked upon a long career in real estate. In 1733 Edward Shippen III received a patent for a large tract of land in western Pennsylvania, about sixty miles southwest of Harris's Ferry. He called the area Shippensburg, and in time began to rent segments of it to settlers who soon flowed into the valley. The next year he purchased 340 acres in Limerick township, Philadelphia County for £8. On the advice of James Logan he also acquired one-sixteenth part of about 450 acres and a copper mine at Perkiomen in Limerick township, in which Logan also had invested.[18]

Although it is tempting to subscribe to a belief that Edward III elevated himself through hard work and perseverance, that would be a distortion of reality. The Shippen family and financial power stemming from its position certainly accelerated Edward III's rise; it had a similar effect on his brothers, sister, and cousin Margaret. Just as an inheritance from his grandmother Shippen in 1724 had provided a large amount of land which served as security when he embarked upon married life the following year, so too in the early 1730s inheritance played a significant role in increasing his stature. In 1731, on the death of his Uncle William Shippen, Edward III received a share of the legacy. This uncle (a half-brother of Edward

III's father) was the second child born of the scandalous marriage of Edward Shippen and Esther (Wilcox) James. On this occasion, however, Edward III received congratulations from his business partner who observed "Your Grandfather's Marriage to that Woman proves not now unhappy to you. Since by it you will have (if I'm rightly informed) a thous^d [pounds to divide] amongst you 4, besides half as much to yor Cousin."[19]

Inheritance also figured significantly in the lives of all the other third-generation Shippens. Ann Shippen's dowry came from her grandparents; perhaps knowledge of the provisions of her Uncle William Shippen's will made her even more attractive for she married about a year before his death. To Margaret Shippen, the only heir of Edward Shippen II, inheritance held the greatest importance. Legacies enabled her to marry. When her father died in 1714, his estate was worth only £279, exclusive of real estate. That amount, although not a paltry sum, would not do much to provide for her maintenance and also acquire a husband in a social station in keeping with that of the family. Ignorant of the provisions of Edward II's will, Margaret's Uncle Thomas Story obtained a tenant for Hillam, the Shippen seat in England, so that Edward II's widow and daughter might be provided with additional income. Joseph Shippen, the rightful heir, complained about this, but Story's pleas that "as Margt Shippen was a near relation he might be contented to let her have the benefit of it for a while as her mother was poor, and the child had nothing left she could then command," struck a responsive chord.[20] Here the great importance of an extended family early in Margaret's life is obvious, for her Uncle Joseph Shippen consented to the plan. Still, the girl's financial status was weak.[21]

Although she was a minor when her father died, she did not marry until twenty years later. Certainly the reason for delaying marriage until her mid-twenties was not a lack of suitors, for at least one young merchant became enraptured by "ye Powers of Miss Peggy's Charms."[22] Margaret and her mother preferred to wait until the young woman's assets would enable her to ensnare a man with a fortune who could provide her with security. When her grandmother Esther Shippen died, she acquired a handsome landed estate in Pennsylvania; she seems also to have enjoyed an income from the Shippen family estate in England. Her Uncle William Shippen's death in 1731 provided her with about £500; presumably this made her a particularly eligible young woman.[23]

In 1734 Margaret married John Jekyll Esq. of Maryland (?–1742), "a Gent, Agreeable in his person, One of admirable Good Sense, & poss'ed of 4 or 600 p[ounds per] annum."[24] Because both he and his chief rival, Stephen Bordley, came from Maryland, it seems plausible that Margaret and her mother had remained in contact with their relations to the south. The details of those connections have not survived. Likewise no record of Margaret's feelings toward her suitors remains. However, the unsuccessful young man believed she chose "one who has no other good quality . . . than a sum of money" instead of "that Love wherein I have ever been ye most deeply engaged."[25] Because Jekyll was many years Margaret's senior ("so near his grave as to be Esteemed by all here to be Sup[er] annuated for business," as Bordley expressed it), and Bordley enjoyed little economic prominence at the time, the interpretation of economic considerations over those of emotions gains validity.[26] Such a decision certainly seems consistent with the motivations of the majority of Shippen marriages in the early eighteenth century.[27]

For some time Margaret enjoyed the companionship of her aunts, uncles, and cousins in Boston. Her husband, however, had indeed been near his grave and was laid in it only eight years after their marriage; hence in 1742 the widow returned to Philadelphia where she owned valuable properties. There she and her three young children would be among her kin who remained important to her until her death two decades later.[28]

That inheritance and the family played the most significant role in determining when one could begin life as the head of a family and regulating the pace of upward mobility is also well illustrated in the cases of Joseph II and William II. While Joseph II's experience largely confirms the positive role of family and inheritance previously portrayed, William II's experience seems particularly instructive, for it indicates the difficulties facing one who lacked similarly strong support. Like Edward III, Joseph II received substantial bequests from his grandmother and uncle Shippen. To this basis in life he added profits in trade. He did not share his elder brother's good fortune of acquiring a reasonably endowed stepsister, and his ambitions in life precluded marrying below his station. In order to marry within the mercantile circles of Philadelphia, Joseph II delayed his union with Mary Kearney until his late twenties. The contrast with his elder brother is apparent. Whereas Edward III quickly moved into the stability of married life, Joseph II preferred to retain a less restricted role several years longer. Furthermore, while Edward III remained cautious in business, investing in land and mines, Joseph more readily displayed aspirations of a gentleman's life style. For example, as early as 1734, Joseph II inquired of William Blair, a cousin in Boston, about the price of a four-wheel chaise. The cousin consulted with the best artisans in town about building a reasonably priced one which might be drawn by one or two horses. He also mentioned that he knew "a gentleman hath a four wheel chaise to be disposed of very good"; the cost in this instance he estimated at £141.[29]

While most Shippens of the third generation benefited from inheritance and certain exertions of the family, the early life of William II, the youngest, remained much more the product of his own initiative. Although not wholly neglected, this youngest son had to fend for himself with considerably less support than his siblings. He never reached the same heights of power and prestige. The more notable advances of his career came after an inheritance from his father. Before the 1740s he remained a minor figure in Philadelphia.

As the last child of Joseph and Abigail (Grosse) Shippen, William II did not enjoy all the benefits of comfort and reassurance which the large kinship network gave his older brothers and sisters. His grandfather died the year he was born, his uncle two years after that, and his mother when he was only four. At about that time his father moved to Germantown; hence the lad became geographically separated from the larger family. Perhaps because his grandmother Shippen barely knew him, she failed to mention him significantly in her will. It is also possible that she expected that he would die young like three of his six siblings, or because she did not wish to divide her property into small segments that she ignored him. In any case, the youngest Shippen was singularly slighted at this time. Only if both his brothers died unmarried was he to receive a share of the two thousand acres in Philadelphia County as a bequest of Esther Shippen. The very next year this property escaped him, for his eldest brother married. In comparison to his brothers, William's fortune on starting adult life would be considerably less.[30]

"Poor Will," as his brother referred to him, evidently received little from his father when he determined to make himself independent of his father's support.[31] Probably William II relied basically upon the substantial bequest of his uncle to set himself up as an apothecary. Although delaying marriage for several years until he became well established and more secure seemed the prudent course to follow, William II paid little heed to caution. He intended to marry almost immediately. Part of the reason for this stems from his intended bride Susannah Harrison's circumstances. Her father, Joseph Harrison, a local shopkeeper, died in 1734; his estate was valued at only £58.18.7, and Susannah's share would not enable her to sustain an independent existence. Each of Harrison's six children or children-in-law received a token bequest of five shillings; his wife Catherine retained life interest in the estate and the entire personal estate. Harrison's modest possessions included 106 gallons of rum in his shop valued at £15.01.4, a Negro woman named Ambo valued at £10, £3.17.3 in cash, a brass snuffer, a copper coffee pot, and a Bible. The remaining items were very ordinary. After the widow's death, his three children were to divide the estate and "my son Joseph Harrison shall have as much again as Either of the others."[32]

In 1735 at the Presbyterian church, the twenty-three-year-old William Shippen II married Susannah Harrison, who was one year his senior. The following year he joined the Presbyterian congregation, a decision which took on greater significance in the future as religious attitudes filled a part of his life previously devoid of such inclinations. Clearly Susannah appealed to him for personal reasons, for she lacked both a satisfactory dowry and high social standing. Besides demonstrating something about his own values, William II's experience indicated that in the third generation the Shippen family could not sustain all its members in the upper ranks of society. The youngest son was at least temporarily cut loose to fend for himself. In this regard, it seems relevant to observe that his rise in stature gained little momentum until his father died, an event which favorably altered the economic position of all third-generation Shippens.[33]

The death of Joseph Shippen affected the development of the Shippen family in several ways. Joseph's role as patriarch involved cultivating his own position as a gentleman, but exerting almost no influence to make his children act in concert with one another. In the 1730s, therefore, his children pursued largely independent careers. Each was aggressive in his chosen realm, but each acted with little reference to his siblings. Little interaction can be observed in their early adult lives. In the 1740s separateness began to give way to a tendency of closer association. For the most part this trend stemmed from deliberate decisions. Because the Shippens were rather well established by the 1740s, they realized that making use of an extended kinship network could benefit the constituent parts. This invigorated extended family is particularly obvious in economic pursuits. It may also be seen in the political realm as well, for as the Shippens became well established economically they entered politics.

The property, both real and personal, released by the death of Joseph Shippen in 1741, together with several properties which he released two or three years before his death gave a burst of energy to his sons. The eldest and youngest became particularly active after receiving their sizable inheritances. All discovered a capability to enlarge their activities and strengthen their position.

When Joseph Shippen died in 1741, Edward III became the oldest living Shippen. Because he was only thirty-eight years old, and an active merchant, it is not surprising that the wealth which had remained dormant while his father lived would now be used. In this regard, the changes transpiring in Philadelphia and Pennsylvania as the new decade opened complemented the aims of the new generation of Shippens. During the 1740s trade revived and Penn's colony prospered. Philadelphia particularly enjoyed a wave of prosperity and its growing population reflected this. By the 1740s Philadelphia surpassed New York in size and with thirteen thousand people became the second largest city in British North America. In 1744 the mayor of the bustling town was Edward Shippen III. This office serves as the dramatic symbol of the rise of Edward Shippen III from relative obscurity in 1730 to one of the town's leading merchants only a decade and a half later.[34]

At about the same time Edward III's father died, his business partner James Logan appears to have lessened considerably his participation in mercantile activities. With sound experience and a sizable inheritance to invest, Edward III made the transition to a more prominent role rather smoothly. He continued or enlarged upon the trading connections already established. Samuel Storke of London, who had been the primary associate of the firm of Logan and Shippen, became a partner with Shippen alone in several trading ventures. For example, in 1742, the *Constantine* carried a cargo of powder, lead shot, flints, knives, jew's-harps and dry goods such as binding, duffels, gartering, bed lace and ribbons valued at £3,385, divided "in equal shares between Storke & myself."[35] Almost concurrently a cargo held in the same fashion valued at almost £1,200 rested on board the *Priscilla*. Identical arrangements pertained to 1743 shipments valued at £1,997 and £861 and a 1746 shipment valued at £770. Besides arrangements as equal partners, Edward III also sold goods on consignment for Storke.[36]

Because no business journal survives, many details of Shippen and Storke's business activities in the 1740s are lost; surviving business papers are suggestive though incomplete. It seems plausible to believe, however, that numerous shipments owned equally by Storke and Shippen traversed the Atlantic before Edward III established a partnership in 1747 with Thomas Lawrence. When Shippen boasted in 1744 that "we live In a very flourishing Province of about 60 years [in age], Our City containing at least 1500 Houses and 15,000 Inhabitants & they are trading toil every Year upwards of 300 vessels which are Loaded with our wheat flour bisket, Tobacco, staves, Beef Pork Gammon Bees wax & Pig Iron, [illegible] sorts of skins such as Deer, Elk, Bear, wolves, Panther, Buffalos, Beavers, fishers, Foxes, Raccoons, Wild Catts Otters Marlins Minks & Muscrats," he realized that his trading activities had helped bring about this prosperous state of affairs.[37]

Shippen's reputation grew. In Boston, his kin who had remained aware of the Shippens although not in regular contact with them, made some attempts to establish relationships. For example, "loving cous" Thomas Greenough had only heard of Edward Shippen III but "rejoyces in his prosperity and hopes . . . he increases in worldly goods."[38] He also urged Shippen to visit or write, a course of action aimed to improve the position of both men. Several years later Greenough ordered £20 worth of the best Philadelphia butter from Shippen; Shippen complied; however, his cousin wanted it for his "own family use."[39] It seems that, although some ties were established with Boston kin, they remained peripheral to the main concerns of the Shippens of Philadelphia.

The more important family ties of an economic nature for Edward III were with his brother, Joseph II. During the 1730s, Edward III confined almost all his merchant activities to the fur trade as Logan's partner. An exception, the sole exception, involved his selling a consignment of soap for Joseph Shute of Charlestown, South Carolina. By the late 1730s, however, Edward III's family connections were not as weak as they had been at the beginning of the decade when he had begun his career. His brother, Joseph II, had succeeded in trade. Part of his business was done with the firm of Logan and Shippen and his account against them for six months in 1736 alone amounted to almost £650. Joseph II dealt mainly in dry goods such as gartering, calico, cambrics, and bed bunk. Several times he ventured to London to establish contacts and do "as much business as he could."[40] There he found Lawrence Williams to be a "very extraordinary cousin" and engaged him as an agent.[41] Williams also served as an agent for Logan and Shippen. Edward III's family contacts were becoming important; he would develop them during the ensuing years.[42]

Although in the 1740s Edward III often acted as a partner in ventures with Samuel Storke of London, at times he involved his brother, Joseph II. For example, in 1745 the two brothers owned the ship *Charming Catherine* and traded with Antigua, St. Christopher, and London. Between 1743 and 1746, Joseph II had an account with Edward III and took goods on consignment from Storke as well. By the mid-1740s, Edward III and Joseph II were closely associated. Doubtless the merits of establishing a more stable partnership crossed their minds. The ambitions and goals of the two brothers did not coincide; hence despite the benefits of experience and fortune each could bring to such a venture, no partnership evolved. By this time Joseph II no longer thought of ways to expand his trading activities. Instead, like his father, he contemplated retiring as a country gentleman before he turned fifty.[43]

His actions had indicated this for some time, although he left few records of his thoughts. Unlike his older and younger brother who purchased land in Pennsylvania, a course of action which might not pay dividends for many years, if not decades, Joseph II devoted himself to ventures which brought more immediate returns. His only known new investment in land paid immediate returns. In 1742 he purchased of John Crutcher, yeoman of Philadelphia, property in Surry, England which Crutcher inherited from his father. For £100.13 Shippen acquired ten acres on the King's High Road together with two malt houses and four dwelling houses and accompanying outbuildings which were already drawing rent. Aside from this, and profits from trade, he relied on returns from short-term loans and renting out parts of his landed inheritance. The conclusion readily drawn from such actions designed to keep his capital readily available is that he wished to be able to retire early in life. Furthermore, in comparison to his brothers, he always had more interest in enjoying life rather than wrestling with it. He had purchased a carriage at a younger age, and in 1748 he joined the Dancing Assembly, an indulgence in luxury which Edward III would not contemplate.[44]

By 1751 Joseph Shippen II wanted to retire from the bustle of business to the calm of the country. He was only forty-six years old, barely six years older than his father had been when he had done so three decades before. His father's example could be followed very closely, for if his brothers were obliging, Joseph II might establish himself in the very house his father had occupied. In 1741 the three Shippen brothers became joint owners of the father's Germantown Plantation; now, a decade later Joseph II proposed buying his brothers' shares and becoming sole owner.

At first Joseph II proposed trading some Germantown lots rated at £250 for his brothers' two-thirds interest in "ye Germantown House."[45] The lots were from among those which he had inherited from his father. Edward III appeared rather receptive to the idea, but William II objected. He complained so strenuously that Edward III finally accepted a role as umpire to reconcile "Brothers [who] are diametrically opposite in opinion."[46] This led to heated tempers. For some time William II remained adamant, and Joseph II leveled sharp criticisms at his brother Edward III. Smarting under these verbal attacks, Edward III urged, "Our Brother J Shippen never had any good pretence in all his Life to complain with any Colour of Reason of either of us because we have always made it a Rule to do him Justice."[47]

Eventually the details of a satisfactory settlement were agreed upon. In February 1752 Joseph II recorded a deed for the "Germantown Plantation" by which he paid his brothers £186.13.4 for their interest in the mansion house and lot.[48] The lot was 84 feet on Germantown Street, 63 feet wide on Green Street, and extended 780 feet between the two. William II and Edward III retained possession of the lots adjoining it on either side. By November 1752, Joseph II was settled in Germantown, a situation which at least his elder brother wished he could duplicate. For Edward III, however, the expense of educating his family and setting up his sons in the world precluded this; William II did not even contemplate such an idle existence. The happy coincidence of an inheritance, success in trade, and having only one surviving son whose career would demand attention made this style of life possible for Joseph II.[49] Although he still called himself a merchant, Joseph II was clearly moving away from that status. After less than a decade of country living and removal from trade, Joseph Shippen II styled himself a gentleman. For various reasons he was the most secure and relaxed, though not most active, of the third-generation Shippens.[50]

All the while Joseph II directed his activities toward retiring from the rigors of economic activities, his brothers, neither of whom could consider retiring, expanded theirs. Aside from Edward III's mercantile activities and William II's apothecary trade which increasingly involved duties as a "practitioner of physick," both became active in real estate.[51]

Naturally because Edward III commanded greater resources, his real estate investments overshadowed those of his younger brother. On several occasions he evaluated his investments; if they failed to produce profits or if capital were required elsewhere, he did not shrink from forceful actions. For example, by 1741 Edward III decided that the Perkiomen mine in which he and his business partner James Logan had invested might be worthwhile as a long-term land investment, but that it was useless as a mining venture. When his partners decided to shoulder additional costs for "Searching & Digging," he criticized the new expenditure as wasteful and pointless, and refused to pay his share of the additional expenses.[52] Although the other owners threatened that he would forfeit his right to the 450 acres at the mine site, Shippen remained fixed in his decision. Although that decision remained the source of contention during the ensuing years, Shippen refused to part with money in this or any other experiment in mining or manufacturing; he also demanded that his right to one-sixteenth of the mining property remained unimpaired. Little sentiment could be attached to a faltering mine in which Shippen had shared only briefly.[53]

Thoughts concerning the family estate in England, however, reveal a great deal. When Edward III's father died, his eldest son expressed considerable interest in "Hillham," which "I have been told has been in our family five hundred years."[54] From about this time onward, Edward III developed interest not only in the Shippens clustered in the provincial town, but also in those in England. He cherished brief missives which he received from some of them. When Edward III sought advice about a way "to dispossess my Cousin Margaret Jeykill (formerly Shippen)," it might appear as if he were consciously seeking possession of a physical symbol of the family's continuity and perhaps its genteel stature.[55] Certainly country seats served as symbols of continuity for the English aristocracy.[56] But Edward III's thoughts on the subject are vividly exposed in a brief postscript to a letter about this ancient family seat. He noted, "I would sell Said Estate for one hundred & fifty pounds Sterling without charge."[57]

Although family had great significance for Edward Shippen III, a country seat in England bore no relevance to it as a symbol. When he looked to the past for "reference ancestors" or figures who played a meaningful role in his origins, he looked no further than his grandfather. From that Shippen emanated great wealth and power, a fact Edward III was reminded of almost every time he wrote an indenture of sale or rent. His ancestry beyond Edward I remained unknown; indeed, he never sought to eliminate the void which existed regarding this subject.[58]

One further implication of Shippen's thoughts on the English property is that after eighty years in North America, half a century of which were spent in Pennsylvania, the Provinces had become home. Although the Shippens looked favorably upon England, they did not wish to live there.

Real estate was one of many forces which rooted the Shippens to Pennsylvania. Of course all three Shippens were engaged in real estate because they inherited large amounts of it in Philadelphia city and county. This they apportioned among themselves. For example, immediately after their father's death the sons by a tripartite indenture divided a sizable amount of property on Cedar Street at the southern city limit. In 1744, they divided a lot between Third and Fourth Streets into nine lots, each brother taking three lots. The following year, by another tripartite indenture, they divided an entire city block (490 feet by 396 feet) between Fourth and Fifth and Walnut and Spruce. But whereas Joseph II remained satisfied with returns from renting or selling these and other inherited lands, both his brothers actively and aggressively enlarged their holdings.[59]

In the early 1740s Edward Shippen III significantly increased his land holdings in both the city and province. These ventures involved an outlay of more than £4,000. The most dramatic purchase was his acquisition at a public auction of an entire city block for £2,102.10. Story square, as people referred to the area (430 feet by 396 feet) between Third and Fourth and Sassafras and Vine streets at the north end of town, had been owned by Edward III's uncle Thomas Story. It was sold by the executors of his estate in 1745 to comply with the will of this Quaker gentleman who had returned to Cumberland, England, shortly after the death of Ann (Shippen) Story about three decades earlier. The following year Edward III acquired for £240 two tenements near the New Market at the south end of town which adjoined property on Second Street which he already owned.[60]

In the few years preceding 1745, Edward III also accumulated gradually more than 3,000 acres divided in a ratio of roughly two to one between Bucks and Chester Counties. In 1745 he decided to lease eleven tracts totaling 2,825 acres to Richard Peters. For this Edward Shippen III, Esq., received the handsome sum of £1,000. At least two schemes in Shippen's mind drew on the capital thus raised. First, he had apprenticed his eldest son to one of the most prominent lawyers in Philadelphia and intended shortly to send him to Middle Temple in London. Second, he was about to enter a new partnership in the fur business.[61]

The new partnership involved two old business associates, for Edward Shippen III and Thomas Lawrence had worked together in the firm of Logan and Shippen since about 1730. As Logan approached his death bed, his friends saw no reason to allow the trading network to wither. The partnership expanded its activities in January 1746/47, when it negotiated a loan of £722 sterling with Thomas Lawrence's father, a Philadelphia merchant. From then on the amounts of credit which the firm extended to traders such as Hugh Crawford of Lancaster, James and John Lawrey of Lancaster, and Thomas McKee ranged from £150 to over £1,000. In addition to shipping furs, Shippen and Lawrence also shipped wheat. When the London market was glutted, their English contacts (Storke and Champion) suggested that they send their shipment to Henry Steer in Lisbon. Although in 1749 Steer observed, "Our market has been very low for wheat lately," he welcomed their shipment, for the "harvest here [was] not so good as expected and English grain is not coming in great supply so the price is rising."[62] London remained the firm's main contact, and when Edward Shippen III's son, Edward IV, arrived in the metropolis to study law, one of his duties involved urging "a pretty large acquaintance with merchants in London" to send consignments of any sorts of goods to his father and Thomas Lawrence.[63]

While Edward III cut the largest figure in the economic world of any third-generation Shippen, and while Joseph II became the first of the generation to style himself a gentleman, the youngest brother, William II, was as aggressive in bettering his position as his more limited opportunities afforded. Even before his father died he embarked on a career in real estate to augment his actions as a chemist. He purchased some property in or near the south end of Philadelphia from his father. During the ensuing decade he added to his holdings in that area of Philadelphia and acquired some in Germantown, Northern Liberties, and Bucks County.

The first opportunity came in 1740 when the widow of Benjamin Fairman, yeoman or gentleman, was unable to meet mortgage payments to the General Loan Office for 68 acres in Shakamaxunk, now called Kensington. William II paid £200 to the sheriff and received title to this property in Northern Liberties on the northwest side of the Frankford road. The following year he purchased for £210 an adjoining 29 acres and dwelling house from the widow and executor of the Fairman estate. Between 1741 and 1745 William II bought two additional lots in Kensington, Northern Liberties. The first was a lot 100 feet by 400 feet which extended from the Delaware River; the second lot of 56 feet by 400 feet adjoined it. Both were purchased from Samuel Hastings, shipwright. Shippen's last acquisition in this area was a plot of two and a half acres on the Frankford road which cost him £530 in 1748.[64]

The other lots which William II bought were located in the city proper. Three he got for £60 from his brother, Edward III. They lay on Cedar or South Street in the area the Shippen family dominated. A few years later his brother sold him a lot at Cedar and Vernon Streets. His other brothers sold him an acre pasture south of the city for £32.6. After negotiations in 1743 with Jehu Claypoole, a tailor of Mt. Holly, New Jersey, William II received a lot on Walnut Street and 150 acres on Neshaminy Creek in Bucks County for £200. In 1745 he added a 20-by-90-foot lot on Front Street which bounded other holdings. Four hundred pounds expended on a building and lot (20 feet by 100 feet) on the east side of Second Street concludes his real estate purchases in Philadelphia city and county during the 1740s.[65]

By the end of the decade William II added another facet to his interests. He purchased three-quarters interest in the Oxford Furnace, an iron works located in Sussex County, New Jersey. Unlike his brother's ill-fated copper mine, this venture paid satisfactory dividends. When his son, Joseph W. Shippen, had completed his formal education, William II bought the remaining interest in the furnace and put his son in charge of operations.[66]

What becomes obvious as one follows the careers of the three Shippen brothers is that although each followed a distinctive course, they were all successful. The degree of success varied, but all three enjoyed considerable upward mobility. Particularly in the case of Edward III and Joseph II, inheritance and ability in trade enabled them to rise rapidly during these two crucial decades of their lives. Although William II benefited somewhat from a goodly inheritance, his impressive rise relied more heavily upon his aggressive character and the still fluid nature of Philadelphia society. At least the two older brothers appeared well on their way to surpassing the position and accomplishments which their father had achieved.

As each brother gained economic security and strength, he experienced a desire to exercise greater powers. These feelings were similar to those felt by their grandfather, Edward Shippen I. Unlike their forebearer who found his political ambitions thwarted in Boston, these men found that Philadelphia's rapid growth, the changing character of its population, the proprietor's favorable opinion of the Shippen family, and increasingly valuable family connections provided political opportunities.[67] The Shippens were able to enter public life from a position of strength. Especially after 1740, they realized the use to which they might put family connections in advancing their members.

The eldest son, Edward III, entered the political life of the city first. Doubtless he entered the Common Council of Philadelphia in 1732 as James Logan's protégé. Five years later his thirty-one-year-old brother, Joseph II, joined him there. After ten years of service, Edward III advanced from councilman to alderman. The following year (1743) the Shippens' brother-in-law, Charles Willing, a wealthy merchant, joined them in the city corporation.[68]

Edward Shippen III also obtained offices on the provincial level. These came because of his valuable connections in the Proprietary party. His business partner, James Logan, was secretary of Pennsylvania and the Penn's most trusted agent in the colony. Another powerful politician was Shippen's Cousin William Allen. Allen's mother was Mary Budd, the sister of Joseph Shippen's second wife. Joseph's son, Edward III, reinforced the family connection when he married Rose (Budd) Shippen's daughter by a previous marriage. The family connection with the Allens proved very important to the Shippens during ensuing decades. As the 1730s unfolded, Allen became an increasingly important leader of the Proprietary party, and soon he exercised substantial influence over the choice of all Proprietary appointees. He enhanced his stature in 1734, when he married a daughter of Provincial Councillor Andrew Hamilton. From 1736 to 1738, while Pennsylvania awaited the appointment of a new governor, James Logan, as senior member of the Council, acted as chief executive of the colony. It is hardly coincidental that in 1737 Edward Shippen III received an appointment as clerk of the County Court of Quarter Sessions of the Peace. Within a decade he acquired other appointive offices.[69]

Certainly family connections explain in part the reason that the closed corporation elected Edward Shippen III mayor of Philadelphia in 1744. More than a third of the members present were related to Edward III or to his kinsmen, such as Cousin William Allen, who would not hesitate to urge support of Shippen.[70] Also Edward III's business associates, James Logan and Thomas Lawrence, voted in the election. Certainly Shippen's great stature as a successful and prominent Philadelphia merchant cannot be ignored, yet one never sees any mention of the role which the family played in obtaining this honor. To carry the point further, family does not seem irrelevant to an explanation of why the mayor's brother, William II, was admitted to the Common Council the following year. Regardless of the reason for his election, William II celebrated his new eminence by seeking "a genteel carriage horse of about fifteen hands high, round bodied, full of courage, close ribbed, dark chestnut, not a swift pacer, if that must much enhance his price."[71]

As the eighteenth century approached the halfway point, the Shippens seemed destined for great stature. All three brothers were successful men of affairs who served the public and rode about in chaises or carriages. At this moment, however, an embarrassing predicament arose. Curiously major scandals or embarrassments plagued all five generations of Shippens who lived during the eighteenth century.

This scandal involved Edward III, who like his grandfather, Edward I, had many agonizing moments following his marriage. Sarah (Plumley) Shippen died in 1735 at age twenty-nine. Although left with three children—ages three, four, and six years—the widower did not remarry immediately.[72] After eight years, Edward III married Mary (Gray) Nowland whom he had known since childhood. It was also Mary's second marriage. Her first spouse, John Nowland, had gone to Barbados several years before; when he failed to contact her or anyone else in Philadelphia, all presumed him dead. In the opinion of the Reverend Aaron Burr, president of the College of New Jersey and friend of the Shippens, Mary was free to marry. Some weeks after the August wedding, the shocking revelation from Barbados that Nowland was still alive, horrified the Shippens. Although Edward III found "many sober People [believe] that she was free many years ago, and that we are justifyable in the sight of God," many harshly denounced Mary Shippen as a bigamist.[73] Shippen's friend, James Logan, advised the couple to separate, but Edward III felt that such action "would cause a great Clamour throughout Town and Country"; hence, he and his wife solemnly "agreed to separate Beds and to inhabit no more together unless that person at B[arbado]s should really be gone."[74]

By 1750 the Shippen's private problem became public knowledge. Although Edward III could convince his brother-in-law, Mayor Willing, to prevent Mary's other husband from entering Philadelphia (the occasion never arose), he could not prevent "Our spiteful Grand Jurys . . . [from] threatening to indite your poor mammy and my Self on Acco[un]t of our marriage."[75] A severe penalty awaited those guilty of bigamy, thirty-nine lashes and life imprisonment. Rather than live "in Terror and danger" Mary went to live with her mother and father.[76] It is doubtful if such a severe penalty would have been meted out against so prominent a citizen. Edward III seemed sure that if he and Mary were convicted, his connections would prevent them from being "tied to a whipping Post & confined to a Goal."[77]

The Grand Jury's threat was not an empty one, for the Shippens were indicted. Fortunately, Governor James Hamilton, the brother-in-law of Edward Shippen III's Cousin William Allen, protected the couple. Edward III scarcely relished the prospect of being under "an everlasting obligation" to the governor; yet he welcomed a pardon for engaging in adultery and for Mary's committing bigamy as well.[78]

Although the Shippens avoided physical punishment, other repercussions from their mistake threatened. The mental anguish created by the affair was considerable. Edward III tried to buoy up his wife's spirits. He suggested that his son, Joseph III, who was away at college, write to comfort his "mother." After denouncing "the malicious Grand Jury" and "so many spiteful Enemies who are always wrongfully condemning us," Joseph III exclaimed, "Oh! May the Author of our Natures' even deliver us from such wicked Passions!" Then in a calmer tone he urged that "you have a Conscience void of offense . . . you have a heart searching God, who is a Righteous & impartial Judge, to deal with."[79] Besides visiting his wife while they remained apart, Edward III struck upon another idea to reaffirm the dignity of his wife and family. He commissioned

Robert Feke to paint a portrait of Mary (Gray) Shippen and one of his son, Joseph III.[80]

A "symbolic family estate" is particularly vulnerable whenever the reputation of any member is questioned. Edward III realized that "it would be grievous . . . [if] all ye Proceedings of ye Court would Stand perpetually on record against us." Even when the record was expunged, Edward III continued to worry that he and Mary would be "twitted in the teeth and our Children after us."[81] Both Edward III and Mary soon embarked upon efforts to compensate for the damage they had done to the Shippen family. Edward III certainly devoted much of the remainder of his life to promoting the welfare of his family and kinsmen; Mary became especially noted for her interest in Edward III's children and grandchildren and also for her piety.

A few months after the Shippens' indictment, Edward III's "brother" Charles Willing obtained letters from his business agent in Barbados which indicated that Mary Shippen's first husband was dead. Both Shippen and Willing sought certified copies of the parish register and statements from people who attended the funeral. When proof arrived, Mary returned to live with Edward III.[82]

To avoid public ridicule, Edward III moved his family to Lancaster, a small frontier town two days by horse from Philadelphia. He might have fled to Shippensburg had his great stone house there been ready. In Lancaster the Shippens, their servant Hance, and Negro woman prayed that the scandal would dissipate. The precipitous flight in 1752 was not entirely irrational. Although the emotional dislocation was severe, the move could make sense from an economic and political standpoint. Residence in Lancaster put Shippen in closer contact with fur traders, and this could benefit the Shippen and Lawrence enterprise. Providing an education for one son in England and the other at the College of New Jersey, while at the same time providing a dowry for his daughter, taxed his resources heavily; living in Lancaster was far cheaper than in Philadelphia. Also, Edward III had already acquired political offices in Lancaster County. In 1737 he became clerk of the County Court of Quarter Sessions of Peace, in 1745 register of Deeds and Prothonotary. He appears to have kept all these offices until 1776, and certainly in the long run his move to Lancaster enlarged his role in Pennsylvania politics.[83]

By mid-century the Shippen family had developed and changed from its early characteristics. Clearly, all three branches of the family were unable to match the prominence of the founder of the family. Furthermore, the Shippens did not remain simply a merchant family. Only Edward III continued in the fur trade; Joseph II lived in retirement as a country gentleman, while William II, the youngest brother, rose in the medical profession. Despite these divergences, all three devoted a significant part of their attention to real estate, the form of investment which had attracted the attention of their grandfather. In the realm of politics, where the founder of the family loomed prominently, the contrast with the third generation is again evident. Of the three brothers, only the eldest made significant progress in accumulating offices in Philadelphia and Lancaster County. Finally, although Edward III and William II experienced the religious enthusiasm of their grandfather, they did so as Presbyterians, for all connections with the Society of Friends had been severed long ago.

Even the structure of the family differed from that of the earlier periods when Edward Shippen I acted as a strong patriarch. Joseph Shippen did little to make the family cohesive. Associations among his children existed; yet they tended to be rather casual. Although Edward III increasingly operated within the context of a larger kinship network, at this time it involved his Cousin William Allen and his connections more than Shippen's siblings.

The Shippen family itself, however, influenced all the Shippens. To a degree, the order in which Edward III, Joseph II, and William II were born into the family influenced the development of their personalities. Inheritance certainly had a bearing on the Shippen men and women of the third generation, and the "symbolic family estate" meant a great deal to Edward III and perhaps to the others as well.

V

The Education and Establishment
of the Fourth Generation:
The Primary Branch

Family life and family structure cannot be comprehended by describing and analyzing the economic and political careers of the third generation Shippens. Their occupations consumed much of the energy of Edward III, Joseph II, and William II. Yet even after those activities receive extensive attention, significant aspects of their lives remain untouched. By the mid-eighteenth century the Shippen family must not be thought of simply as individuals; to approach them as such is to misconstrue their lives. Only after one has become familiar with the Shippen's family life and structure can one understand what it meant to be a Shippen. From this standpoint the lives of individual Shippens can be dealt with intelligently.

Some of the information about family life and structure involves demographic considerations such as how many children the third generation had and at what ages these children married. Beyond this is the question of geographical mobility. To what extent did the Shippens remain concentrated in Philadelphia? It is important to know which Shippens left and why. Often the answer is intricately bound up with the degree of control which the father exercised over his children. In this regard it seems important to determine whether children were treated equally, the degree of differentiation among them, and how they responded to these influences. Family, especially the father, played a significant role in the education of the fourth generation. If generous, the older generation can measurably advance the ambitions of the young; in other circumstances a strong patriarch can retard or even destroy youthful plans. In this realm of activity, as elsewhere, the patriarch as a real historical and human figure emerges; he should supplant or cast aside stereotypes or idealized conceptualizations. Although the older generation exerts strong influences upon its offspring, the younger generation has an impact on its parents. Whether positive or negative, this impact cannot be ignored.

Little evidence survives concerning the childhood of the fourth generation. Letters and other Shippen papers of this period revolve about their fathers' businesses and public lives; private lives remain relatively obscure. This does not mean, however, that nothing is known. Although information about child-rearing practices (such things as weaning, toilet training, and the like) does not survive, several significant aspects of the early life of the fourth generation can be reconstructed from demographic information.[1] By analyzing the existent information and drawing upon insights derived from certain psychological studies, one may suggest the relevance of this information to their later lives.

The relationship of the size of family to the father's activities merits some attention. Each branch of the third generation had a rather large number of children at roughly two-year intervals. Only Edward III married more than once, but all his children came by his first wife. Edward III and Sarah had seven children; Joseph II and Mary had nine children; Anne II and Charles Willing had ten; and William II and Susannah probably had several more than the four who reached maturity. Only Sarah died before menopause; hence with that exception each branch of the family had as many children as they could. Sarah is the only Shippen of the thirteen in the third and fourth generation who died "in child bed." She was only twenty-nine when she died and had borne a child every year or two since her marriage. Even though childbirth caused her decease, that cause seems grossly overrated as a force in the colonial family if the Shippens are in any way representative. There is reason to believe they are.[2]

More important to the development of family life and a child's personality than the total number of siblings is the number with whom the child must compete. Although the three Shippen fathers of the third generation sired more than twenty children, none of their families ever teemed with children. Only Joseph II and Mary cared for as many as six at the same time; for William II and Susannah, the number was four, and for Edward III and Sarah, it was three.

Because there was a moderate number of children in the family, each child had ample opportunity to attract his parents' attention, love, and care. Beyond this, because the number of children remained relatively small, each child could develop a particular personality by distinguishing himself from his peers. Surviving evidence concerning the fourth generation's adolescence and mature years indicates this occurred. The number of surviving children bears directly on the future of the Shippen family as well, for it influences the degree of dispersion of the father's resources both while he lives and after his death.[3]

Also important to the structure and future of the family is the proportion of males and females in each branch. Edward III had two sons and a daughter; Joseph II had only one son and five daughters; William II had three sons and a daughter. For example, the entire descent of Joseph II's branch of the family rested on one son; when that young man died, his father's interest in the extended Shippen family noticeably diminished. The future of Edward III's branch of the family seemed secure with two sons, and although he treated them differently, his substantial wealth could aid both and not impair the family's standing. William II had the least financial assets and the greatest number of male heirs; he had to provide somehow for three sons. His decisions also reflect differential treatment. One strong characteristic of the third generation which seems to distinguish it from previous generations is that the fathers expended considerably more energy, attention, and money on the eldest sons. A lack of evidence prevents fixing precisely when in the son's life this began. The circumstance that each eldest son was his father's namesake, however, seems suggestive. Younger sons still received considerable attention, and daughters certainly were not ignored.

As the fourth generation reached adolescence, evidence regarding its members increases. Analysis of their early life and their functioning within the family, especially in relationship to the head of the family, becomes possible. Their lives express vividly the role of

family, and in the process the characteristics of the Shippen patri-
archs become explicit.

The first member of the third generation to emerge as head of a
family and to assume the role of patriarch was Edward III. His sons
Edward IV (1729–1806), and Joseph III (1732–1810), and daughter
Sarah II (1731–1784) leave a fuller picture of intra-family relationships than either of the other branches of the Shippen family.
Edward III paid close and continuous attention to the development
of his children. He directly involved himself in their education and
exerted considerable efforts to improve them. Consistently he employed numerous techniques to keep the family tightly bound together; for a long while he remained closely involved in the major
decisions of his children's lives.

Edward III took particular care to groom his elder son Edward
IV for a significant career in Philadelphia. The fourth Shippen in
America bearing the name Edward would have much to live up to;
both his father and great-grandfather had cut large figures in economic and political circles. To launch the lad who bore these large
responsibilities, Edward III apprenticed his teen-age son to Tench
Francis, "an able lawyer" in Philadelphia who served as attorney
general of the province. By 1744, Edward III had already entered
his son's name for admission to Middle Temple, London. Clearly
this young man's career was important to his father, for these educational plans cost dearly.[4]

Shortly after his nineteenth birthday, Edward IV concluded his
apprenticeship and embarked for London to further his training in
the law. He described his winter ocean voyage as "terrible," for
"when the ship was on its side" he thought surely they would per-
ish.[5] He shuddered as he described the calamities of his first trip
away from home and marveled at his safe arrival after several
perilous weeks. To lessen the feeling of being in another world,
Edward III suggested that his son dine with Richard Penn, a friend
of the family, and also meet with some of his father's business contacts. To provide the youth with some sense of security, his father
encouraged him to correspond with his brother, sister, "Uncle
Billy," and himself. The young man also conveyed a letter of introduction from Mary Shippen to an English cousin, requesting that

"civilities" be extended "to my said son."[6] This and other acts made Edward IV "sensible of, & grateful for Mammy's interesting herself so much in my Welfare." During the year he spent abroad, consequently, Edward IV remained in constant contact with his family.[7]

Needless to say Edward IV marveled at educational opportunities abroad, and reflected upon education in the colonies which he felt far inferior by comparison. After about a year of study he hoped to be called to the bar. Some problems arose and prevented him from completing the requirements in time and forced him to postpone donning a wig and gown. Rather than return home empty-handed, he requested his father to allot him an additional £30, for "with this necessary Sum . . . I may be enabled to compleat my Affairs with Advantage and quit England with Credit."[8] During the summer of 1749, after completing his studies, Edward IV ventured to France, for he thought that "a man that comes to England to see the world is inexcusable in peaceable times, if he does not visit that Metropolis of the polite worlds." Paris particularly impressed him, and he enjoyed speaking in French to the people, whom he found cordial and hospitable, a "character of that Nation."[9] Edward III thoroughly approved of his son's conduct and confided to him "notwithstanding you will cost me a good deal, yet if I had money to spare, I would send you as much more and allow you to stay there another year. You must conform to my circumstances; I've done the best in my power to serve you."[10]

With the advantages of fine English legal training and the broadening experience of foreign travel, Edward IV acquired a rather high opinion of himself. From this time onward he remained the more dominant and forceful of the two brothers; he was also given to displaying a somewhat haughty manner on occasion. For example, having completed his own education, he took "the Liberty to press you [his younger brother Joseph III] to pursue Learning with a great deal of Assiduity; you are now in a time of Life the most proper to lay a Foundation for being a Man of Consequence." Reflecting on his own experience which loomed large in his mind, he observed, "If ever you travel you'll find how men of Letters are every where respected, you'll see the ascendancy the knowing man has over the Blockhead."[11]

On his return to Philadelphia in 1750, Edward IV clearly expected to be "a Man of Consequence", and he likewise assumed that he would enjoy ascendancy over the many "Blockheads." Brother Joseph III rejoiced that "Neddy has attained so good a Character in England which certainly will resound greatly to his Advantage."[12] Neddy's father's connection with the Penns, Cousin William Allen, and other influential Philadelphians enabled him to realize this potential. At first, however, Edward IV merely pursued life as an attorney at law. He handled a case for his "brother" James Burd, one for a college friend of his brother, Joseph III, and some miscellaneous legal work for his uncle, William Shippen II. Soon his practice expanded.[13]

As Edward IV's reputation grew, he sought public offices in which to display his talents and increase his income. The overriding importance of family connections demands attention, for family ties and influence rather than merely ability enabled him to acquire his first offices. Fortuitously, in 1748, James Hamilton became deputy governor of Pennsylvania, and two years later his brother-in-law, William Allen, was appointed chief justice. With the support of these kinsmen, Edward Shippen III solicited Thomas Penn for employment for his son Edward IV. In 1752, Penn informed Governor James Hamilton that "I have succeeded in getting a Commission for Mr. Edward Shippen to be Judge of the Admiralty. . . . I am very well pleased to have succeeded in the application as I have a Regard for the young Man and think it may be of Service to him as well that it is desired by yourself, Mr. Allen, and others of our Friends."[14] In this instance, because Cousin William Allen and his brother-in-law James Hamilton controlled most of the patronage in Pennsylvania, a kinsman's career advanced. When Edward IV entered the Philadelphia Common Council in 1755 at age twenty-six, nepotism again served him well.[15]

The family, both immediate and extended, also played an important part in one of the most consequential events in young Edward IV's life—his marriage. The "very affectionate and dutiful son" admitted to his father that he found Peggy Francis, the oldest daughter of his preceptor, "the most amiable of her Sex." He averred that though other young women possessed larger fortunes or would have been more agreeable to his father, "yet . . . our affections are not always in our Power to command, [and] ever since

my Acquaintance with this Young Lady I have been utterly in-
capable of entertaining a Thought of any other." In seeking his
father's consent, without which there could be no marriage, he confessed, "If I had obtained a Girl with a considerable Fortune no
doubt the World would have pronounced me happier," but his
thoughts on contentment and happiness centered about "internal
Satisfaction and contentment of the mind." Although love figured
prominently in Shippen's decision to marry, something which
descriptions of marriages among the colonial elite ignore, passion
could not rule a man of his breeding. "Without a Prospect of a
comfortable Subsistence, tis madness to marry" announced Shippen,
and certainly he never contemplated excluding considerations of
"Money Matters" altogether.[16]

Although Edward IV's potential to amass a fortune seemed good,
his present status counted most. Were he to rely solely on his own
resources he could not marry at this time or, if he did, his choice of
partners would be severely proscribed. The young man depended
on the Shippen family to launch his married life. Unlike the members of the third generation, all of whom inherited considerable
amounts which enabled them to marry, Edward IV saw no early
prospect of an inheritance. Because of this, he depended on the
good will and cooperation of his father. In this case parents' consent was no impotent legal phrase. Edward III proved obliging,
even if very timid. After considerable deliberations he proposed
turning over to his son a house on Walnut Street in Philadelphia
and £250. Edward IV informed the father of his intended bride of
this offer. Tench Francis expressed "some Disatisfaction That you
have given me nothing more."[17] Francis pointed out that the house
could burn down; thus it represented little security for his daughter.
The dowry which he attached to his daughter was £500 sterling.
Although a great part of the money would be spent for furniture
and to build up Shippen's library, which the older man found
sorely inadequate, perhaps as much as half might remain to be put
out at interest. This provided a ploy which might induce Edward
III to raise his offer, for Edward IV promised that "if it can be
contrived That you should take the £250 upon Interest . . . I shall
chearfully acquiesce."[18]

Negotiations continued several months. Edward III relied on

some of his kinsmen for advice. Cousin William Allen's opinions always carried much weight, and the two corresponded about this matter several times. Cousin Allen discussed the matter with his mother, "as both she and I have always had a sincere regard for you and your family and heartily wished their welfare."[19] After analyzing Shippen's thoughts and while recognizing that Shippen knew his own circumstances better than they, they still felt compelled to speak freely and urge him to raise his son's interest. Shippen asserted that he could do no more because of his precarious hold on the office of prothonotary. Already some men had attempted to dislodge him; Shippen feared the loss of revenue. William Allen assured him that only the commission of a crime could precipitate his expulsion from office, for it was held for good behavior as in England. The chief justice continued his reassurances in a way which again underscores the importance of family to securing significant government posts in colonial Pennsylvania. If the proprietor tried to remove you, Cousin Allen promised, you can "believe that your interest with the present governor and his friends, your alliance with Mr. Francis by family to say no more would . . . be sufficient to prevent any thing of the sort being put into execution."[20] In this connection, it seems appropriate to comment that as the marriage negotiations progressed Tench Francis "talks of getting me [Edward Shippen IV] appointed Attorney General in his Room."[21]

All in all, Allen believed that Francis offered much more than Shippen and that if the match were broken off it would reflect poorly on the Shippens. The trouble with his own recent marriage which threatened a scandal made Edward III especially sensitive to any threat to the family's reputation. Perhaps this proved the deciding argument, for when Allen speculated that people will think "it strange that upon the marriage of your eldest son you should not give him a house to live in," Edward III realized how essential the whole matter was to his son and the unity within the family which he sought to foster.[22]

Through various lines of reasoning, therefore, Allen gradually convinced his cautious cousin to increase "your assistance in settling him [Edward IV] forward in the world."[23] In 1753, Edward Shippen IV took Margaret Francis as his wife. He was twenty-four; she was only eighteen. Both appear slightly younger than the average colonial couple at marriage. The great wealth of both families made the young marriage possible. The union lasted over four decades until Margaret's death. Her husband never remarried, preferring to spend the last twelve years of his life as a widower.

According to many scholars, when a son marries, moves out of his father's house, and establishes his family under a new roof, that son has created a nuclear family.[24] In the case of the third- and fourth-generation Shippens, however, such an opinion is extraordinarily superficial. Despite a degree of independence which Edward IV enjoyed because he supported himself and lived a distance of two days away from his father, he continued to function in the context of an extended family. "Isolation of the conjugal unit" failed to take place. Edward Shippen III remained in almost daily contact with his sons through business and personal correspondence. Although his role as father gradually altered, his close association continued long after Edward IV reached maturity, even until the older man's death.

In addition to economic and political activities which illustrate the relationship between father and son, perhaps the following personal advice from Edward III to Edward IV serves best to summarize crisply not only the father's continuing role as adviser, but also the life style which the Shippens believed young members of the elite should display. After describing his own busy day as an example worth emulating, Edward III told his son, "Young married Men shou'd be very diligent, frugal & carefull, that they may not only be able always to support a Wife & a housefull of Children, but also to lay up a hundred or two pounds for every one of them when they go out into the Wide World."[25] He denounced at length a "too common thing [which was] for Young Men when they first appear upon the Stage of Action to Aim at grandeur and Politeness . . . to entertain . . . in a genteel Manner . . . to sit at table two or three Hours tipling Wine, and punch, which . . . [renders them] unfit for any business. These frivolous and pretentious youth would then waste away the rest of their time on the bowling green or at the billiard table and later go to the tavern until midnight, and finally "stagger away home to Snore, Spue, and Groan."

"Avoid what the world calls pleasure," warned the father, for

"Pleasure is only for Crowned Heads and other great Men who have their Incomes sleeping and waking." Clearly Edward III contrasts himself and the Shippens generally with the "great Men" of the English aristocracy. His comments, which continue in a similar vein by recommending temperance, sobriety, diligence, and other virtues, cannot be dismissed as simply phrases expected of a father. In large measure they describe Edward III's values. Having spent his early adult life struggling hard to emerge from obscurity during economically depressed times, Edward III internalized values which helped him rise. Even at age fifty the father could not seriously entertain thoughts of leading a life not "closely employ'd all day"; hence the relevance of these words of caution continued. The question soon to arise would be whether or not Edward IV, experiencing a different sort of entrance into the adult world, would find it necessary or convenient to adhere to such a life style.

Foreseeing the temptation to disregard this advice, Edward III pressed his opinions strenuously. To indicate the universality of these dictums, and add to the weight they carried, he pointed to various kinsmen who might serve as models for the young man. "Go to your Cousin Allen, opulent as he is," noted the father, and "you will find him up early & busily employ'd until Coffee house hours. And when he invites any number of Gentlemen to dinner . . . he soon desires the favour of being excused from drinking, and this without Blushing." The other examples of "temperate Industrious Gentlemen" Edward III selected were Tench Francis and Charles Willing, his son's father-in-law and his uncle. Again the important role of family in the lives of the Shippens receives recognition, for of all the successful gentlemen in Philadelphia, Edward III chose his kinsmen as models for his son.[26]

As a merchant, Edward III could not refrain from illustrating his point once more by references to self-interest and cost. After some calculations he exorted his son, "Remember if a Man should spend 3/ in Liquor necessarily or otherwise in his own House every Day, and 3/6 at Club every night, and £3 a Year at the Assembly and £4 pr Ann. for the Concert. It will require £125.12.6 to support such proceedings." Edward III's reiteration of his advice several times within the same letter underscores the importance of these concerns in his own mind. As a "Most Affectionate Father" he deemed it his role to instruct his son, a role which would not diminish with years. During the rest of Edward IV's life, he would never be far from paternal authority and never free of paternal influence and concern. Consequently Edward IV cannot be understood without comprehension of the relationship which existed with his father and the Shippen family.

Although Edward IV became the most important Shippen of the fourth generation, his brother and sister were directed by many of the same forces as he. Their lives are not carbon copies of their elder brother, a circumstance hardly surprising, yet highly important. A comparison of the variations in the lives of the three provides a better understanding of them all.

Like their older brother, these children must be understood in the context of the family, for it served as the single most important influence in their lives. There was nothing inevitable about this; the influence of family varies directly with the degree of intensity with which its members try to make it influential. Very consciously the third and fourth generation of this branch of the Shippen family strove to make family important. The patriarch, Edward III, tersely summarized the essence of the power of the family over the lives of its members when he expressed the hope that "you will all three of you be always ready and willing to obey my Instructions."[27] To an extraordinary degree they were. Basic to these instructions was the principle of loyalty and obligation to the members of the family. This proved to include not only one's parents and children, but also one's siblings, nephews, nieces, grandchildren, and to a lesser degree uncles, aunts, and cousins.

At about the same time Edward IV set off for Middle Temple to forward his career, his brother and sister left home for the first time. Joseph III went to Newark, New Jersey, to attend college; Sarah became the wife of James Burd. Although physical separation occurred, most significant ties to the family remained intact.

Edward III paid close attention to the development of his son Joseph III. He took an active role in the education of this son and for a long period of time dominated many of the thoughts and actions of the young man. Joseph III seems to have remained under his father's tutelage until about age seventeen.[28] When Edward III decided that his son was ready to attend college, actions to implement Benjamin Franklin's "Proposals relating to the Education of Youth in Pennsylvania" had not yet converted the Charity School into the Academy of Philadelphia. The father's actions in the years clustering about 1750 indicate that he particularly sympathized with the first object in a 1749 petition to the Common Council of Philadelphia for such an academy; that is, "That the Youth of Pennsylvania may have an opportunity of receiving a good education at home, and be under no necessity of going abroad for it, whereby not only considerable expense may be saved . . . but a stricter eye may be had on their morals by their friends and relations."[29] Despite the merits of the proposal in its entirety, it met firm resistance from the proprietor of Pennsylvania who thought the "proposal for the education of youth is much more extensive than ever I designed, and I think more so than the circumstances of the Province render necessary."[30] Although he promised to consider the matter further, he opposed any charter on the grounds that "you set out too great at first."[31]

A viable alternative existed. Although Edward III could scarcely afford to send this son to England, colonial facilities remained within his reach. One outgrowth of the Great Awakening, a religious revival which helped shape the lives of many colonists including Edward III and William II, was an increased interest in education. In the middle colonies the College of New Jersey serves as the most lasting monument to that religious fervor. Edward Shippen III and his brother William II showed considerable interest in that institution; the former by acting as a founder and trustee for twenty years, the latter by sharing his ideas with Robert Smith in drawing up architectural plans for the college at its permanent site in Princeton. Both fathers also sent their sons to the college.[32]

Many characteristics made the college appealing from Edward III's point of view. First, it was not too far away; hence he could visit his son on periodic business trips to Perth Amboy and elsewhere in New Jersey. Second, its New Light affiliation meant important religious components of education would not be neglected. Beyond this, as a trustee and a close acquaintance of President Aaron Burr, Sr., Shippen would be well attuned to all training his son received. Third, because the entire college met at the Reverend Mr. Burr's house in Newark, a close and intimate environment would flourish. There were, after all, only six members in the first graduating class (1748) and while Shippen attended the total enrollment remained small.[33] Daily prayers and church attendance on Sunday were mandatory; beyond this the belief that the college served *in loco parentis* is apparent in the rigid rules of conduct including severe penalties for any student who might "frequent a tavern," play "cards or dice or any other unlawful game," or "keep company with persons of known scandalous lives." Young Joseph III would not be suddenly wrenched away from a rather sheltered existence.[34]

Edward III was not about to grant his son an independent existence. Both economic and emotional bonds received constant attention during Joseph III's college years. But when he went away from home, certain new responsibilities had to be accorded to the youth. An important one would be handling money. Edward III had already begun to train his son regarding the importance of money, keeping accurate accounts of any money expended, and similar financial matters. He accomplished this by keeping an account with his son for at least the year preceding Joseph III's departure to Newark.[35] In 1749, for example, Edward III and his son had an account which ran on for fully ten pages, although the entries consisted of small sums, such as nine pennies which Edward III loaned Joseph III at the market or eight pennies for postage on Neddy's letter. The entire account between father and son amounted to but £8.8.1. Clearly the purpose was didactic rather than monetary. The son did not receive a fixed and adequate allowance, but instead had to request funds periodically, a circumstance calculated to continue a feeling of deference to his father.[36] Numerous other favors, material and emotional, fostered this attitude.

More than mere material considerations, emotional ones bound Joseph III to his father. His father consciously cultivated this feeling in all his children. The most effective device to keep emotional ties tight and the sense of family a highly honed instrument was to establish family correspondence. As soon as any members were away from the father, letters began to flow in both directions. This was one of many concrete expressions of what being a "very affectionate and dutiful son" or "very affectionate father" meant. Generally at least several letters a week were exchanged. In this way all members of the family remained informed of anything affecting the lives of their kin. They also developed a very strong sense of family identity. Beyond this, they remained constantly aware of the huge reservoir of strength and security available to them. From the 1750s onward, no Shippen need have feared that he faced the world or the future alone.[37]

In the years to come the Shippens often drew on the emotional as well as the material support of the family. The support remained available regardless of the seriousness of whatever happened to create a need for it. During the era of the American Revolution the family, attempting to deal with problems of great seriousness, provided succor and support. In 1750, however, Joseph III's anxieties stemmed from an attack of homesickness. He confided to his father that he found it hard to live so long away from his parents "from whom I have never lived before." Clearly he appreciated news of the family, about whom he constantly inquired, and also the lad experienced "a great desire to know how Affairs &c. goes in my native Habitation," and hoped his father would allow him to subscribe to the *Pennsylvania Gazette*.[38]

Although Joseph III found Newark "a solitary village," he soon adjusted to college life and pursued his studies conscientiously.[39] As he explained to a West Indian classmate, he sought a knowledge of the "Arts and Sciences, so that when I arrive to Man's Estate, I may set out in the World with the same Advantages as others."[40] More specifically this meant study of Latin, French, mathematics, philosophy, and some natural philosophy.

A basic requirement for entry into the college was a sound knowledge of Latin. Under President Burr's direction, Joseph had increased his facility with the language during the months preceding July 1750 when he entered as a freshman. He borrowed his brother's copy of Cicero and Dryden's translation of Virgil. Within a year he had read four volumes of Horace which he borrowed from his cousin Tommy Willing. A translation of Cicero also proved useful to him. As he improved, Joseph III corresponded in Latin with his father and a few classmates.[41]

Although competent in Latin, Joseph III relished a more practical language, namely, French.[42] When he was about eight or nine years old his father had taken a Frenchman into the house for about fifteen months to teach French to his daughter Salley. All three children appear to have benefited from the experience. By the time he went to college, Joseph III had achieved such fluency in the language that during the ensuing years "Votre tres obeissant et affectionè fils" frequently corresponded with "Mon tres cher & honoré Père" in French. Delighted, therefore, best described Joseph III's feelings when his father suggested that he use the summer of 1752 to study French with a family in New Rochelle, New York. Joseph III spent his time "for such an excellent purpose" at Monsieur Galliet's.[43] The young man observed that the whole family spoke excellent French, and promised that he would "endeavour to speak nothing else."[44] Several other classmates stayed at the quiet house on a hill. There, every morning they studied, and in the afternoon they read French books which Joseph III supplemented with his father's French letters.[45]

As with Latin and French, so too with mathematics, logic, and natural philosophy, Edward III acted as a positive force promoting his son's education rather than a parent who had turned the responsibility over entirely to others. Naturally he sent his son books for the courses such as Watt's *Logic,* Whiston and Brent on eclipses which proved useful in understanding astronomical calculations, and two papers concerning the "Lectural Experiments of the Several Branches of Philosophy." Beyond this came words of encouragement. For example, on one occasion when writing to his son about mathematics, Edward III recalled, "Spherical Triangles . . . . used to delight me much when at School; & indeed at present I take great pleasure to think of these pretty things"; he felt certain that with practice his son would enjoy "these pretty things."[46] Here and elsewhere Edward III provides himself as an example which he hopes, and expects, his son will emulate. Like his father, Joseph III later displayed considerable interest in astronomy and astronomical calculations. Another example of Joseph III's obvious adulation of his father's intellectual interests, which inspired his own, were the lectures on electricity which had delighted Edward III and his son Neddy IV before they were forwarded to Newark. Joseph III experienced "great Satisfaction to think that the very same things . . . are taught at this College."[47] Several months later Lewis Evans performed the experiments for the students; Joseph III was impressed, for after every experiment he hastened to his room to write down all he remembered. When Joseph III questioned the value of certain other areas of study such as philosophy, his father strongly urged, "I would not have you neglect the School Knowledge, tho' you may never have occasion to use it, it may enable you to detect False-hood when disguised as a syllogism."[48]

From all existing evidence, Joseph III remained a very obedient and dutiful son throughout his college years. Rather than challeng-ing his father or attempting to break free on his own course, he continued to live up to his promise: "You may depend upon it, Sir, I shall take your agreeable Advice in every particular."[49] Conse-quently although his teachers and others regarded him as "a diligent student" who delighted in reading (a need for spectacles substanti-ates this), he remained immature in the sense that he lacked much independence. His father's close attention to his son's every action contributed to this. Not only did he involve himself with his son's subjects, but he entertained tutors when they visited Philadelphia and as a trustee remained aware of happenings at the college. The fact that Uncle Doctor (William Shippen II) also served as a trustee and visited the college, especially after he entered his own son, cer-tainly did nothing to encourage any action on any basis independent of family considerations. The influence of the family clearly ex-tended Joseph III's adolescent years well into his twenties.[50]

This immaturity reveals itself frequently in his correspondence. For example at age eighteen he accepted enthusiastically his father's "excellent comparison of the Bee to my State which I shall en-deavour to make as similar as possible."[51] The analogy seems more appropriate for a much younger person. Two years later as the end of his college career approached, he thanked his father for "the sincere Concern, which I am very sensible you have ever had on my Acco[un]t, as well for my Education, as the promotion of my Happiness in all other Respects, ought to fill me with the highest sense of Gratitude & Esteem for so affectionate a Father."[52] The sentiments, though admirable and appropriate, when taken in con-junction with Joseph III's actions as a whole, again point to his marked sense of dependency upon his father. This attitude of great deference to his father and even belittlement of his own abilities receives full laboration in a letter requesting his father to attend the commencement ceremonies at the College of New Jersey in 1753 at which he received his degree "Ill would it suit with a Disposition I ought to cherish of not appearing ostentatious if I were to express the Satisfaction I shall feel in seeing you at this Commencement"; confessed the graduate, "for such a Thing at this particular Time would seem to insinuate that I should be proud to grate your Ears with what I suppose will be deem'd a wretched Oration." "But for me to imagine that a good Oration can be produced from so barren a Soil as my own Brain," he continued, "would in short be the highest Conceit & Arrogance, (Evils I would despise with the utmost Contempt)."[53] Upon graduation, therefore, Joseph III turned to his father for direction; he did not strike out on his own.

At one time Joseph III had hinted that he wished to receive additional education in Scotland and England.[54] This proposal required far more money than his father's resources would allow; hence the latter squelched it abruptly. Edward III had already expended "a good deal" on his elder son's education in the colonies and abroad. At roughly the same time he also strained his financial resources to enable his other children to marry. Even after relinquishing his own desire to retire from the fur trade, his circumstances could not enable him to grant Joseph III's request. Although Edward III rejected primogeniture and instead exerted strenuous efforts to assist all his children, limitations of his wealth forced him to make an important decision. Either he could treat all three with equality, or he could give preferential treatment to his namesake. He chose the latter course. Significantly, even the resources of the Shippen family which by mid-eighteenth century were more extensive than those of most Pennsylvanians, had their limits.

Despite the inability to further his younger son's career as well as his elder son's, the former had received and continued to receive considerable attention. At this time Edward III decided to take his son into the fur trade with him. In doing so he more deeply etched his imprint upon his son's habits and outlook. Edward III described their business day as well regulated and rather regimented. He described their habits to Edward IV, for he thought the example merited attention.[55] "My Son Jo & myself rise every morning at about Sun rising," explained Edward III. "We then sit close to our Business till 9 a Clock and we find that we can do more by that time than in all the rest of the Day; as we are afterwards often interrupted in our necessary affairs; neither do we receive Visits, nor return any until it is near Sun sett." Pleasant diversions or interruptions were scrupulously avoided, for "if a best friend should happen to come to saunter away an hour or two with us we make it a fixed Rule plainly to tell him, that we are so engaged, that we cannot possibly wait upon him." During the day both Shippens ate moderately and refrained from drinking strong liquor; consequently "the whole day seems like a long morning to us." Not long after eating a light supper and imbibing a little wine, they retired at ten in the evening. Life seemed fulfilling even if not particularly exciting.

Joseph III continued to work with his father. Although he received a legacy of over £100 which his father had held in trust for him, he harbored no specific design for its use. Occasionally Josey went on errands for his father, as when he went to a sheriff's sale of property against which his father held a substantial lien; in this instance his assignment consisted of bidding up to £300 and demanding immediate cash if anyone outbid him. For the most part, however, Joseph III remained in Lancaster passing time in his father's office. Edward III, however, could actually run his business by himself with the assistance of an apprentice or two and reliance on occasional favors by his kin in Philadelphia. While in Lancaster his son Josey essentially marked time.[56]

Josey lacked the ambition which fired his father and older brother and displayed little if any initiative. Perhaps his father's overprotective attitude had stifled the development of these traits.[57] That a young man with Joseph III's education and connections would entomb himself in a small backcountry village puzzled his friends. When his aggressive cousin William Shippen III, a former college companion mildly arraigned him for his shrinking from public life, Joseph III responded weakly, "I have found during the few years I have been in the world, that every scene of life from my cradle upwards has rather created fresh troubles, than satisfied my expectations of pleasure & happiness."[58]

Even Josey's brother Ned commented to his father about Josey's lethargy. It was he who struck upon an idea which eventually drew Josey into the larger world. In 1754 the French and Indian War commenced in the wilderness area to the west of Lancaster. As a leading figure in the county Edward Shippen III rode about contacting settlers urging them to stand their ground against the Indians.[59] Joseph III admired his father's diligence and public spirit. He also became aware of military preparations, for Edward III acted as paymaster for provincial forces in 1755–1756. As a result of government contracts which Cousin William Allen obtained for him, Edward III involved himself in supplying the ill-fated Braddock expedition. With his eye ever open for a good chance to advance, Neddy pointed out to his father, "If my Brother Jo has an Inclination to go into the Army there never was a better Opportunity and perhaps will never be so good a one as now." Neddy felt confident that were Josey to enter the army the connections and influence of the Shippen family could quickly obtain him an officer's commission, for "Young Fellows of less Merit and with much fewer Friends are continually promoting."[60]

The suggestion made a great deal of sense. It influenced Edward III because his forceful elder son knew well how to convince his father, a talent he increased during the ensuing years without ever appearing undutiful. He touched upon values they both revered. Because Josey had "nothing to do in the World at a Time of Life when Activity would be of the greatest Use," Neddy feared that "he will probably spend his Youth in Idleness."[61] The lack of "some Scheme of Life" obviously rankled both men. An army career would provide one, and it made more sense than other avenues for advancement such as trade which at the time seemed more precarious.

With or without enthusiasm Joseph Shippen III, "who will unquestionably follow your [his father's] Advice in this as well as every thing else," grasped hold of a main chance to success and prominence.[62] By April 1756 the young officer was already organizing defenses and recommending men for ensign's commissions. Even before this he had drawn a plan for a fort by method taught him by Governor Robert Hunter Morris. This and his subsequent ardor for things military suggest that rather than cajoling and forcing Joseph III into the army, his father merely prodded him.[63]

What made the military experience all the more attractive was the happy coincidence that he found himself stationed with his "brother" James Burd. The two got along particularly well during the war and remained close friends throughout their lives. Scarcely had Josey arrived in camp than he and Burd decided "to live in one tent together."[64] Like Joseph III, Burd's entry into the army received its impetus from the Shippen family. Also like his "brother," Burd had indeed found that "every scene of life . . . rather created fresh troubles, than satisfied by expectations of pleasure & happiness."

James Burd (1726–1793) left his home of Ormiston, near Edinburgh, Scotland, and in the 1740s established himself as a merchant in Philadelphia. The Scottish merchant seemed prosperous, and his promised share of his family's estate in Scotland appeared as solid security against the uncertainties of the future. In May 1748 he married Sarah Shippen II, the only daughter of Edward III. The fact that he was an immigrant Scot and she a fourth-generation Pennsylvanian of English stock posed no impediment. Edward III perceived the match as an excellent opportunity to provide for his seventeen-year-old daughter's happiness and security. At the same time the match augmented the Shippen family with another useful member.[65]

When acting on his own, James Burd imported from London dry goods such as superfine broadcloths, flannels, osnaburgs, silk, velvet, lace, and other miscellaneous items, which he sold at his store on Carpenter's wharf, opposite William Coleman's. Soon Burd became neatly enmeshed in the Shippen trading network which extended from Philadelphia to Boston, London, and the West Indies with coastal trading in the Chesapeake Bay area. In the summer of 1749, for example, Burd, his "father," and "Uncle" Joseph Shippen II sent a shipment of deer skins to Neddy IV who was then in London. Other relatives such as Cousin Thomas Fayerweather of Boston, John Wilcox of Philadelphia, and Walter Stirling (who later became a cousin of Burd's) transacted business with them as well. The names of "Mrs. Jekill" (Sarah II's cousin) and "Dr. William Shippen" (her uncle) also receive mention in Burd's account book of 1750–1756. At times business demanded that Burd be absent from his young wife as in October 1749 when he ventured to Maryland, or 1751 when he personally oversaw transactions in Jamaica. The sacrifice of being away from Sally II seemed worthwhile, for Burd anticipated large profits.[66]

As if to celebrate his rising fortune and increasing happiness,

Burd displayed his wealth in a way which somewhat alarmed "Father" Shippen. Burd began his adult life in a world of expanding opportunities, circumstances which contrasted with the more dismal period of Edward III's formative years. At this time in his life he felt his "father" carried to excess his veneration of the virtues of hard work, frugality, and cautiousness. Although Burd's family grew rapidly, a daughter within eight months of the marriage and eight more children at about two-year intervals, his thoughts rarely dwelt upon laying up money to launch them into the world. The young man enjoyed the dancing assembly. Although only twenty-four, he believed that his accomplishments merited considerable expenditures on certain luxuries. A prized possession was his chaise for which he purchased a new harness made of "ye Best Neets Leather, Sow'd white, & Pattern'd, [with] Brass Square Buckels, Brass Round ye Skirts & Brass Staples, Screw Rings, & Rowlers."[67] Pride abounded in his countenance, as he rode about town with the "Scarlet wosted Rein" held tightly in his hands. By mid-century only a few of the most successful merchants and prominent officeholders owned carriages; no wonder Edward Shippen III doubted the appropriateness of the young man's activities.[68]

Despite Edward Shippen III's propensity to discern reasons for concern and anxiety even when they seemed remote, in this instance his fears were well founded. Like any other merchant Burd expanded his enterprises by relying on credit. Although not actually in partnership with the Shippens, his connection with so successful a family encouraged men to grant Burd's requests for loans. Within a few years he had greatly overextended himself. In 1751 a venture to Jamaica failed to realize the expected profits, and by 1752 Burd found himself floundering. He owed Walter Stirling more than £1,000 sterling; other called upon him for smaller amounts. The situation augured disaster.[69]

To avert this the Shippen family stepped in to provide succor and protection. Although Edward III complained bitterly that Burd had "brought an intollerable burthen upon my Shoulders," he accepted responsibility for his "son's" actions.[70] While he attempted to make arrangements to satisfy Burd's creditors, he also urged Burd to move from the city and thus lessen his expenses. Burd abided by the decision, partially out of gratitude and also to escape the sneers and villification which his failings might call forth.[71]

Although shaken by his misfortunes, Burd retained a desire to succeed and attract admiration. He cleverly suggested that Shippensburg become his new home; its founder assented to the proposal, later recalling, "I located Shippensburg Plantation for a nest egg for my Self and Children and happy for us I did so."[72] At Shippensburg Burd would be looked up to as the "son" of the powerful man who owned the town and many of the surrounding farms rather than pitied or spurned as an unsuccessful merchant. This image received strength from the founder himself. Edward III believed that his obligations as an affectionate father included setting up his children in a fair degree of comfort. When he visited them at Shippensburg in May 1752, for £10 he got possession of a whole plantation for them. After dickering with local farmers, he acquired some sheep and five fine milch cows as well as a fine flock of laying hens. Breeding ducks and Burd's own work horses rounded out the livestock. Shippen also bought hay, oats, and certain other necessities for his children.[73]

Edward III admitted, "I have always had a great inclination to live in the Country;" hence he enjoyed watching the Burds establish themselves.[74] He also delighted in sending them advice about farming, such as how and when to plant and the proper use of cow dung. Periodically he even sent seeds with instructions on how to plant them. Always he expressed words of encouragement and his unfaltering love for both his children.[75]

Burd responded to all this by applying himself to his new occupation. By October he planted a crop of winter wheat and made other improvements. As he gained experience, he developed a certain fondness for farming. His friend, brother Joseph Shippen III, acknowledged Burd's enjoyment of the science of agriculture when he sent him a poem on raising hops. But Burd was not content to remain simply a farmer. As early as 1753 people referred to him as a merchant and in the fall of that year he ventured to Virginia on a business trip. When he suggested that Edward Shippen III erect a great stone house on a hill overlooking much of Shippensburg, in the back of his mind he pictured himself as its occupant. The idea was not so farfetched as it seems, for Shippen liked his "son" very much and mulled over several ideas which might enable Burd to become the figure in town all men looked to. For example, Edward III promised his "Dear Children" that "If I should build a mill or mills, at Shippensburg, I shall let you have the management and benefit of it or them." In fact he contemplated not only a grist mill, but also a saw mill, for otherwise he would be "paying through the nose" for lumber.[76] At least the grist mill reached fruition, for by March 1755 Burd rode "all over the country" to solicit contracts for flour."[77]

Characteristically, Burd overstepped the boundaries of propriety while he expanded his enterprises. In January 1756 he presented Edward III with a substantial bill for building a large barn. Edward III complained, "I have not money to spare, and so I always told him."[78] Burd, however, had calculated well; he knew the Shippens would cover the expenditures. Sure enough Edward III, the ever indulgent father, directed his son Edward IV "you must if possible collect as much of Salleys [Burd's wife] money as will do it [pay for the barn, for] if he does not discharge the debt he will be arested." Before his anger abated, Shippen swore, "I shall let him know when he comes here that I will never pay one six pence for him directly or indirectly, more."[79] Edward III could not long remain at odds with his daughter's husband. The two men enjoyed each other too much for that. Furthermore, Josey seemed always ready to support his venturesome and somewhat extravagant "brother." Only Edward IV continually expressed a rather hard line toward Burd, but without his father's support he could not thwart Shippen support for most of Burd's future projects. Burd, of course, earnestly repented at the time, but he retained his old attitudes.

Shortly after the Burd's took flight to Shippensburg, the great Anglo-French conflict resumed. Like Edward IV, James Burd saw it as an opportunity for advancement. Besides, as the probability of war increased, the chances of succeeding in business or as more than a subsistence farmer diminished. Rumors of Indian scalping parties caused many to flee the frontier areas of Pennsylvania. Soon even the possibility of remaining unscathed in Shippensburg appeared questionable. In August 1755 Burd thought seriously about taking his children to stay with the Shippens in Lancaster.[80] He delayed that move. Edward III and "Mammy" Shippen remained anxious about their safety. Only a month before Edward III informed his "son" that "I was apprehensive of all your perishing in the wood."[81] The Shippens' concern had amplified with Edward III's firsthand encounter with the barbarities of an Indian war. Indians had murdered fifteen soldiers near a camp in which Shippen stayed while supervising government business; on the same trip he encountered four others hanging by their heels.

As accounts of the "Melancholy & Distress'd Situation of the Inhabitants of this & other Frontier Countys"[82] and of "the cruel Ravages, and Murders daily committed by Our Savage Enemies"[83] inundated Governor Morris, actions to defend those areas began. Among those recommended strongly for a position of responsibility and leadership by powerful political figures such as Chief Justice William Allen and Edward Shippen of Lancaster was James Burd. Although family connections figured prominently in his appointment, solid evidence of his capabilities were not lacking. During 1755 Burd worked in conjunction with Shippen to manage the cutting of a government road through western Pennsylvania. Burd satisfactorily managed accounts under his care and also displayed a talent for leadership as he directed the activities of road cutters, wagoners, and provisioners. Burd soon learned that Chief Justice Allen "hears a good Character of you & says you have recommended your self very much to the Governments which pleases him very much."[84] No hypocrisy figured in Edward III's strong recommendation of his "son" to Cousin Allen. Before Burd received a commission in the provincial service, those responsible for it considered his past failings. Because of the war crisis and because Burd had acted responsibly and demonstrated characteristics valuable to defense activities, his former foibles dimmed in importance.[85]

Thus it was that venturesome Major James Burd and tractable Captain Joseph Shippen III came to share an army tent in the wilderness. As officers they enjoyed prestige, and they reinforced their status with obvious symbols which set them above their men. Along with gingerbread, chocolate, newspapers, and other goodies which "Mammy" and Edward Shippen III sent came pewter teapots, silver buckles, regimental uniforms, and other luxuries. By August, Ft. Augusta was nearing completion and both young men seemed well adjusted to their new situation. Although separated by many wilderness miles, they remained constantly aware of the Shippen family and their relationship to it. Edward III, an avid correspondent, greeted almost every person en route to Ft. Augusta and asked them to carry letters to his sons. Both Burd and Josey III set aside time almost daily to keep their father informed of their situation.[86]

Edward III continually sent advice as well as information, but if he believed that he could continue his strong guidance over young Josey umimpaired, he miscalculated. At age twenty-four Joseph Shippen III was on his own for the first time. Although he did not cut ties with his father, for the first time in his life he had his own responsibilities and also a degree of economic autonomy. These changes enabled him to mature considerably. When he left the army about four years later, he had achieved an ability to make decisions for himself and to act on his own. This does not imply that he came to disregard the Shippen family; it means that he became a more forceful figure within it.

The catalyst in this transformation was "my Dear Brother" James Burd. Josey liked the major who was six years his senior and looked to him for direction. Although the change in Joseph III evolved over time, it received a large boost early in the war. Pennsylvania was particularly stingy when it came to voting funds to prosecute the war and provide for her own defense. This rankled the frontier in general and its military defenders in particular. Major Burd, who was not noted for weighing very carefully the consequences of his actions, decided to complain vigorously and forcefully. The admiring Captain Shippen joined him in signing a remonstrance to the governor, threatening to resign unless they and their men were paid for their services.[87]

The insolent letter caused an uproar in Philadelphia. Edward Shippen IV, the rising government official, saw his future threatened by the rash action of his "brothers." "It was surely the Height of Imprudence," he exclaimed, "to run the least Risque of making Enemies of their best Friends."[88]

He tried to allay the anger of important officials who exploded that the letter was "rude" and "mutinous." Neddy convinced the governor that his brothers' "Height of Imprudence" was simply an ill-judged compliance to their colonel's design. Although Neddy had no way of knowing this, the governor believed him and avowed that he remained inclined to do anything for either of them. The fury of the other gentlemen abated but slightly. When Neddy informed his father of the incident, the latter wrote to Cousin Allen, Governor Morris, and Mr. Hamilton. Edward III felt confident that he won them over. He also mentioned to Burd and Josey the displeasure Cousin Allen and others expressed; however, his letter lacked Neddy's emotional overtones and indicated all had been set aright. Weeks later he offered Josey the poignant observation that "there is a time to Speak one's mind, and a time to be Silent: the great art is to understand how to time things well."[89] His refusal to castigate Josey and Burd harshly for their actions implies a certain pride that Josey had begun to take initiative and act on his own.[90]

Joseph Shippen III took a real liking to military life, ordered a sword and books on military discipline from England, and became a recruiting officer. Needless to say family connections proved useful in obtaining the appointment. When he arrived home in Lancaster on leave in May 1757, he found the governor, James Hamilton, Colonel Stanwix, and some officers of the Royal Americans at the Shippen house drinking tea. During their conversations that afternoon, the position was offered to him.[91] Always affable and more easygoing than his elder brother, he did well as he traversed the countryside signing up men for Colonel Stanwix's Royal Americans. For every man who enlisted for three or four years, Shippen got £4; he received £5 if the recruit enlisted for life.

Recruiting activities occasionally took Joseph III to Philadelphia. There at the center of preferment he visited William Allen and other kinsmen. His career benefited from the contact. When it seemed that Burd would be part of an expedition against Ft. Duquesne, "Cousin Allen . . . [thought] Capt. Shippen ought to stay behind to Command Fort Augusta."[92] Joseph III, no longer an immature youth, was thought of as a capable adult. A few days after seeing Cousin William Allen, Joseph III happily informed Colonel Burd that certain new duties as brigade major would delay his return to the fort. By the end of the month Joseph Shippen III received his commission as a lieutenant-colonel.[93]

Seventeen hundred and fifty-nine proved the *annus miralibis* for Great Britain. After James Wolfe's stunning victory on the Plains of Abraham, French defeat seemed imminent. Never anxious to expend funds for defense, Pennsylvania began to reduce its expenditures. An indignant Colonel Shippen found himself in command of Fort Bedford and only one hundred men. "I don't look upon the Command of 100 men only at this Post, equal to my Rank," he complained. "Indeed it seems something unmilitary for a Lieut. Colo.[nel] to be left with a Captain's Command."[94] December 1759 and January 1760 were miserable months for the soldiers at the fort. Little reason for an army seemed to remain, and Joseph III described his orders to march from Bedford to Lancaster as affording him "the Honour to bring up the Rear of a general Retreat."[95]

Military careers should end with a bang, not with a whimper; Joseph III was not to be disappointed. One of his last acts in the Great War for Empire was to quell a mutiny among his troops. It broke out violently on January 21, 1760 when the garrison heard that, after January 15, they were to receive no pay. The men refused to do their duty and forced the release of a sergeant whom Shippen had confined. As Shippen described the encounter, their action "obliged me to march at the Head of the Guard with my Sword drawn among them, & swear that I was determined to run the first man thro that attempted to . . . do any kind of violence."[96] By storming, threatening death and forfeiture of pay, and pointing out the disgrace and infamy of rebellion, the colonel appeased the spirit of his troops. Though not the sort of engagement an officer cherishes, Shippen's actions in the mutiny serve as a fitting symbol of the new man who emerged from the war. He was at ease with responsibility and able to make decisions wisely; he also had sufficient courage and ambition to carry them out. The colonel would not shrink from life after the war as he had before it commenced.

Colonel Burd decided to remain in the army for a while. Periodically, especially after 1760, he devised other schemes for his future, but for the present he silently agreed with the Shippens who thought "he acts more in Character as a Soldier. And perhaps his present Office is the most profitable." To have peacetime command of Ft. Augusta seemed very advantageous "as no Danger is apprehended [there and] the Absence of an Officer from his Post would be in a great Measure winked at."[97] His other "brother" concurred, averring that at Ft. Augusta Burd "may live cheaper, better & more happy than at any one [of the other forts] on the Communication to Pittsburg."[98]

Before trying to acquire that post, however, Burd spent some time at Ft. Pitt. In July 1760 General Stanwix appointed him Assistant Deputy Quarter Master General. The assignment paid 7/6 sterling per day and included the honor of a seat at the general's right hand at the officers' table. The proud colonel told Edward Shippen III "I am very thankfull as I hope it may be of some service to my agreeable Family."[99] Salley thought it "very genteel in the General, to be so Considerate, as to reward merit where it is due."[100] His "father" was pleased as well, and hoped Burd would be allowed something for the preceding two years as well.[101]

As the war drew to a close Burd's rank changed several times. In 1761 he became captain of a Pennsylvania infantry company. Later it seemed he might be a major. In 1762 he received £500 for expenses to go to Pittsburg to receive prisoners, a position for which he was unanimously chosen. In 1763 as many plans and rumors circulated concerning future military establishments in Pennsylvania, the Shippens and their friends actively intrigued to obtain preferment for Burd. For example, when Joseph III learned that the British intended to station twelve thousand troops in America, he reasoned that a regiment might be stationed in Pennsylvania. If the governor were given power to appoint officers, "I imagine no one will stand a better chance, or can claim so good a Right to the Command."[102]

Burd, however, now gave serious thought to retiring from the army and settling down with his family. Rheumatism and certain other physical disorders had weakened him, and he wished to recuperate. The events which transpired during the ensuing months prevented this. During the summer of 1763 Indians again took up the hatchet and scalping knife, and settlers fled the frontier. Burd agreed with his "brothers" that under the circumstances "that it would be very unadvisable [to] mention a Syllable of it [retiring] to the Governor."[103] Edward III also liked Burd's "Resolution of leaving the Service as soon as you can resign Your Commission with Reputation," but likewise thought it inappropriate to quit in the midst of a serious threat to the colony.[104] By January 1764, Burd believed that the time to retire with honor was fast approaching.

He declined to accept a new command to fight the Delawares and Shawnees, though his "brothers" assured him "you will have command of a battalion if you want it."[105] He informed Joseph III that he also wished to resign his command at Ft. Augusta.[106]

By August, with his health impaired, Colonel Burd had entirely withdrawn from the army. Edward III received with mixed emotions Burd's announcement that he had decided to enter "some other way of Life that might be more agreeable to myself & my Family; but what that will be I cannot as yet inform you."[107]

In the meantime the uncertainties concerning Edward III's youngest son's way of life dissipated. When he retired from the provincial service in 1760, Joseph III decided to take a trip to Europe. He conceived of his intended voyage as a profitable business venture and also a pleasant contrast with the past few dreary months in the wilderness. Although he had amassed a fair amount of capital while in the provincial service and could augment it with money inherited from his Uncle William Shippen, Joseph III could not venture forth without additional financial backing. He immediately turned to his brother Edward IV for support. Edward IV readily accepted the opportunity to help his brother and at the same time make use of some "idle capital." He and Joseph III agreed to invest £750 each in the venture. Edward IV also interested some of the Shippen relatives in Philadelphia. Cousin William Allen agreed to put up £1,000 for his son John Allen who would accompany Joseph III. Cousin Tom Willing gave an additional £500. Several other investors brought the total value of the cargo to £6,000. By the time Joseph III set sail, he and his brother held twenty-five percent interest in a £7,000 cargo of sugar.[108]

Initially Joseph III contemplated a trip to London, but when Edward IV informed him, "All my friends are hearty to serve you, and all concur in advising Ag[ain]st the London Scheme," Joseph III acquisced to setting out for Leghorn which offered greater profits.[109] Soon the Shippens assembled a cargo of sugar and looked forward to what promises to be a grand voyage."[110] By the beginning of March, most arrangements were completed. Characteristically Joseph III's father sent him instructions concerning the trip, but Joseph III's family role in this instance was to guide rather than be guided. Cousin William Allen desired Joseph III to accompany his son John through Italy and on to England for he once "spent six years . . . in England and am very sensible they are to go thro' a fiery Trial—The Many Temptations youths are exposed to in your City [London], and Vice & Luxury that is too predominant, make me very anxious."[111] The Shippens, who so often benefited from their connections with Chief Justice Allen, were requested to adhere to family duties and return a compliment. While a Grand Tour sounded exciting, it also entailed great expenses. Because Joseph III's financial position was dwarfed by comparison to Cousin Johnny's, Cousin William Allen proposed that he would pay two-thirds of the joint expense. Joseph III agreed to the proposition, but as his brother critically observed, "I am afraid this Scheme tho' it may do very well for Mr. Allen's Son with a heavy purse at 22 Years of age Will by no Means answer for Joe who is but beginning the World at 27." He added philosophically, "However, if Mr. Allen can be obliged without any Detriment to Joe, it must be done."[112]

By April the snows melted, the roads became passable, and the seas calmer in winter. Edward IV accompanied his brother to Gloucester where the latter embarked for Europe. Despite "strong Gales of Wind & very rough Seas almost the whole Way," Joseph III arrived at Gibraltar only four weeks after rounding Cape Henlopen.[113] The foul weather hardly affected Joseph III, and although his cousin suffered from seasickness most of the trip, Joseph III informed their families in Philadelphia that they were "extremely hearty and well, having lived very happily together during our short Passage."[114]

After a fortnight in port, they resumed the voyage to Leghorn. Because a French privateer had chased them into Gibraltar and privateers swarmed about the Mediterranean, they welcomed the chance to continue in a convoy protected by two British men-of-war. Besides, they dined with the captains of the *Shannon* and *Favorite* and enjoyed other civilities. During a two-week quarantine upon arrival in Leghorn, Joseph III experienced second thoughts about the impending Grand Tour. With some misgivings, he resolved the dilemma; he decided, "I cannot bring myself to think of disobliging Mr. Allen in so material a thing, as leaving his Son in this Strange Country to himself without a Companion to travel or advise with; especially as he consented to his coming to this part of the World on an Expectation that I would accompany him."[115] Although the decision was his, Joseph III appreciated learning that it "meets with my Father's approbation."[116]

Having reaffirmed his plans, Joseph III set about disposing of his cargo. He dealt with Jackson and Rutherford, Englishmen who welcomed the cousins into their house during their stay at Leghorn. "The indifferent Market our Sugars have come to here," disappointed Joseph III, but he worked quickly to dispatch a vessel to Philadelphia so that "we shall gain a small profit."[117] He dispatched the ship in July. It stopped in Barcelona to take on brandy, then at Malaga for wines, and finally joined another British naval convoy. Upon receiving it, Edward IV happily informed his father that "we shall make a very respectable voyage of it. The first Cost of the Cargo amounts to £2700 sterl[ing] and we have no doubt of making it turn 8 or 9000 £ this money." He hoped to realize a fifteen percent profit on the sugar sold at Leghorn, "but the principal Profit . . . [is expected] upon the homeward bound Cargo."[118]

After completing their business, Joseph III and his cousin decided to begin their diversion through Europe. They visited parts of Tuscany during the late summer before going south to Rome. Florence impressed Joseph III most, and he marveled at "a Collection of some of the greatest Rarities & pieces of Antiquity in all Italy." In that city, Sir Horace Mann, "who is extremely polite & civil to all English Gentlemen," made their stay all the more memorable.[119]

In January 1761, the cousins arrived in London, "this long wished for City." In the first letter he wrote the family in months, Joseph III alluded to the happy times augmented by "the great Civilities we received from the Ministers at the different Courts & a number of worthy English Gentlemen we met with on their travels in Italy," but saved details of his impressions of Italian cities for his father's "Fire Side at Lancaster."[120] Although Joseph III avowed, "I cannot reproach myself with the least extravagance," clothing and travel expenses from Leghorn amounted to about £200.[121]

London appeared as a "great hurrying & busy City," yet Joseph III felt very comfortable there. As soon as he arrived he sought out Mr. Francis (his brother's brother-in-law) "who immediately took

Lodgings for us both having quitted his own to live with me." Francis, in London on merchant business, introduced Shippen to commercial figures and did "everything in his power to assist me in purchasing an assortment of Goods."[122] While in London, Joseph III also visited and dined with Cousin Dolly (Willing) Stirling who only recently moved there from Philadelphia. This was an important family obligation which could not be ignored. Indeed, before she learned that Shippen and Francis were touring the manufacturing cities of England, Cousin Stirling complained to her mother in Philadelphia about her discourteous cousin who avoided her for several weeks. This compelled Joseph III to request his "sister" Peggy (Francis) Shippen to clear up the matter with Aunt Willing or Cousin Nancy. Pleasant plans to meet Cousin William Shippen III who was studying medicine in Scotland misfired when William III's dissertation delayed his return to London.[123]

Joseph III returned to Philadelphia in 1761, where he set up shop in Market Street as a dry goods merchant. Despite his useful contacts in London, Leghorn, and other parts of Italy, he remained a merchant but a few months more. Doubtless through the efforts of a grateful Cousin William Allen and other relatives in politics, Joseph Shippen III was commissioned secretary and clerk of the Governor's Council in January 1762. The proprietor heartily approved the appointment, for "from the Character I have had of you, and from my own observation while you were here [London], I conceive the Offices to be very well filled."[124] Joseph III served the province and Penn family as secretary for the next decade and a half until the American Revolution altered his situation. Fees and commissions for performing duties as secretary of the province complimented his salary of £15 per year.[125] According to a tax assessment made a few years later, the office's value amounted to £100 or £200 per year. "The honourable & profitable Employment" enabled Shippen to quit "all thoughts of trade."[126]

Soon the secretary moved from Market Street to a smaller house near the governor. There he lived for several years with a clerk and housekeeper; the latter, significantly, was the same woman who had served his father years before. But life as a bachelor seemed not wholly satisfying. In time Joseph III responded to questions and prods by friends such as John Morgan who asked, "Are you afraid of Matrimony, or have ye refined elegancies of European Ladies impaired your relish for ye exquisitely soft & native Charms of our Americans?"[127] In October 1762, Joseph III married at Christ Church, Philadelphia, Jenny Galloway of Maryland, "a most amiable and accomplished young Lady."[128] At age thirty-six Joseph III married later in life than any other Shippen in the eighteenth century. By December, however, according to a nephew, "Aunt Shippen . . . [was] settled at home and behaves very agreeably. . . . She is a young Lady of a most amiable Disposition & [I] have a very great Esteem for her. The Loneliness of a Batchelor's House seems to wear off and I believe Uncle's present Manner of Living with so good a Companion gives him a great deal of Happiness & Satisfaction."[129] Thus the last of Edward III's children was finally well settled.[130]

Edward III took great pride in his sons' achievements and great interest in his only daughter and her family, and his involvement in their development justifies and explains it. As patriarch, he exerted a strong influence upon all his children's lives. Not all his children received identical treatment. His sons were more important than his daughter, and his elder son, most important of all. This differentiation is particularly evident in the amount of education he provided for each child. Although Edward III strongly shaped the lives of his children, limits to his powers existed. He sought to inculcate in them the values most applicable to his own life, yet succeeded only partially. As part of the maturing process, his children achieved identities of their own by creating a new synthesis of values. Finally, the fourth generation emerged into well-established positions, not simply by their own efforts, and not simply by the efforts of their father. An extended family fostered their growth and progress. This involved not only them and their father, but also certain cousins and significant inheritances from deceased members of the Shippen family. The influence of the extended family remains a continuous feature in their development throughout the rest of their lives. This larger context remains vital to understanding the Shippens.

⤝⊐⟩⊏ VI ⊐⟩⊏⟨⊐⟩

The Establishment of the Fourth Generation: The Secondary Branches

If, as Jonathan Swift remarked, "censure is the tax man pays to the public for being eminent," certainly not all Shippens found themselves in the same tax bracket. In the third and fourth generations, the Edward Shippen III branch bore a far heavier share of the load than did the branches founded by Joseph II and William II. The latter two may be described, therefore, as secondary branches of the Shippen family. Although ten adult heirs represented the secondary branches, knowledge of the activities of only William Shippen III (usually referred to as "William Shippen, Jr.") survived the passage of time.[1] Obscurity engulfed the others soon after their deaths, if it had not already begun to do so before.

Regardless of their stature, however, these Shippens must be retrieved from oblivion. After that they may remain secondary figures in the family's history and obscure if not forgotten people in any broader context, but they will add an essential dimension to an understanding of the Shippen family. Importance need not connote greatness or eminence. These secondary Shippens were important. Their lives have meaning which must be explored.

As each Shippen of the third generation married, he set up a separate household. Although association with his brothers continued, and although he might rely upon them for assistance, he retained primary responsibility for his family. As Joseph II and William II assumed this responsibility, it becomes possible to compare their actions with those of their older brother, Edward III. For example, how did they involve themselves in their children's lives, what controls did they utilize and how effectively did they use them, and did they treat all children the same or emphasize one? Also, it seems significant to determine to what degree they utilized the resources of an extended family. Finally, where did their children go, in terms of economic and social mobility as well as geographical mobility?

In 1752 Joseph Shippen II retired to the family plantation in Germantown. There he and his wife, Mary, reared their six surviving children: Catherine (1740–1812), Joseph IV (1743–1766), Mary (1745–?), Abigail (1746–?), Ann III (1749–?), and Margaret (1751–?). Probably because this branch of the Shippen family failed to perpetuate the family name beyond the death of Joseph II, almost all records and evidence of the family disappeared before the end of the century. Only a suggestive sketch of the lives of these Shippens may be presented.

While in retirement Joseph II depended for support upon profits accumulated in trade and income from real estate. In time he also invested in an iron works with his brother, William II. The farm at Germantown supplied much of his food, and all indications are that he was content. Fevered economic exertions lay beyond his interest, and he entertained no strong ambitions regarding the exercise of political power. Like his father, Joseph II seems to fit rather neatly the pattern existing in England in which a successful merchant, upon accumulating sufficient resources, retired to a country seat to lead the life of a gentleman.[2]

Joseph II was not averse to schemes to augment his income if they would not interfere with his chosen style of existence. That, in essence is what he told his nephew, Edward Shippen IV, who informed him in 1757 that "Mr. Allen asked me whether I thought Uncle Joseph would accept the Post" of receiver of customs for Delaware Bay. Joseph II expressed interest in the position if it would not oblige him to reside at Lewes, Delaware, otherwise he declared that he would not accept it "even at twice the salary."[3] The young man suggested that his uncle speak further with Cousin Allen about the conditions, assuring him that the chief justice "is heartily disposed to serve him and will do all in his Power to get him the office upon the most advantageous terms possible."[4] Joseph II's terms seemed agreeable to all concerned. Although at this time the proprietor bowed to the wishes of Thomas Pelham who urged another's candidacy. Thomas Penn informed Joseph II that if he served now as a deputy it would advance him toward a collectorship of his own. He also pointed out to Shippen that the office required "but little attendance, [and] might be executed without your removal from the Place where you are."[5] By 1760 Joseph II acquired the office of surveyor of customs for Delaware Bay. Barclay and Son of London served as his security and William Allen gave a counter security. Although the office paid £50 sterling per year instead of £150 sterling as he had earlier been led to believe, there were "no Prerequisites attending the Office," and the income from it was "enough to buy him wine & a few odd trifles besides."[6]

The additional revenues began arriving at a most propitious time. Around 1760 obligations to his children demanded that Joseph II expend significant sums of money. His eldest daughter, Catherine, had arrived at a marriageable age (twenty years old), and his namesake's education was about to become decidedly more expensive.

Money and gentility figured prominently in Joseph II's mind as he negotiated with Richard Wallin, Esq., who sought his daughter's hand. After reaching an agreement, Joseph II seemed "highly delighted with the Match."[7] His pride of accomplishment appears justified, for as he explained to his nephew, Edward IV, over dinner, "this Gentleman has an Estate in Jamaica worth Five thousand Pounds ster[lin]g p[er] annum." In 1760 Wallin lived in retirement in Philadelphia upon about £600, because he had borrowed a large sum (about £25,000) in order to improve his estate. Within about two years, however, the encumbrances on his estate would dissipate, and Shippen envisioned his daughter and her husband rolling "in his coach and Six."

Edward IV left the only known description of his cousin's intended mate. According to Edward IV, his character was that of "a good natured Man, without much Understanding or the least Knowledge of any kind of Business; He had a great part of his Education in England, where he acquired a genteel Taste and polite Behavior at the Expense of a few thousands." Despite Wallin's extravagant proclivities, it seemed he "cannot possibly squander such a princely fortune." Marriage negotiations were concluded in September, and in December 1760, Edward IV informed his father that "Cousin Kitty is to be married to Morrow."[8] Joseph II expended a considerable sum on his daughter's dowry to achieve such a desirable union for her. Regrettably neither the Shippen papers nor deeds recorded in Philadelphia preserve any description of it.[9]

Like his elder brother, Joseph Shippen II provided his son with the advantage of a college education in the colonies and the added benefits of continued improvement in European institutions. Joseph Shippen IV attended the College of Philadelphia as a member of the class of 1761. Like his cousins, he intended to pursue a professional career. After studying theology in England, the young man returned to Philadelphia. Youthful ambitions snapped in 1766; at the young age of twenty-three, Joseph IV died. He had not married, and his life hardly begun, was scarcely remembered. Of the twenty-one adult Shippens in the first four generations, only two others (both men) died unmarried. Because all three died before they were thirty years old, it seems safe to assert that all Shippens born before the Revolution contemplated marriage as a normal part of their development.[10]

Joseph IV's death had serious repercussions for the Joseph Shippen II branch of the Shippen family. Joseph II had no other sons to carry on the family name, and his wife was beyond the child-bearing age. He became the last representative of his branch of the family. Not surprisingly, Joseph II's interest in the larger Shippen family diminished. For example, he failed to attend the 1770 meeting of the Common Council of Philadelphia at which his nephew, Joseph Shippen III, was elected a member. The death had other repercussions. Because Joseph II no longer needed to anticipate expenditures to help his son's career advance or assist him in establishing his own household, financial provisions were available for other purposes. In the following year, 1767, when his twenty-one-year-old daughter broached the subject of marriage, Joseph II gave his consent. Abigail married Edward Spence of Jamaica. The couple then moved to the West Indies where Abigail would be near her older sister.[11]

Joseph II's daughters, Mary, Ann, and Margaret, remained at home a while longer. Not until 1774 did her Uncle Edward III spread the news that "Nancy [Ann] Shippen is married to Isaac Jones's son."[12] Another kinsman "rejoiced to observe the Marriage of Uncle Jo's Daughter and that the Family are Comfortably settled in Philadelphia."[13] Ann III married at age twenty-five, a bit later in life than most women among the Philadelphia elite. Her husband, Robert Strettel Jones, was a successful merchant whose father had served in the Common Council for many years and also as mayor on two occasions. Robert Strettel Jones's inheritance upon his father's death in 1773 enabled his happy father-in-law to brag that "Nancy is as well married as any Lady in the province and keeps the best of company."[14] Few details regarding the marriages of Joseph II's other daughters survive.

In retrospect Joseph II could look upon his activities as a father with pride. Three of his daughters married very well, and he had done all he could for his son during the lad's short lifetime. In part because he produced no male heir, Joseph II's role as a father differed considerably from that of his brother, Edward III, in that he did not continue such close scrutiny of his children's activities. Beyond this, the structure of his branch of the Shippen family was collapsing. Since he had no male heir, his line of the family would soon die out. Furthermore, the family was dispersed, as two daughters had permanently left the province with their husbands. Only his younger daughters remained nearby. Although a Revolution was brewing in the colonies, it could not have catastrophic results for this branch of the Shippen family. The catastrophe had already occurred; the Joseph Shippen II branch of the family was destined for natural extinction.

By contrast natural extinction seemed highly unlikely for the William Shippen II branch of the family. Four of his children reached adulthood, namely, William III (1736–1808), Joseph W. (1737–1795), John (1740–1770), and Susanna (1743–1821). The problem challenging William II's capabilties and resourcefulness as a father stemmed from producing a fairly large number of heirs and his lack of economic stature in comparison to his brothers. William II was ambitious and had plans to propel his children upward in society. Although his own efforts and ingenuity in this endeavor partly explain his success, the role of the extended Shippen family must also be considered. At crucial moments his older brother rendered assistance. Again the error of looking upon Shippens simply as individuals will become apparent.

While Edward III and Joseph II reaped large profits from coastal and trans-Atlantic trade, their younger brother, William II, diligently practiced his trade as a chemist "at the Sign of Paracelsus Head (opposite the Prison in Market Street)."[15] Beyond the schemes he nurtured to advance his own stature, William II was fixed in his determination that his sons would begin life with more advantages than he had. Education appeared the most appropriate means to achieve this desire. Like his brother, Edward III, William II promoted the Great Awakening as a New Light Presbyterian. The opportunity to intertwine a classical education with firm religious guidance existed at West Nottingham, Chester County, Pennsylvania, where the Reverend Dr. Samuel Finley, later a president of the College of New Jersey, conducted a boarding school. William II's son, William III, soon joined the small group of boys who lived in Finley's home. There he learned something of farm work and social graces in addition to formal knowledge of Latin and the New Testament.[16]

In 1750 William II inquired about entering his son in the College of New Jersey. President Burr offered to tutor the lad so that he would be ready to enter the freshman class in September 1751. In March, Billey (III) set off for Newark, accompanied by Cousins Josey (III) and Neddy (IV), and their kinsman Chief Justice William Allen. On the way they dined on "good Rock fish and a fine Loin of Veal."[17] Edward IV and William Allen went on to conduct some business matters leaving the two students at the college. Although Joseph III was four years William III's senior, the two saw each other frequently, for William III lived in President Burr's house, and besides the college was so small that daily contact was inevitable.[18]

Superior preparation, motivation, or intellect enabled William III to surpass the achievements of his cousin. Whereas Joseph III took three years to complete his studies, William III required only two. In 1754, eighteen-year-old William Shippen III delivered the valedictory address at the commencement exercises. He impressed the audience with his abilities. Ezra Stiles, for example, applauded the "ingenious oration," and George Whitefield compared Shippen's eloquence to that of Roman orators.[19] More than a half century later, an eulogist recalled that the valedictorian had "attracted the eye of every beholder [by] the elegance of his person, the ease and gracefulness of his whole deportment," and that "a power of fascination seemed to issue from his tongue."[20] Shippen's cousin, who had read the oration and made certain suggestions concerning its contents, requested a copy as soon as it appeared in print.[21]

Upon graduation William III returned to Philadelphia to begin a medical apprenticeship under his father. By 1754 William Shippen II had risen considerably above his origins as an apothecary. As his business expanded with ever-increasing success, he broadened the scope of his medical activities. His rise was assisted by the circumstance that during the first half of the eighteenth century, few physicians with M.D. degrees practiced in the provinces. Those with knowledge of drugs often expanded their activities to serve the community as doctors. By mid-century William Shippen II was prominent among such people, and from then on he usually described himself as "practitioner of physick." Philadelphians called him Dr. Shippen. His appointment as physician to the Pennsylvania Hospital in 1753 (a post he held until 1778) attested to the high respect people had for his abilities, for he was the only informally trained practitioner thus honored.[22]

Despite the great usefulness of vocational training acquired under the guidance of a talented father, obvious advantages lay in securing a medical degree. If current conditions continued, William III would have a vast advantage over most competitors. On the other hand, if the practice of medicine were to become more professional, William III could reap the benefits of entering the field at the beginning and acting as one of the major contributors toward the improvement of the profession.

No medical schools existed in the colonies at the time; hence additional training would be very expensive. Although William II's prosperity continued during the 1750s and 1760s, the cost of schemes to educate his children and to augment his income exceeded his immediate resources. As important as his children's advancement might be, he refused to forfeit opportunities in real estate and manufacturing which would advance his own position. During the two decades following 1750, William II expended more than £2,000 to acquire additional land and a substantial sum to gain possession of an iron works.[23]

The Shippen family enabled William II to promote both plans simultaneously. Here, as in many instances after mid-century, the Shippen family connotes a broad range of kinsmen rather than a nuclear family. The bonds between the William II and Edward III branches of the family, for example, received frequent reinforcement from services members of one branch performed for the other. In September 1757 William II informed his "Dear Brother" Edward III that "I am casting about to raise a Sum for Billey's Improvement abroad."[24] Edward III's interest in William III's progress and his efforts to assist his nephew Joseph W. Shippen (William II's second son) make it likely that he responded favorably to his brother's request.[25] Besides, the expense of establishing his own children had passed, and he currently enjoyed new revenues from his position of supplying troops battling the French in western Pennsylvania.

In September 1758, having secured what his father immodestly described as "the best Foundation that can be had in this country," young Shippen set sail for England.[26] At this time he expected "to spend this winter in London with ye finest Anatomists for Dissections, Injections &c. in England; at ye same time visit ye Hospitals daily & attend Lectures of Midwifery with a Gentleman who will make that branch as familiar to him as he can want or wish to have it."[27] In the spring or summer he anticipated going to France through Leyden "where he gets graduated & sees all the operations of Surgery that can be performed by those Monsieurs." William III seemed determined "to understand Surgery perfectly," and upon his return to Philadelphia, he expected with naive confidence that "no Case can happen in his business that he cannot undertake to manage with Ease & freedom."[28]

"After an unpleasant & dangerous Voyage of 7½ Weeks," William III arrived in Belfast.[29] Rather than resume the discomforts of travel by sea, he rode on horseback to Dublin. After briefly admiring the "very fine City," he crossed over to England and soon settled himself in "dirty London."[30] During the following months Shippen came to know much of "this little World," the remarkable city which in size and complexity contrasted so much with the provincial town from which he came.[31] Matchless medical facilities and experiences lay before him, and he benefited as fully as possible from his sojourn there. Beyond this, physical separation from his father and the Shippen family provided some opportunity to resolve certain conflicts between the old values which seemed so sensible in his youth, and the new tastes which accompanied his rising status. A tersely written journal kept from July 1759 to January 1760 and a few surviving letters provide some illumination on the subject.[32]

As a "student at large," William III began to broaden tremendously his practical experience within his first few days at St. Thomas's Hospital in Southwark. On occasion he also observed at other principal London hospitals such as Guy's, St. George's, and St. Bartholomew's. There he observed physicians make their rounds, examine patients, perform surgery, and treat diseases, illnesses, and accidents. Obstetrics fascinated Shippen and he learned about midwifery from Dr. Colin Mackenzie and enrolled to study anatomy under the enormously famous William and John Hunter.[33] To introduce man-midwifery to Pennsylvania, where as in most colonies strong prejudices existed against it, Shippen must be very adept. Mackenzie's manner of teaching facilitated such expertise. On July 31, 1759, he first records observing "a labour at Crucifix Lane this Morning, a natural presentation."[34] Mackenzie presumably had a small lying-in hospital there, and Shippen often made similar entries in his journal. Toward the middle of the following month, Shippen spent seven hours with "my Barbors Maid who was in Labour," and there "I delivered her of a Daughter," his first recorded delivery.[35] From then on deliveries became commonplace, and on one occasion he examined seventeen pregnant women in one day.[36]

Shippen's training in anatomy consisted of equally practical endeavors coupled with brilliant lectures delivered by a gifted speaker. William Hunter, his mentor, had studied under Alexander Monro and William Cullen at Edinburgh and under John Douglas and William Smellie in London, all of whom were regarded as the outstanding men in their fields. By mid-century Hunter had surpassed them, and among the many accolades he received, appointment at Physician Extraordinary to Queen Charlotte in 1761 was perhaps most impressive. His unschooled younger brother, John, gave up the trade of a wheelwright and more than a decade in the dissecting room made him excellent in that calling, as well as an enthusiastic young teacher. The enthusiasm of the Hunters proved contagious,

and for weeks Shippen became thoroughly engrossed in dissections.[37] William Hunter provided "each of his pupils with one
entire body and from time to time . . . [inspected] the dissections
himself."[38] John Hunter taught Shippen the art of anatomical injec-
tion, a skill useful in expanding one's knowledge as well as convey-
ing it to others. The impression of the men upon Shippen was great.
Often in the evenings the student visited the Hunters and chatted
about anatomical particulars. Clearly Shippen "was receiving the
soundest instruction which the eighteenth century could offer in the
specialties which he most wished to cultivate."[39] When Shippen
brought his mentors' high standards in anatomy and obstetrics to
the colonies, he played "a leading part in the establishment of medical education in America."[40]

While residing in London, William Shippen III particularly impressed his teachers with his industriousness and serious dedication
to his pursuit of medical knowledge. He, and most other medical
students from the colonies, provided a favorable contrast to most
students from the British Isles.[41] Even Shippen once referred to the
latter as "young boobies."[42] The adoption of such an orientation
by a first-born son is not surprising. In William III's case, this seriousness gained impetus from the guidance which the Shippen family
provided. Although this influence remained detectable in his personality, the independent existence he enjoyed overseas enabled him
to modify the values of the older generation to coincide more adequately with his own desires. No severe conflict with his father
ensued, but a divergence occurred.

The Great Awakening looms as one of the most important events
shaping the outlook of William III's father and Uncle Edward
Shippen III. Both rejected the religious indifference of their father
and involved themselves in the movement as New Light Presbyterians. Both men followed closely the progress of the great evangel-
ist the Reverend George Whitefield; both encouraged the growth of
the College of New Jersey, a product of the Awakening which
sought in part to instill religious concern among its students.[43]
William II became a founder of the Second Presbyterian Church of
Philadelphia in 1742 and remained a member for nearly seventy
years. Many of the values which his friend, Whitefield, commended
became integral parts of his life. The medical biographer, James

Thatcher, probably repeated the words of one who had known the old doctor well when he wrote:

As proof of the influence of the religion he loved, it is worthy of notice that in the whole course of his long life he never was once heard to swear profanely, nor to take his Maker's name in vain . . . admidst the bright cluster of his virtues conspicuously shone his humility, modesty, integrity and truth. His temperance was so great that, till within a few weeks of his death, he never drank wine, nor any other spirituous liquor . . . even his dress conveyed his ideas of simplicity, for he was opposed to ostentation in everything.[44]

Although any eulogist tends to exaggerate, in this instance William II's characteristics were simply magnified rather than imaginatively created. Those traits might easily apply to a Quaker, such as Edward Shippen I; hence, it seems that certain aspects of the Shippen family's "symbolic estate" helped form the habits of William Shippen II.

Uncle Edward Shippen III's spiritual concerns paralleled in many regards those of his younger brother. His business partner once described him as "too religious," and his correspondence throughout life often reflects a tendency to dwell upon religious subjects. The life characterized by diligence, frugality, sobriety, temperance, and other virtues which he urged upon his son, Edward IV, coincided well with the style of life most Great Awakening preachers advocated. What made such a life style particularly relevant to William II and Edward III was that it coincided so closely with the characteristics essential to their own progress in a society of relatively limited opportunity. To a large degree hard work, thrift, and avoidance of luxuries enabled the rather insignificant merchant and the apothecary to prosper during economically hard times. Even after success and inheritance presumably lessened the need for such discipline, both men clung tenaciously to the values inculcated during the formative period of their lives.[45]

William II delighted in informing the Reverend Mr. Whitefield "of a very hopeful appearance among the Students in Jersey College . . . [where] all save 3 or 4 almost all at once became deeply distressed about their Souls—a great number of whom continue to behave very becomingly," and hoped his own son would develop in the same direction.[46] To encourage this, the father requested Whitefield and Dennys DeBerdt, a Methodist merchant of great repute, to counsel and assist the young man "with regard to Manly, Genteel frugality, in his Expences & living."[47] As William II explained to his most trusted friend in England, "You are well acquainted with the Temptations & Dangers a young Fellow is exposed to in such a city as London." Hopefully William III could room with an "awakened" family near the hospital as well and thus be more likely to avoid the evils.[48]

Before embarking, William III had listened to his uncle berate the "rakes and fops" of London and enjoin the necessity of frugality and diligence. Consistent with the obligations of "your dutiful Nephew," William III corresponded with his uncle and informed him "your Remarks [are] all just."[49] Although William III found "ye ways of Vice & Wickedness as many and as various as I expected," he assured his uncle that "I find very little Difficulty shunning them." Whether or not the Shippens went so far as some "New Lights" as to condemn the theater and such amusements, William III felt no reluctance in admitting that occasionally he went to see the famous actor, David Garrick, perform. He hastened to add, however, that "I do not spend it [my time] trifling, about Play Houses, Opera, reading romantic Tales, or trifling Newspapers at Coffee Houses &c., as I find many have done before me, but in right improvement of those Advantages which are not to be had in my own Country."[50]

Close analysis of William Shippen III's journal reveals that the young man accurately described his stay in London. On the average he saw about three plays a month and frequented the coffee house only about once a month. For the most part, however, the journal dwells on his medical experiences. More importantly, the brief entries in the journal indicate that his tastes tended far more toward working hard at his studies and then enjoying sociable relaxation, than toward reflecting upon the state of his eternal soul.[51] Aside from Sundays, only on Thanksgiving,[52] on Christmas, and on two occasions when Whitefield preached, did Shippen engage in any religious activity.

While in London William III moved farther and farther away from the religious enthusiasm of his father and uncle; at the same time, his dedication to his profession and affinity for convivial social occasions increased. Except for Whitefield's consistent excellence, William III's interest in religious orations noticeably wanned as the months passed. This becomes evident as successive entries in the journal lose the detail of the first Sunday he described. That notation indicated a certain degree of attachment to his father's values. Sunday, July 22, 1759, had been "One of my most pleasant Days, heard in the forenoon Mr. Read . . . Dined with my kind friend Mr. De Berdt, heard Mr. Elliot in the afternoon. . . . In the evening heard Mr. Kinsman an excellent Preacher at Tabernacle. . . . About 10 went home . . . having spent the Day with much peace and pleasure."[53] Never again was Sunday crammed full of religion morning, noon, and evening.

In time attendance at the Tabernacle or religious orations became simply a matter of habit, a ritual which evoked little interest. For example, on Sunday, August 12, 1759, William III simply noted, "Spent as before at Meetings etc.", on Sunday, November 4, 1759, he noted "as usual at Mr. DeBerdts," and subsequently his entries stressed the customary aspect of what he did with occasional references to speakers' names.[54] Never did he comment upon the content of sermons; at times he evaluated the manner of presentation. Aside from Whitefield who was "always agreeable," few moved him to record praise and several annoyed him enough to evoke criticism.[55] For example, he heard Mr. Stevens "preach or rather Grunt miserably!"[56] He thought Mr. Condor "a scholar and bad preacher," and dismissed "the famous Fordyce [as] an affected stiff orator."[57] That Shippen attended church almost every week must not be forgotten, yet the ritual cannot overshadow his increasing delight in other activities.

Aside from medical endeavors which took precedence over everything, Shippen gave ample time to recreation and diversions.[58] He preferred the intimacy of tea time, social visits, jaunts about the country, and coaching parties more than large public amusements such as fairs. As a handsome young bachelor, Shippen enjoyed social visits and taking tea, for they provided him with the opportunity of meeting many attractive young women. For example, after having tea with the Huthwaites, he enjoyed one of "the most enchanting rides I ever had" with Miss Jeffreys "very good and agreeable chatty etc." and "Miss Huthwaite kind."[59] On another visit to the Huthwaites he took particular notice of "Miss Laneton . . . a very sweet good Face, very pretty too. [And] Miss Cleves worth 10,000 too etc."[60] One of his happiest memories was of a small gathering of about fifteen young people. He spent the afternoon with Miss Jeffreys, and later sang with her to the accompaniment of a flute. Then, "We danced all minuets and in short spent the afternoon as merrily as you please."[61]

The medical student loved dancing and attended several assemblies. At the Camberwell Assembly in September he again danced with Miss Jeffreys, although "40 [other] young Ladies most of them pretty and genteel, elegantly dress'd in flounced Trollopes" composed the gathering.[62] The Lord Mayor's Show and Ball consumed an entire autumn day. In December at a ball in London graced by "35 Ladies genteely dress'd," he danced with "Miss Knox an agreeable Lady and good Dancer."[63] Usually he returned home from any diversions by about ten or eleven o'clock. Only once, with "a very Pretty soft agreable Girl," did he make merry until three the next morning.[64] Because he saw the sun rise before retiring, he "slept till 1 oClock Tuesday afternoon."[65]

Plays encompass almost all William III's public entertainment. He applauded the famous David Garrick in several performances including his great roles as Archer in *The Beaux Stratagem* and Ranger in *The Suspicious Husband*. Other plays and farces evoked various responses from the young man regarding their quality. Shippen stopped by the coffee house infrequently, played cards, once, and entered a tavern never. He went to three fairs; he thought Bartholomew's Fair "very vile and ridiculous,"[66] the Borough Fair "very foolish,"[67] and the Chamberwell Fair unworthy of any comment.[68]

In essence what transpired while William III was in England was a process of maturation in which the young man worked out a particular identity. His dedication to his profession, his enjoyment of social amenities at teas and dances, and his admiration of fine country seats made him similar to his cousin, Edward Shippen IV, the lawyer. Both young professionals came for New Light Presbyterian backgrounds, yet they represented a new order which became increasingly distinguishable in the British Empire as the eighteenth century evolved. Many aspects of urbane and polite society in

England helped them modify the views of their youth to fit their own circumstances in the middle and late decades of the eighteenth century. Both men returned to Pennsylvania where they still resembled their fathers in terms of seriousness and ambitiousness. Beyond this, their life styles revealed a much larger degree of affinity for pleasurable pursuits and displays of rank than did their fathers. This served as an obvious contrast between the two generations.[69]

Before returning to the colonies, however, William Shippen III, hoped to achieve greater competency in his profession. After completing two years of practical training, William III prepared for the last phase of his European education. He sought a M.D. degree. War between England and France precluded study in the Continent as he originally planned. Besides Dr. John Fothergill of London, a powerful influence on the lives of many Pennsylvanians in particular and the promotion of science in the colonies in general, advocated most convincingly the advantages of studying under the Monros, William Cullen, and others at Edinburgh.[70]

During the following year he engaged in theoretical study at the University of Edinburgh and wrote his dissertation entitled *De Placentae cum Utero nexu.*[71] He dedicated it "to the best of fathers WILLIAM SHIPPEN, A most expert physician of the same [Pennsylvania] Hospital, to whom for fostering care and the singular liberality with which he has always encouraged the education of his son, the fullest tribute of a greatful heart is rightly due," and five other physicians of the Pennsylvania Hospital.[72]

The young doctor then returned to London just in time to see the coronation of George III. He joined John Morgan, another Philadelphian seeking medical knowledge abroad, and a couple of ladies to watch the procession as it left Westminster Abbey. Shippen's impressions probably approximated Morgan's who marveled, "It is impossible by words to give any idea of the richness of the Coronation Robes of the King, the Queen, the Peers and Peeresses or of the august appearance they all made—nothing could exceed it."[73]

Shortly after this Morgan set off for Edinburgh to garner medical knowledge, and Shippen embarked for France to enhance his stay abroad. They parted cordially; within four years they became inexorable foes. As physician to a pulmonary consumptive patient,

William Shippen III managed to go to France despite the war. After conversing with Paris physicians, including the celebrated Senac, he returned to London.[74]

As one of his last acts before returning to Philadelphia, Shippen married Alice Lee of Virginia at the Church of St. Mary le Strand, Middlesex. At age twenty-six, Alice Lee had been living with her cousins the Ludwells. Although she received an annuity of £40 sterling, doubtless her personal attributes and the prestige of her family attracted William III. The annuity, while not inconsequential, represented all Alice Lee received from her father's estate. This had come about from the heavy-handed actions of her eldest brother. Those activities also instilled wrath in the younger sons and helped promote strong bonds between them and the Shippens during and after the American Revolution.[75]

The couple returned to Philadelphia in May 1762. As they settled down in William III's father's spacious house at Fourth and Prune (Locust) Streets, how small and intimate the provincial town must have seemed.[76] There in the south side of the city within short walking distance resided his father, Cousin Edward Shippen IV and his young family, Cousin Joseph Shippen III, and his widowed Aunt Anne (Shippen) Willing with his numerous unmarried cousins.[77] Only eight miles away lived his Uncle Joseph Shippen II, and because Uncle Edward Shippen III kept in almost daily contact with Philadelphia, he scarcely seemed absent. William III's move to Front Street did not change the situation. Although William III had visited and dined with Cousin Dolly (Willing) Stirling in London and even tended her illness, attempted (unsuccessfully) to meet his Cousin Joseph Shippen III who voyaged there, and encountered numerous Pennsylvanians including Benjamin Franklin, James Hamilton, John Morgan there, that metropolis was fundamentally different.[78]

Having such a large group of kin constantly observing one's activities produces different results depending upon the individual observed. It can stifle and constrict, or it can support and strengthen. Because William III returned from England confident of his own abilities and with a firm idea of what he wished to do, subsequent influences of the family proved highly beneficial. William Shippen III joined his father as a partner. In addition to practicing what he learned abroad, the younger Shippen, like several young contemporaries, wished to inspire others with the contagious enthusiasm of his mentors. In particular he cherished the hope of bringing to fruition "a School for Physick amongst you [in Pennsylvania] that may draw many students from various parts of America & the West Indies & at least furnish them with a better Idea of the Rudiments of their Profession than they have at present on your Side of the Water."[79] Shippen lacked the organizational and promotional abilities needed to launch a medical school, but with his father's assistance he inaugurated a series of lectures on anatomy. The course of lectures "for the advantage of young gentlemen . . . whose circumstances and connections will not admit of their going abroad for improvement," dwelt upon anatomy and surgery, and gave "a few plain directions in the study and practice of midwifery."[80] They were also available as "entertainment" to curious gentlemen. The demonstration of anatomy by dissecting cadavers precipitated resentment on the part of some. On at least one occasion William Shippen III felt compelled to deny rumors that he engaged in grave robbing. Not all were convinced; opposition to his activities found periodic expression in well-aimed missiles which shattered windows in his laboratory and nearby public lamps.[81] Shippen also offered to lecture twice a month at the Pennsylvania Hospital where he expounded upon Fothergill's gift of a valuable "set of Anatomical Paintings & Castings in plaister of Paris representing different views of Several parts of the Human body."[82] By the beginning of 1765 he felt confident enough to offer to men and women a complete course in midwifery, a proposal bound to stir up controversy. But then, Shippen seems to have thrived on controversy, for he became involved in it so often.[83]

At about this juncture John Morgan returned from four years of study abroad with a very definite and highly polished proposal concerning the direction in which medical education in the colonies should develop. In many ways he resembled Shippen. Born in 1735, the son of Evan Morgan, a Philadelphia shopkeeper, John Morgan attended the Reverend Dr. Finley's academy, served a medical apprenticeship under Dr. John Redman, graduated from the College of Philadelphia with commendations for his "Genius & Application,"[84] and then went to England and Scotland for additional medical training. In London he studied under the Hunters and then he went on to Edinburgh where "Dr. Morgan has graduated . . . with such Reputation as few, if any, have ever obtained."[85] Like Shippen, he impressed all with his intelligence and ambition. Morgan then did additional work on the Continent and finished his sojourn with a dazzling Grand Tour which even included an afternoon with Voltaire at Ferney. He arrived in Philadelphia with an impressive array of honors including membership in prestigious learned societies such as the Society of Belles Lettres in Rome, the Royal Society of London, the Académie Royale de Chirurgie de Paris, the Royal College of Physicians of London, and the Royal College of Physicians in Edinburgh.[86]

With such sterling credentials, Morgan contemplated an illustrious career in Philadelphia, doubtless expecting to become the most significant medical figure in the most important medical center in the colonies. Specifically, he sought to implement his *Discourse upon the Institution of Medical Schools in America.* Morgan's reputation, written support from the Proprietor Thomas Penn and former Governor James Hamilton, and tactful consultation with several trustees of the College of Philadelphia wrought great success. On May 3, 1765, the trustees of the college unanimously elected John Morgan professor of the theory and practice of medicine. Morgan, not Shippen, became the founder of the first medical school in British North America and held the first medical professorship.[87] In the eyes of the public the innovation and triumph were all Morgan's. But the plan itself had been the product of several minds, especially Shippen's and Fothergill's. Although Morgan went beyond their contemplations of 1762, he made no mention of their role and took "full credit for the Medical School."[88] Furthermore, Shippen's lectures in anatomy seemed a significant forerunner of the medical school, yet they were ignored in publicity given "Morgan's plan." Morgan had ignored his colleague and offended him deeply.[89]

The insult had grave consequences for the development of medicine in the colonies. Although Morgan recommended Shippen for a post as professor of anatomy, the wound remained raw and festering. Morgan did little to allay Shippen's wrath, and in 1766 exacerbated the situation by again ignoring Shippen when he founded a medical society. This widened the breach within the medical profession in Philadelphia. By the time classes opened in the fall of 1766, reconciliation was impossible. Shippen and Morgan continually feuded both publicly and privately concerning who originated the medical school. The other physicians in the city invariably chose sides.[90] This poisoned atmosphere continued over the years until Morgan's death in 1789. Periodically their antipathies overflowed all bounds, and during the Revolution the career of neither was well served by their animosities.[91]

William Shippen II always took greatest interest in his eldest son, but by no means ignored his other children. In assisting them start out in life, as in many endeavors, William II discovered the verity of what his eldest brother, Edward III, taught him "when a Small Shaver," that is, "Nil tam difficile est quod non Solertia vincat."[92]

Both John and Joseph W. Shippen entered the Academy of Philadelphia in 1751. Details concerning their early training remain obscure and somewhat puzzling. Neither seems to have completed studies for a degree in Philadelphia. By 1755 John attended the College of New Jersey, and in 1758 at age eighteen, received a B.A. degree. Like his eldest brother, John then returned to Philadelphia to serve a medical apprenticeship under his father. In this way William II avoided a considerable outlay of capital. The savings mounted up over a few years and when added to other funds available from business transactions enabled Shippen to send a second son abroad for advanced medical training. John went to France; he earned a M.D. degree at the University of Rheims.[93]

Upon his return to Philadelphia in the mid or late 1760s, he decided, doubtless after consultation with his father and brother, William III, that he should practice elsewhere. Perhaps the thought of embroiling himself in the Shippen-Morgan feud made practice in that city unattractive. By siding with his brother, he would instantly make powerful enemies who might impede his advancement. This became evident in 1770 when Morgan and his friends defeated his application to become professor of natural history.[94] Then again, his reason for leaving may have been positive rather than negative. The Shippens had kin in Maryland with whom they maintained some contact. Perhaps that explains why Dr. John Shippen moved to Baltimore during the summer of 1770 where he "got into a good business."[95] Like his Cousin Joseph Shippen IV, however, the young man's talents were hardly displayed or tested. In December his Uncle Edward Shippen III lamented over "the Melancholy news . . . which is, that Johnny Shippen is dead at Baltimore after 4 days ilness of billious fever."[96] The doctor was but thirty years old.

John's brother, Joseph W. Shippen, had also permanently moved from Philadelphia by this time. Again this move and much of Joseph W. Shippen's life can be understood best in the context of the Shippen family. After leaving the Academy of Philadelphia, the young man appears to have gained some knowledge of business in Lancaster with his Uncle Edward Shippen III. In the spring of 1756 William II thanked his brother for "your kindnesses to my son Jo," who had "finished his Ledger to pretty good purpose."[97] About a year later William boasted that "Josey is in the best place in Town among Merchts."[98] For some time after that Joseph W. Shippen earned a living as a merchant. The Shippen's family connections in Boston served him well, and he dealt particularly with Cousin Thomas Fayerweather. Cousin Fayerweather had dealt with other Shippens before that time; hence their trade pattern connecting Boston, Philadelphia, and the West Indies was already established. Furthermore, Fayerweather liked the Shippens and enjoyed doing favors for them such as sending lobsters and other New England delicacies. In 1760 Joseph W. Shippen ventured to New Providence, Jamaica, where he took on a cargo of molasses and limes valued at 2,257 pieces of eight in which Fayerweather held an interest. That he sent a cargo of indigo to his cousin in Boston the following year is the only other surviving bit of information regarding his career as a merchant.[99]

One reason for this is that Joseph W. Shippen ceased to be a merchant some time during the 1760s. When Joseph W. Shippen convinced his father that he could keep ledgers accurately and that he had obtained the maturity and skill necessary to manage a business enterprise satisfactorily, he became the manager of the Shippen family iron works. This explains why he moved to Sussex County, New Jersey.[100]

Back in 1749 William Shippen II purchased a three-fourths interest in the Oxford Iron Works. The Iron Act passed by Parliament in the following year apparently produced no ill effects upon its operation; indeed, Shippen probably benefited from the British bounty on pig iron.[101] To cut transportation costs Shippen applied for a royal license to operate a ferry connecting Sussex County, New Jersey with Pennsylvania at "the foul Reef on the said River Delaware." In 1755 George II granted him "the sole [right of] keeping a Ferry over the Delaware River at the place aforesaid and Two miles above and two miles below." The ferry would benefit others as well by "Shortening and making Easy . . . Journeys from one Province to another as also in Transporting Horses Cattles and Goods."[102]

In 1759 William II and his brother, Joseph II, agreed to buy from Jonathan Robeson of Kingswood, New Jersey, the Oxford Furnace in Sussex County and four thousand acres belonging to it, along with all houses, buildings, Negroes, horses, cows, wagons, and utensils. They paid for it by delivering £350 in cash or pig iron (valued at £5 per ton) that summer and a like amount the following summer. In addition to this the brothers promised to sell Robeson one hundred tons of pig iron a year for three years at £6 per ton. From then on brief notations concerning the furnace appear in the Shippen Accounts and William Shippen II's Daybook. Surviving letters indicate that William II visited the furnace several times before the Revolution.[103]

Although William II and Joseph II contemplated selling the furnace in 1764, it remained in the Shippen family until the nineteenth century. Joseph W. Shippen continued to manage the works until his death in 1795. His father refused to turn the property over to his son. This tended to keep him in a subordinate position. He may have resented this; in an analogous situation his brother, William III, expressed annoyance at their father's hoarding money which William III wished to expend on his son's education. Regretably Joseph W. Shippen left almost no evidence about his life. He married Martha Axford and had nine children, the first of whom he named after his father. When he died in Sussex County, his father acted as administrator of his intestate estate. Thus from birth to death, the influence of the father over the son never ended.[104]

The same sort of observation applies to Shippen's only daughter Susanna. Born in 1743 and named after her mother, this last surviving child flourished under fond attention. Sukey was "1 spoilt Girl" as her brother, William III, once affectionately reminisced.[105] For example, when she was thirteen years old her father took her in his carriage to Newark to visit her brother John, President Burr, and Governor Belcher. The next year he thought of letting her accompany Mrs. Burr to Boston where she might feast on lobsters and other treats at Cousin Fayerweather's. Although William II expended less on her education than on her brother's, she learned "besides what belongs to a compleat Housewife, now & then a little Geography, Arithematick & Grammar—and what is best of all a Habit of Strick Honest[y] & real Religion."[106]

Perhaps that explains why in 1767 she married the Reverend Mr. Samuel Blair (1741–1818). He was twenty-six, she, two years his junior. At twenty-four, Sukey was an older bride than any Shippen to date. This reflects her father's lack of economic standing in comparison to his brothers, father, and grandfather as well as the impact of his sons' expensive education and perhaps a father's reluctance to give away his daughter.[107]

Blair was born in Chester County, Pennsylvania, the son of an immigrant Irishman. His father, "probably the most gifted intellectual among the Presbyterian partisans of the revival" or Great Awakening, had attended William Tennent's Log College before leading "one of the most remarkable of the Middle Colony revivals" and opening his own ministerial school.[108] The son attended the College of New Jersey at about the same time as Sukey's brother John. After graduation in 1760, Blair became a tutor in the College and thus better acquainted with William Shippen II, a trustee. The year before his marriage the young minister accepted a position as pastor of Old South Church in Boston. Although elected president of the College of New Jersey at age twenty-six, he declined the honor so that John Witherspoon might head the institution.

After the marriage "Cousin Sukey Shippen" left a broad network of kin to reside in Boston.[109] There of course Cousin Fayerweather cordially welcomed the young couple. Only two years later, however, the couple returned to Philadelphia with a "lovely bounding Daughter."[110] They remained in Philadelphia where for a time Blair preached "now & then . . . to any Congregation whose pastor happens to be abroad."[111] In 1776, Blair served as chaplain of the

Fourth Battalion of Pennsylvania troops. This action explains the Blairs' flight to Sukey's father's furnace in New Jersey during 1777. Several years later Chaplain Blair preached a sermon at Preakness, "well calculated to inculcate religious principles, and the moral virtues," to the troops of Washington, Greene, Knox, and others.[112] After the war the Blairs returned to Pennsylvania and spent the rest of their lives surrounded by numerous relatives. Blair served as chaplain to the House of Representatives from 1790 to 1792 and received a D.D. from the University of Pennsylvania. He and his wife retired to property William II owned in Germantown. Upon his death, they received title to it and other property. In time they built a house for their son Samuel, Jr., on an adjoining lot. The Reverend Samuel Blair assisted in the founding of the First Presbyterian Church of Germantown and Chestnut Hill. The Blairs died in Germantown after experiencing longevity which characterized a rather large number of Shippens.[113]

Like his brothers, William II took satisfaction in his performance as an "honored and affectionate" father. He provided for his children very well considering his resources. At least two sons exceeded him in terms of education and the prestige one gains from entering a profession with the highest university degree obtainable. His daughter also married a professional. Only his second son did less well in terms of prestige; however, his economic situation was certainly adequate.

Although the secondary branches of the Shippen family never attained a position in the front ranks of Philadelphia society, as the progenitor, Edward I, had, their experiences provide a positive comment upon the opportunities available in the middle colonies as the Revolution approached. But they need not reflect the situation facing most colonists at the time. Although hard work and the cleverness to exploit opportunities particularly helped William II raise the stature of his branch of the family, both he and his brother also benefited from valuable inheritances. Beyond this, William II especially utilized a vibrant extended family which was not available to all Philadelphians.

Developments within the family, the tendency to emphasize sons, particularly the eldest son, reflect the same pattern revealed in the primary branch. This pattern is strengthened by the similarities in the personalities of William III and his cousin Edward IV, both of whom were serious, ambitious, and most successful. Moreover, the successful attempt to provide for all children compels recognition. In terms of family structure, the tight-knit nature of the William II branch approximates that of Edward III's although the same does not hold for Joseph II's.

Yet certain contrasts with the primary branch require attention. The secondary branches failed to achieve the eminence of Edward III's. Only William III stands out as significant, though neither great nor likable. Edward Shippen III had maintained better control over superior resources. This is particularly true in terms of political connections. No secondary fourth-generation Shippen held a political appointment before the Revolution.

Although evidence precludes recreating the lives of the secondary branches as fully as those of Edward III's, perhaps Joseph II, William II, and their children would no longer complain with Joseph Addison: "We are always doing something for posterity, but I would fain see posterity do something for us."

VII

Interaction as a Family
Before the American Revolution

In the second half of the eighteenth century the Shippen family reached its zenith of power and complexity. Intra-family relationships of various kinds developed and intensified. As members of the Shippen family exercised their roles as parents, grandparents, uncles, aunts, nephews, nieces, and cousins, they influenced the lives of other members of the extended family in significant ways. Certainly in many instances family considerations and actions explain why these people acted as they did. Repercussions might be felt beyond the confines of the kindred group.

All this becomes clearer as certain aspects of the lives of the third-, fourth-, and fifth-generation Shippens receive analysis. In some respects this involves elaboration upon traits described during the establishment of the fourth generation; beyond this, however, certain new roles are undertaken. For example, Edward Shippen III becomes the first Shippen in the colonies to relish the role of grandfather and to add that dimension of influence to the lives of numerous descendants.[1]

The Shippen family activities which occurred before the Revolution can be observed best by viewing the primary branch of the family, which left a wealth of evidence regarding their lives. By contrast, for instance, almost nothing survives concerning the Joseph II branch. Besides, grandchildren of the primary branch reached maturity before the Revolution, whereas the outlines of the development of their younger cousins remain barely discernible. The other Shippens will not be ignored, for a comparison promises use-

131

ful benefits. But they, like some of their counterparts in the primary branch, merit mention during a consideration of the last quarter of the eighteenth century.

As the second half of the century commenced, the geographical dispersion of the Shippen family created the illusion that family cohesiveness was disintegrating. The bankrupt Burds took flight to Shippensburg in 1751; the following year Edward III moved to Lancaster and Joseph II, to Germantown. For the Shippens, however, geographic separation merely modified an increasingly close-knit family organization. Emotional and economic bonds received reinforcement. As patriarch of the primary branch, Edward III consciously promoted this development. His affectionate concern for his younger brother, William II, helped foster kindred feelings with that secondary branch. Only Joseph II's branch seems somewhat detached from the multitude of family concerns, and this detachment may simply reflect the lack of surviving evidence.

As Edward III constantly strove to keep members of the primary branch of the family interested and involved with one another, certain events beyond his control assisted him. In particular, the Great War for Empire had this effect. As fellow officers during the war, Joseph Shippen III and James Burd came to be close friends as well as formal "brothers." Efforts to advance their careers involved Edward III, his son Edward IV, and Cousin William Allen, among others. The war brought about another effect upon the Shippen family. It was paradoxical. On the one hand James Burd remained physically absent from his wife and young family for many years, yet at the same time, the Burds lived in a strong family environment. Increasingly the Burds came under the influence of the Shippens. This paradox lies at the heart of several matters which help explain the structure and function of the Shippen family and what it meant to be a member of this kinship group.

When James Burd decided to enter the provincial service, he must have done so with mixed emotions. Although he could advance more rapidly there than as a farmer-merchant in a backwoods town and perhaps extricate himself from heavy debts, he would have to leave his wife and young children. Besides, there also loomed the possibility of death, and it required little effort to conjure up the brutalities of an Indian war. Burd, however, to judge

WILLIAM ALLEN, 1704–1780

By J. Augustus Beck after original variously attributed to Benjamin West and Robert Feke (*Historical Society of Pennsylvania*)

EDWARD SHIPPEN IV, 1729–1806

By Gilbert Stuart *(Collection of the Corcoran Gallery of Art)*

JOSEPH SHIPPEN III, 1732–1810

By an unknown artist after original by Mary Peale *(Historical Society of Pennsylvania)*

JANE GALLOWAY SHIPPEN, 1745–1801

By Benjamin West *(Historical Society of Pennsylvania)*

WILLIAM SHIPPEN III, 1736–1808

Attributed to James R. Lambdin after original by Gilbert Stuart
(Historical Society of Pennsylvania)

MARGARET (SHIPPEN) ARNOLD, 1760–1804, AND CHILD

Attributed to Daniel Gardner *(Historical Society of Pennsylvania)*

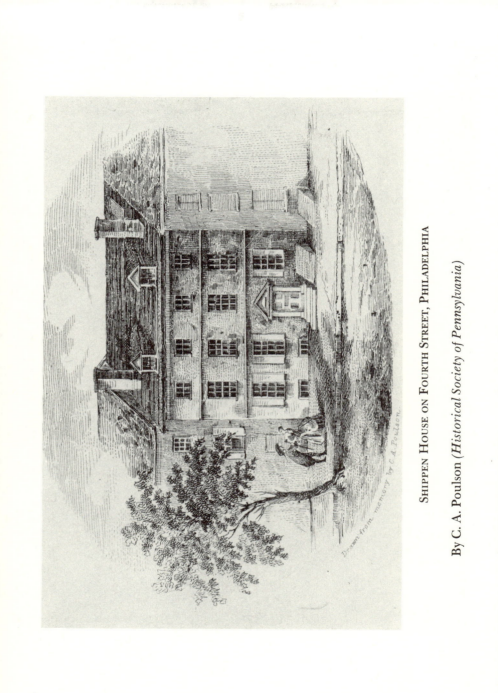

SHIPPEN HOUSE ON FOURTH STREET, PHILADELPHIA

By C. A. Poulson (*Historical Society of Pennsylvania*)

Drawn from memory by C. A. Poulson.

Map of the Province of Pennsylvania in 1770

By William Scull (*Historical Society of Pennsylvania*)

from his subsequent actions, nurtured responsibilities as head of his family and intended to provide for his dependents to the best of his ability.

Burd departed for the wilderness of Pennsylvania in 1756; for the next eight years he visited his family only periodically when he obtained leave. Sarah (Shippen) Burd ameliorated the situation of a fatherless family by moving to Lancaster where she lived under the care of her father and mother. Edward III delighted in "the ducky children" and exerted a strong influence over their lives.[2] He paid particular attention to their education. "Mammy Shippen" aided her "daughter" in subsequent childbirths and helped her take care of the increasing flock of young Burds.[3] Beyond this the Shippen family in Lancaster included several other people. By 1757 the widowed Granny Gray (Edward III's wife's mother) and Cousin Patty Gray lived with Edward III. Although Sarah Burd rented a separate dwelling, family contact was frequent; indeed, according to Edward III, "There is not a day in the week but we see one another."[4] As a result of constant contact her children thought in terms of many kin rather than simply their parents and siblings when they considered their family situation. For example, on one occasion when Sarah dined at Pappy Shippen's, her eight-year-old daughter Sally remarked, "We only want two here, Pappy & uncle [Joseph Shippen III] to make us happy."[5]

Aside from caring for her children, Sarah had the responsibility of running the household. This entailed directing the activities of servants and expending funds for expenses she deemed necessary. The colonel sent her money from time to time, and she appreciated his regard for her, especially "I am sensible of [it] in giving me so much Liberty to act in your absence." Though she remained ever "anxious to do what I know is agreable to you," she exercised considerable discretionary power.[6] Often Sarah relied upon her father's knowledge and experience for guidance. For example, during the summer of 1760, Shippen and his daughter traveled about the area looking for cattle. "Daddy" found stock and prices near Lancaster unsatisfactory and only after going beyond York did the two strike a bargain with a farmer. On another occasion Sarah purchased three dozen sheep which she thought a bargain at twelve shillings a piece. Sometimes she could not negotiate so successfully. For instance, although she and "Daddy" inquired of everyone, they encountered great difficulty purchasing hay, and finally paid an inflated price.[7]

Complicating Sarah's activities were fairly frequent pregnancies. The colonel visited his wife and the families at Lancaster on periodic leaves; during those eight years Sarah was "in a thriving condition" four times.[8] Not surprisingly "that Situation" was hers during the summer of 1759 when Mr. Barton, her landlord, urged "poor Salley" to move. The emergency forced her to lease "a very handsome house" in a section of town her husband thought undesirable.[9] Thoroughly disappointed with those arrangements, she soon contracted to move into Dr. Neff's new house as soon as it was completed. In the meantime she and her father prevailed upon Barton to allow her to continue several months longer where she was. Sarah thus postponed the onerous burdens of moving until a more convenient time.[10]

In the spring of 1760 Sarah, her six children including "a lumping fat girl" born only months before, and the servants moved into "our house."[11] "Daddy & Mammy" assisted.[12] Although Sarah regretted the high rent of £25 per year, she delighted in its location, for "its near Daddys."[13] Knowledge that the house met with her husband's tastes also reconciled her to the expense. A while later she reported to James Burd that "Daddy, Mammy, children, & both familys are well, we live very amiably together."[14]

By this time James Burd had emerged from his status as a debtor and contemplated relocating his family in Shippensburg. His thoughts focused not on the "good house"[15] and modest meadows he occupied before the war, but on Edward Shippen III's great "Stone House & a plantation round it."[16] Such surroundings seemed more appropriate for an officer and gentleman, and James requested the privilege of residing there.

Edward III encouraged Burd's "Shippensburg Scheme," but with important qualifications. He offered certain tracts adjoining the great house and even promised to subsidize the erection of certain buildings for Burd's use. The stone house and four hundred acres which formed "the Cream of the whole Tract" of Shippensburg, however, played a significant role in Edward III's own ambitions. He harbored a desire to retire one day to the house on the hill and live as a country gentleman. Burd's proposal threatened that dream, for were Shippen to "allow you to occupy my Plantation . . . every year the fields will grow worse and worse . . . [while] you will reap the Same advantage from it as if it were your own and . . . any fences you may make upon it will be rotten in ten years time & so of no advantage to me." Edward III closed the matter with an earthy observation; Burd had a good farm to return to, "& my advice to you is to spit in your hands & hold it fast."[17]

Although Burd's plan simply evoked a refusal from his "father," it drew outraged objections from his "brother," Edward IV. "Is it possible he can think you so weak as to put any thing in his power after the wild conduct & very bad Oeconomy he has heretofore discovered?" exclaimed the young lawyer.[18] Often contemptuous of this wayward "brother," Edward IV malevolently suggested to his father that Burd would not hesitate to sell the plantation for his own advantages.

During the ensuing years, Burd's resettlement caused sharp dissension within the family. Always ambitious, Burd pressed plans which greatly upset Edward IV who acted as his major antagonist. The weak economic status of the colonel and expenses of his large family made most of his schemes dependent upon assistance from the Shippen family. Fortunately for Burd, Edward III, who felt strong obligations to assist his daughter Sarah and her husband, directed the family's activities. Furthermore, despite James Burd's shortcomings, the older man liked him. Edward III therefore not only restrained Edward IV's periodic antipathy for Burd, but even drew Edward IV into efforts to promote the Burds' welfare.

When his own "Shippensburg Scheme" met with a rebuff, James Burd rejected his "father's" alternative despite clear knowledge that Shippensburg was a flourishing place. Briefly, he pondered the possibilities of returning to the colonial capital where he thought he could become a wealthy merchant. Edward IV tried to discourage this "mad Scheme,"[19] for if Burd settled "near this town the Consequences . . . might be easily forseen without much of the Spirit of Divination."[20]

Burd also declined subsequent urgings by the Shippens that he settle at Shippensburg or nearby Carlisle. Finally, Burd decided to have a house built at Northampton, Cousin William Allen's town.

Just as the house neared completion a harrowing yet humorous experience caused Burd's ever active mind to drop this scheme for another. When he arrived in Northampton in January 1764, he encountered bedlam created by frightened frontier people seeking refuge from Indian war parties. As an officer and experienced defender of the frontier, Colonel Burd tried to organize the people and save them and the town. Much to his chagrin he found there were "only four Guns in the Town, one of which was my own, two out of order & no ammunition."[21] Fortunately a confrontation failed to materialize, but Burd admitted "this new Indian War has altered the Situation of my affairs greatly . . . I must not expose my Family to the mercy of such unhuman Crea[tures."][22]

Undaunted by this turn of events, Burd inquired about several plantations. Because their prices lay beyond his financial grasp, he relied on his "father" and "brothers" for assistance; they in turn provided advice and worked on the details of the purchase. The Boyd plantation was available for £1500, and Sarah sighed, "I am very anxious to buy the plantation, as I am in Great hopes . . . we may get settled at last."[23] Unfortunately Edward IV and Joseph III had much of their money tied up in a cargo to England; thus Burd was unable to acquire this property.[24]

Next the families considered John Gillelyn's 470 acres on the Brandywine Creek in Chester County. Edward praised it strongly, for " 'tho there are finer Plantations in our County . . . [they are] not to be sold, & if they were, ye same Quantity of Land & sort of Improvements could not be had for the Money."[25] James therefore asked his "father" to buy the plantation for him, for "it seems agreable to my Wife, & Recommended by you, two Considerations that weigh with me."[26] Although Sarah Burd had only £400 on hand and James none at all, several people and the government owed the Burds money, and James thought he could easily pay £1,000 or £1,200 for the plantation. Edward III and Edward IV went to see Gillelyn, knowing full well the implications of Burd's observation, "To a Plantation I must go with my Family Immediately as it will not do for me to set down and spend what little I have scrap'd together with much difficulty and hardship."[27] But when Edward III actually toured the plantation, he decided it was not worth the money. Sarah informed her husband that "Daddy . . . thinks by waiting a little longer you will be able to get a place for Eight or Nine hundred pounds, as money begins to be very Scarce & people will be obliged to sell their plantations for to pay off the Mortgage at Vendue."[28]

Colonel Burd journeyed from Ft. Augusta to Lancaster for the last time in the summer of 1764. His "broken constitution," frustrated ambitions, and responsibility for a large family caused considerable anguish. For the next few years this feeling rarely abated and occasionally precipitated fits of ill temper. The joy of reunion with his family was dampened by the recent death of Burd's ten-year-old son, Allen, which caused "a severe shock upon us."[29] When only three, this youngster called himself "Mr. Allen Burd . . . upon all occasions,"[30] and was "too unruly a member to make tea at his Aunt's Tea Tables," thus displaying a personality somewhat akin to his father's.[31] James entertained large plans for this son who began a hornbook at age three and just before his death "was greatly advanced in his Education beyond all the Boys here so young he could read Latin, Dutch & Greek & was a very good Arathmatition & an Extream fine Scholar."[32]

Other deaths and further frustrations occurring at about this time may explain Burd's rather irascible state during the next few years. Burd's brother George, who had run off from a medical apprenticeship to London and then to the army, died in 1764, and the only surviving son wrote his parents in Scotland expressing condolences on "the great loss our Family has Sustain'd."[33] James's other brother, John, had died a few years before in Jamaica. Now his father was writing his last will and testament and James felt a strong emotional desire to see his family in Scotland. He informed his father that "nothing in this Life would be more pleasing to me than to . . . see my Dear Parents & Sisters." Were James Burd's parents to die before he accomplished this, "it will be unsupportable Grieff to me."[34]

Only a year later Burd's father died. He left his estate in confusion. Although Edward Burd (James's father) owned three farms, a mansion house, gardens, parks, and a town house, his debts amounted to £2,441. The executor of the estate informed James that provisions of the will could not be met, and he suggested that James turn over his lands for the support of his mother and sister.

Stricken with grief, Burd signed a power of attorney to expedite matters. According to James Burd, within six years, "The person I sent the Power of attorney to, has pocketed all my money, and my Sister's also."[35]

These deaths evidently enervated the spirited colonel, for until 1766 Burd frittered away time in Lancaster. At the same time the Burds enjoyed living with Edward III, and he in turn liked having "the flock" around him. This however upset Edward IV who decried "what trouble and Expence Mr. Burd and his family have heretofore put you to."[36] Family resources should not be squandered in this way reasoned the eldest heir, and thus he gave "Mr. Burd a Spur about going into the Country."[37] Edward IV demolished Burd's last hopes of setting up as a merchant at Lancaster and still wished Burd would settle at Shippensburg. Finally Edward IV stopped his hints, for "I am afraid there would be such grumbling and Dissatisfaction that neither he nor my Sister would be happy."[38] Even the suggestion that Burd work "a good farm" put the colonel "in such a temper of mind," that Edward IV finally declared, "If he is so very stout & self-willed as not to take advice, I for my part shall never think of him or his Affairs any more."[39]

With that outburst the crisis spent its remaining energy, and the next month, May 1766, Edward Shippen III purchased a farm for the Burds. Tinian, as Burd called the seat, lay on the Susquehanna River in Paxton township, Lancaster County. The price of £900 pleased all, and Edward IV and Joseph III promised their father that "we will so manage the matter that after some time if Mr. Burd is to owe anything, it shall be to us; so that he need not be in dread of creditors."[40]

Workmen quickly erected a log house, and work on a permanent stone house commenced the following spring. The Burds planted crops long before their permanent abode was completed. In September 1768, the Burds moved into their new house. Other improvements such as a barn, kitchen, and stable took shape as well. On several occasions the Shippens readily loaned Burd money to improve the plantation, and Edward III delighted in sending seeds and advice as he had years ago when his "son" and daughter farmed at Shippensburg. The Burds were finally happy and content. Grateful to the Shippens, they named the first child born at

Tinian, Joseph, after Colonel Jospeh Shippen III.[41] Burd's only regret was that family visits would be less frequent than in the past. He let Edward III know that "I often wish . . . that you either lived at Tinian, or [the] next Plantation; that we might spend as many happy days, & hours together as we did when we lived at Lancaster."[42] Edward III missed "the flock" as well, but took pleasure in contemplating that although "old folks must not expect to live forever, yet if our lives are spared to be useful to our Children . . . it is accounted a blessing."[43]

Edward III might have added that being useful to our children's children also seemed a blessing, for by this time he was already deeply involved in their lives as well. Because the Burds practically lived under his roof for several years, Shippen's influence upon them was greater than upon those grandchildren bearing the Shippen name. Indeed, because James Burd was absent from his family for almost a decade, the grandfather's influence upon several young Burds even exceeded their own father's. Shippen alluded to this when he pointed out to the colonel that "if this war should prove fatal to you, which God forbid, it must give you a great pleasure whenever you reflect upon it to think that your wife and Children have Such Friends as your mammy and myself to take care of them."[44]

In this regard, the young Burds, whom Edward III affectionately dubbed "the Ducky Children," were particularly fortunate. Edward III had not only a strong desire to help his grandchildren, but was particularly well equipped to do so. His financial resources were large; his family connections were well cultivated, and his interest in education, remarkable. As he entered the last third of his long life, he no longer had to struggle to elevate his own position and provide for his own children; thus he could devote time and energy to what became a significant concern of his life. Clearly the Shippen family's exertions explain why the Burds began life as well as they did; their own father's financial resources, for example, were barely enough to support the family. The Colonel depended on the Shippens' aid to establish his children in the world when they reached maturity.

In the main only information concerning Edward III's role in the formal education of his grandchildren survives, yet his influence

certainly extended beyond that. Clearly Edward III sought to make
his life an example for his children and grandchildren; on several
occasions he acknowledged this role explicitly. Deeply concerned
with spiritual matters himself, the New Light Presbyterian attempted to implant strong religious convictions in his grandchildren. For instance, on one occasion his instructions to James Burd
were "Please to tell your Children that as soon as ever they awake
in the morning to lift up their hearts to God, & open them to him,
as much as possible they can, & to avoid all thoughts about the
world until their morning Devotions are over."[45] Shippen went on
to express his religious thoughts, such as, "The Great Principals of
Religion are Faith, Knowledge, Remembrance, Love & Fear, all
which the Holy Scripture useth to express the whole Duty of
Man." Because all his lengthy thoughts on this occasion were on
God and Jesus Christ, he told Burd to "Let the Children Copy this
Letter."[46]

During the 1750s Edward III devoted considerable time to improving his facility with several languages. Particularly his correspondence with his good friend James Read of Reading indicates
his fascination with Latin and French. He purchased many books,
borrowed others, and jotted down copious notes. He had actively
helped his son Joseph III acquire proficiency in French and arithmetic; now he encouraged similar interests in his grandchildren.
This helps explain why Allen Burd was so advanced in languages
and arithmetic when only ten years old and why "Cousin [William]
Allen . . . says [Neddy Burd] is a Clever Boy."[47] In 1764 Edward III
paid the three tutors who worked with Allen Burd, "not to mention
ye daily advantage he gets of 7½ Minutes under my [attenti]on; &
you know the great opinion I have of my Self,"[48] bragged the grandfather. At age thirteen, Neddy Burd had already left the direct
scrutiny of his grandfather for training at the College of Philadelphia, but when he came home for a vacation, his grandfather
inquired closely into his progress. After "an Examination with me,"
Edward III proudly reported, Neddy Burd "has acquitted himself
to my approbation."[49] James Burd, always aware of his debts of
gratitude to the Shippens, replied, "My Sons are both much obliged
to you for your Paternall care and affection and it gives me great

pleasure to Observe that they Improve their opportunity & answer your Expectation."[50]

When Allen Burd died, Edward III naturally intensified his interest in his namesake. Edward Burd attended the College of Philadelphia until 1765. Then his grandfather, who evidently paid for young Burd's education, hinted to Edward IV that Neddy become his apprentice. Edward IV needed someone in his law office at the time, and although he thought it too early for his nephew to leave school, he agreed. In August 1765 Edward Burd was indentured "to be taught to be an attorney at law" to his uncle. Uncle Edward IV generously refused any fee for the training. He thereby helped Neddy Burd receive an education which his father could not have afforded to provide.[51]

Another significant aspect of this family indenture was that the customary section of the document indicating that the master would provide food, clothing, and lodging was crossed out. Edward IV had five children ranging in age from five to ten years of age. He did not want the bother of another young person in his household. Furthermore, upon the birth of his youngest child, "a fine Baby . . . of the worst Sex . . . yet heartily welcome," Edward IV gently lamented that he must wait "a few Years longer before I ride in my Coach."[52] Although births were inevitable, the prominent lawyer and officeholder refused to postpone acquisition of a conspicuous symbol of his eminence by taking his nephew into his house.

During his apprenticeship Neddy Burd lived with his Uncle Joseph Shippen III. The house on Fourth Street, which Joseph III rented from his brother, lay just down the street from Edward IV's "Great House." The arrangement pleased everyone, and because Colonel Shippen and Neddy Burd's father were such good friends, the young man's stay in Philadelphia was pleasanter than it might otherwise have been. The south side of Philadelphia appeared to Neddy Burd much as it had to his "cousin" William Shippen III when the latter returned from London and Edinburgh. A vast kinship network helped him define his place; his mother was a Shippen, and thus any who recognized the Shippens as kin extended this recognition to the Burds. This brought about some divergence from strict kinship nomenclature. Neddy Burd talked of "Uncle J. Shippen" who was actually his mother's uncle; he knew "Cousin Sukey Shippen," and "Cousin Jemmy Willing" who were really his mother's cousins, and "Cousin Billy Allen" who was a bit more distantly related than that.[53] Of course Neddy Burd felt closest to members of the primary branch of the Shippen family. On one occasion he remarked, I have "so great a Regard for my Namesakes [Uncle Edward Shippen IV and Cousin Edward Shippen V (Edward IV's son)] that I make them as nearly related as possible by incorporation" in my daily walks.[54]

In the law office of his successful and ambitious uncle, Neddy Burd learned a great deal. Shippen imparted knowledge gained through professional study abroad and more than a decade of practice. Young Burd utilized his preceptor's library and took many detailed notes on important legal terms and procedures. In addition to study of the law, which consumed most of his intellectual energy, Neddy also studied Greek, German, and French. Uncle Joseph Shippen III gladly paid for his nephew's French books and schooling with Professor Paul Fooks of the College of Philadelphia. Because Pennsylvania contained a large German population, Uncle Joseph III also convinced Neddy to learn "Dutch." Grandfather Shippen, ever eager to assist Neddy, sent a "Dutch Grammar"; unfortunately the rules of grammar were also written in that tongue; hence his grandson found it useless.[55]

As time passed it became apparent that the Shippen family's ability to train Neddy Burd in the legal profession and to launch him successfully into the world could easily compensate for his premature departure from college. Neddy claimed, "I did not seem sorry for having quitted," when he attended "the Commencement when I should have stood a Candidate for the Degree of Bachelor of Arts if I had remained at College."[56] His comments on the occasion, however, betray a degree of envy and uneasiness. He observed that "my Class . . . braved it thro [the ceremony] undauntedly & indeed some of them bordered on the presumptuous Extreme."

Neddy Burd's anxiety came from his clear perception of his total dependence upon the Shippens. When he contemplated launching into the world, he realized, "It will be difficult for me to maintain myself at first but I must exercise Frugality and put my Shoulder to the Wheel—Grandpa, I believe, will lend me some assistance at my setting out." As Neddy contemplated his resources and those of his father as well, he reached the conclusion that "I should be hard punished I fear if Grandpa did not give me an assisting hand."[57] The Shippens held the reins controlling his advancement; more than Neddy's particular talents, the Shippen family would determine his immediate future.

Sound reasons for both optimism and pessimism existed. Already the Shippens had helped Neddy a great deal, and they had also assisted Neddy's parents and sisters as well. Although nothing indicated a waning of the desire to nurture the Burds, past efforts proved expensive, and Neddy was not wholly certain of the Shippens' ability to continue their support. Edward III, the patriarch of the Shippen family, underwent some financial strain toward the end of the 1760s. To a large degree this grew out of family obligations which he took upon himself. For example, in addition to subsidizing Neddy Burd's education, purchasing Tinian for the Burds, making additions to his "Great House" in Philadelphia which he rented to his son Edward IV, Edward III also contributed to the dowries of two granddaughters.

Events surrounding the marriages of Sarah and Mary Burd (also called Molly Shippen Burd) provide several insights into the way the Shippen family functioned. Sarah, the Burd's eldest daughter, met Jasper Yeates, her future husband, at her grandfather's house in Lancaster. In the fall of 1764, Edward Shippen III engaged in a fierce quarrel with his clerk. When the clerk quit, Edward III accepted his son's offer to "send up my apprentice Yeates to your Assistance."[58] Jasper Yeates (1745–1817), son of John and Elizabeth (Sidebotham), was born in Philadelphia and in 1761 received a B.A. from the College of Philadelphia. Although the grandson of an associate justice of the Supreme Court of Pennsylvania and member of the Provincial Council, Yeates "depends intirely upon me for his promotion," Edward Shippen IV averred in 1764.[59] Not surprisingly Yeates and his father readily acquiesced to Shippen's request to help out at Lancaster. Edward IV rejoiced at the opportunity to help his father, and Yeates happily took a place at the table of Edward Shippen III of Lancaster, a prominent man in his own right.[60]

The clerkship was temporary, for Edward IV acknowledged that his apprentice's "Knowledge in the Law and the Ambition natural to a young Man of Good Education will soon push him higher."[61] His potential and good character made Yeates wholly acceptable to the Shippen family; thus in 1767 Sarah Burd felt no qualms in accepting "in the kindest Manner . . . to cement our mutual affection by the firmest Union."[62] Jasper Yeates informed her father, "I am happy beyond Expression in the anticipation of the Moment when I shall see her mine; . . . I have the sincerest & most disinterested love for her, derived from the many opportunities I have enjoyed of viewing her in the Exercise of every Virtue & Grace which can dignify the female Mind."[63] The colonel consented to the proposal, and a few weeks later his daughter married the young lawyer.

Sarah's brother, Neddy Burd, wrote to congratulate her. He also praised his parents for "forbearing to influence your conduct in the least sufficiently evinces how dear your happiness is to them. And as you have been left entirely at your own liberty I doubt not but that where you have resolved on giving your hand it will be also accompanied by your heart."[64] Without wishing to deprecate the lofty sentiments and the marriage which lasted fifty years, we might draw attention to several other relevant considerations. James Burd faced financial difficulties in trying to support his large family; Sarah's marriage would decrease expenses somewhat. Furthermore, Yeates seemed likely to advance in his profession and that would provide comfort and security for his daughter; a lack of wealth precluded James Burd from negotiating a marriage contract with men with established fortunes. Although provisions of the dowry are unknown, presumably Edward Shippen III contributed to it.[65] Beyond this Jasper Yeates also benefited from an alliance with the powerful Shippen family. James Read of Reading is only one of many who took notice of Edward Shippen III's "worthy Grandson Mr. Yeates."[66]

A few years later, in the autumn of 1771, Burd's second daughter reached her maturity and wished to marry Peter Grubb, a rich iron master. James Burd consulted the Shippens for advice. A while later Molly's grandfather Edward Shippen III replied, "Mr. Yeates thinks very well of that Gentleman for a relation & so do your Mammy and myself."[67] He also indicated that his sons, Edward IV and Joseph III, voiced no objections. Again Neddy Burd commented approvingly upon the proceedings; he thought it "a suitable Match for my Sister as I am very certain that he would not have received so much Countenance from those of her Relations whose Duty and Delight it is to take Care of her Interest and provide for her Welfare unless he was every way unexceptionable."[68] That the marriage involved more than the young couple and their parents was obvious to others as well. For example, James Read wished Edward Shippen "and Coll. Burd with your good Families much Joy in the Marriage. . . . You have hitherto been happy in the Marriages which have arrived in your Family, and I pray . . . it may always be the Case with all of yours."[69] At the wedding which took place in November at Tinian, Molly's grandfather "was as merry as any," and though almost seventy years old expressed his joy at the union by his "Activity in dancing the Cobbler's Jig."[70]

Molly and her husband, "a man of good Character, and possessed of a considerable Estate," went to live at Hopewell Forge.[71] During the next few months family visits from the Burds occurred frequently. Beyond the normal expression of affection, these trips also indicated concern for Molly who soon began to experience pregnancy. Molly's fifteen-year-old sister Jenny helped her considerably during her last months. Molly finally sent her home just before the birth so that if "I should take ill sooner than I expect & send for you [her mother] in a hurry," her sister could take care of the younger Burds.[72]

Soon Peter Grubb came to take Sarah Burd to Hopewell to be with her daughter. Grubb's mother and sister were also present when Sarah announced the "good news" of the birth of another grandchild. James Burd's view of the news was somewhat mixed, for he wondered whether the child had been conceived before the marriage vows were taken. Edward Shippen III assured his "son" that "it is a very common thing for young women with their first Children to come 3 or 4 days or a week short of ye usual time."[73] He even mentioned that "P[egg]y A[lle]n was brought to bed 3 days before her nine months were completed." Burd had forgotten the precise date of his daughter's marriage; actually a few days more

than the usual time elapsed between the marriage and the birth.[74]
Molly was pregnant every year of her married life. The strain
was more than her health could withstand. In November 1773,
Sarah Burd became very uneasy about Molly's condition, for
"though I have often heard of womens taken sick a month before
the time & it has gone off, til the right time & done very well, but I
can't say I L[ike] it as their is a risque of bad Consequences."[75] Her
fears were not entirely unfounded. Although the baby did not
arrive until February, her mother and sisters who attended her
during her labor worried about the severe pains which continued
after the birth. Within a few weeks, Molly Grubb died. The trauma
of death deeply affected her sister Sarah. "Her Sleep is frequently
interrupted by sighs, which she represses as much as possible, in the
Day," observed her husband.[76] Although "the great Love she had
for her Sister & her extreme Sensibility, gave Reason to fear the
worst Consequences," in time Sarah recovered her usual spirits.[77]

Back in 1771, of course, Joseph Shippen III had no way of foreseeing the abrupt end to this promising marriage. It was then that
he expressed the hope that "my other Nieces at Tinian, as they
grow up, may be as fortunate as their Sisters in marrying so well, &
so early in Life."[78] Coincidentally both women married at age
eighteen. That was young not only according to their uncle's standards, but also according to the general tendency in the eighteenth
century.[79] Furthermore, because their father was not rich, indeed
quite the contrary, they seem to contradict the eighteenth-century
tendency of age at marriage to vary inversely with wealth.[80] The
Shippen family connection explains the exception to the rule.
Edward Shippen III contributed toward their dowries. Also connections with the Shippen family which exercised great influence in the
political and economic affairs of the province proved an inducement. Certainly Yeates benefited from it. Less than two years after
Molly's marriage to Peter Grubb, her mother informed Edward
Shippen III that Grubb wished a commission as a justice of the
peace. Shippen had helped his daughter's husband secure such a
post a few years earlier, and now he asked Cousin William Allen,
who controlled the distribution of these political plums, for one for
another relative. Grubb received the commission.[81]

Because Edward Shippen III readily assisted men who became

grandsons by marriage, it is not surprising that he also helped his daughter's son whom he had known so much longer. Edward III followed Neddy's activities through correspondence with the lad and also with Neddy's uncles. Neddy always thanked his grandfather for sound advice, gladly ran errands for him, and of course sent his love and duty to the families at Lancaster and Tinian.[82]

By 1771 Neddy Burd's apprenticeship drew to an end; preparations to settle him in a practice received serious attention. His grandfather and Uncle Edward IV took responsibility for this. Uncle Edward IV always thought Northampton a sensible spot, for Neddy's father owned a house there which was "dead" to the colonel, "but would be of much service" to Neddy.[83] In August 1771, Edward III gave his approval to the proposal, which pleased Edward IV who was convinced that it "is the best opening for a young fellow at this time."[84] The colonel dissented. He knew that the prothonotary of that county "can't hardly live by the Income of his office; by this, [I] Judge there must be little to do, and I think it is a poor County." Besides "Easton is a Doghole of a Place, Remote from all the World."[85] Because his financial resources precluded defying the Shippens, James Burd softened his objection by indicating that if Neddy found the place agreeable, that because it was "recommended by his friends he may make a Tryall of it in the Manner you mention."[86]

Needless to say, Neddy Burd was "much better pleased" when Uncle Edward IV turned his attention toward Reading instead.[87] Many things made the Berks county seat more attractive. Though only four years older than Easton, Reading (founded in 1748) with a population of about 1,100 was already the fourth largest town in Pennsylvania. Easton had only about 400 inhabitants. Not only was Reading larger and more prosperous than Easton, but it lay closer to Philadelphia and much nearer Lancaster and Tinian. Furthermore, James Read, who held all county offices except sheriff, was a good friend of Neddy's grandfather, and "Uncle was so good as to promise his Interest for me with the principal People of his Acquaintance in that county."[88] Neddy's grateful father profusely thanked the Shippens "for your great goodness and Bounty to our son Neddy—we are very happy He is to Settle at Reading & hope Mr. Biddle will be prevailed upon to shew him his Countenance, and that our son will meritt his favour—I make no Doubt but Mr. Jas. Reed [*sic*] your Daily Correspondent will also favour our son with His smile, which will likewise be of service to him."[89]

Appropriately, when Neddy Burd arrived in Reading in the spring of 1772, he wore a new suit which his grandfather Shippen bought him for the occasion.[90] Neddy lodged at Mr. Whitehead's for about £26 a year and kept an office at Mr. Lightfoot's, whose house was closer to the court house. The young lawyer intended to be "extremely industrious & frugal" and hoped that during the first year his income would at least cover the cost of his lodgings, office, traveling, and other necessary expenses. "If I do not get much Business at first," he told his grandfather, "it will give me the greater Opportunity of improving my Knowledge."[91] Trips to clients in surrounding areas of Lancaster and Northampton Counties soon augmented fees from local clients.

Although the Shippens no longer observed Neddy's every movement, they remained concerned for his welfare and advancement. Though on his own in some ways, the young man remained within their sphere of influence. Neddy acknowledged this, for example, when he forfeited at his grandfather's request a trip he wished to make, because I "shall always think it my Duty to obey you in your Commands."[92] A more vivid example occurred a few years later when Neddy's Uncle Edward IV learned of his nephew's involvement in "a most scandalous and iniquitous practice of gaming" with "a Set of Sharpers." Neddy's "very affectionate uncle" delivered a sharp rebuke, for "my love & friendship for you will not permit me to be silent when I see you on such a precipice." "The Reputation of a young Man just setting out in the world is extremely tender," continued Edward IV, "and early Impressions concerning him generally last for life. The Confidence placed in them is always in proportion to the prudence or discretion with which they act, and nothing in this world is more likely to destroy that Confidence than risking Money at Play."[93] The young man wisely stopped gambling, and his reputation in Reading, Philadelphia, and elsewhere remained unscathed.[94]

Shortly after that incident, for example, James Read praised Neddy's diligence and other virtues and told his grandfather that

"Mr. Burd has in all his Conduct much of the Character of your valuable Son Mr. Edward [IV]." Certainly wrote Read, "this must give . . . all your Family, and me a great Deal of Pleasure."[95] Neddy, meanwhile, continued to practice law at Reading and also served as the King's attorney at Northumberland. By the time he was twenty-three, he attained a notable promotion to the office of clerk of the court of *nisi prius*. Again family connections served him well, for his "brother," Jasper Yeates, who had held the position resigned in his favor. The new position introduced Neddy "to the particular acquaintance of the first Men in the Province and the Income of the office is a clever thing for a young Fellow."[96] To his grandfather, he wrote, "I am exceedingly obliged both to Mr. Yeates & my Uncle—to the one for resigning in my favor, & to the other for giving it to me with such Chearfulness."[97] Others in Pennsylvania may not have regarded overt nepotism with equal enthusiasm, but there is reason to believe that it was characteristic of several other prominent families besides the Shippens. For example, when James Read congratulated Edward III on his grandson's promotion, he mentioned that he had resigned as deputy register for Berks County in favor of his own son. Read concluded, "Is it not agreeable to find our Descendents thus honoured?"[98]

All this while the number of descendants multiplied. In all, Edward Shippen III's three children had twenty-eight children, twenty of whom reached maturity. In each case, all children came from one marriage, for no one remarried upon the death of the spouse. One reason for this was that the marriages lasted so long; the average was almost thirty-seven years (Edward IV's forty-one years, Sarah's thirty-six years, Joseph III's thirty-three). In this regard not one member of the fourth generation and only one member of the fifth generation married more than once. That provides a ratio of forty-one people to one. Such a lopsided pattern based on a significant number of people suggests that this may have been typical of late eighteenth-century Pennsylvania families.[99]

Although the Shippens did not write many details about the early years of the young additions to their families, certain things can be said about them and their parents' and grandparents' attitude toward them. Again literary evidence covers only the primary branch of the Shippen family in any significant way. Because considerable space has already been devoted to the young Burds, these few remarks will concern Edward IV's and Joseph III's children.

Edward IV and Margaret Francis had eight children at roughly two-year intervals; one boy and four girls reached maturity. Joseph III and Jenny Galloway's ten children came at irregular intervals until Jenny was forty-three; four males and three females reached maturity. To these Shippens, children probably seemed inevitable, boys preferable to girls, and expressions of emotion about them natural. Naming children served as an important means of building family identity, and it was a family duty that these children know and be known by their kin. Edward IV informed his parents of the births of his first three children, but in 1758 all the bells in Philadelphia rang rejoicingly, and Edward IV jubilantly illuminated his house for joy; "My Peggy was safely delivered of a fine lusty BOY."[100] They named him Edward; the sixth Shippen of that name to live in Philadelphia in as many decades. Shortly after Joseph III married, Edward IV observed, "How my Brother struts since he has got a *Son*."[101] Girls were not unwanted, and when Jenny Shippen was pregnant with her third child, Edward III hoped for a granddaughter, "for we all know that asortment is very acceptable."[102] The attention the Shippens lavished on daughters of the fourth, fifth, and sixth generation is further evidence of this appreciation of what Edward IV once referred to as "the Worst Sex."[103]

Almost all evidence suggests that the Shippens viewed children as an inevitable consequence of marriage. Aside from the large number of offspring, both Edward IV and Joseph III mentioned on at least one occasion a desire that children not be born at a particular time. In both cases the large expenses of child rearing forced alterations of immediate goals. For example, upon the birth of his fifth child, Edward IV remarked that he would have to wait a few years longer before riding in a coach. When Joseph III's second child in as many years of marriage was about to arrive, he confided to his father that "if Events were always to correspond to our own particular Desires, I should have rather wished this to have been postponed a Year or two longer. But let God's will be done; and whatever that may at any time be, I hope I shall always be entirely contented and resigned to it."[104] Joseph III's less ambitious personality in comparison to his brother's was fortunate, for the former had a larger number of children and more of them survived. At age thirty-one Edward IV's wife gave birth to her last child. Most women in the eighteenth century carried their last child later than this. No concrete evidence concerning her use of birth control measures survives, but because demographic evidence suggests that some Philadelphians had knowledge of such means, this possibility cannot be ignored.[105]

The Shippens expressed their love for their children by overt emotional actions. If the number of kisses delivered in person approximated the number sent through the mail by parents, children, and grandparents, the little ones were almost smothered with affection. Even if that exaggerates the situation, as it doubtless does, spoiled children abounded. This tender attention began at birth when the child was taken to its mother's breast. When Jenny Shippen feared that she would be unable to nurse one of her sons, it gave her "no small concern."[106] A few years later Joseph III and Jenny "both met with a severe Stroke of Affliction, in the Death of our little Daughter."[107] Joseph III found that "this Loss has so much affected her [Jenny], that it will require a Length of time before she can recover her usual Spirits and Chearfulness."[108] Fortunately the birth of a daughter the following year gave "great Joy [to] both . . . the Father & Mother, as it supplies the place, in some measure, of the dear little one we lost."[109]

At birth an important step in reinforcing family identification occurred. The child was given a name. After the second half of the eighteenth century began, the Shippens not only identified with a large number of living kin, but also looked back across many generations as well. This is a matter of inference, for the Shippens used fairly common names such as Edward, Joseph, William, Ann, Mary, Margaret, and Sarah. But of all the names to choose from they tended to select from a relatively small number, even when that led to considerable confusion. For instance, at one time four different Joseph Shippens walked about Philadelphia. There was Joseph Shippen II, son of Joseph Shippen, and Joseph Shippen III whom contemporaries called Joseph Shippen, Jr., to distinguish him from his uncle; Joseph II had another nephew called Joseph W. Shippen, and a son, Joseph Shippen IV, who was undoubtedly confused with the others.

Even the Shippens realized the problems they created, but this made no difference. For instance, to indicate affection for their father's second wife, Joseph III and Jenny agreed "to name her [a baby] after Mammy and generally call her Polly, to distinguish her from one of my Brother's Daughters, who is called Molly."[110] When the Shippens selected a name which had not been used by them in America, they reinforced family identification in other ways. In the fifth generation the Shippens began using middle names such as John Francis Shippen (1762–1763), Joseph Galloway Shippen (1783–1857), Molly Shippen Burd (1753–1774), and Thomas Lee Shippen (1765–1798). Joseph III named his firstborn Robert, "in remembrance of Dr. Robert Shippen Vice Chancellor of Oxford my [Edward III's] Father's first Cousin."[111] Instead of reaching into the past, the Shippens might look laterally. Joseph III's second son was named "*John,* after Jenny's Father."[112] Upon the birth of Joseph III's third child, Edward III suggested "may be you will name it John. I only mention this as there was one of that name, brother of William Shippen ye Parliament man . . . from who I once received a very kind letter, which I have preserved."[113] Because Joseph III already had a son of that name, he declined. As that was Edward III's twenty-second grandchild, he can certainly be forgiven the confusion; the error is comforting to others who view the genealogical jungle.

These children quickly became acquainted with the members of the Shippens' vast kinship network. Because so many lived close by in the south side of Philadelphia, that was easy. Dr. William Shippen II and his son William III served as family physicians to the Edward III branch of the family.[114] Children required inoculation against smallpox and treatment for other ills. The old doctor knew them well. Because Edward IV's and Joseph III's children did not see their grandparents as often as their cousins the Burds, other means substituted. Whenever Edward IV or Joseph III ventured to Lancaster, they returned loaded down with presents from their parents to their children. On one occasion, as Joseph III prepared to depart, he found neither his father "nor my Mother would be contented without stuffing them full of good Things"; they even exceeded their usual generosity. With a smile on his face, Joseph III jested, "I shall be equipped for an East India Voyage."[115] The grandchildren beamed with excitement whenever presents from their grandparents arrived. When old enough to make the two-day journey, the grandchildren visited Lancaster. The visits were of unquestionable delight and importance; for example, in 1775 Edward III so enjoyed the visit of his granddaughter Peggy Shippen, that he promised that upon her next visit, "I will ride out more than once to meet her, tho[ugh] it is even on a Court day."[116] As soon as they learned to write, the grandchildren engaged in the familial duty of writing letters. A few youthful efforts survive. For example, ten-year-old Sarah III (Edward IV's daughter) wrote her "Grandmamma," whom she addressed as "Honoured madam":

> Sister Betsy tells me she is writing a letter of thanks for the presents you were so kind to send by papa; I hope she won't undertake to write for me, as I am able to write for myself; what signifies a year and a half's difference in our Ages and perhaps four or five Inches in our Height; I think as much of myself as her Ladyship; and as my papa has had me taught to write, I don't see why my own pen may not convey my own Thanks.[117]

As the second half of the eighteenth century unfolded, the structure and functioning of the Shippen family explained more about its members than in earlier years. The family contributed to their sense of identity in many ways, and the Shippens consciously worked at directing interpersonal relationships. The Shippens functioned as an extended family and derived the economic and political benefits which such a structure can provide. Although this structure is more often associated with past societies than the present, the extended family functions in many parts of the modern world. Strikingly "modern" in character also were the emotional attitudes of the Shippens toward children and death, among other things.

VIII

The Shippens and the
American Revolution to 1781

During the years before the American Revolution, the structure and functioning of the Shippen family helped give a certain character to the society in which they functioned. Their roots extended to the founding years of the province. With the exception of the interlude of the second generation, Shippens played significant roles in the colony's development during almost that entire three-quarters of a century through the exercise of familial, economic, and political power. Particularly after mid-century, their actions as a family influenced more than simply members of their kinship group. On the eve of the Revolution, the third, fourth, and even fifth generation of Shippens composed one of the old established families of Pennsylvania. Few other families rivaled them in terms of power and influence.

Even before the Great War for Empire, the power of the Shippen family evoked hostility and envy as well as respect. Indeed, because the power of the Shippen family and especially the Allen-Hamilton-Shippen kinship network was associated with the proprietor, many politicians felt strong resentment and helped precipitate attempts to overthrow the Proprietary government. In time the old-style politics which the Allen-Hamilton-Shippen network represented engendered enough resentment so as to become a cause of the Revolution in Pennsylvania. In several respects the proprietor's major antagonists were not fundamentally different. The Pennsylvania Assembly was not particularly representative of the people of the province. It was dominated by the Quaker party which in turn was

154

strongly influenced by a Philadelphia-centered oligarchy. Groups attached to the Logan, Pemberton, and Norris families roughly paralleled rivals in the Proprietary group. After 1770 both leading factions of the old party system increasingly recognized their common ground and a common threat, for by 1776 the Quaker and Proprietary parties became functionally indistinguishable. Emerging political groups recognized the similarities, despised the old system, and overthrew it. The concept of a "conservative revolution" fails to explain the protest movement in Pennsylvania; on the other hand, an "internal revolution" was not only attempted, but it met with a significant degree of success.[1]

Although questions concerning the nature of the American Revolution and its impact upon this old established family merit additional treatment, 1781 marks a significant terminal point to one phase of the history of this family. Edward Shippen III, the strong patriarch of the primary branch of the family, died. His death roughly coincided with the cessation of hostilities at Yorktown, but the dividing point in a family study derives from private, not public concerns.

Before the 1740s the Assembly, dominated by the Quaker party, gradually took over many prerogatives which the proprietor had enjoyed. In 1746 Thomas Penn gained majority control of the family holdings in Pennsylvania; soon he revealed determination to change the situation. Although not a tyrant, Penn desired stronger authority as executive of the province. As a result, struggles between the proprietor and Assembly over taxation, courts, and secret instructions for the governor became endemic. In the 1750s the talented and aspiring politician Benjamin Franklin entered Pennsylvania politics in a significant way. For a time he acted as an independent. Although both the Quaker party and Proprietary group courted Franklin, by 1755 he decided that the former offered the better means to promote his plans. Shifts within the Quaker party and the inclusion of Franklin and his admirers notably widened the Quaker or Assembly party's base. Often the power of the proprietor or his supporters such as the Allen-Hamilton-Shippen group frustrated Franklin and his adherents and associates.

Outraged by what it considered the proprietor's inflexible and arbitrary government, the Quaker party gradually resolved to attempt an overthrow of the proprietor. The effort culminated in the 1764 campaign to make Pennsylvania a royal colony. That campaign, the key to Pennsylvania politics according to one leading authority, convulsed politics and precipitated important realignments in political parties.[2]

In the mid-1750s difficulties between the proprietor and Quaker party intensified. By 1757 Franklin was in England to urge Penn to give up his government. Frustrated in his dealings with Penn, Franklin overestimated the amount of English support for eliminating private colonies. After a brief lull, Pontiac's Rebellion and the march of the Paxton Boys placed the Assembly in a precarious position with regard to Penn. In 1763 Indian raids on the frontier and inadequate protection caused the Paxton Boys, a vengeful group of Scotch-Irish Presbyterians, to murder a group of friendly Indians at Conestoga and Lancaster. In March 1764 the frontiersmen marched on Philadelphia to lodge their complaints. Philadelphia mobilized to fend off the impending onslaught of "white savages." Although the Paxton Boys turned back after meeting at Germantown with various officials including Governor John Penn and Benjamin Franklin, a significant event had transpired. The Quakers' intense verbal attacks on Presbyterians, blaming them for the Paxton march and the threat to law and order, encouraged Presbyterians to rally as a political group. The Presbyterians entered Pennsylvania politics and became a significant force. They felt that the Quaker Assembly neither listened nor responded to the people in general and displayed indifference to frontier complaints in particular.

The Quaker party, fearful of anarchy and of losing ground to the proprietor, came to the conclusion that a change in government was now imperative. The intense campaign for royal government commenced. The Quaker-dominated Assembly passed resolutions criticizing the Proprietary government and urging its replacement. A petition supporting that end gathered 3,500 signatures. Assembly resolves criticized Thomas Penn's governing from afar and use of arbitrary power when he issued instructions to his governors or appointed judges for good behavior. Furthermore, Penn's appointees corrupted public morals and attempted "to demolish and annihilate the Priveleges granted" by William Penn.[3] In the campaign, detractors portrayed Thomas Penn as a tyrant; indeed the proprietor and his friends supposedly sought to reduce Pennsylvanians to a "servile Condition of the . . . worst slaves of the worst absolute Monarch."[4]

Despite efforts by Franklin, Galloway, and much of the Quaker party, resistance to the attempt to overthrow the Proprietary government mounted. The Presbyterians led the opposition. The families, politicians, and policies associated with the Quaker party became increasingly anathema to them; furthermore, they viewed the movement for royal government as an attempt by the Quaker Assembly to draw attention away from frontier complaints. Several influential figures of the Quaker party such as Israel Pemberton and John Dickinson sided with the ill-organized Proprietary group. About fifteen thousand people signed a petition opposing royal government. After the heated and exciting election campaign, notable casualties at the polls included Franklin, his lieutenant Galloway, and several other ardent promoters of royal government. Although the proprietor had not been popular for decades, Pennsylvanians refused to relinquish the advantages they enjoyed under the Proprietary government for unknown consequences. Unperturbed by this setback, for years Franklin and Galloway urged the Quaker party to continue attempts to replace the Proprietary government.

The Shippens had affiliated with the Proprietary party ever since their arrival in the colony; in 1764 Edward III, Joseph II, Edward IV, and Joseph III, and several of their kinsmen depended upon the proprietor for much of their stature and income. Furthermore, by this time the Presbyterians in the province generally aligned with the faction led by William Allen. Naturally the Shippens applauded the defeat which the opposition suffered in the fall elections.

The tendency to look favorably upon Franklin, Galloway, and their supporters for a royal charter exists. Usually their effort is considered an attempt to promote sound principles and improve the government. Leaders of the Proprietary group customarily stand in contrast because of their selfish opportunism. Although the Proprietary party leaders wished to keep their offices, many in the Assembly party appear motivated to a large degree by a desire to obtain preferment. Such was the charge by their opponents. Even Galloway's friends frequently teased the talented lawyer about his ardent craving for a judgeship. Franklin's son was governor of New Jersey, and many believed the father wanted to govern Pennsylvania.

Campaign charges cannot be accepted at face value; however, even Franklin and Galloway's scholarly defenders and other analysts describe both politicians as ambitious and find that many of their merchant and professional supporters anticipated offices under a royal establishment.[5]

Supposedly convincing considerations against the charge that Franklin and Galloway favored royal government to advance their own interests are that previously both declined the opportunity to join the Proprietary side and that both felt compelled by events.[6] True, in the previous decade both had had the opportunity to join with the Proprietary group, but that alternative no longer existed. Not only was the old route blocked to them, but the Proprietary group prevented them from realizing their aspirations. A royal government could present a reasonable, perhaps the only, chance to satisfy political ambitions. The compelling event could have been the inefficient, archaic Proprietary government; however, the campaign's failure severely undercuts the contention that events or the people made royal government the wave of the future. The lack of opportunity which would exist if no alteration of government occurred remains a plausible alternative explanation.

The opinion that material considerations reinforced principles or perhaps overshadowed principles gains more credence because the support of Franklin, Galloway, and their party for a royal charter continued well into the period of imperial crisis when colonial antipathies toward the extension of tighter control erupted. Franklin, Galloway, and their associates promoted royal government through the Stamp Act crisis; Franklin continued until he recognized defeat in 1768, and as late as 1769 Galloway urged the project upon the Assembly.

Efforts to reorganize the empire soon made questions regarding Proprietary rule lose their urgency if not relevancy. Far more significant issues involving colonial rights and the authority of Parliament replaced them. When Grenville's Stamp Act precipitated forceful and even violent opposition in some colonies, Pennsylvania responded more moderately. In England Franklin came to view the act as inevitable and even nominated friends for appointments as stamp distributors. Under Galloway's leadership the Quaker party, still hoping to gain the ministry's approval of their request for a royal charter, attempted to prevent violence. The White Oaks, the working-class base of the party, even defended the stamp distributor from a mob led by the son of Chief Justice Allen. The ominous forebodings of the election of 1764 and the Stamp Act crisis disturbed the Proprietary group. When the Townshend Act reopened the imperial question, parts of that group tended to fear internal developments almost as much as imperial threats. Actions of the frightened Quaker party caused it to lose its working-class support by 1770. From 1770 to 1776 both the Quaker party and disintegrating Proprietary group moved closer together. Many observed that executive-legislative relations never had been smoother. It was the new party, the Presbyterian, which became the moving element and emerged in a forceful way as independence was declared. To them, both the old, established parties represented a style of politics which they sought to repudiate.

As the imperial crisis developed, the Shippens were caught in an ambiguous position. They not only opposed the effort to increase British control by converting Pennsylvania into a royal colony, but also disapproved of broader efforts to tighten the empire. On the other hand, they did not sympathize with aspects of the protest movement which might be directed against them as participants in the old-style politics. In time the Revolution acted upon the Shippens, and their reactions to it became an important aspect of the family's history.

The paucity of manuscripts regarding the attitudes of the secondary branches during the decade and a half preceeding the Declaration of Independence again necessitates focus upon the major branch of the Shippen family. Though lamentable, that relative void inflicts less damage than might be supposed. In regard to the imperial crisis, all evidence indicates that all Shippens opposed the "tyrannical" British measures. Not until the issue of independence was raised do serious divisions appear. In regard to any local problems which imperial problems precipitated, the lack of evidence hampers full comprehension of the Shippen family response. Fortunately certain actions and sparse bits of correspondence by the secondary branch suggest differences of opinion. The integrity of the Shippen family actions during this period can be preserved adequately.

When the Stamp Act crisis began, Edward Shippen IV remarked that his namesake was born just in time "to breath[e] about three weeks the Air of Freedom; for after the first of November we may call ourselves the Slaves of England."[7] Edward IV's brother Joseph III and nephew Neddy Burd (Edward IV's apprentice) echoed those sentiments. Joseph III sent pamphlets criticizing the Stamp Act to his father at Lancaster. The patriarch thought Daniel Dulany's *Considerations on the Propriety of Imposing Taxes in the British Colonies* a "masterly performance" and also liked the one attributed to John Dickinson.[8] With some misgivings Edward IV and Joseph III agreed to defy the parliamentary measure; their cousin, Dr. William Shippen III, signed the Non-Importation Agreement designed primarily for merchants, thus perhaps indicating fuller endorsement. Aware of the Stamp Act riots in New England, Edward IV feared "these violent Methods will tend to fix Chains upon us sooner than they would otherwise come. . . . Poor America! It has seen its best days."[9] A great sense of relief and elation filled the Shippens the following spring when repeal of the hated act temporarily abated anxieties and resentments regarding British authority.[10]

Upon resumption of the imperial controversy brought on by the Townshend Acts, John Dickinson published his *Letters from a Farmer in Pennsylvania,* and William Allen sought to nullify the inaction of the Assembly by calling a mass meeting at the State House. There Dickinson and Charles Thomson ("the Sam Adams of Philadelphia") enunciated the colonial grievances. The ensuing petition gained the endorsement of most "men of the best understanding among us."[11] Allen's cousin, Edward Shippen III, the leading political figure in Lancaster County, espoused similar sentiments. He exclaimed to his friend James Read, the most prominent politician in Berks County, "What confusion does a corrupt Ministry cause to a people born to freedom! You see that the People of New England will struggle for Liberty, even tho' Regiments are threatened to be sent over to reduce them to obedience."[12]

Though Philadelphia merchants chafed under the non-importation agreement, William Allen and "many judicious people" urged continuance of the colonial policy of economic coercion.[13] When New York merchants finally abandoned the boycott in July 1770, another large meeting at the State House in Philadelphia occurred. The principal speaker was Charles Thomson, who drew support from local mechanics and "radicals." But others applauded him as well. For example, Joseph Shippen III, secretary of the province, praised Thomson for his "long, animated and sensible harangue."[14] Shippen was pleased that all but one of Thomson's resolutions carried, and thought that "patriotic sentiments" characterized the entire proceedings that day. Although the embargo soon ceased, the Shippens doubtless appreciated the increasing strength which the Proprietary party enjoyed in Philadelphia.[15]

Several years later news of the Boston Tea Party electrified the colonies. Parliament's rigorous response with the Coercive Acts precipitated colonial organizations of resistance which cooled the ardor of many in the Proprietary party in Pennsylvania. William Allen and others began to fear that the protest movement might degenerate into overt treason and anarchy. Among Allen's closest friends were his kinsmen, the Shippens. Although for some time Edward Shippen III and his "son" James Burd lashed out violently against British "tyranny," Edward IV and Joseph III became reticent. Their correspondence with their father tended to convey the course of events as newspapers and rumors presented them; both brothers deleted their own reactions to these occurrences. As the secretary of the province explained to his nephew after military confrontations commenced, "I do not think it prudent at this time for me to trust in a Letter any Remarks or Sentiments respecting the present Transactions in America."[16] The actions of Edward IV and Joseph III, however, strongly suggest their thoughts even before they finally breached their resolution to keep silent.

Meanwhile out in Lancaster County, Edward III constantly commented upon the news he received from his sons in Philadelphia before he passed it on to James Burd at Tinian. Shippen's opinions were well known to his fellow townsmen also. He subscribed £10 for the relief of Bostonians suffering under the effects of the Coercive Acts. That sum amounted to almost twice as much as any other donor in Lancaster County gave; in fact more than ninety percent of the subscribers in the county contributed £1 or less.[17] Shippen wrote to James Burd complaining, "The merchants in England look upon us in *this* part of the world as their Slaves, having no more regard for us than Seventy Wealthy Creoles who have bought themselves Seats in the Parliament House have for their Negroes on their Plantations in the Western Islands." He continued, "[they think] It is our duty to work for them and while the white & black servants send the Merchants gold & Silver & ye Creoles Spirits Sugar & Mollasses etc. . . . they may take their pleasure and roll about in their Coaches." But, he concluded, "they must not expect to have their labor & eat it too."[18] Presumably Shippen conveyed similar opinions in conversations about town, for only a few days later he was elected chairman of the Lancaster County Committee of Correspondence and of the Lancaster County Committee of Observation.[19]

James Burd repeated Shippen's thoughts to friends in Middletown and the surrounding area; "the People of England . . . [believe] that it was not only Lawfull, Reasonable, Just, humane & proper, but absolutely Necessary to make Negroes Slaves & further that *Political Necessity* . . . required that all the People of North America should be slaves also."[20] The colonel also condemned Lord North's "most Iniquitious, Cruel, ungenerous, unjust & unconstitutional Plot."[21] In time James Burd emerged as the chairman of the committee at Paxton.[22]

Late in 1774, however, Edward Shippen III began expressing great fears lest civil war break out. Though convinced that "the Ministry have no hopes of Succeeding against us unless it be by bombarding ye Town of Boston & so beginning an Unatural [*sic*] War with us who are neither natural or unatural [*sic*] Rebels," Shippen began to hedge.[23] He sought to protect himself rather than to commit himself further to the resistance efforts. Because he realized "the great Impropriety" of being chosen to the Provincial Convention, Shippen "as if by accident . . . let a few of our leading People, both of Town & Country, know of my misfortune."[24] Ill health and old age served as an acceptable excuse, and Shippen happily avoided the embarrassment of election to that "definitely revolutionary" body.[25]

James Burd also equivocated. Though eager like Edward III to see the colonists delivered "out of the hands of our murdering Enemys,"[26] in August 1775 the colonel resigned his military commission and also his position in the Paxton Township Committee.

Only a month later, however, he resumed both duties. Edward III approved, for otherwise Burd "would have appeared suspicious, and your Influence might have been greatly injured in your Neighborhood."[27] Colonel Burd remained in command of armed rebels until December 1776. Then "at this time of Public Danger," he resigned for the last time; his confused explanation claimed that inability to muster sufficient troops for his battalion evoked retirement.[28]

By contrast young Neddy Burd acted decisively in a manner carefully calculated to serve his own best interests. If British troops put down the rebellion, Neddy Burd's family connections would continue to serve him well; yet if a civil war ensued and displaced his grandfather and uncles, Burd's position as kinsman of "traitors" and son of an almost impoverished father would become precarious. Consequently Neddy Burd viewed a military career in the rebellion as an opportunist. As he explained after about three months' service in a Pennsylvania Rifle Battalion from Berks County, "I think I have acted as a Volunteer . . . long enough to shew my hearty Disposition & wish for the [succ]ess of the Cause. We are engaged in & have sacraficed as much in proportion to my Circumstances voluntarily & freely as any One of them can boast."[29] His parents and the Shippens were relieved that Burd had "fully satisfied your Couriosity, and answered all the purposes of your going to the Camp," and because the young lieutenant harbored no intention of seeking a promotion, his Uncle Joseph III advised him to hasten home.[30] Although Neddy Burd engaged in no battle, he thought "that Consideration ought not to keep me here to the Ruin of my Business"; hence he took his uncle's advice and left Boston.[31]

Lieutenant Burd's departure for the scene of hostilities, however, was made in defiance of family advice. Uncle Edward IV thought it "a ridiculous thing for a young man bred in an office to attempt to command . . . Men bred in the woods and enured to Hardships."[32] Likewise grandfather Shippen disapproved of Neddy's plan and censured him for "not consulting his Friends" before he volunteered.[33] Cousin Thomas Willing supported the Shippens with an additional note to the same effect. Only Burd's "brother" Jasper Yeates thought the lieutenant's "Intentions were so virtuous & laudable . . . that they appear . . . to palliate if not justify" the action.[34] Although the Shippens bore no ill will toward Burd for his headstrong determination, the subsequent Loyalist proclivities of Edward IV, Joseph III, and Thomas Willing suggest duplicity in the particular objections which they raised.[35] Hindsight misconstrues things. For example, shortly after Neddy Burd returned to civilian life, Edward IV urged James Burd to retain his colonel's commission, for "it is safest in these times, especially at that distance to have a Military Command."[36] Furthermore, in November 1775, Joseph Shippen III hoped that success of Continental forces in Canada would "induce the Ministry to bring about an Accommodation."[37] His identity lay with rebel arms, for he believed that "our having possession of Canada, with the Canadians & Indians in our Interest will be of immense Advantage to us."[38] As late as the end of 1775, the Shippens' sympathy lay with the protestors; their advice to Neddy Burd stemmed from concern for his personal safety.[39]

The attitude of the primary branch of the Shippen family toward the protest movement changed abruptly. "A most extraordinary *Pamphlet* entitled, *Common Sense* . . . was published here last Week," exclaimed Joseph III in mid-January 1776, "[and] to the great Surprize & Alarm of many People . . . it openly avows an absolute Independency of Great Britain."[40] The shocked secretary believed that extreme would be "fatal to America in its Consequences," but suspected that the Continental Congress would adopt it if "the Government shall actually . . . employ foreign troops to reduce us."[41] Upon hearing this news Edward III declared, "I dread the Consequences of a State of Independency. . . . May God forbid it."[42] These sentiments reflected Edward IV's thoughts at the time as well. During the following months the Shippens hoped that Lord North's Conciliation Plan or efforts by moderate men in the colonies would thwart the designs of "violent wrongheaded people."[43]

Disappointment followed disappointment. The Shippens, who for so long took for granted the idea that the "better sort" should lead and the "inferior sort" should follow, now expressed fears that the social structure was endangered. When "a few Gentlemen" on the Philadelphia Committee of Inspection failed to block Timothy Matlack and "a number of other violent wrongheaded people of the inferior Class" who wished the Provincial Convention to transact business instead of the General Assembly, Joseph III envisioned "the greatest Confusion Anarchy & discension."[44] Moderates in the

Assembly added seventeen new members to that body from Philadelphia and the back counties in an attempt to strengthen the
legally constituted organization against the schemes of "those violent Republicans."[45] The newly constituted Assembly still lost
ground to the extra-legal body. Like his brother, Edward III denounced "a design on foot to reduce the affairs of this province to
as great a State of Anarchy as will put us on a level with some of
the Colonies to the Eastward." He hoped that Cousin Andrew
Allen and "a few other good Men" in Congress could stop "the
cunning men of the East."[46]

At length the Shippens realized that "whatever Objections we &
thousands of others may have to an Independence, it appears . . .
beyond a Doubt, that a public Declaration will be made."[47] All they
could do now was pray "for the preservation of our *Liberty* &
Prope[*rty*]" and make preparations for their own safety.[48] The Shippens of the primary branch of the family decided that "every moderate thinking Man must remain silent and inactive."[49] In April
1776 Joseph Shippen III moved his family to his country house in
Germantown. Several weeks later his brother, Edward IV, settled his
family in Amwell, New Jersey, on a farm which he had recently
purchased as a retreat. Even Edward III contemplated riding out
the storm of revolution on his plantation at Shippensburg.[50]

Significantly, the secondary branches of the Shippen family do not
reflect the major group's response to the course of events after the
Great War for Empire. Joseph II, surveyor of customs for Delaware
Bay, must have dreaded independence, although his thoughts concerning the British measures, at least those which might increase
his declining income, very likely conflicted with those of the primary branch. Unfortunately his opinions do not survive. The
William Shippen II branch displayed continuous support for the
protest movement even after it became treasonous.

William Shippen III eventually headed the medical department
for the Continental Congress. Because physicians enjoyed a large
degree of political immunity during the war, for example, they
could pass through enemy lines to care for the wounded, William
III need not have disagreed with most of the sentiments of his
cousins. His wartime activities deserve further attention, but for the
moment it seems worth noting that his conduct can be explained

largely by professional considerations and opportunism. Only William II openly supported the Revolution in word and deed. Although he remained on cordial terms with the neutral or Loyalist Shippens, he did not share their opinions of independence and its possible consequences.

In July 1776, William II wrote to his older brother, Edward III, "I give you joy of the late declaration of Independence." Thankful was the doctor that neither weakness nor passion prevented "so desirable an Event." Instead of fearing the consequences of this drastic step, William II welcomed what he thought of as an unique "opportunity of forming a plan of government upon the most just, national & equal principles; not exposed as others have . . . been to caprice or accident or the influence of some mad conqueror, or prevailing parties or factions of men," but upon deliberate council directed solely to the public good by wisdom, impartiality, and disinterestedness. Although that observation doubtless evoked a resounding denial from Edward III, William II's closing remarks rang true, even if he and his brother evaluated them differently. William II struck upon a significant cause of the Revolution in Pennsylvania when he wrote:

I don't wonder to see some of our Friends offended & full of resentment upon the change—who have heretofore been at ye head of affairs & in short have in many instances behaved as though they thought they had a sort of Fee simple in them, & might dispose of all places of Honor & Profit to such as pleased them best now to be ousted or at least bro[ugh]t down to a level with their fellow Citizens.[51]

William Shippen II voiced a resentment which many Pennsylvanians experienced. Most colonists believed that something had gone wrong in the empire; many outspoken rebels also believed that all was not well at home either. Because Loyalist, rebel, and neutral contingencies attracted an impressive number of people from every social station, this internal conflict cannot be comprehended by a simple class-conflict theory. In Pennsylvania, however, sharp criticism of the social structure and life style of many people after mid-century occurred too often to be ignored. Beyond this existed violent detestation of the way in which provincial politics operated. The style and functioning of the Shippen family played a significant part in creating this internal disenchantment. The Shippens were not unique in this regard; hence an analysis of their role provides vital insights into the nature of the Revolution.[52]

Analysis of the ideology of the American Revolution reveals that the colonists exercised great care in selecting authors and ideas to support their case. Those authors who seemed particularly revelant detested the tendencies of their own day, especially the growth of luxury, vice, corruption, and arbitrary power. This was especially true of classical writers such as Plutarch, Livy, Cicero, Sallust, and Tacitus, and also of the English Radical Whigs, John Trenchard and Thomas Gordon. Sound reasons exist to support the thesis that these ideas held "real personal and social significance for those who used them"; they were neither propaganda nor hollow abstractions.[53] The rhetoric expressed the reality as these writers perceived it.

When the Reverend Andrew Burnaby, who traveled through the colonies in 1759–1760, arrived in Philadelphia, he marveled, "Can the mind have a greater pleasure than in contemplating the rise and progress of cities and kingdoms? Than in perceiving a rich and opulent state arising out of a small settlement or colony? This pleasure every one must feel who considers Pennsylvania."[54] But to many who made the colony their home, such rapid changes evoked a certain uneasiness. The great influx of immigrants, especially the Scotch-Irish and Germans, for instance, not only promoted prosperity, but also created the most heterogeneous population in British North America. Even the physicial environment altered almost yearly; new farms were carved out of the wilderness, and towns sprang up as well. With "progress" and "opulence" came increasingly elegant life styles and greater contrasts in wealth than in the past.

Many colonists, such as Chief Justice William Allen, entertained ambivalent feelings regarding these tendencies. On the one hand, he felt pride in the advances and took a leading part in bringing them about; on the other hand, he feared the loss of a more virtuous past. For many, the sense of foreboding intensified after midcentury. Countless contemporaries swelled the throng of critics of the tendencies which they perceived.

Nowhere in Pennsylvania were the alarming tendencies as pronounced as in Philadelphia, the political, economic, intellectual, and social center of the province. And few people did more to set the tone of that society than the Shippens and their kinsmen such as the Allens, Willings, and Francises. Their activities hastened what has been identified as "the Europeanizing of the urban centers."[55] Particularly after mid-century fine town houses and country seats appeared in the Delaware Valley. Their occupants enjoyed fine foods and wines, and wore expensive clothes; an increasing number also rode about town in fancy equipages. Dances, balls, social clubs, the theater, and like pursuits also consumed their interests.

"Urban elegance" in Philadelphia began with the substantial brick edifice erected by Dr. William Shippen II in 1750.[56] About a decade later many began to follow suit; the doctor's brother, Edward III, and nephew, Edward IV, were among the more notable emulators. Although many country residences dot the environs of Philadelphia on the Nicholas Scull and George Heap *Map of Philadelphia and Parts Adjacent* of 1750, the tendency to construct more luxurious country seats occurred after mid-century. The Shippens' Cousin William Allen, built "Mt. Airy" and provided the "real impetus to the rage for elaborate country estates."[57] By the 1770s eighty-two Philadelphians owned places clearly defined as country seats in Philadelphia County alone. That figure does not include those in surrounding counties, nor many more modest plantations. For example, Joseph Shippen III's "Shippen's Grove" was assessed for tax purposes merely as a dwelling, and his uncle Joseph II's plantation in Germantown was his only residence and rated as such.[58]

Like many of their contemporaries the Shippens of Philadelphia enjoyed lobster, oysters, and other fine food; although William II refrained from drinking wines, his son William III, nephews, and brothers imbibed. They all possessed fine furniture and furnishings including silver pieces for the table and imported carpets for the floors.

As people expended money on elaborate houses and furnishings, they tended to purchase appropriate means of transportation. During the decade after the Great War for Empire, the number of coaches in Philadelphia tripled, and the number of carriages (including coaches, chaises, laudaus, and chariots) increased from thirty-eight to about ninety. The Shippens owned carriages appropriate to their social rank. Joseph III owned a chair; his father and uncles owned carriages, and his brother Edward IV coveted a coach. In fact, even as the first shots of the Revolution sounded, Edward IV contemplated spending about £200 to erect a brick coach house, large enough to accommodate a four-wheeled carriage. Edward IV's Cousin William Allen, Cousin Thomas Willing, and "brother" Tench Francis were among the nine Philadelphians who owned coaches by the 1770s.[59]

Because the Shippens used titles such as esquire or doctor, they did not usually describe themselves as gentlemen.[60] Their values and actions, however, indicate they conceived of themselves as such. And they represented a growing number of successful Philadelphians who fit much the same pattern at least in terms of embracing symbols of gentility. No evidence suggests that the fourth-generation Shippens felt uncomfortable in the role as gentlemen. For years before the 1770s, they seemed neither anxious nor frustrated.[61] While the style of life the Shippens easily embraced became more prevalent, it caused concern in many minds. Edward III, his brother William II, and Cousin William Allen sometimes remarked unfavorably open the tendency of the times. All three men whose formative years took place during a period of relative austerity never fully shook attitudes inculcated years before. It seems as if the diatribes each uttered against the luxury, extravagance, vice, and corruption which they believed prevailed in England (especially in London) haunted their minds as they viewed their own society. Yet even they were not sufficiently disturbed to desist from continuing what many considered extravagant practices.[62]

A number of contemporaries commented both publicly and privately about the extravagance, immorality, and debauchery which seemed increasingly to describe their society. Much, though not all, of this criticism focused on those with wealth. For example, in 1770 Samuel Coates effortlessly depicted the debaucheries of a dozen scions of leading Quaker families, and in 1773 the *Pennsylvania Chronicle* ridiculed the city's fishing clubs in an account of "Glutton Hall."[63] Especially after 1745 ministers denounced the decline of morality. For example, in 1762 upon the announcement of a lottery to erect "public Gardens, with Bath and Bagnios" in Northern Liberties, the ministers threw their support behind a law to outlaw lotteries, dice, cards, and other games of chance. They specifically denounced the "immoderate and growing Fondness for Pleasure, Luxury, Gaming, Dissipation and their concomittant Vices."[64] Benjamin Rush, a young doctor who soon became an ardent advocate of social reforms, lamented in 1764, "Religion is at a low ebb among us . . . Our young men in general . . . are wholly devoted to pleasure and sensuality."[65] In a lighter vein, the Grand Tour which became popular after mid-century drew criticism from some, for Edward IV, Joseph III, William III, and their Cousins Allen represented but a fraction of the number of Philadelphians who enjoyed it. For example, Col. John Alford expressed mock amazement that Joseph Shippen III and his cousin Johnny Allen traveled so far just for the honor of kissing the Pope's great toe.[66]

Neither criticism of the social developments nor use of Radical Whig ideas dictates a particular stance in the Revolution. For example, the equivocating James Burd wrote of "our flesh & blood in England . . . [who] live a life of dissipation," and Edward III, who received the letter, refused for some time to sign an oath of allegiance to the revolutionary government.[67] Perception of the tendencies in England alarmed people; belief that they existed in the colonies made many anxious about the future and more apt to act vigorously. The increase of luxury and vice formed only part of the ideology of the American Revolution. Frenzied fear of conspiracies and plots to create arbitrary power also dominates the protest literature. Again the suggestion that the intensity of concern cannot be explained simply by alienation from a relatively weak British imperial system appears fruitful.

The functioning of the Shippen family and its kinship network before 1776 and its experiences during the Revolution supply ample evidence to substantiate the thesis that many in Pennsylvania were caught up in "a revolutionary situation, deeply alienated from the existing sources of authority and vehemently involved in a basic reconstruction of their political and social order."[68] In this case almost all Shippens saw the internal political situation from the inside. They did not view it with alarm. Only William II, who criticized those at the head of provincial affairs who "dispose of all places of Honor & Profit to such as pleased them," grasped the view from the outside.[69]

This observation received more emotional and public expression when "a tradesman" decried "a family compact of Pennsylvania" which existed to "get all the profit[,] will soon reduce and control the people as the East India Company controls Bengal."[70] The "tradesman" might easily have been a resentful member of a higher rank in society. In the case of many officeholders in Pennsylvania and Philadelphia, family connections often received preferment over money, education, or talent alone.[71]

Any who aspired to political office in Pennsylvania quickly became aware of the tremendous degree of nepotism which characterized the system of government. The name Shippen figured prominently in this trait. For example, by 1770 all three Shippens of the third generation held at least one political office, and two of the three Shippens of the fourth generation who lived in the province also held office. That was only the beginning of a vast network of power which included cousins, uncles, nephews, grandsons, and brothers-in-law (who were considered "brothers"). In the Common Council of Philadelphia sat Edward Shippen III,[72] Joseph Shippen II, William Shippen II, Edward Shippen IV, Joseph Shippen III, Cousin William Allen and his three sons (Andrew, James, and John), Cousin Thomas Willing, Cousin Allen's brother-in-law James Hamilton, and several more distantly related figures. Edward Shippen, founder of the family in Pennsylvania, had served at the beginning of the century surrounded by many kin; many of their descendants, however, were no longer closely associated with the Shippens. In the more recent past, Charles Willing (Edward III's "brother") and Tench Francis (Edward IV's "father") served in the Common Council. There is no need to reiterate how so many relatives came to hold office in this closed corporation. The Shippens were unique in only the degree of their influence, not their use of nepotism. For example, during the eighteenth century the Morrises and Redmans produced four common councilmen, ten other families had three, and eighteen had two; of course this only scratches the surface of the other kinship networks.[73]

On other levels of government the Shippens and their family associates figured significantly. For example, Edward Shippen III was prothonotary of Lancaster County and also recorder of wills and deeds. His son Edward IV filled the offices of judge of the Admiralty Court, prothonotary of the Supreme Court of Pennsylvania, and in 1770 with his Cousin Andrew Allen was appointed to the Governor's Council. Edward IV's brother, Joseph III, was secretary of that body and the province. Joseph Shippen II derived income as surveyor of customs for Delaware Bay. The Shippens' connection with Cousin Allen served them well. William Allen, one of the most powerful figures in Pennsylvania, served as chief justice during the quarter of a century preceeding the rebellion, and for twenty of those years he also sat in the General Assembly. His son Andrew served as attorney general of Pennsylvania and on the Governor's Council, and managed to obtain a seat in the General Assembly as well. His younger brother, John Allen, was a justice of the peace. William Allen's "brother" James Hamilton, also a justice of the peace, sat on the Governor's Council, and like his father had served as pronthonotary of the Supreme Court. James Hamilton was deputy governor from 1748 to 1754, 1759 to 1763, and acting governor in 1771 and 1773.[74]

Other officeholders whom the Shippens recognized as kinsmen were justices of the peace such as James Burd, William Allen, John Allen, Peter Grubb, Thomas Willing, Tench Francis (who died in 1758), and Charles Willing (who died in 1754). Tench Francis had been attorney general and judge of the Admiralty Court when Edward IV married his daughter. Neddy Burd and Jasper Yeates also obtained legal appointments because of the Shippen family connection.

Such a preponderance of kinsmen in public offices was not coincidental.[75] Frequently family connections explained the appointments. In 1764 Edward III appointed his "son" James Burd deputy prothonotary of Lancaster County; in 1767 Edward Shippen IV appointed his wife's "brother," James Tilghman, his deputy commissary of the Vice Admiralty Court.[76] Written evidence substantiates many other instances of admitted nepotism; Edward IV's appointment to the Admiralty Court, Neddy Burd's appointment as clerk of the court of *nisi prius,* and clerk of the circuit court and James Burd's and Peter Grubb's appointments as justices of the peace are but a few examples.[77] William Allen's control over the distribution of the office of justice of the peace was well known to contemporaries, and the influence that the Allens, Hamiltons, and Shippens exerted over many provincial appointments can scarcely be exaggerated. Symbolic of this influence with the proprietors was the marriage of William Allen's daughter Ann to John Penn.[78]

The Allens and Shippens also exerted influence upon the nomination of candidates for the General Assembly. William Allen actually served in the Assembly from 1731 to 1739, and from 1756 to the Revolution he represented Cumberland County. References scattered through the Shippen papers indicate the role of William Allen and Edward Shippen III in gaining the nomination of certain individuals and using their "influence" in the area to get their candidate elected. Although control of popularly elected offices was far less strict and reliable than it was over appointive offices, the Allens in Northampton County and the Shippens in Lancaster County were forces with which to reckon.

The Shippens and Allens made no attempt to conceal their ties of kinship, and in a small town of about twenty-five thousand it was fairly easy to ascertain familial bonds. Contemporary observers need not have held precise knowledge of the Shippen family structure to become alarmed. In fact, imprecise knowledge probably exaggerated the degree of nepotism and accentuated a sense of apprehension.

Resentment unquestionably existed. It received expression in the newspapers before the Revolution and vindication in the Pennsylvania Constitution of 1776 and other acts of the Revolution.

The Pennsylvania Constitution of 1776 serves as a ringing denunciation of many activities and practices of the Shippens and other families during the colonial period. The radicals who drew that document did not simply seek to confirm the colonial past. These men and their followers abhored many characteristics of the old society and the way in which it functioned. Whether or not they achieved a better society remains debatable; that they attempted to alter past patterns is undeniable.[79]

Political concerns dominated the constitution; however, comments upon certain social trends received mention. After declaring that "Government is or ought to be Instituted for the Common Benefit Protection and Security of the People, Nation or Community, and not for the particular Emolument or advantage of any

Single man, Family or set of Men," the authors of this revolutionary document adopted at least thirteen more statements which stand as indictments of the Shippens and their friends.[80]

In the future the people, meaning all male taxpayers and their adult sons, had the right to elect public officials or the body which appointed them. Justices of the peace, one of the most obvious plums in the Proprietary patronage system, were singled out in Section Thirty. Henceforth they were to be elected, not appointed, and justices of the peace were prohibited from sitting concurrently in the General Assembly. Other provisions regarding the General Assembly apply more to the Shippens' kinsmen and other families than to the Shippen family, for they rarely aspired to serve in that body.[81] Under this constitution, members had to reside in the county which elected them, and no man could serve more than four years in seven. Furthermore, the use of meat, drink, money, or promise of patronage to acquire votes disqualified the offender.[82]

Concern that rotation in office occur and that multiple office-holding be abolished received reiteration in sections dealing with representatives to the Continental Congress, members of the Supreme Executive Council, and judges of the Supreme Court. The experience of the Shippens, as well as their kinsmen, during the colonial period had been diametrically opposed to these concepts. Pennsylvania limited the tenure of its representatives to the Continental Congress to two years and required an interval of three years before reelection. Another innovation was the Supreme Executive Council which took the place of the governor. Again tenure in office was short, varying from one to three years depending on the county one represented, and after a term in office followed four years' mandatory retirement from the Council. In this way the reformers believed that "the danger of Establishing an inconvenient Aristocracy will be effectually prevented."[83] This Council, not a governor, proprietor, or William Allen, exercised appointive powers in the state. Finally, judges of the Supreme Court of Pennsylvania received fixed salaries and commissions of only seven years; although eligible for reappointment, the Assembly could remove them for misbehavior at any time. As with others, these judges could not sit in the Continental Congress, Supreme Executive Council, or Assembly, "nor hold any other office Civil or Military, nor . . . take or receive Fees or Perquisites of any kind."[84]

While mentioning drastic changes regarding officeholding, we must observe that changes took place in local government which affected the Shippens. After 1776 five Shippens, four Allens, and their kinsmen no longer sat in the Common Council of Philadelphia. That body's abolition occurred in 1776, and it was not reinstituted until 1789. Then the principles of rotation in office and terms limited to specific periods of time were introduced.

The ideology of the American Revolution decried social as well as political developments. Consistent with that body of thought, the Pennsylvania Constitution of 1776 declared that "a frequent recurrence to fundamental principles and a firm Adherence to Justice, Moderation, Temperance, Industry and Frugality are absolutely necessary to preserve the Blessings of Liberty and keep a Government free." They admonished the people to "pay particular Attention to these points in the choice of Officers and Representatives."[85] One of the last sections of the document affirms that "Laws for the Encouragement of Virtue and prevention of Vice and Immorality shall be made and constantly kept in force."[86]

Beyond any doubt the radicals in 1776 wanted to change significant characteristics of the prewar society. They gave formal expression to the grievances in the revolutionary constitution adopted in that year. Although Pennsylvania was noted for widespread loyalist and neutral sentiments during the course of the Revolution, enough people shared the prejudices of the radicals or felt powerless to oppose them so that this constitution lasted for sixteen years. The degree of change wrought by the Revolution can only be ascertained by examining the postwar decade as well as those preceeding Yorktown, but it is clear that many colonists were alarmed by what they perceived and wanted to change it.

This view of the Shippens, the way they operated as a family in politics, the elegant life style they enjoyed, was obviously subjective. Though by no means self-sacrificing public servants, the Shippens generally fulfilled their public duties competently. For the most part there was nothing intrinsically wrong in what they did.[87] But to ambitious people frustrated by the operations of the Shippen family or to people in general who became unsettled by changes unleashed particularly after mid-century that scarcely mattered. Regardless of whether or not their society was actually endangered, these people believed that it was, and many acted forcefully upon that assumption.

The radicals demanded loyalty oaths as a means of compelling adherence to the reforms which they announced in the constitution. Repelled by the idea of enforced conformity to a system hostile to their interests, the Edward Shippen III branch of the family prepared to lose their offices. These men raised in the traditions of "the private city" contemplated neither heroics nor foolhardiness.[88] They were not Tories; they harbored no desire to increase the royal prerogative.[89] No Shippen contemplated bearing arms or providing civilian services for the British, and Edward III even continued to pray for "the glorious news of ye Defeat of our murdering Enemys" the British.[90] Family considerations had always come first; they remained uppermost in importance. Private considerations, not lofty principles or class consciousness, continued to explain their activities during the ensuing years.[91]

In general the Shippens followed Joseph III's advice to avoid running "any Risque of disobliging the public in these critical times," and pray that God "grant Wisdom to those who may govern this once happy Country, . . . that all may terminate in Peace Liberty & Safety."[92] For Edward IV and Joseph III, temporarily leaving Philadelphia proved the best way to implement this suggestion. Edward III remained at Lancaster; James Burd stayed at Tinian, but both contemplated flight to Shippensburg if necessary.[93]

Edward IV and his family passed the summer of 1776 at "our place of Retirement" in Amwell, New Jersey.[94] "The place is very pretty," remarked Major Neddy Burd who was on his way to fight the British when he visited his uncle.[95] The proximity of Cousin John Allen only twelve miles away helped compensate for the inconvenience of moving. The two families enjoyed visiting. James Burd however wished that his "brothers" had "both come to Lancaster County."[96]

At his seat in Northern Liberties, Joseph III felt almost as secluded as his brothers; he rarely heard of occurrences in town, and when he went to Philadelphia, he stayed mainly in his house.

Although Joseph III ceased "conversing or writing on the subject of politics,"[97] he realized, "I must very shortly surrender my Office; [hence] I am under the necessity of going into the Country . . . to look out for a small Farm for the Support of my Family."[98] The loss of his office as secretary of Pennsylvania would entail a severe financial setback; hence Joseph III lamented, "I have not in my power at present to purchase a large one without involving myself in Debt."[99] This explains why he declined his brother's suggestion to buy the Lowrey plantation in Amwell. Though "a very clever place" of 230 acres of "extraordinary good land" with a substantial house and many improvements, the owner asked £1,700.[100] Even when Edward IV lauded it as "an extraordinary Stand for Business, [for] Mr. Lowrey has made a fortune at it, partly by keeping Store & partly by buying large Quantities of Wheat for selling again to Merchants in Philadelphia," and offered to join his brother in partnership, Joseph III said no.[101] To begin such an enterprise at this juncture seemed too precarious.

When Joseph III found that he could not obtain a satisfactory farm "in your [Edward IV's] Neighborhood," he decided "to endeavour to find out some retired Situation in Chester County, so as to be within a days Ride of my Father's Family."[102] Eventually he succeeded and purchased Joseph Musgrave's farm on Nottingham Road in Kennett Square.[103] It lay twelve miles north of Wilmington, twenty miles west of Chester, and forty miles from Lancaster. The new two-story brick house had three small rooms on each floor; the entire dwelling was only 32 feet by 22 feet. A brick kitchen with two small bedrooms above stood behind it. Another small brick building, a stone dry goods store, two good frame barns, excellent stables, and a log tenement completed the list of structures. An apple orchard, seven acres of meadow, twenty acres of bottom land, and forty acres of wooded upland describe most of its other attributes. Joseph III thought the price of £1,100 not too dear, and "on the whole I hope it will accommodate my Family tolerably well, & that they will be content with their Lot till we are blessed with better times."[104] While Joseph III prepared to move, his nephew, Neddy Burd, stopped by; according to Burd the purchase was of "a little plantation of about 100 acres of Land of wh[ich] there is 30 acres Meadow Ground with a Neat House Office Barn etc."[105]

Another nephew, Edward Shippen V, added that because Uncle Joseph III's farm lay within "half a mile of all sorts of Tradesmen . . . & an exceeding good School . . . [he has] advantages that very few in the County have."[106]

In September 1776, Joseph Shippen III moved his family to Kennett Square. Almost a year later the rebels finally decided to arrest the officers of the old Proprietary government. This offended Joseph III who exclaimed, "I am not conscious of having merited, by any part of my Conduct, being put under so disagreeable a Restriction and Confinement."[107] Upon reflection the secretary "judged it most prudent to make no Complaint of the Hardship, and so without any shew of Difficulty submitted."[108] He signed a parole as a prisoner whereby he agreed to remain within six miles of his house and promised that "I will not do any Thing injurious to the United States of America by Writing, Speaking or otherwise nor give any Intelligence to the Commander in Chief of the British tories nor any Person under him."[109]

Almost all other officers of the old government remaining in Pennsylvania also signed paroles without hesitation. About a fortnight later the revolutionary government enlarged the bounds of the paroles of Joseph Shippen III, Edward Shippen IV, James Hamilton, and some others to the entire state. Both the arrest and the advance of the British army on Philadelphia caused Joseph III to send his and his brother's papers to Lancaster for safekeeping with their father. Not for several years however did the new state government think the records of the provincial secretary might be useful. By then it was too late, for in 1776 Joseph III turned them over to John Penn.[110]

Although Joseph Shippen III lost his office and revenues derived from it, no other property was confiscated. Some of it, however, was damaged during the course of the war. British soldiers plundered his house in Philadelphia during the occupation of 1777 and destroyed his lot in Northern Liberties. His and neighboring farms in Kennett Square were plundered of food, and in 1778 Joseph III pleaded that American armies not encamp "at *this place,* [for] my Farm must inevitably be ruined, . . . And I shall be totally undone as a Farmer."[111] Though spared another encounter, Joseph III soon found his farm too small. Not until after the war did he find a more satisfactory one. In the meantime he opened a small store where he sold sugar, coffee, and various other commodities which his nephew, Neddy Burd, sent from Philadelphia. By the time hostilities ceased in 1781, Joseph Shippen III had suffered serious setbacks. The Revolution, though not utterly disastrous, significantly altered the life of this neutralist.[112]

The same might be said of the other Shippens, although important differences characterized each individual's experience. Though farther removed from the theater of the war, neither Edward Shippen III nor his "son" James Burd found the Revolution agreeable. Independence from Great Britain seemed a serious error to Edward Shippen III whose life began in the first years of the reign of Queen Anne. Of course difficulties had beset his life at times; yet he evaluated the past benignly. He could not easily discard his identity with the mother country; his ancestor William Shippen, "the Parliament Man," not Lord North whom he called "that Great Murderer,"[113] seemed typical of English rule. For this reason his last years proved very unhappy.

For months after the Declaration of Independence, Edward III refused to take the oath of allegiance to the revolutionary government. Although he resolved to "say nothing about Politicks in Letters," he clearly expected that his action would cost him his offices.[114] He had held some of them for almost four decades, and although in 1776 he lamented "[I] scarcely [receive] enough to buy salt for my porridge," they had been lucrative posts in the past. He contemplated "casting about for a country settlement as well as my Children & Mr. Allen & his three sons."[115] Upon hearing this his "son" James Burd immediately offered his stone house at Tinian; for he was willing to move his family into the roomy wooden buildings on the plantation. Shippen thanked "his son" for the generous offer, but averred "out of Love to your Selves & family, it would be with the greatest Reluctance for us to accept it."[116]

Despite the fact Edward III received no income from his offices, and people hesitated to record wills and deeds during civil turmoil, Shippen's retention of his offices until 1777 provides a curious comment upon the temper of the rebellion. Finally, Peter Hoofnagle, who had served as Edward III's apprentice and then clerk, decided to run for the office when Edward III remained firm in his refusal to abjure King George III and swear allegiance to the new govern-ment. Although he doubtless agreed with his son that "in these times I shall consider a private Station as a post of Honour," with no business and almost no income, Edward III's circumstances be-came uncomfortable.[117] In a moment of desperation, he even con-sidered becoming a farmer at Shippensburg. But, as his son pointed out, "the Management of a farm is more proper for a man in the prime of Life than in his decline, then Nature calls [for] Ease of body as well as Ease of mind."[118]

Nature would be satisfied in neither demand. Many things trou-bled Edward III's mind, including adversities affecting his family in Lancaster and elsewhere, political turmoil, financial difficulties, and a sense of uncertaintly which pervaded everything. Because contemporaries considered Edward Shippen III a very rich man, his financial difficulties require scrutiny. The loss of his offices stopped some of his income, and tenants in Philadelphia and Shippensburg fell in arrears in their rents, thus drying up that source as well. The Perkiomen mine had yielded no profits in years. None of this is surprising, but in 1777 Edward III ruefully admitted that "tho' I have been here four and Twenty years, I have not been able to lay up anything."[119]

This statement reflects reality, yet distorts and belittles the profits Shippen made during his years at Lancaster. During those decades he spent huge sums of money. Most often expenditures involved duties which he assumed as the Shippen patriarch. For example, he built great houses in Philadelphia and Shippensburg; he gave sub-stantial sums to his sons, Edward IV and Joseph III, and several grandchildren upon their marriages, and expended a considerable sum on the education and establishment of his namesake Edward Burd. Edward Shippen III had also helped support his "son" James Burd and assisted him in the purchase of Tinian. Household ex-penses for the family at Lancaster which consisted of Edward III, his wife, her mother and sister, and a slave or two were far from paltry. Guests in the Shippen house during those years were fre-quent. For instance, Edward IV always dropped by as he rode the circuit, and he, his brother Joseph, Sister Sally, Jasper Yeates, and their families often enjoyed sojourns there too. In addition, taxes on his real estate consumed a portion of his income. Much of his

land in Philadelphia, Germantown, and Shippensburg lay undeveloped, yet as land values rose, as they did in Philadelphia, taxes
went up. In regard to land, it also seems pertinent to remark that
even before the war many tenants were in arrears, and a few ran off
with no intention of ever paying.

Regardless of where the money went, the war caused painful recognition of its disappearance. Actually only the intensity of recognition was new. Back in 1770, creditors pressed Edward III. He sold
some lots in Philadelphia to his sons to raise money to discharge
his debts. Both sons responded beyond this in a way which typified
part of their conceptualization of being "dutiful sons." Joseph III
promised to collect money which various people owed his father,
and Edward IV also endeavored to raise money to get his father out
of debt. "Whenever you should be press'd to discharge any particular Demand," Edward IV informed his father, "my Brother and I
. . . [will] make it our Business to pay it off or take it upon ourselves."[120] As had been the case when James Burd ran into similar
difficulties, the Shippen family stood ready to assist a kinsman.
Usually the family's financial, political, or emotional support protected members of the family from the full impact which similar
occurrences would have upon most other people. This is one benefit
of an extended family. Because the financial, educational, and political resources of the Shippens were great, only a few of the other
extended families functioning in Pennsylvania could succeed so
well in the protective role.[121]

Much of this pattern recurred a few years later. When pressed
for money, Edward III checked his books and found several people
indebted to him; hence he asked his son Edward IV to see the gentlemen involved. "I know it will not be a pleasant Task for you,"
apologized the father, "but do it as well as you can."[122] Edward IV
also arranged to sell some of his father's property in Germantown
and purchased some of it in Philadelphia for himself. Although
laws of the revolutionary government prohibited non-jurors from
alienating or acquiring property, the Shippens evaded the proscrip-
tion.[123] William Shippen II, the Radical Whig, assisted in these
machinations and also offered to purchase his brother's house and
fifty acres in Germantown.[124]

Financial difficulties continued to plague Edward Shippen III throughout the Revolution. Taxes on his extensive landholdings exascerbated his situation. For instance, in 1778 he paid £48 for state taxes on his Shippensburg property while muttering that they were too high. When notice of an additional tax of £106 levied for Continental purposes arrived, he complained to the commissioners. His accounts of rents received persuaded them to give an abatement. Upon hearing his father's complaints, Edward IV hinted, "Considering the high taxes you pay for your Shippensburg Estate & the little Income it affords . . . [might it] not be worth your while to think of Selling it & laying out the Money in something else that would afford you a better annual Interest."[125] Several decades earlier Edward III had viewed the Shippen family seat in England more as a source of revenue than a symbol of the family; now his son expressed the same sentiments toward Shippensburg. Edward IV thought the sale could raise at least £10,000. Because no better investment opportunity arose, the Shippens retained possession of Shippensburg; however, when taxes more than doubled in a year, Edward III sometimes questioned the wisdom of that decision.[126]

Though he continued to lament "that ever old England should fall out with their American Children," Edward III accommodated himself to the change.[127] By paying taxes to the revolutionary government, he gave recognition to its authority. A desire to retain his property rather than belief in its legitimacy explains that action. When in the fall of 1778 he applied for an office in the radical government, he indicated a belief that the Revolution would succeed. More than this, his sentiments, which had always been with colonial grievances if not independence, caused him to question some traits of society for the first time. For example, on one occasion as he allotted beer for his table, his two servants' table, and his two slaves' table, he pondered, "I would consider the Condition of these poor Slaves; indeed, Strictly Speaking, I think none of any colour ought to be bound longer than Seven Years."[128]

Edward Shippen freed his slaves by his will; he did not however advance in the new society. Certain radicals admired his benevolence. They refused to accord him an office as a symbol of their esteem. Instead Timothy Matlack, one of the most active revolutionaries in Pennsylvania, resorted to verbal rewards, saying, "Your virtues and distinguished attention [to] improve mankind, create a respectful affection—and, that cheerfulness and health of mind which . . . can only spring from temperance and conscious integrity excite the most pleasing sensations among those who have the pleasure of observing your conduct."[129]

Respect, old age, and Shippen's limited overt opposition to independence protected him from the worst hazards of the Revolution. Relative isolation protected his "son" James Burd. The colonel finally resigned his commission in December 1776 when he found it impossible to raise a company. His miseries compounded. "I have not got one shilling in my office these 6 mo[nth]s," noted Burd; "neither can I get a farthing from my Tennants tho 2 years Rents almost due."[130] As a matter of fact, several families lived rent free on his plantation during the war. Burd's resignation, the suspected Loyalist proclivities of the Shippens, and rumors that he refused to take an oath to support the new government precipitated a mob which attacked Tinian and threatened to carry Burd "under a strong guard no body knows where!"[131] Fortunately Burd avoided rough treatment from the hostile crowd, yet financial and emotional problems troubled his mind, and his health suffered because "my Constitution is become very Crasy" because of the last war.[132] The Shippens and his "son" Jasper Yeates sent periodic financial and legal advice and incessant family news; yet Burd's "Last Frontier," like his entire life, remained plagued with problems, frustrations, and failures.[133]

Burd's "brother" Edward Shippen IV, the most powerful member of the fourth generation, was unaccustomed to frustration and failure. With concern for his family and his professional stature uppermost in his mind, he dextrously moved through the tortuous course of events in the Revolution. Despite one monumental error in judgment, at the end of the war he stood ready to attempt recovery of his past eminence in Philadelphia and Pennsylvania.

After quietly spending the summer of 1776 in Amwell, New Jersey, Edward IV who feared Howe's advance through New Jersey, moved his family back to Philadelphia only to encounter rumors of an impending invasion of the capital. When General Thomas Mifflin erroneously confirmed the fears, Edward IV followed the example of his Uncle William II and left town. Edward IV and his family spent the winter at his place near the Falls of the Schuylkill in the Northern Liberties of Philadelphia. Only a maidservant remained in his town house to prevent its being used by American soldiers. Almost daily, Edward IV rode about six miles to town to make himself conspicuous about his house and reinforce the illusion that the house was occupied.[134]

Though he resented the loss of income from his offices and found life "extremely difficult for those, who have large families and no Share in the present Measures," he decided to remain neutral for the time being.[135] Depending upon one's sympathies, the characterization realism or opportunism fits this neutral's view of the rebellion until late 1778. "I think another Summer must necessarily shew us our Fate," he told his father. "If the War should continue longer than that we are all ruined as to our Estates, whatever may be the state of our Liberties."[136]

Much to Edward IV's chagrin, his only son and namesake jeopardized the family's neutrality by associating with the British army in New Jersey. The young man had gone to New Jersey as much to avoid serving in the rebel militia as on business for his master. There he met his cousins Johnny, Andrew, and Billey Allen (sons of Edward IV's Cousin Andrew Allen) who convinced him to go with them to General Howe. When the Continental army surprised the Hessians at Trenton, Edward V was taken prisoner. Fortunately he took no commission from the British; hence Joseph Reed, a good friend of the Shippen family, "got me immediately discharged without giving my Parole."[137] The young man returned to his family in Philadelphia, feeling lucky to have lost only his horse, saddle, and clothes. This essentially is the story which Edward IV and his son conveyed to Edward III who was deeply concerned about the occurrence. "Though I highly disapproved of what he had done," Edward IV told his father, "yet I could not condemn him so much as I should have done if he had not been inticed to it by those who were much older and ought to have judged better than himself."[138] The Shippens' neutrality remained intact; no serious repercussions, such as an attainder for treason, followed.

Having survived the incident, Edward continued his neutrality, impatiently waiting definite indications of the outcome of the conflict. This is not to suggest that the Revolution did not affect him. During 1777 he lived in almost constant fear of arrest by the radicals, and increasingly felt the burdens of trying to support his family which included four daughters, ages seventeen to twenty-three. His daughters had expensive tastes; although his eldest daughter assured her father that when they could purchase no more "finery . . . [we will] make ourselves look tolerably smart in homsespun," he hoped to avoid that necessity.[139] Increasingly however he grumbled about rising costs and the need for retrenchment.[140]

The twelve months or so following August 1777 proved crucial to Edward IV in resolving certain problems connected with his expensive family and also the question of political allegiance. In August 1777 rumors regarding an invasion of the capital of the rebelling colonies became reality. The Yeates offered their kinsmen the Shippens asylum in Lancaster, but Edward IV's first parole forbade his traveling there. Great anxieties troubled the group gathered at "the Cottage" near the Falls of the Schuylkill, for as Elizabeth Shippen told her cousin Sally Yeates, "Papa is in a very disagreeable . . . [situation] as he is liable to be removed from his family at a moments warning. . . . If he was to be torn from us," she knew her composure "would forsake me entirely."[141] Like most of the officials of the old government, Edward IV signed the necessary paroles; thus he avoided exile in Virginia. The group of Quakers who refused the oath suffered considerably for their testimony against the war.

The British took Philadelphia, and like many people from all ranks of society, Edward Shippen IV stayed in town. Presumably he did so for several reasons. First, he hoped to protect his house against plundering, and second, he sought to gain some sense of the prospect of a British victory. His daughters proved attractive to the young officers, Major John Andre courted Peggy Shippen, and a brazen young lord kissed Sally Shippen in the street. Edward IV asked for and received an apology for the latter occurrence. Beyond that Edward IV tried to avoid identification of his family with the occupying force.

Although American fortunes seemed at a low ebb while Washington encamped at Valley Forge, the British failed to convince Edward IV of their ability to win. Only after great difficulty did they finally reduce Mud Island in the Delaware River; hence they could not really begin to consolidate their position until the winter of 1777–1778. The capture of the capital proved meaningless. Congress escaped, and the rebellion refused to die. In the spring of 1778 rumors that General Clinton was going to replace Sir William Howe suggested that England admitted failure up to this point. As the British prepared to evacuate the city, they reinforced that opinion in the minds of many.

It comes as no surprise that Edward Shippen IV did not join the throng of three thousand civilians who accompanied the British army in June on its retreat from Philadelphia to New York. Such commitment would certainly precipitate an attainder for treason and confiscation of all property by the revolutionary government. To judge from Edward IV's actions immediately following the evacuation, we can conclude that that event played a decisive role in committing Edward Shippen IV and his family to the rebel cause. Before the end of the year he happily announced to his father, "I gave my daughter Betsy to Neddy Burd last Thursday Evening, and all is Jollity and Mirth. My youngest daughter is much sollicited by a certain General on the same Subject."[142] Neddy Burd had recently gained modest fame by fighting for the Americans and now held an office in the revolutionary government; the "certain General" was Benedict Arnold, one of the more successful American officers. The Shippens never let their children enter marriage on whims or emotions alone if they could help it, and particularly with their daughters, approval of the family was all but obligatory if the union were to transpire. Though the fighting of the War for Independence continued three more years, for Edward Shippen IV the war was over; the Americans had won.

Both these marriages demonstrate vital aspects of the functioning of the Shippen family, and both had important consequences. Neddy Burd had wanted to marry his cousin Betsy Shippen when he returned from the battlefields of Boston in December 1775, but his Uncle Edward IV declined the request. Edward IV explained that tumultuous times and precarious business conditions made such a step imprudent. Neddy Burd admitted these are "bad times for us poor Lawyers," and as the weeks passed, his business almost ceased.[143] People thought he might ride off to battle again. "This is the reward for my Losses & Expenses in the Service of my Country," he complained.[144]

As late as March 1776, Neddy Burd remained "against Independence if we can possibly be reconciled upon Terms consistent with our Safety . . . [and] our essential Rights."[145] If the British peace commissioners offered only pardon, he was uncertain what action he would take. Soon he resolved that dilemma. After the Declaration of Independence, the county expected Burd to turn out as a major in the militia. Although he declared, "If an Oath similar to that of Convention Men was proposed to me I should most certainly refuse," that problem never arose.[146] With no other prospects in view, Burd reentered the military, for "I have no Notion of any Man's refusing his Service when his Country Calls on him."[147] As he set off for New Jersey and New York, the major naively reassured his father, "The Service will not be attended with much Danger."[148] Only two months later William Shippen III informed his father, who wrote to his brother, who in turn wrote his "son" James Burd that Neddy Burd had been taken prisoner by the British. After spending several months in a prison ship in New York harbor, Neddy Burd was released when Washington exchanged prisoners with the British. Upon his release, the major went to enjoy his freedom at his Uncle Edward Shippen IV's house.[149]

Neddy returned to civilian life in Reading. In August 1778 the revolutionary government of Pennsylvania appointed him prothonotary of the Supreme Court, the position which his Uncle Edward IV held for many years before the Revolution. When he married Edward IV's eldest daughter in December, he compounded this amazing instance of continuity. The lavish wedding served notice that Edward IV and his family had not been cast aside by the Revolution. Elizabeth Shippen had no less than twenty-five bridesmaids, which prompted her delightfully witty Cousin Elizabeth Tilghman to tease, "How is it with your highness now, have you got over all your little palpitations . . . shameless girl, how could you be so naughty as to have so many witnesses to your actions?"[150] The Edward Burds lived with Edward Shippen IV for about three months until they set up housekeeping. Before settling in their house, they visited Uncle Joseph Shippen III at his farm in Chester County.[151]

Right after the wedding Edward IV reviewed his situation. Although his public image exuded confidence, he confided to his father that "the Stile of Life my fashionable daughters have introduced into my family and their own Dress will I fear before long oblige me to change the Scene." Edward IV calculated that "the Expence of supporting my family here will not fall short of four or five thousand pounds per annum, an Expence unsupportable without Business."[152] The sale of his 370-acre farm and gristmill in New Jersey for £9,000 helped finance the marriage and dowry of Betsy and Peggy. When the burden of supporting them fell to their husbands, Edward IV felt some relief; yet affectionate regard for their well-being, not simply monetary concerns explain his consent to their marriage.

For the next few years he often contemplated moving to Lancaster where the style of living was far less expensive than in Philadelphia, and where he could be near his father. For example, when he purchased a farm in Chester County, one of its attributes was its proximity to Lancaster. Edward IV however chose to continue complaining about the expense of living in Philadelphia rather than leaving. Despite the costs, that was the best place for this ambitious man with extensive legal training and experience to be if he wished to regain his former stature. Edward Shippen IV wanted greater rewards than his private practice gave. By 1780 he confessed to his father, however, that high taxes "and the necessary Expences of my family reduced [me] frequently to great straits in Money Matters— and I see no likelihood of matters mending in any short time."[153] By now the taxes on his house in Fourth Street amounted to £3,000 per year; those on parts of "my little Estate" in Chester County and Merion Township, Philadelphia were £2,400 and £1,800 respectively.[154] Despite the inflation caused by paper money and the war, those sums forced Edward IV to consider selling some real estate, a distasteful prospect which he managed to avoid.[155]

Edward IV's financial difficulties made his anxieties surrounding the marriage of his youngest daughter all the more acute. In 1779, General Benedict Arnold, whose gallantry at Ft. Ticonderoga, Quebec, Valcour Island, Ridgefield, Norwalk, Ft. Stanwix, and Saratoga had helped make him one of Washington's favorites and military commander of Philadelphia, was one of the most able and conspicuous American war heroes. Many things went through Edward IV's mind as he encouraged the marriage of his nineteen-year-old daughter to a widower twice her age. The discrepancy in ages was extraordinary by eighteenth-century Philadelphia standards; a more than cursory appraisal of marriages indicates the normal age difference between marriage partners was usually under six years, and often much less than that. Presumably a significant consideration must have been the benefits to be derived by associating the Shippen family with an ardent supporter of the American cause. To judge from Edward IV's actions in the 1780s and 1790s, he earnestly wished to resume public offices and repossess the honor and income he felt appropriate to a gentleman.[156]

That Arnold had been a druggist and bookseller before the war mattered not at all, for the Shippens viewed Arnold as "a fine Gentleman."[157] The dowry of "Mt. Pleasant," one of the finest country seats in North America, helped express the father's good wishes for the couple's happiness. Comments of kinsmen indicate only approbation of the marriage.[158]

Only a month after the couple moved into "Mt. Pleasant," Arnold began his treasonous correspondence with the British. Although romantic tales attribute this and subsequent treasonous actions to the charms of Peggy Shippen, no evidence substantiates that notion.[159] Although Peggy and her sisters had been courted by British officers and her brother even briefly stayed with the British army, no solid evidence indicates that any Shippen held strong Tory convictions. All had viewed British actions before 1776 as tyrannical; after that, although many opposed independence, none seemed to desire a British victory. Furthermore, Edward IV, Peggy's father who had so carefully guarded his neutral stand for two years, had just committed the family to the American cause. The Shippen papers lack their usual completeness when they deal with Peggy Shippen before the discovery of Arnold's plot, and someone could have purged them of incriminating evidence. The recorded actions and thoughts of Peggy and her family consistently indicate utter disapprobation of Arnold's conduct. Because all surviving evidence suggests Arnold acted on his own and American authorities declined to imprison her as a spy, and because Peggy's complicity does not make sense, she stands exculpated.[160]

Peggy's contemporaries viewed the situation differently. In September 1780 Arnold's plot to betray his new command of West

Point created a furor. Although his British associate, Major John Andre, was executed as a spy, Arnold escaped. The British rewarded him with a commission as brigadier general, £6,315 cash, and an annual pension of £500 for his wife, commissions for three sons by his first marriage, and later £100 pensions for each of Peggy's children.

A few days after General Arnold's flight to the *Vulture,* Peggy Shippen Arnold returned to her father in Philadelphia. There her family and friends rallied to protect her. Edward IV and his nephew ("son") Neddy Burd "tried every Means to prevail on the [Supreme Executive] Council to permit her to stay among us & not go to that infernal Villain her Husband."[161] Edward IV and his daughter offered to desist from writing to Arnold and to show all letters received from him to the government. For a time this and other entreaties seemed about to succeed. "Such treachery [which] chills . . . [the] very soul" overshadowed all considerations.[162] Although Peggy Shippen Arnold was not imprisoned as a spy, thus indicating that Pennsylvania authorities dismissed accusations of her involvement in the plot and other intrigues, on October 27 they ordered her into exile. About two weeks later her father escorted her to New York.[163]

"This Circumstance has involved the whole family in the deepest Distress," mourned Neddy Burd who detested his sister's unwilling and forced reunion with "a Man who appears to be so very black."[164] Understandably the Shippen family began to create explanations of how this disaster had befallen them. As early as November 1780, they formulated the myth that "the Sacrafice was an immense one at her being married to him at all."[165] In reality, the Shippens had misjudged Arnold, and lacking clairvoyance, they had strongly approved his proposal of marriage.

Considering the fact that Benedict Arnold became synonymous with treachery and villainy in America, the Shippen family's setbacks seem mild. No other members of the family were prosecuted. Only a few years after the episode Peggy Shippen Arnold's father and "brother" Neddy Burd both held positions of trust and power in Philadelphia and Pennsylvania.

In some ways the activities and connections of the William II branch of the family helped salvage the Shippens' reputation.

Despite public abuse of William Shippen III for his handling of the Continental Medical Department, William II, William III, and the latter's "brothers" Richard Henry Lee and Arthur Lee were strongly identified with prominent roles in serving the revolutionary movement. Because differences of opinion regarding politics between William II and his favorite brother, Edward III, did not impair the personal cordiality between the two branches of the family, a closer look into the activities of the secondary branch seems imperative.[166]

Though sixty-four-years old when the Declaration of Independence was signed, William II welcomed the Revolution and actively participated in it. He identified with the radical group in Pennsylvania, served on revolutionary committees, and in 1778 and 1779 sat in the Continental Congress. His commitment was such that he could believe, "It is pretty clear we shall have great Slaughter but I am very clear that all will work together for good."[167] William II benefited from conditions created by the Revolution. While his brother Joseph II's eyesight and money disappeared, William II easily surpassed him in stature and wealth. By the end of the war, the youngest brother was no longer the humblest in terms of worldly possessions.[168]

Because of his activities, William II thought it prudent to flee Philadelphia on several occasions when a British invasion appeared imminent. During one such flight in the winter of 1776, the doctor helped tend wounded soldiers at Bethlehem, Easton, and Allentown who were under the care of his son, Dr. William Shippen III. The younger doctor's activities during the war complicate this branch of the family's attitude toward the Revolution. Paucity of evidence regarding William III demands caution, yet several things suggest that he lacked the radical convictions of his father.[169]

William III's brief experiences as a young man in Georgian England helped form his values which departed significantly in some respects from those of his New Light Presbyterian father. Although William III retained affiliation with the Presbyterian church, his religious enthusiasm faded. In its place developed a strong sense of professionalism, which to the doctor connoted tight control over his emotions, among other things. To judge from his subsequent behavior that he was not inclined to reject the idea of nepotism or of public offices existing for the emolument of the officeholder. Although he held no offices before the Revolution, no lucrative medical posts existed then, and William III was not covetous of other political appointments. Finally, William III's life style confirmed the tendencies since mid-century; like his Cousin Edward IV the lawyer, Dr. William Shippen III could not fathom the older generation of Shippens' concern about increasing signs of luxury.

Private ambitions to advance professionally, socially, and economically explain William III's wartime career; principles and political theory figured hardly at all. According to his main detractor, Shippen once confided to the director-general of Continental hospitals a desire to stay in the service "as a more *Gentlemanly* life . . . than that of a drudging private Practitioner."[170] Even if we allow for the fierce prejudice of the source, that characterization rings true. In July 1776 William Shippen III became chief surgeon of the Flying Camp in New Jersey. His ambition and influence could only intensify the insurmountable problems facing the director-general, John Morgan. Enemies and rivals in the past, the two doctors soon renewed the antipathies with amazing virulence.

When Congress appointed John Morgan director-general in October 1775, they selected the best qualified physician in terms of training, experience, and widespread acclaim. Despite Morgan's talents and visions of performing a great and humane service for his countrymen, he failed. A lack of supplies, ill-qualified personnel, restricted authority, and incessant bickering overwhelmed him. Neither Congress nor military commanders adequately understood the vital functions of hospitals in the war effort. The director-general bore the brunt of criticisms for the horrors and sufferings of the sick and wounded during the winter of 1776–1777. Abruptly in January 1777, Congress relieved Morgan of command; neither charges nor opportunity for a defense were given. Deeply hurt, Morgan spent the next four years seeking vindication. Almost immediately this involved malicious attacks upon William Shippen III.[171]

Blinded by vindictive rage, Morgan forgot the many causes which brought about his dismissal. He fixated upon the "Machiavelian . . . conduct" of William Shippen III and his fellow conspirators.[172] Several considerations made Morgan single out Shippen in addition to their decade of disagreements. Shortly after Shippen became chief surgeon to the Flying Camp, he challenged Morgan's jurisdiction over the entire medical department. Shippen's interpretation of Congressional resolves made the two men equals with jurisdiction over distinct areas. Shippen's lay west of the Hudson River. Because the Continental army retreated into New Jersey, Shippen gained the upper hand by late 1776. Furthermore, Shippen's reports to Congress of his successes contrasted favorably with Morgan's complaints of untenable conditions. In Morgan's mind what clinched the idea of a conspiracy was Shippen's appointment as director-general in April 1777 (only three months after Morgan's dismissal). Surely, thought Morgan, Shippen, his brothers-in-law the Lees of Virginia, and their friends lay behind the events of the past few months.[173]

Though Morgan repeated his charges publicly and often, no one paid heed to them until Dr. Benjamin Rush, first privately and later publicly, began to enunciate growing concern that "our hospital affairs grow worse and worse. . . . The fault is both with the establishment and in the Director-General. He is both *ignorant* and *negligent* of his duty."[174] The accusations brought action from Congress which relieved the director-general of the power to supply the hospitals in February 1778 and slashed his budget in April 1779 amid rumors that Shippen used supplies for his own personal profit. Morgan, who sought personal vindication and revenge, allied with Rush whose concern centered upon the need to reform the hospitals and alleviate unnecessary suffering. Although Rush earlier feuded with Shippen in civilian life, base motives seem absent from this ardent republican and reformer. Only a weak or wholly unprincipled individual could have seen what Rush saw, and not be moved to action.[175]

Rush refused to divulge his evidence except to a court-martial board. The reason, he explained, was that "the Doctor had two Br[others] in law in Congress, and as I had before experienced the partiality of a large body of the house to the D[octo]r, I objected to appearing" before a Congressional committee.[176] As a court-martial became likely, Morgan and Rush gathered more evidence against the director-general. In January 1780 Shippen was arrested and five specific charges presented.[177] Essentially his accusors claimed that Shippen speculated with supplies such as wine and sugar when the sick and wounded needed them, and second, that his incompetence caused needless suffering and death. The court-martial began in March 1780; although no formal records of it survive, it has been deftly reconstructed, and its irregular nature recaptured. For example, the members of the court-martial board changed through the proceedings so that almost no one heard all the testimony; on one occasion Shippen had Morgan jailed with excessive bail in an unsuccessful attempt to prevent collection of evidence; and Shippen even entertained members of the board at a party where he served fine delicacies brought from Philadelphia and delighted his guests with mocking imitations of John Morgan.[178]

By a single vote the court-martial board acquitted Shippen of all five charges. The members however were "clearly of the opinion, that Dr. Shippen did speculate in and sell hospital stores . . . which conduct they consider highly improper and justly reprehensible."[179] General Edward Hand cast the deciding vote. The fact that he was distantly related to the Shippens cannot be dismissed as irrelevant, although that need not explain his vote.[180]

In Congress, Shippen's brothers-in-law found it difficult to restrain their outraged colleagues. Although motions to censure or discharge Shippen failed, Congress refused to confirm or sanction the acquittal. After considerable debate it merely indicated that the director-general was released from arrest. After his release in August 1780, Shippen remained in office for five more months. Upon his return to civilian life, he was challenged by a harshly worded handbill written by John Morgan. Shippen's arch foe had opened a newspaper attack on Shippen in September which grew in intensity when Shippen finally responded in November. Both writers proved adept at hurling acrimonious epithets until that public scandal left the press late in December.

Even Shippen's defenses of his conduct suggest little to exonerate him. In general he appeared insensitive to the human suffering about him; he never claimed that as director-general he visited the sick, dressed wounds, or comforted soldiers in his care. On the other hand, he, the court-martial board, and Congress agreed that he speculated with needed hospital stores. Although the practice of officeholders using public funds and public provisions for private gain was a rather common practice in the eighteenth century, it can scarcely be defended in this instance. In sum, William Shippen III violated many basic tenets of the ideology of the Revolution. Shippen failed to refute satisfactorily the charge that he made "his own place a mere sinecure, and an engine of corruption and power.[181]

Dr. William Shippen III returned to civilian life; scandal neither restrained his ambition nor chastened his style of living. The luxurious entertainments of "Lord Worthy," as his admiring daughter called him, indicate no regrets over spending money accumulated during his tenure in office.[182] The tendency to place monetary considerations and advancement above emotional well-being which characterized the doctor in public life carried over into his private life as well. Although his relationship with both surviving children was affectionate to the point of prolonging their immaturity and emotional dependence, this powerful father managed to destroy the life of his daughter and granddaughter, and strongly contributed to the state of melancholy which engulfed the latter third of his wife's long life.[183]

Although much of this unhappiness occurred after the war, it began during it. Ann Home Shippen, or Nancy as everyone called William III's only surviving daughter, attracted the attention of several suitors including Bushrod Washington, Henry Beekman Livingston, and Louis Otto. She had many accomplishments; she sang, danced, played the harpsichord, knew some French, and wrote charming notes and letters. Clearly she and Louis Otto, a young member of the French legation in Philadelphia, loved one another in a romantic sense. She accepted his proposal of marriage in March 1781. When Otto broached the subject of marriage to her parents, Nancy's mother gave a favorable response. William III reacted differently. Love seemed no assurance of happiness, comfort, and security. As her father he felt it his duty to act in her best interests, even if he interfered with her current infatuation. Colonel Henry Beekman Livingston was the father's choice. That's whom Nancy married, and her father candidly explained the reason to his son,

Nancy is much puzzled between Otto & Livingston. She loves ye first & only esteems the last. L—— will consummate immediately. O—— not these 2 years. L—— has 12 or 15,000 hard. O—— has nothing now, but honorable expectations hereafter. A Bird in hand is worth 2 in a bush.[184]

Only days after Nancy accepted Louis Otto's proposal, she married Colonel Livingston at her father's house. Although a marriage thus arranged might have led to happiness, in this case it failed abominably. Within a year Nancy separated from her husband; she returned to her father's house for the rest of her life. There the meaninglessness of her existence eventually overwhelmed her with melancholy. Before that finally happened, her father indulged her with great affection and attention, and she totally suppressed any feeling of resentment toward him.

Not since Edward Shippen, founder of the family in America, thwarted his daughter Ann's desire and had her marry a gentleman of his choice had such trampling on personal preferences characterized a marriage in the Shippen family. Money and advancement had always been important, but never to the exclusion of all other considerations. Undoubtedly Nancy's marriage proved the unhappiest and least successful of any Shippen marriage during the century. Although certain other Shippen marriages became involved in controversy, almost all seemed agreeable, and specific evidence characterizes several with warm emotional attachments. Poetic justice seems detectable in the last twenty years of Nancy's father's marriage which became strained and unhappy.

For the Shippens the 1780s began with an almost overwhelming sense of despair and grief. In addition to problems involving marriages, scandals, and treason, came an expected yet painful loss. Edward Shippen III, the oldest living Shippen, patriarch of the major branch of the family lay dying at Lancaster.

Though Edward Shippen III wrote a will in 1763, he remained in good health well into his sixties and mentally alert and active until at least age seventy-five. By the late 1760s he and "Mammy" Shippen felt the effects of old age as rheumatism periodically incapacitated them. Edward III also wore a truss which his son purchased for him in Philadelphia. Edward III's brother, Dr. William Shippen II, often prescribed medicines for them by mail, even though doctors resided in Lancaster. He also personally attended Edward III's family in Philadelphia, and sometimes at Lancaster as well.[185]

In 1777 both Edward III and his wife became very ill, Edward III recovered and lived four more years, but Mary only survived

several months. Mrs. Shippen strained the patience of several kinsmen during her last year. Her "grandson" Jasper Yeates remarked
at one point, "She can have no Pretensions of Lodging at Tinian.
Her political Sentiments, bad Temper, whimsical Disposition &
religious opinions would make her continuance there improper."[186]
Apparently she detested independence even more than the other
members of that branch of the family. She died in 1778 before that
event was accomplished. Her death deeply affected her husband; he
wrote a long eulogy of her which began,

> Her whole Life was a Heaven upon Earth; for I was acquainted with
> her from a Child. Her pious example was a blessing, and portion to every-
> body under her roof. in Short, She was a great Christian. How many
> hundred Times have I found her in our Chamber with the Word of God
> in her hands; & when I ever missed her there, she had [illegible] into ye
> Chamber humbling her self before the Blessed God our gracious heavenly
> father in Prayer & adoration; to whom She is gone, to receive the Regards
> of her fidelity.[187]

From then on, Edward III's thoughts which had often focused
upon religion did so more frequently. He conveyed religious
thoughts and quotations to his family, especially the Burds at Tinian, to whom he remarked, "While I am catcechizing my Children
I am learning myself."[188] Then in September 1780, Edward III
learned of the death of his old friend Cousin William Allen. His
associate in so many activities was seventy-six, about a year younger
than Edward III. About this time, at his son Edward IV's prompt-
ing, Edward III finally gave up management of his friend James
Hamilton's estate in Lancaster which he had attended for several
decades. The patriarch needed rest, but even that and continuing
prescriptions from his brother William II could not postpone death
much longer.[189]

The family sensed this, and several grandchildren came to pay
their "Dutiful acknowledgements."[190] By April 1781 Edward III lay
very ill, and his grandson Jasper Yeates confided, "It gives me the
greatest Pain to declare, that in my opinion he can remain but a
small Time amongst us."[191] That summer both sons visited their
father. The emotional strain was considerable. For example, Ed-

ward IV's stroke was probably brought on by the impending death
of his father, the depressing situation of his exiled daughter Peggy,
and his own financial straits.[192]

The end came in September 1781. On the twenty-fourth Jasper
Yeates confessed to Neddy Burd

> I have just left your Grandfather & fear I shall not see him again alive.
> Poor Gentleman! He is tired of Life & can articulate nothing but his Wish
> to die. Even this is scarcely intelligible. He is as weak as 'tis possible for
> a living Creature to be. He takes no Sustenance, is feverish & laxative.
> Under these Circumstances it would be a Happiness to him & his Friends,
> who feel all his Groans, that he should take Leave of this World.[193]

Edward III's children were also present. Barely able to control
her feelings, Sarah admitted, "I thought I had Fortitude to bear this
great shock but I think we must summon all our resolution to bear
it."[194] Her younger brother Joseph III recalled a few weeks later,
"The Situation of my Mind, while at Lancaster was such, that I
could not think of writing. . . . The Loss I have sustained in the
Death of an affectionate & good Father has been truly distressing."[195]

The death of Edward Shippen III symbolized the end of the era
during which the Shippen family rose to its greatest heights.
Although he and his brothers descended from a wealthy and distinguished grandfather, the founder of the family in America, the
real wealth and power of the family came later in the eighteenth
century. The actions of the third generation created that. They also
provided the environment of the extended family which played such
a large role in the advancement of so many. Although the three
branches remained distinct, particularly after mid-century they assisted one another; this was particularly true of the Edward III and
William II branches. By the time of the American Revolution,
though their fortunes and political persuasions differed, all three
branches reflected the meaning of being an old, established and
successful family of colonial Pennsylvania.

When the Revolution came the family divided. No evidence of
Tory sympathies survives. Although the Edward III branch opposed
independence and maintained neutrality, it remained on intimate
terms with the William II branch which held revolutionary offices.
Only William II ardently supported a radical ideology; in several

ways the fourth generation professionals resembled each other more than their fathers, despite the superficial similarity in the side they supported. Private interests such as safety or advancement of the family stood above any ideology for them.

The Revolution caused significant changes for the Shippens. By 1781 it seemed to be reversing the relative stature of the two branches which could continue to produce Shippens. The opportunity to profiteer in an office helped William Shippen III considerably. The loss of offices tumbled the Edward Shippen III branch from power, preferment, and profits and threatened to push them far below their prewar stature. If we consider their wealth and power before the war, their decline was startling. Although the Shippens lost no property other than offices, something more important was destroyed. The elaborate extended family network, covering three generations, and lateral kinsmen such as fathers, sons, brothers, uncles, nephews, cousins, and others received extensive damage. Aside from the fact that almost no kinsmen held office, several of the most important figures were permanently gone. For example, Edward Shippen III, Cousin William Allen, and two of Allen's sons were dead; Andrew Allen, heir apparent of that family, remained in exile. The Allens' family alliance with the Penns declined tremendously in value as the government and vast lands in Pennsylvania were taken from them.

Despite sound reasons for despair, hope survived. More importantly, many familial and financial resources remained. The effects of revolutions cannot be ascertained immediately; the recuperative powers of the Shippen family were yet to be tested.

The End of an Era

Almost all living representatives of the Shippen family still resided in Pennsylvania when the Anglo-American conflict ceased.[1] No one had been attainted of treason, and no one had suffered confiscation of property. Survival, though important, only touches upon one of the consequences of the American Revolution upon this old established family. The Revolution had already brought about some dramatic changes, but the Revolution was not over when the war ceased.

Revolution can mean either a complete change or a completed cycle in which one returns to the starting point. Desires that both these ideas reach fruition existed in Pennsylvania during the 1780s and 1790s. The question was which connotation would prove a more appropriate evaluation of the American Revolution. Those who believed they or society benefited from the course of events after independence sought to promote the new order of things. On the other hand, many who accepted the reality of independence hoped that they could recapture much which characterized the old order. The experience of the Shippen family reveals dynamic tension.

Although the death of the patriarch of the Edward Shippen III branch removed a potent cohesive force from those Shippens, the constituent parts did not embark upon independent paths. The extended family network binding Edward IV, James Burd, Joseph III, and their dependents continued until at least the beginning of the nineteenth century. Emotional and economic ties remained intact, as did the tendency to rely upon the extended family for numerous other functions. In general members of this branch of the family continued to operate in a familial atmosphere.[2]

Economic concerns remained the most tangible evidence of family cohesion and means of reinforcing identity with the larger kinship network. The three brothers kept running accounts with one another until James Burd's death in 1793; after that Edward IV and Joseph III continued the practice until the former's death in 1806. Real estate, both in Philadelphia and undeveloped areas of Pennsylvania, also contributed to family identity as it had throughout the eighteenth century. For many other economic functions the Shippens continued to rely on the family rather than outsiders.[3]

Real estate fostered the continuance of close family identity and association for several reasons. Both Edward IV and Joseph III owned real estate in Philadelphia which had been in the family for four generations. Whenever they leased or sold it, they recounted certain aspects of the family's history in the indenture. They also inherited some Philadelphia lots from their father which they continued to hold jointly until at least 1794. Because Joseph III lived a day or two away from Philadelphia for the rest of his life, he relied on others to manage details of negotiations regarding his property there. He chose kinsmen to perform the services. Often his brother Edward IV collected rents or arranged rentals of property. When Edward IV tried to sell his brother's house at an auction, he employed a shill to increase the bids. During the depression of the 1780s, Joseph III's nephew Edward Burd also exerted considerable energies trying to extract rents and recover arrears from his uncle's tenants. Burd's tact and ability in this and other business endeavors for his uncle became a formal arrangement in 1792 when Joseph III gave his power of attorney to his nephew.[4]

Aside from real estate in Philadelphia, Edward IV and Joseph III owned land elsewhere in Pennsylvania. The brothers still remained absentee landlords in Shippensburg and continued to collect rents from tenants three, and James Burd also had a right to some of the income from that estate. Although arrears in rent mounted during the 1780s, in 1789 Joseph III happily informed his brother that "Shippensburg appears now in a much more thriving State than it has ever been and will probably improve & increase . . . every Year . . . [because of] the Trade of the back Country by means of the great State Road to Pittsburg leading into it."[5] In time some of Joseph III's descendants actually settled there.[6]

During the decade after the Great War for Empire, Edward IV and Joseph III acquired land and claims in less developed areas of Pennsylvania in what became Northampton, Bedford, Cumberland, Allegheny, and Westmoreland counties. Their largest holdings lay in Northumberland County; counting tracts they had neither patented nor paid for and those held in other names, as well as some for which they held clear title, their holdings amounted to about 3,150 acres. Edward IV valued this holding at £3,000 in 1786, but no prospective buyer did; hence the Shippens retained possession of this land for some time. The confusion and disappointment which characterized the largest holding appears rather typical of their undeveloped holdings. Often their knowledge of the holdings was imprecise, usually they overvalued them, and only occasionally did they make a satisfactory sale. For example, in 1784 they wanted £800 for their unpatented tract at White Deer Hole Creek; four years later they would have settled for £600. Edward IV's complaints in 1788 about the "Circumstances of the times and the great fall of Lands" in value seem to characterize the brothers' outlook on their landed investments in the 1780s and 1790s.[7] And in the mid-90s he decried "the Embarrassments we have experienced and may yet experience" from people entering contracts, occupying land, and then defaulting.[8] Neither were the Shippens particularly responsible when it came to their undeveloped lands; they often failed to pay taxes on their lands until they feared their holdings might be sold by the sheriff for defaulting in payments.[9]

Although the brothers sold some of their holdings, Edward IV's observation that "as we are growing older, it seems better to convert Land, encumbered as these [holdings] seem to be, into money . . . than to keep them upon the expectation of there hereafter being a greater price" seems essentially an unfulfilled dream.[10] For the Shippens, their undeveloped acres in Pennsylvania remained largely a frozen asset.

Disappointments and frustrations generally characterized postwar economic experiences of Edward IV, Joseph III, and James Burd. The latter two suffered particularly in this regard. Joseph III found his farm in Kennett Square and the small amount of trade he carried on inadequate to support his family. The birth of four more children after 1780, all of whom reached maturity, in addition to his three teen-aged children, increased family expenses considerably. In 1783, with hopes of improving his faltering position, Joseph III moved to Lancaster. His experiences there failed to commend the move. Almost immediately he informed his nephew Edward Burd, "I find my Expences here much greater than they have been for some Years past."[11]

Aware of Joseph III's predicament, Edward Burd and Edward Shippen IV probably suggested to Edward Shippen V, a merchant, the potential benefits of a family connection in the strategically located town of Lancaster. In the spring of 1784, Edward V offered his service in the mercantile line to his Uncle Joseph III. When Edward V formed a partnership with Richard Footman a few months later, he reaffirmed the offer to Joseph III. "As you must have a considerable Influence with the shopkeepers of Lancaster County," wrote Edward V, "we shall take it as a favor if you will mention us to such of them as we may depend on."[12]

Shippen and Footman imported from London, Bristol, Amsterdam, and France, and expected to enter the West Indian trade as well; hence they bragged "there will not be a more general wholesale store in Philad[elphia]."[13] But Joseph III hesitated. He still thought of himself as a gentleman and appended "Esq." to his name.[14] Though unable to afford the luxuries which previously accompanied that status, he could easily look back upon his life at Kennett Square as that of a simple country gentleman rather than that of a farmer.[15]

Lack of sufficient income eventually caused Joseph III to compromise a bit. In the eyes of the family Joseph III's stature would not suffer from engaging in trade; indeed, Edward IV informed his brother that Jasper Yeates (their nephew by marriage) felt certain that Joseph III could succeed well in the dry goods business at Lancaster; "he is so well convinced of it, that he would gladly join you in it."[16] In May 1786, Joseph III announced that Shippen and Funck opened a new store in Lancaster where dry goods, merchandize, and groceries might be obtained "on reasonable terms."[17] Shippen and Funck transacted business with Footman and Shippen of Philadelphia. Joseph III quickly became disenchanted with the situation, and complained that sales during the winter of 1786–1787 proved remarkably dull and that a scarcity of cash in the area made it impossible to collect debts. Joseph III's friend, ex-Governor John Penn, accurately evaluated the six-year sojourn at Lancaster when he observed, "I cannot suppose you can spend your time very agreeably at Lancaster where your company must be confined & not always the sort you would choose or as you have been used to."[18]

By 1788 Joseph III wished to return to a country life. He considered buying William Penn's old manor of Pennsborough in Bucks County and several other farms in the area. The reason for his interest in that region was a desire to be near his kinsmen Dr. William and Mary (Shippen) McIlvaine who lived in Bristol, Pennsylvania.[19] After a vain search for a satisfactory location in Bucks County, Joseph III decided to return to Chester County. Early in 1789 he purchased "a very good Farm on Chester Creek" with good buildings, improvements, and meadows.[20] It lay in Westtown, about four miles from West Chester and twenty-three miles from Philadelphia. He named it "Plumley," in memory of his mother, Sarah (Plumley) Shippen.[21]

One of the attractions of this new location was its relative proximity to his wife's kinsmen in Maryland. Jenny Shippen often regretted that her "nearest relations . . . [were] perfect strangers" to her children.[22] Shortly after the Shippens settled at Westtown, that changed. The Ringgolds visited the Shippens and invited Jenny's eldest daughter to pay an extended visit to Chestertown. Mary Shippen's visit to Maryland and subsequent visits to see kinsmen in Philadelphia are especially important. More than simply confirming the continuing significance of the extended family, these visits reveal a great deal about the effects of the Revolution upon Joseph III and his family.[23]

Born in 1773, Mary Shippen never experienced what it meant to be a member of the primary branch of the Shippen family during its ascendancy. Like most fifth-generation descendants of Edward III, her formative years felt the impact which the strain and setbacks of the Revolution produced. Her thoughts concerning the summer of 1790 which she spent at Chestertown, Maryland, and the winters she passed in Philadelphia before her marriage in 1793, indicate much about what it meant to be a Shippen after the Revolution.

Mary thoroughly enjoyed her stay at Chestertown; everyone seemed so open and friendly. The style of life there, however, contrasted sharply with her past experiences. "I shall never envy the Marylanders the lives they lead, though exceedingly easy and well," she informed her mother, and added that the "sweet retirement" of Westtown remained preferable.[24] As Mary prepared to go to Philadelphia several months later, she described herself to her Cousin Molly Yeates as a rather serious girl whose head could not be turned by the gaiety of the capital.[25]

Although readily accepted into the most fashionable company because of her Aunt Bordley's introductions and the Shippens' past eminence, Mary found, "This life is very different from what I have been accustomed to & I must confess it is not altogether agreeable to me."[26] She looked askance at the "trifling ceremonious morning visits," the "necessary etiquette," the parties, balls, and so forth.[27] In short, she enjoyed a simpler retired life and "would most unwillingly give [it] up for the *unsatisfactory* pleasures of a dissipated life."[28] With varying degrees these sentiments reflected the view of her father, brother John, and Uncle Edward IV of the "pleasures" of "the gay folks about us."[29] The Shippens now viewed the wealthiest and most powerful ranks of society from the outside.[30]

More than this, however, Joseph III and his family had accommodated themselves very well to their reduced circumstances.[31] Lacking the drive and specialized talents of his older brother which might encourage an attempt to retrieve past eminence, Joseph III endowed the metamorphosis of his circumstances with virtuous connotations. Although he did not refer to it as such, the country gentleman lived in "republican simplicity."[32]

Edward Shippen IV refused to accept a similar fate. This ambitious professional harbored strong desires to regain the power and influence which he previously enjoyed. During the 1780s he grasped at opportunities for advancements; he seemed determined to succeed. Although Edward IV still derived some income as a lawyer, from rents, and from the occasional sale of real estate, and also reduced his living expenses by relying on products from his farm, the loss of his offices in the Revolution dealt him a severe financial blow. His initial attempt to keep up appearances could not continue. He moved out of the Shippens' great house in Fourth Street into a more modest dwelling.[33]

His father's will gave the great house to both sons; because neither could afford to purchase the other's share and because they both needed money, they decided to sell it. Edward IV asked £5,000. After viewing the house, one potential buyer offered less than £4,000 because of the extensive repairs he foresaw. "The Report of the ruinous Condition of the house has been so prevalent," complained Edward IV, "that I fear we shall have no new offers."[34] Edward IV acknowledged the dilapidated condition of the house, gardens, gates, and yard; he resolved to spend about £100 to £300 for repairs and lowered his price to £4,500.[35]

Edward IV also garnered other sources of revenue. He received power of attorney from William Hamilton, and thus assumed the duties which his father previously performed for James Hamilton. Edward IV checked over family ledgers, accounts, and papers, and attempted to recover debts due his father's estate. Some of them were almost twenty-five years old; the attempt to retrieve any that old reflected his desperate financial straits. When a cargo of dry goods arrived in Philadelphia from France in 1782, Edward IV exclaimed, "This must prove a good Spec[ulation]" and invested £1,000 in it.[36] Before the war he used "idle cash" when he invested in merchant ventures. During the 1780s Edward IV had no "idle cash," and in this instance, he admitted to Jasper Yeates, "I have not the Money [to invest] & must depend on you for it."[37] His kinsman gladly joined Edward IV in the venture. Edward IV's financial distress during the 1780s became so severe that the lines he copied on the inside cover of his cashbook must have elicited grim determination rather than a smile.

One penny put out at our Savior's birth to 5 per Cent *Compound* Interest, would before this time have increased to a greater Sum than would be contained in two hundred Millions of Earth all solid gold—But if put out to *simple* Interest, it would have amounted to no more than Seven shillings & six pence—[38]

The entire family felt the effects of Edward IV's deprivation. Along with many material indications came personal ones as well. For example, Edward IV's eldest son and namesake did not marry until he was twenty-seven, three years later in life than his father had. In part the reason stemmed from the postwar depression which made it difficult for the young man to establish himself, but the inability of his father to moderate the influence of the times played a role too. Similarly, Edward IV's difficulties in accumulating dowries for his daughters Sarah and Mary meant they did not marry until ages twenty-nine and twenty-eight, respectively. They were the oldest Shippen brides of the eighteenth century.

Demographic evidence regarding the children of Joseph III and James Burd reflect similar predicaments. Joseph III's two youngest daughters never married; his eldest daughter married at age twenty-six, and his youngest sons married at ages thirty-one and twenty-nine respectively. Joseph III and Jenny strongly censured their eldest son for his marriage, and although he was only twenty-two, he received no financial support from his parents. The evidence regarding Burd's children conforms to the same pattern. Jane and Margaret were twenty-five and twenty-six, respectively, and Elizabeth, the youngest child, seems to have remained a spinster. James Burd, Jr., outraged his family by marrying "a low bred Dutch girl"; information regarding the only other son of James and Sarah Burd is incomplete.[39]

Neither Joseph III nor James Burd ever approached the level of material prosperity which they enjoyed before the war. Joseph III's postwar financial status has already been discussed. In the political realm, although Joseph III became a justice of the peace of Chester County in 1791, the prestige and emoluments of that office provide an extraordinarily sharp contrast with those enjoyed as secretary of Pennsylvania. James Burd regained no political office after the war. Always pressed for money before the war, he found that the death of the indulgent Edward III and financial straits of Joseph III and Edward IV meant the benefits of his family connections depreciated significantly. Burd's constant refrain until his death in 1793 centered upon expenses which his circumstances could barely afford because of his lack of affluence. In short, as far as economic and political affairs were concerned, neither Joseph III nor James Burd partook in any counterrevolution, if indeed one ever occurred in Pennsylvania.[40]

On the other hand, Edward IV seemed determined to return to power. His first opportunity came in 1784 when he received a commission as justice of the peace and president of the Court of Common Pleas for Philadelphia County. Though humble positions to a man who had served as prothonotary of the Supreme Court and judge of the Admiralty Court, Edward IV accepted the chance to end his eight-year stint as a private citizen. When elected a magistrate in Philadelphia in 1785, Edward IV candidly expressed his opinions of the office to his brother Joseph III. "Tho[ugh] I dislike the business & know it will be burthensome," admitted Shippen, "I shall however take it, under an Expectation that having been in this instance the Choice of the People, I may be in the way of something more to my mind."[41] At the same time Shippen also became judge of the Orphans Court, a position which he held until 1789.[42]

Edward Shippen IV soon found the burden of several offices not worth the effort; thus in 1786 he resigned as justice of the peace and president of the Court of Quarter Sessions of the Peace in order to devote his energies to the more important office of president of the Court of Common Pleas for Philadelphia County. He retained the latter position until 1790.[43]

Upon the creation of a federal judiciary system in 1789, Edward Shippen IV's friends, including his kinsman James Tilghman and Pennsylvania's Attorney General Rawle recommended Shippen as district judge of Pennsylvania. Though they claimed "he has too much modesty and merit to push himself forward," those words seem more a reflection of proper etiquette than of Shippen's character.[44] The office required knowledge of common law, as well as civil and maritime law, and the petitioners believed that "Mr. Shippen posses[ses] far superior knowledge and Capacity for the station" than the leading candidate.[45] Although Shippen would have accepted the position, it was not offered.

This rebuff failed to discourage the sixty-year-old lawyer. A while later the government of Pennsylvania relied in part upon Shippen's advice in setting up an entirely new arrangement of the courts in the commonwealth. His standing with influential politicians was such that he received an appointment to the Pennsylvania Supreme Court in 1791. To a significant degree the fortunes of Edward IV's life at last revived. Soon he wrote to his kinsman Jasper Yeates, "Nothing for some time past has afforded me so much pleasure as your acceptance of a Seat in the Supreme Court."[46] Neither Shippen nor Yeates had welcomed independence, yet within fifteen years of its declaration both men sat in the highest state judicial body. Shippen continued in that body for fifteen years; Yeates served twenty-six. In 1799 Edward Shippen IV became chief justice of Pennsylvania and served in that capacity until 1805, the year before his death.

The reemergence of Edward Shippen IV qualifies facile generalizations about the revolutionary characteristics of the American Revolution in Pennsylvania. Despite the qualifications, however, the revolutionary nature of the movement outweighed the continuity. Before the rebellion when Shippen sat in the Supreme Court with his cousin, the chief justice, they were part of a vast kinship network which had amassed many offices for its members. Now only Edward IV, Jasper Yeates, and a few other kinsmen held offices; in general their power was far less extensive and far fewer kinsmen shared in it. Although neither nepotism nor the tendency of elite domination vanished from Pennsylvania, the particular people involved and the tremendous power formerly concentrated in one kinship network changed to a significant degree.[47] Although the Revolution appears a bit ambiguous in its effects, the degree of change in significant areas suggests the revolution in Pennsylvania was more thoroughgoing than many care to admit.

Because twice as many members of the fifth generation survived in comparison to the fourth, doubtless alterations in the structure and functioning of the Edward III branch of the family were in the making even if no revolution had occurred. What might have happened remains speculative, but what did happen often reflected the relative deprivation which the Revolution saddled upon these Shippens. As already indicated, after 1776 significant changes in the economic and political functions of the family occurred. No longer could the Shippens launch their children into the world with such great confidence in the likelihood of their success and at least local eminence. Indeed it became rather difficult to launch them upon adult careers or into attractive marriages.

Beyond this, the tight cohesion of the family lessened after the death of the patriarch Edward III. True, Edward IV, Joseph III, and James Burd conducted business with one another until they died, and Edward IV and Joseph III corresponded faithfully and frequently. Family visits between Joseph Shippen III's and James Burd's families were not infrequent and efforts to have kinsmen know each other were not neglected. Nevertheless, geographic dispersion and the loss of the patriarch caused the three families within the primary branch to drift somewhat apart and to concentrate more upon immediate kinsmen than in the past. For example, Edward IV tried to situate his children as well as he could; he handled investments in land and the Bank of North America for his daughter Margaret (Shippen) Arnold, yet his association with his brother Joseph III's children was neither economic nor political in nature. He offered only familial friendship. For the most part, that was all Joseph III could offer in return. For example, when Edward IV's son James became depressed while working on a ledger and journal and developed "too much fondness for the looseness of the other Sex," his father sent him to Lancaster to stay with his Uncle Joseph III.[48] Although Joseph III probably gave the young man "gentle hints," the rapport which previously characterized the relationship between Edward IV and his nephew Edward Burd never developed.[49]

In short, neither Edward IV nor Joseph III could assume the family role and responsibility which their father had. Neither one provided leadership over the three constituent parts of the Edward III branch; indeed, their relationship with their own children and grandchildren proved a pale image of the patriarch's. Symptomatic of the decline of cohesion was the geographic diffusion of the fifth generation. Edward IV's children resided in Philadelphia, Bristol, and London; Burd's children lived in Philadelphia, Lancaster, and Tinian; Joseph III's dwelled at Philadelphia, Shippensburg, and Westtown. Disintegration exaggerates what was transpiring; however, it is clear that major reorientations and realignments characterized the Edward III branch of the Shippen family after the American Revolution.

More catastrophic changes befell the Joseph II branch of the family. Although this branch was destined for extinction before the war, the Revolution made the collapse complete. In 1766 Joseph II's only male heir died unmarried. Two daughters married and went to the West Indies. Another daughter married well and remained in Philadelphia. Those three successful marriages strained Joseph

II's resources; the Revolution crushed him. Although almost no details survive, it is clear that the loss of his offices left the seventy-year-old man in a predicament. His precarious position is reflected in the marriages of his daughters, Mary and Margaret. Both women remained single until about age thirty, and neither's husband matched the stature of the successful suitors of Joseph II's other daughters. In 1784 he felt obliged to sell seven lots in Germantown to his brother William II. By 1787 he defaulted on a mortgage he had taken out thirteen years earlier on a lot 80 feet by 780 feet on Green and Main Street in Germantown. His brother William II bought the property at a sheriff's auction for £95. The next year Joseph II sold for £500 a large adjoining lot together with "the Brick House thereon Erected by the name of Roe Buck Tavern" and all his other lots in Germantown.[50] The old Shippen country house, first occupied by Joseph Shippen I shortly after Queen Anne's War, was now in the possession of his youngest son. In 1795, William II proposed to purchase the remaining Shippen lots in Germantown from Edward IV and Joseph III. Five years later they complied.[51]

Unlike the other two branches of the family, the William II branch benefited from the course of events after independence. From a material and social standpoint, their position became decidedly better than before the war. On a human level, however, their situation became morbid. Familial love and duties failed to produce the pleasures and positive results previously enjoyed by the Edward III branch; instead, they intensified the discomforts brought on by several unfortunate occurrences.

The William II branch merits treatment because the consequences of their use of the extended family were so different from those derived by the Edward III branch.[52] The functioning of the family and its members can be summarized by focusing upon the consequences of Ann Home (Shippen) Livingston's marriage and certain aspects of the life of Thomas Lee Shippen. Only months after the marriage of Henry Beekman Livingston, overcome with possessive jealousy he became convinced of his wife's infidelity. Though even his own mother dismissed the accusation as proposterous, the "Wretched Unhappy man" abused and persecuted his wife until she fled to her father's house in Philadelphia.[53]

Ann's distraught state of mind continued for years as she tried to reconcile herself to an impossible situation. At first she tried to resign herself to her fate. As she lavished attention upon Peggy, "the sweetest child that ever was born," she could escape coming to grips with what had happened.[54] For some time she consoled herself with "the reflection of having conformed to the will of my parents in the most important action of my life."[55] The actions of her husband made her believe that "men are generally tyrannical," but she exempted "Lord Worthy," her father, from that characterization.[56] Even when William Shippen III hold his daughter that Peggy Livingston must live with her grandmother Livingston, because the child's "fortune depends on the old Lady's pleasure," Ann bemoaned her fate rather than admit hostility toward her father.[57] This suppression of her emotions toward her father proved difficult, especially when she heard an anecdote about "a young Lady who was sacrificed to the avarice & ambition of her parents to a man She hated."[58] Although Ann remained subject to fits of weeping and melancholy, she maintained fair control over her emotions; in mid-1783, when she allowed her daughter to go to her grandmother in New York, the fact that "I have done my duty" still provided solace.[59]

All the while Ann lived with her parents she spent many enjoyable times visiting friends, attending dances, giving teas and parties, and entertaining several gentlemen who found her attractive. To her, therefore, William Shippen III had "the sweetest disposition in the world, affable & polite to everybody, & to his Wife & children he is sweetly indulgent."[60] While Ann clung to the rhetoric which expressed what was supposed to be, her mother confronted stark reality. A tremendous sense of guilt concerning her daughter's circumstances and inability to cope with the death of her own infant son caused her to withdraw from life. Early in 1784 Ann noticed a "visible alteration" in her mother's character which became "more composed, more serene, more indifferent about worldly matters than ever I saw her.[61]

Ann resisted any impulse to give up, although she already glimpsed the reality of her existence. "I am twenty years old," she wrote in her diary; "when I look back . . . what account can I give

of myself for not having made a better use of it."[62] Despite the fact
that she gave delightful parties, entertained friends and family with
her singing, playing the harpsichord, and charming conversation,
and read French and could reflect on other accomplishments, "the
most important action in . . . [her] life," her marriage, was a failure.[63] While growing up, she developed certain concepts concerning
being a dutiful wife and affectionate mother. Although at age twenty
she resolved to spend her next twenty years in a better manner, her
ability to hide from the meaninglessness of her life (measured by
her definition of meaningful) proved limited.

Ann's daughter spent the winter of 1783–1784 in Philadelphia; in
April Ann returned the child to Grandmother Livingston in New
York. Upon Ann's return to Philadelphia she found that her father
had rented the Shippen house to the Spanish ambassador and moved
into the small house next door. The impending expenses of his son's
education abroad necessitated the move, and his wife's desire to live
in the country to recover her health became an additional incentive.
Mrs. William Shippen III stayed at Mt. Peace in Germantown, the
country house of William Shippen II. With amazing shortsighted-
ness, William III urged Ann to stay there also to care for her depressed mother. Within a week Ann found the situation so disagreeable that she broke down and "cried heartily for my nerves are
weak."[64] This made her father "angry [and] tho' I saw he was sorry
for me, he ask'd me who was so proper to take care of Mamma as
her own child?"[65] Fortunately Ann's Aunt Bordley intervened,
and William III agreed to hire someone to assist Ann. Still the
summer proved particularly disagreeable, and in the fall William
III asked his daughter to come live with him in Philadelphia, "as
Mamma is so fond of solitude & I am not."[66]

Given Ann's family environment and the control exercised over
her, changes in her personality were hardly surprising. For example,
while Ann continued secluded with "a Mother whose situation is
by far more distressing than anyone can conceive," she mused "how
much shou'd I have suffer'd . . . if those prejudices which are customary to people of my birth had holden . . . over me—if for example I had annexed much value to luxury & showy dress."[67] In
February 1785, a few months after her return to Philadelphia, the

change became more pronounced when the young woman recorded, "Within these last three months my time has passed in a continual round of insipid amusements & trivial occupations."[68]

Within the next few years the remaining sparks of life were wrung out of her. In 1785, upon her father's urging, she refused her husband's offer to attempt reconciliation. Two years later she told Livingston to proceed with an application for a legal separation; however, his refusal to provide support for his child protracted deliberations. All the while Nancy's daughter lived alternately with her mother and grandmother. In 1788, Ann contemplated keeping her daughter to herself, but decided against it for both William Shippen III and Uncle Arthur Lee thought it inexpedient "to deprive her [Peggy] of the patronage of such a Grandmother."[69]

Between 1789 and 1795 Henry Livingston threatened to take the child away from his wife; however, Madam Livingston (Henry's mother) sympathized more with Ann. Perhaps more than a selfish desire to possess her granddaughter caused Madam Livingston to help thwart her son. In any case, toward the end of the 1790s she took Peggy away from her mother entirely. Even before that Ann became overwhelmed by the emptiness of her life. On Christmas 1791, she made the last meaningful entry in her diary; after that nothing seemed worth recording. Between 1791 and 1812 she wrote about a half dozen more entries about what she heard in church. She merely recounted the sermon without comment.[70]

Ann's mother, a religious recluse, died in 1801 at age seventy-five. In a house which Ann's grandfather William Shippen II provided and later bequeathed to her, the melancholy woman lived alone until her daughter finally left Livingston Manor to spend the rest of her life with her mother. Not until 1841 did seventy-eight-year old Ann Home (Shippen) Livingston die. Her daughter never married and lived on until 1864, dying at age eighty-two. Rarely has longevity been so painful.[71]

Although the life of William Shippen III's only surviving son was short, the last years of it proved only somewhat less agonizing than his mother's, sister's, and niece's. In his case, however, the actions of an indulgent father and the extended family network served him rather well. He avoided certain pitfalls; however, an incurable disease frustrated his father's medical talents as well as his ambitions. After spending several years at Mr. Booth's Academy near Frederick Town, Maryland, Thomas Lee Shippen studied law in Williamsburg, Virginia. There he visited his uncles Arthur and Richard Henry Lee, and also met many of his cousins. In 1784 he returned to Philadelphia where he "was so fortunate as to have my studies directed by" his kinsman Edward Burd.[72] William Shippen III harbored great ambitions for his son's advancement and prepared to spend a large amount to provide his son with training at Middle Temple and further refinements from a Grand Tour.[73]

Thomas Lee Shippen wrote to Thomas Jefferson inquiring about an European education. The minister to France advised against it and armed the young man with appropriate American prejudices. After lauding the usefulness of an American education, Jefferson enumerated the disadvantages of a youth venturing to Europe. "If he goes to England he learns drinking, horse-racing & boxing . . . he acquires a fondness for European luxury & dissipation & a contempt for the simplicity of his own country," said Jefferson as he painted a distorted contrast between the old and new world. After berating other presumed influences of Europe which included among other things "a passion for whores" and disdain for the marriage bed as "an ungentlemanly practice," Jefferson summarized his case by concluding that an American educated in Europe "returns to his own country a foreigner."[74]

Despite the warning, alone and undaunted, Thomas Lee Shippen embarked for Europe in 1785. Shippen met Jefferson in Paris and the latter recommended that Shippen tour parts of the Netherlands, Germany, Italy, and France before going to England. In August 1786 Shippen arrived in London and entered Middle Temple. Although Jefferson and many other Americans feared the evil influence of Europe, Thomas Lee Shippen assured his mother, "There is no difference between this and any other City that I have ever seen except in the size and number of the buildings and the noise and hurry of the streets."[75] He found the manners much the same, channels of vice no more numerous, and temptation not so strong as in America. He informed his father that "I am so transformed already by dress that you would hardly know me, curls to my hair, round hat, raven's gray coat, black sattin vest, white cassimer breeches and white silk stockings, my scarlet coat is renouvelled a la mode."[76]

Despite his life style and polished manner, the young gentleman developed an ambiguous stance toward the British. On the one hand he aped much of the style of European aristocrats. On the other hand he detested their "hauty ignorant overbearing and presumptuous" attitude toward Americans.[77] He could scarcely, he said, restrain "my indignation when I observe worship bestowed on star'd and coroneted fools, rich Apes, and dignified villains" as he described "the nobility of this degraded Country."[78]

Shippen reconciled the paradox by deprecating distinctions in England as "not founded in nature" but created "to feed the vanity, and flatter the ambition of weak and designing men." Myopically he exclaimed, "Thank God similar causes produce not similar effects in this respect in America, as long as we are free and incorrupt we shall have no titles, no distinctions but those of virtue and vice, of wisdom & folly."[79] A more impartial observer might object to his comments; for example, a prominent leader of the Revolution recommended that Thomas Lee Shippen acquire the title "My Lord" and declared that "the elevation of mind which *Birth & Rank* impart" was essential to creating a good statesman.[80] Many Philadelphians also remembered how the ambitious father of Thomas Lee Shippen acquired much of his fortune.[81]

Several things promoted young Shippen's hostility toward the English aristocracy in particular and European aristocracy in general. Thomas Lee Shippen arrived in London only two or three years after the Peace of Paris ended the War for Independence. Often he found himself on the defensive, and particularly so when he met Tory exiles such as the daughter of Andrew Allen, a distant cousin. Second, Thomas Lee Shippen's family was not in the very highest ranks of Philadelphia or Pennsylvania society. For example, neither the political nor financial assets of William II approached those Edward Shippen IV enjoyed before the American Revolution. And before the late war, William Allen, James Hamilton, and certain other men in Philadelphia exceeded Edward IV's stature. Furhtermore, the expenses of Thomas Lee Shippen's sojourn abroad taxed his father's financial resources to their limit, in contrast, for instance, with the effect on William Allen of similar provisions for his three sons. Little wonder that Thomas Lee Shippen realized the great discrepancy between his family and the wealthy and powerful European aristocrats he met.[82]

Because William Shippen III readily acquiesced to the increasing financial demands of his son even during the depression of the 1780s, his love and indulgence of his son, as well as his ambitions for the young man, cannot be denied. In 1787 Thomas Lee Shippen asked his father to finance a year's stay in France; his father agreed to raise the needed 200 guineas, but reminded his son to handle the funds with the greatest economy, "for money never was so scarce." To emphasize the point, William III related, "When you pass the Hotel d[e] Londre in the Rue Honore remember your Father lived 3 months there on a very little money."[83] Because William III found that "tis so very hard to procure it [money]," he requested his father's assistance.[84] "Your Grandfather hears your letters with parental eagerness," wrote William III to Thomas Lee Shippen, "but advancing a shilling . . . he has not ye most distant idea." With characteristic avariciousness, William III said of his bearded father, "He will not part with a shilling while in ye body. I wish he may do so properly when he dies."[85]

When in 1788 Thomas Lee Shippen requested an additional year abroad, his father again agreed, although he indicated the need for "great Economy & you must embarke early in the Spring for America—my Finances make this *absolutely* necessary."[86] A friend criticized William III as "capricious in . . . [his son's] education"; yet the doctor brushed aside the comment as narrow-minded, and reveled in the comment of Madame Faucauld that Thomas Lee Shippen was "the most polished American she has seen."[87] The next spring Thomas Lee Shippen again imposed on his father for another extension. Though compelled to sell a prized possession for £200 sterling, William III again indulged his son. The son went to Versailles where the splendor simultaneously awed and repulsed him, to Geneva where "there are very few genteel houses where I am not acquainted,"[88] Sardinia where he observed "the shocking effects of a tyrannical government and a tyrannical religion,"[89] on through Italy. He returned to London that winter. "I am without a farthing," he confessed; he denied extravagance on his part and requested at least £300 sterling so that he might "return with credit to my native Country."[90]

At last in the spring of 1789, after over three years abroad, Thomas Lee Shippen prepared to return to America. Had he an independent fortune, he might not have returned, for he informed his father of his distaste for practicing law. "There is something in the indiscriminate advocation of right & wrong adverse to my Nature," he declared, "and besides that the wrangling and altercations of the bar can never be agreeable to me." Perhaps anticipating the explosion of wrath if he pressed such sentiments, Thomas Lee Shippen added, in a self-pitying manner, that though "the road to travel which you wish me to pursue will prove a rough & thorny one . . . I will follow it, tho' I should bleed myself to death." He concluded, " 'Tis yours to order, mine to obey."[91]

Although William III chose his son's profession, Thomas Lee Shippen made the vitally important choice of his own wife. William III tried to influence his son at least once. In 1787 the doctor wrote that General Dickinson had a high opinion of Thomas Lee Shippen and "a charming girl of 15 . . . [who] is improving rapidly . . . [and] will have 15 or 20,000."[92] Doubtless recalling his sister's misery, Thomas Lee Shippen did not reply affirmatively to the hint.

In 1791 Elizabeth Carter (Farley) Bannister, a seventeen-year-old widow from Virginia became his bride. Although money must have entered into the decision, in one of several love letters to her before their marriage Shippen wrote, "I have been as well since I left you as a lover can be in the absence of his mistress."[93] William III and his wife approved the marriage, and both urged the couple to settle nearby in Philadelphia. The newlyweds moved into their own house around mid-1791. The marriage lasted only seven years.[94]

Two years after the marriage while in New York, which Shippen thought a "wretched unfeeling inhospitable Jewish town," he became very ill.[95] His doctor informed the young gentleman that he would not recover quickly, and thus the patient returned to Philadelphia in a litter.[96] Dr. William Shippen III described his son as being "in a very dangerous way" that fall.[97] Dr. Benjamin Rush claimed that he nearly cured the young man of "a pulmonary consumption by 25 bleedings after he had been deserted as incurable by [Dr. Adam] Kuhn and most of the physicians of the city."[98]

Thomas Lee Shippen never really recovered. At age thirty-three he died of tuberculosis while under his father's care. Ironically, Benjamin Rush, antagonist of the father but friend of the son, wrote an epitaph:

> Friends of Science, liberty, and virtue, . . . do homage by your Tears to the character of *Thomas Lee Shippen*. . . . The mind of this accomp[lishe]d & excellent young man was rich stored with every kind of useful knowledge, acquired by study, travelling and conversation. His Eloquence was alike pleasing, and instructing. His person was elegant. His manners were particularly correct and graceful. His benevolence embraced the whole family of mankind. . . . In an age of infidelity he was not ashamed of the cross of Christ, dying he gloried in it.[99]

William Shippen III took his two grandchildren away from their mother and into his own house. Alice Lee Shippen informed her son's widow, "Our Charming Tommy . . . charms everybody . . . his Grand Father is fonder of him than I ever saw him of any child, he says 'tis because he sees a great deal of his precious Father in him."[100] The informal adoption enabled the young widow to remarry.

William Shippen III's wife and father died in 1801. At last William III received a sizable inheritance. Although Dr. William Shippen III continued to lecture on anatomy at the college, his health soon failed. In 1808, at age seventy-two, he died from an attack of anthrax at his home in Germantown. Caspar Wistar, a former student, delivered a glowing eulogy.[101]

In 1810 William Shippen III's cousin Joseph III died. The last Shippen of the fourth generation was buried at Lancaster. Although the Shippen family lived on, the activities of the nineteenth and twentieth century lie beyond the scope of this study.

X

The Shippens in Retrospect

This study of the Shippen family began in the mid-seventeenth century and spanned the following century and a half. It dealt with more than seventy-five people who bore the Shippen name, and with many other people who functioned within their kinship network or were affected by it. The founder of the family left Yorkshire, England, in 1668 and settled in Boston, Massachusetts. There the Quaker merchant increased his fortune by his own efforts and inheritance. Tired and frustrated by his condition as an "outsider," he moved in 1694 to the recently established colony of Pennsylvania. Because of his fortune, zeal in support of "the Truth," and family connections, he immediately became one of the most prominent "insiders." His success in Philadelphia proved sufficient to attract both his sons to migrate to the city as well. The nascent extended family network expanded. The wealth and land he accumulated before his death helps explain why no major migration of Shippens from Philadelphia took place for five generations. When Edward Shippen died in 1712, he left an impressive legacy in terms of his mercantile and landed wealth, the extended family network, and "symbolic estate."

Within a short period of time the original family structure collapsed. Death soon reduced the second generation to only one surviving heir, Joseph Shippen. When he left the Society of Friends, he returned the family to the status of "outsiders." His efforts as a merchant and a large inherited fortune enabled him to retire as a country gentleman at age thirty-seven. In order to sustain this position, however, Joseph Shippen retained tight control over his assets. Although his only daughter married a wealthy merchant and his eldest son was apprenticed to James Logan, a successful merchant and secretary of the province, Joseph exerted little effort to forward the careers of his children and almost no effort to cause the family to function as an extended family. Though the oldest living Shippen in America until his death in 1741, he scarcely can be described as a powerful patriarch. His eldest and youngest sons tended to reject the example he provided. Both displayed more the character of Edward I, their grandfather. They were ambitious and strongly influenced by religious enthusiasm. Only Joseph I's namesake approved his father's actions and tried to repeat them.

The third generation began their adult lives as heads of essentially nuclear families and as "outsiders." Edward III, Joseph II, and Charles Willing were merchants, William II, the youngest son, an apothecary. By mid-century a dramatic transformation occurred. Although they began their careers in a period of relative economic stagnation, hard work, grasping opportunities, and changes in the colony made them all successful. As Pennsylvania grew rapidly in size after 1740, their inherited land began to provide additional income, and as the colony lost its predominantly Quaker composition, the Shippens returned to the condition of "insiders." All three brothers and Charles Willing gained political offices as well as fortunes of varying sizes. After mid-century, one of the most significant changes in the family occurred. Because of the efforts of the brothers, their families began to function as an extended family in politics, economic concerns, and the promotion of members of the fourth and fifth generations. This was particularly true of the Edward III and William II branches, and the reason stemmed from the closer personal relationship between the eldest and youngest brother.

Many Shippens enjoyed longevity and rather long marriages; hence intergenerational activities increased after mid-century. Support, whether material or emotional, came from grandparents, parents, siblings, spouses, and other family connections. In an atmosphere of strong personal relationships, deep feelings about love, children, and death became typical. Interpersonal relationships also helped mold personalities.

During the decades approaching the Revolution the Shippens reached the zenith of their power. To a remarkable degree this resulted from the workings of the extended family. Because of the extended family and the acceptance of familial duties, almost every male member of the fourth generation received a college education and most became professionals. Women were not forgotten, although their training was less extensive. Furthermore, the involvement of kinsmen in the training and advancement of members of the family became increasingly important. The extended family not only advanced its members; it also protected them from problems or dangers such as the loss of offices or the worst effects of bankruptcy. The working of the family made a deep impression on all associated with it. All Shippens remained constantly aware of their existence within a family environment. The family figured in most major decisions of life, and individual Shippens cannot be comprehended unless they are perceived in this broader context.

The Shippen family's significance lay not only in its importance to members of the kinship network, but also in its impact on the society in which it functioned. During the 1760s and 1770s many colonists perceived dangerous trends in their society which seemed omens of disaster. Their thoughts focused not simply upon parliamentary measures, but also upon developments in the colonies as well. Love of luxury and a lust for power epitomized what was going wrong. The Shippens' life style and functioning as a family in politics provided concrete substantiation of a need for alarm and action. The radicals in Pennsylvania indicated in newspapers and elsewhere a desire to change basic characteristics of provincial society and the way it functioned. The Constitution of 1776 reads like an indictment of the nepotism of the Shippens and their kinsmen as well as a criticism of their entire way of life.

Until 1776 all Shippens looked adversely upon British measures which contributed to the imperial crisis. When they looked at colonial society, only William II perceived the view from the outside and ardently supported the Revolution. The others opposed independence but remained neutral or acted as opportunists. No Shippen was a Tory. Despite differences of opinion, all branches of the family remained on cordial terms. One reason for this is that the family came first in the minds of most of these people raised in the tradition of "the private city." This in no way implies the Revolution was not a revolution for the Shippens. Though none of their property was confiscated, the loss of offices irreparably cast the Shippens from their prewar position. Neither the rise of the William II branch nor the partial recovery by the Edward III branch substantiates the idea that the Revolution simply confirmed past experiences. In a broader view, because the power which the Shippens, Allens, Francises, and other kinsmen wielded before the war ceased and was not immediately replaced by another extensive family network by their descendants or their rivals, the revolution in Pennsylvania brought about a meaningful change.

At the same time the family continued many functions on through and after the Revolution. It rallied to protect William Shippen III from conviction for negligence and speculation while director-general of the Continental Medical Department, and tried unsuccessfully to prevent the exile of Peggy Shippen Arnold after the discovery of her husband's treason. After the war, however, indications that a restructuring of the family would occur became evident. In part the modification seemed likely even without the Revolution, but that event had a significant impact as well. The termination of the Joseph II branch of the family, the death of Edward III (patriarch of the primary prewar branch), and the geographical dispersion of the fifth generation indicated the family tree was being pruned and that new shoots would provide new variations.

As far as the extended family was concerned, it did not cease. Although serious modifications occurred, it still linked all Shippens to a certain degree. Because the Shippens remained very much aware of the family's "symbolic estate," which encompassed several generations operating through more than a century of time, the likelihood of the eradication of the extended family at the end of the eighteenth century seemed remote. Within the larger kinship network, subsidiary ones functioned. The operation of the William II branch as an extended family, which involved the third, fourth, fifth, and even sixth generations reveals many unpleasant aspects of the extended family. While the Edward III branch usually succeeded in making the extended family function for the benefit, advancement, and protection of its members, this other branch realized those benefits to a lesser degree and experienced constricting, stifling, and destructive effects.

During the course of research on the Shippen family, considerable evidence emerged to demonstrate that many people and events in the colonial and Revolutionary era can be understood only in the context of the family. Reconstruction of families in their entirety, regardless of the public reputation of particular members, combined with prosopographic treatment of such people will further enhance our knowledge. What makes this a particularly delightful and fascinating process is that, by dealing with all members of a family or kinship group, we discover a huge range of human activity. Analysis of families provides a wealth of new information regarding the structure of the family and how it functioned. That and probing the external relations of the family, its economic base, and life style reveal significant insights into the economic, social, and political life of early America which ordinarily might elude us. Viewing the Shippens across five generations provides an escape from untested conventional wisdom about families and the early American era. The complexity of the past reemerges, and our understanding of it deepens.

Notes

CHAPTER I

1. Edward N. Saveth, "The American Patrician Class: A Field for Research," in *Kinship and Family Organization,* ed. Bernard Farber (New York, 1966), pp. 257–268; Bernard Bailyn, "The Beekmans of New York: Trade, Politics, and Families, A Review Article," *William and Mary Quarterly,* 3d ser., XIV, no. 4 (October 1957), p. 608; William Goode, *World Revolution and Family Patterns* (New York, 1963); Patricia Joan Gordon, "The Livingston Family of New York, 1675–1860: Kinship and Class" (Ph.D. dissertation, Columbia University, 1959); Bernard Farber, *Kinship and Class: A Midwestern Study* (New York, 1971).

2. Bernard Bailyn, *Education and the Forming of American Society: Needs and Opportunities for Study* (New York, 1960), p. 25. *Ibid.,* pp. 16, 24; Oscar Handlin, *The Uprooted: The Epic Story of the Great Migration That Made the American People* (New York, 1951), pp. 4, 6, 9.

3. John Demos, "Families in Colonial Bristol, Rhode Island: An Exercise in Historical Demography," *William and Mary Quarterly,* 3d ser., XXV, no. 1 (January 1968), p. 40. In this regard, Michael Gordon, a sociologist at the University of Connecticut, recently rejected the notion that every household with an additional kinsman (such as a maiden aunt) was necessarily an extended family. See Michael Gordon's review of Richard Sennett's *Families against the City* (Cambridge, Mass., 1970), in *Journal of Marriage and the Family,* vol. 33, no. 2 (May 1971), 391–392.

4. Philip J. Greven, Jr., *Four Generations: Population, Land, and Family in Colonial Andover, Massachusetts* (Ithaca, 1970).

5. For the definition of these terms in sociology and the debate over the extended family, see Goode's *World Revolution and Family Patterns.*

6. Edmund S. Morgan, *The Puritan Family: Religion and Domestic Relations in Seventeenth-Century New England* (Boston, 1944); John J.

Waters, *The Otis Family in Provincial and Revolutionary Massachusetts* (Chapel Hill, 1968); Alice P. Kenney, *The Gansevoorts of Albany: Dutch Patricians in the Upper Hudson Valley* (Syracuse, 1969); James B. Hedges, *The Browns of Providence Plantations: Colonial Years* (Cambridge, 1952); Richard S. Dunn, *Puritans and Yankees: The Winthrop Dynasty of New England, 1630–1717* (Princeton, 1962); Aubrey C. Land, *The Dulanys of Maryland: A Biographical Study of Daniel Dulany, the Elder (1685–1753) and Daniel Dulany, the Younger (1722–1797)* (Baltimore, 1955).

7. For an enlightening discussion of prosopography, see Lawrence Stone, "Prosopography," *Daedalus,* vol. 100, no. 1 (Fall 1971), pp. 46–79.

8. For a fuller treatment of "the symbolic family estate," see chapter five of Farber's *Kinship and Class.*

9. The ordinal designations used in this study and their eighteenth-century equivalents are given in the appendix. Some authors who deal with the Shippens have adopted another system of identification which seems an unsatisfactory alternative. In it, for example, "Edward Shippen, Sr." is always referred to as "Edward Shippen of Lancaster" while his son "Edward Shippen, Jr." is always "Chief Justice Edward Shippen," and "Joseph Shippen, Jr." is "Colonel Joseph Shippen." This is misleading and conjures up erroneous impressions. "Edward Shippen of Lancaster" spent less than half his life at Lancaster; his son Edward was chief justice of Pennsylvania for fifteen years but only at the end of his life, and "Colonel Joseph Shippen" was many things besides a colonel; he served in the military only about three or four years.

10. When Lester J. Cappon pointed out the importance of local studies in "The Colonial Period Reexamined" (in *Research Opportunities in American Cultural History,* ed. John Francis McDermott, [Lexington, 1961], p. 6), he noted the necessity for the historian to understand "the provenance of the records and the character of the people whose thoughts and actions are recorded in them. Here are cultural data on individual persons and on family kinships which are easily lost in the impersonal tabulations and correlations of statistical data."

11. For example, see Jackson Turner Main, *The Social Structure of Revolutionary America* (Princeton, 1966). In regard to geographic mobility, Main equates movement out of an area with upward economic mobility. The reverse was usually the case with the Shippens, their kinsmen, and many others in Pennsylvania. Living in the country definitely reduced the expenses for members of the upper ranks of society. Jessie Lemisch argues in "The American Revolution Seen from the Bottom Up" (in *Towards a New Past: Dissenting Essays in American History* [New York, 1969], p. 7), "Geographic mobility was extremely high among the poor." An under-

standing of the Shippen family and the way it operated also calls into question the practice of equating increases in taxable estates with general economic opportunities in the province. Even if the individual became richer, the additional wealth could have come from an inheritance.

12. Saveth, "American Patrician Class," p. 26.

CHAPTER II

1. John W. Jordan, ed., *Colonial and Revolutionary Families of Pennsylvania* (3 vols., New York, 1911), vol. I, pp. 96–109; Charles P. Keith, *Provincial Councillors of Pennsylvania* (Philadelphia, 1883), pp. 46–47; Baptismal, marriage, and burial records of the Shippens transcribed from the Parish Register of Monk Fryston in the Diocese of York and the County of York, 1538–1624, HSP.

2. Joseph Shippen, genealogical entries in his Bible, in Thomas Balch, *Letters and Papers relating to Pennsylvania* (5 vols., private printing, Philadelphia, 1855), p. 6.

3. Jordan, *Families*, vol. I, pp. 97–99.

4. *Ibid.*, pp. 99–101; Betsy Copping Corner, *William Shippen, Jr., Pioneer in American Medical Education: A Biographical Essay* (Philadelphia, 1951), p. 5; Balch, *Letters relating to Pennsylvania*, p. 24; Carl Bridenbaugh, *Cities in the Wilderness: The First Century of Urban Life in America, 1625–1742* (New York, 1962), p. 6.

5. Richard T. Vann's "Nurture and Conversion in the Early Quaker Family" (*Journal of Marriage and the Family*, vol. 31, no. 4 [November 1969], 639–643) is particularly helpful for explaining Edward Shippen's conversion to the Society of Friends. Vann finds that the overwhelming majority of early converts to Quakerism were younger sons of mobile families. He explains that, for younger sons, "there were substantial discontinuities in growing up and when children had to improvise their occupations and to some extent their lives, religious conversion, as a psychological drama of alienation from and then reconciliation to a loving, if stern, father, might help make superior sense of life." Although the Shippen family in England was not mobile, Edward's move from England to Boston makes his experience consistent with Vann's findings.

6. [Governor] Coddington [of Rhode Island] to ———, Boston, 16 August 1677, quoted in Balch, *Letters relating to Pennsylvania*, vol. I, p. 24; Thomas Story, *A Journal of the Life of Thomas Story . . .* (London, 1718), pp. 195–196. For treatment of the persecution of Quakers in Massachusetts see Brooks Adams, *The Emancipation of Massachusetts: The Dream and the Reality* (Boston, 1962, c. 1887), chap. five, especially pp.

198–248 and Rufus Jones, *The Quakers in the American Colonies* (New York, 1966, c. 1911), bk. one, chap. five. Adams and Jones fail to mention Edward Shippen.

7. Joseph Shippen's genealogical entries in his Bible, quoted in Balch, *Letters relating to Pennsylvania,* vol. I, p. 11.

8. Bernard and Lotte Bailyn, *Massachusetts Shipping, 1697–1714: A Statistical Study* (Cambridge, Mass., 1959), pp. 38, 73, 132–133; Edward Shippen to Jonathan Dickinson, Philadelphia, 21 6 Month 1699, R. R. Logan Collection, HSP.

9. Deed, Hannah Hull to Edward Shippen, 18 January 1676, *Suffolk Deeds* (14 vols., Boston, 1880–1906), vol. IX, pp. 449–450.

10. Deed, Edward Shippen to Samuel Eells, 11 March 1679[80], *Suffolk Deeds,* vol. XI, p. 297. Deed, Thomas and Abigail Bingley to Edward Shippen, 28 December 1677; Deed, Anne Perry to Edward Shippen, 19 December 1679; Deed, John Wall to Edward Shippen, 3 July 1679, *Suffolk Deeds,* vol. X, p. 241; vol. XI, pp. 259, 195.

11. Deed, Joshua Scottow to Edward Shippen, 27 June 1681, *Suffolk Deeds,* vol. XII, p. 78.

12. Deed, Simeon Stoddard to Edward Shippen, 5 May 1682; Deed, Jonathan Jackson to Edward Shippen, 15 March 1683/4; Deed, Benjamin Davis to Edward Shippen, 9 June 1684, Samuel White to Edward Shippen, 12 July 1684, *Suffolk Deeds,* vol. XII, p. 187; vol. XIII, pp. 95, 135, 155.

13. Edward Shippen's petition to Sir Edmund Andros, 12 September 1687, in Balch, *Letters relating to Pennsylvania,* vol. I, pp. 28–29.

14. *Ibid.,* p. 24; Edward Shippen [III] to John White, Chester, 9 7bre 1741, Maria Dickinson Logan Papers, HSP; *Appleton's Cyclopaedia of American Biography,* ed. James Grant Wilson and John Fiske (6 vols., New York, 1894), vol. V, p. 511.

15. Bernard Bailyn, *New England Merchants in the Seventeenth Century* (New York, 1964), p. 135.

16. *Ibid.,* pp. 108, 111, 112, 135, 137, 168, 190.

17. Rebekah Richardson to Anthony Morris, New York, 17th of ——— Month 1688, Francis Richardson Letterbook, 1681–1688, HSP.

18. The last ten pages of Francis Richardson's Letterbook, 1681–1688 at the Historical Society of Pennsylvania, contain letters of Rebekah Richardson written "After ye decease of my Husband" concerning unfinished merchant business of her husband. They include a reference to "Edward Shipin in Boston."

19. Jordan, *Families,* vol. I, p. 49. The 1689 marriage of Edward and Rebekah Shippen in Rhode Island is recorded in the Philadelphia

Monthly Meeting's Book of Marriages, Arch Street Meeting House, Philadelphia.

20. A brief sketch of Anthony Morris appears in Jordan, *Families,* vol. I, pp. 49–50. It seems that many early settlers of Pennsylvania remarried shortly after the death of their spouse. For example, Morris married four times; the last three unions took place within a year or two of the decease of his spouse.

21. Balch, *Letters relating to Pennsylvania,* vol. I, p. 29. *Appleton's Cyclopaedia,* vol. V, p. 511, agrees that "Mr. Shippen was either banished or driven to take refuge in Philadelphia." James Thatcher, *American Medical Biography,* with a new Introduction and Bibliography by Whitfield J. Bell, Jr. (2 vols., New York, 1966, c. 1828), vol. II, p. 80, claims that Shippen was driven from England and Boston because he was a Quaker. Carl Bridenbaugh's *Cities in the Wilderness,* p. 103, indicates that after 1677 Quakers enjoyed immunity in Boston. Brooks Adams's *Emancipation of Massachusetts* concurs with Bridenbaugh.

22. For a fuller discussion of the concept of insiders and outsiders see N. Elias and J. L. Scotson, *The Established and the Outsiders: A Sociological Enquiry into Community Problems* (London, 1965), and W. M. Williams's *Gosforth: The Sociology of an English Village* (Glencoe, Ill., 1956) and *A West Country Village, Ashworthy: Family, Kinship, and Land* (London, 1963).

23. Bridenbaugh, *Cities in the Wilderness,* p. 6; John J. Walters, Jr., *The Otis Family in Provincial and Revolutionary Massachusetts* (Chapel Hill, 1966), p. 50; James A. Henretta, "Economic Development and Social Structure in Colonial Boston," *William and Mary Quarterly,* 3d ser., vol. XXII, no. 1 (January 1965), pp. 75–92, especially pp. 79–80.

24. Frederick B. Tolles, *Meeting House and Counting House: The Quaker Merchants of Colonial Philadelphia, 1682–1763* (New York, 1963), pp. 38–40; Gary Nash, *Quakers and Politics, Pennsylvania, 1681–1726* (Princeton, 1968), p. 11.

25. Nash, *Quakers and Politics,* p. 52.

26. *Ibid.,* p. 26; also pp. 3, 15–16, 49–50; Edwin B. Bronner, *William Penn's "Holy Experiment": The Founding of Pennsylvania, 1681–1701* (Philadelphia, 1962), pp. 21, 27–28, 31–32, 55, 77–86.

27. Nash, *Quakers and Politics,* pp. 49–56, 277–286; Tolles, *Meeting House and Counting House,* pp. 116–117.

28. Nash, *Quakers and Politics,* p. 280; List of Taxables, Pennsylvania, 1693, HSP. Nash's observations on the first proprietary rent roll of 1689 at the Historical Society of Pennsylvania (*Quakers and Politics,* p. 53) must

be handled with care. Less than 600 names appear on this list, yet Pennsylvania population was about 8,000. Families were not large enough to account for the discrepancy; hence inhabitants other than wives and dependent children were omitted from the compilation which Nash analyzed. There are also some problems with his analysis of Philadelphia's tax structure. He deals with Philadelphia city and county as a unit. Although many decades later they became almost synonymous, at this time the city was a town in whose inhabitants lived in reasonably close proximity to one another; Philadelphia county was still farmland. This distinction suggests that the social structure of Philadelphia city may have been slightly more stratified than Nash admits; nevertheless, this slight qualification does not appreciably alter his conclusion, for the range of wealth on the list is not great.

29. Nash, *Quakers and Politics*, p. 181.

30. *Ibid.*, pp. 283–285.

31. *Ibid.*, pp. 285–286; also pp. 278, 280–284.

32. Because the Morrises and Shippens lived within short walking distance of each other, there was no need for written correspondence. An indication of the close relationship exists in Mary Morris's will in which the widow names "my brother Edward Shippen" executor of her estate. Philadelphia Will Book A, p. 516, No. 220, 1699, Philadelphia Recorder of Wills.

33. The proprietor, William Penn, seems an exception to this statement, yet because he did not settle permanently in Pennsylvania the qualification lacks relevance. Some idea of the immensity of £10,000 sterling may be gained by realizing that the annual British imports to the entire colony of of Pennsylvania from 1700 to 1710 averaged only £9,687 (Nash, *Quakers and Politics*, p. 320). See also United States Bureau of the Census, *Historical Statistics of the United States, Colonial Times to 1957* (Washington, 1960), p. 757, Robert Proud, *History of Pennsylvania, from . . . 1681, till after the Year 1742* (2 vols., Philadelphia, 1797–98), vol. 1, pp. 264–265, 271; Arthur L. Jensen, *Maritime Commerce of Philadelphia* (Madison, Wis.: 1963), pp. 292–296.

34. Nash, *Quakers and Politics*, pp. 282–284.

35. Keith, *Chronicles of Pennsylvania from the English Revolution to the Peace of Aix-la-Chapelle, 1688–1748* (Freeport, N.Y., 1969 c. 1917), vol. I, p. 139, gives no evidence for his assertion that Shippen was hardly exalted above ordinary men. The inventories of estates which suggest a contrary opinion can be consulted conveniently at the Genealogical Society of Pennsylvania where photographic reproductions exist in bound volumes.

The originals are available at the records office of the Recorder of Wills in the Philadelphia City Hall Annex, however the Annex has neither the means nor the inclination to facilitate examination of these records.

36. Nash, *Quakers and Politics,* p. 53.

37. Deed, Gunner Swenson to Edward Shippen, 29 September 1694, Miscellaneous Manuscripts, Brayton Collection, HSP. Patent, William Penn to Edward Shippen, 28 January 1693; Patent, William Penn to Edward Shippen, 12 October 1701, Annie Hare Powel Brayton Collection, Deeds, 1681–1701 (referred to in card catalog as Parchment, Brayton Collection), HSP; Balch, *Letters relating to Pennsylvania,* vol. I, pp. 28–29.

38. W. E. Horner, "Address," in Samuel Hazard, *Register of Pennsylvania* (16 vols., Philadelphia, 1834–1836), vol. X, p. 66, writes of Shippen that "he was invited by Penn."

39. Edward Shippen to Jonathan Dickinson (in Jamaica), Philadelphia, 21 6 Month 1699, R. R. Logan Collection, HSP.

40. Edward Shippen, Jr., Letterbook, 1700–1701, Etting Papers, Miscellaneous Manuscripts, vol. I, p. 36, HSP.

41. See especially Edward Shippen [Jr.] to John Crouch, Philadelphia, Tenth Month 30, 1700, Edward Shippen, Jr., Letterbook, 1700–1701, Etting Papers, Miscellaneous Manuscripts, vol. I, p. 36, HSP.

42. Edward Shippen [Jr.] to John Crouch, Philadelphia, Ninth Month 21 1700; Edward Shippen [Jr.] and Joseph Shippen to John Eccleston, Philadelphia, 22 Ninth Month 1700, Edward Shippen, Jr., Letterbook, Etting Papers, Miscellaneous Manuscripts, vol. I, p. 36, HSP.

43. Deed, Enoch Yardley to Edward Shippen, 21 September 1696; Patent, William Penn to Edward Shippen, 2 October 1701; Patent, William Penn to Edward Shippen, 24 October 1701, Brayton Collection, Deeds, 1681–1701, HSP; Deed, ——— to Edward Shippen, 1701, Pemberton Manuscripts, p. 24, Library Company of Philadelphia; Deed, John Goodson to Edward Shippen, 3 March 1703, Brayton Collection, Deeds, HSP.

44. Gabriel Thomas, *An Historical and Geographical Account of Pennsylvania, and of West New Jersey in America* (London, 1698), p. 43.

45. Balch, *Letters relating to Pennsylvania,* vol. I, p. 43; John F. Watson, *Annals of Philadelphia and Pennsylvania, in the Olden Time* (2 vols., Philadelphia, 1857), vol. I, p. 368.

46. Photographs and engraved reproductions of Edward Shippen's portrait are in a collection of Shippen portraits, Simpson Plates, No. 207, and Gratz Collection, Mayors of Philadelphia, Case 3, Box 9, at the Historical Society of Pennsylvania.

47. "A Paper from our Yearly Meeting at Burlington '98. A true Copy

taken by Ann Shippen," 21 April 1698, Gratz Collection, Quakers, Case 14, Box 1, under Burlington, HSP.

48. Watson, *Annals of Philadelphia and Pennsylvania in the Olden Time* (2 vols., Philadelphia, 1857), vol. I, p. 39. Tolles, *Meeting House and Counting House,* pp. 123–132, discusses the Quaker attraction for "the best sort, but plain"; the particular phrase was used by John Reynell in a letter of 25 November 1738 to Daniel Flexney, Reynell Letterbook, 1738–1741, HSP.

49. Keith, *Chronicles of Pennsylvania,* vol. 1, p. 47. The Provincial Council was an elective body from 1682 to 1692; it became an appointive body from 1692 to 1694 when Pennsylvania existed as a royal colony. After that short interlude, the Council was again an elective body until the reorganization of the colony at the turn of the century. From then until the American Revolution, provincial councillors were appointed to office.

50. William Penn to ———, Philadelphia, 28 Eight Month 1701, Shippen Papers, Box 1, HSP.

51. Tolles, *Meeting House and Counting House,* p. 117.

52. Frederick B. Tolles, *James Logan and the Culture of Provincial America* (Boston, 1957), p. 26, says that Logan as secretary of the commissioners of property "was saddled with most of the work, for Shippen he soon found was 'too thronged in his own affairs,' and Owen and Story were too unworldly for such mundane business." This opinion should be temporized by acknowledging the existence of Edward Shippen's accounts of quit rents and other business of the proprietor, 1709–1712, Logan Papers, vol. 2, p. 117, HSP.

53. Keith, *Chronicles of Pennsylvania,* vol. I, pp. 87, 296; John Hill Martin, *Martin's Bench and Bar of Philadelphia* (Philadelphia, 1883), p. 166, and about a dozen manuscript collections at the Historical Society of Pennsylvania reveal Shippen's offices.

54. *Minutes of the Common Council of the City of Philadelphia, 1704–1776* (Philadelphia, 1847), begin with Edward Shippen serving as an alderman, and he appeared to vote for officers and members of the council as late as 1711. For a discussion of the function and structure of the Common Council of Philadelphia see Bridenbaugh, *Cities in the Wilderness,* p. 145 or Keith, *Chronicles of Pennsylvania,* vol. I, pp. 207, 400, 403–404, 434–435. Martin, *Martin's Bench,* p. 102.

55. Tolles, *Meeting House and Counting House,* p. 75.

56. *Ibid.,* pp. 64–65, 73, 75; Bronner, *William Penn's "Holy Experiment,"* pp. 53–54.

57. Philadelphia Monthly Meeting, Minutes, 3 Fourth Month, 2 Tenth Month, 27 Tenth Month 1695, 31 Eleventh Month 1695/96, 29 Eleventh

Month 1696, 30 Fifth Month 1697, Arch Street Meeting House, Philadelphia.

58. Philadelphia Monthly Meeting, Minutes, *passim*.

59. Jordan, *Families*, vol. I, pp. 99–100; Tolles, *Logan*, pp. 6–11, 76–77. Tolles, the noted authority on the Logan family, explodes the myth of Logan's lofty origins which Jordan among others has perpetuated. Ann Shippen's dowry is described in a deed of July 1706 from Edward Shippen to Thomas Story, Philadelphia Deed Book E.3, vol. 6, pp. 11–13, Philadelphia Recorder of Deeds. By this deed Edward Shippen, "for consideration of the Natural Love and affect[n] which he hath and Bearest unto and for the said Ann his Daughter," granted a lot 40 feet by 200 feet on Second Street, "that New Brick House Messuage or Tenement now building by the said Edward Shippen upon the hereby granted land," and use of a wharf built at the end of the lot.

60. Philadelphia Monthly Meeting, Minutes, 28 Fourth Month 1706, Arch Street Meeting House, Philadelphia.

61. Marriage Certificate of Thomas Story and Ann Shippen, 10 Fifth Month 1706, Shippen Family Papers, LC.

62. Isaac Norris to ———, 11 Fifth Month 1706, quoted in Balch, *Letters relating to Pennsylvania,* vol. I, p. 65; Balch, p. 60; Philadelphia Monthly Meeting, Minutes, 31 Third Month 1706, Women's Monthly Meeting, Minutes, 31 Third Month 1706, Arch Street Meeting House, Philadelphia; Edward Shippen et al. to David Powell, Philadelphia, 12 April 1703 (under Owen), American Physicians, Gratz Collection, Case 7, Box 32, HSP; Patent to Thomas Story, 3 Eleventh Month 1703/04, Shippen Family Papers, Box 16, LC.

63. Jordan, *Families,* vol. I, p. 100, incorrectly gives Shippen's third wife's name as Elizabeth; he also wrongly identifies Esther's first husband as Thomas James. Verification of her name and marriage to Edward Shippen appears in the Deed of Charles Jones to Edward Shippen, 3 November 1711, Miscellaneous Manuscripts, Brayton Collection, HSP. Jordan probably drew his information from Balch's *Letters relating to Pennsylvania;* Balch (p. 65) not only gives the wrong name, but also errs on the date which he reported as 1704. Because controversy surrounded Shippen's marriage in 1706, it is treated fully in the minutes of the Philadelphia Monthly Meeting, and there can be no doubt regarding when it occurred.

64. Philadelphia Monthly Meeting, Minutes, 28 Fourth Month 1706, Arch Street Meeting House, Philadelphia. William Wade Hinshaw, ed., *Encyclopedia of American Quaker Genealogy* (3 vols., Ann Arbor, 1936–1944), vol. II, p. 445, indicates that Philip and Esther James had a son Philip born in 1702. Deed, Charles Jones to Edward Shippen, 4 November

1711, Deeds, 1703–1759, Brayton Collection (referred to in card catalog as Parchment), HSP; Esther Shippen to John Branch, Philadelphia, 2 April 1714, Brayton Collection, Miscellaneous Manuscripts, HSP.

65. James Logan to William Penn, Jr., 12 August 1706, Penn-Logan book compiled by Deborah Morris Logan, HSP.

66. Women's Monthly Meeting, Minutes, 25 Eighth [month] 1706, Arch Street Meeting House, Philadelphia.

67. Philadelphia Monthly Meeting, Minutes, 29 Ninth Month 1706, Arch Street Meeting House, Philadelphia.

68. *Ibid.*, 13 Sixth Month 1706.

69. *Ibid.*, 28 First Month 1707/08. *Ibid.*, 23 Sixth Month, ——— Seventh Month, 25 Eighth Month 1706, 27 Tenth Month, 31 Eleventh Month, 28 Twelfth Month 1707; Women's Monthly Meeting, Minutes, 27 Tenth Month 1706, 26 Twelfth Month 1707/08, Arch Street Meeting House, Philadelphia. The Philadelphia Monthly Meeting refused to record this union in their Book of Marriages.

70. Thomas Murray to the Monthly Meeting of the People Call'd Quakers Held in Philadelphia, 30 Eleventh Month 1707/08, Miscellaneous Papers of the Philadelphia Monthly Meeting, 1682–1737, Arch Street Meeting House, Philadelphia.

71. Philadelphia Monthly Meeting, Minutes, 26 Tenth Month, 27 Twelfth Month 1707, 30 Fourth Month 1710, 30 Ninth Month 1711, 31 Eighth Month 1712, Arch Street Meeting House, Philadelphia; Monthly Meeting of Philadelphia to Friends in London, 25 Ninth Month 1709, under M. Lisle, Society Collection, HSP.

72. Philadelphia Common Council, *Minutes*, October 1707; Marriage Certificate of Samuel Powel and Abigail Wilcox, 19 February 1701, Marriage Certificates, Am 10155 folio, p. 42, HSP. The way in which these men were related may be ascertained by consulting the appendix for a schematic representation of the Shippen family kinship network during the first and second generations.

73. Edward Shippen et al. to [Lieutenant Governor] Charles Gookin, Esq., 12 April 1709, Documents of the Provincial Council, Large Volume, Logan Manuscripts, p. 45, HSP.

74. Philadelphia Monthly Meeting, Minutes, 26 Sixth Month, 30 September 1709, 25 Third Month 1711, 26 Seventh Month 1712, Arch Street Meeting House, Philadelphia; James Logan to Col. John French, London, 26 June 1710, MHS.

75. Keith, *Chronicles of Pennsylvania*, vol. I, pp. 150–151.

76. Edward Shippen's Will, No. 241, 1712, Philadelphia Will Book C, p. 303, Philadelphia Recorder of Wills.

77. Edward Shippen III claimed that his grandfather Edward I told "my Uncle Edwd. Shippen . . . at ye time of making his will if it was not for the aversion he always had for entailing Estates, he would entail Hillam Estate on his family." Edward Shippen [III] to John White, Chester, 9 7bre 1741, Maria Dickinson Logan Papers, HSP.

CHAPTER III

1. A comparison of the first- and second-generation Shippens with the fourth- and fifth-generation Otises produces a very close analogy. See John J. Waters, Jr., *The Otis Family in Provincial and Revolutionary Massachusetts* (Chapel Hill, 1968), especially pp. 126–131.

2. Marriage Certificate of Thomas Story and Ann Shippen, 10 Fifth Month 1706, Shippen Family Papers, LC.

3. Indenture of William Shippen to Israel Pemberton, 31 October 1723, Pemberton Manuscripts, 1660–1855, p. 28, LC.

4. *Ibid.*

5. Of Israel Pemberton's ten children, only Israel, Jr. (1715–1779), James (1723–1809), John (1727–1795), and Charles (1729–1748) reached maturity. In 1729 their ages were, respectively, fourteen, six, two, and less than one years old.

6. John W. Jordan, *Colonial and Revolutionary Families of Pennsylvania* (3 vols., New York, 1911), vol. I, pp. 288–293; William Shippen's Will, No. 174, 1730, Philadelphia Will Book E, p. 144, Philadelphia Recorder of Wills.

7. Almost nothing is known of Joseph Shippen's first wife, Abigail Grosse. Thomas Balch, *Letters and Papers relating to Pennsylvania* (5 vols., private printing, Philadelphia, 1855), vol. I, p. 66, makes the vague statement that "her connections in Boston appear to have been most respectable." Edward and Joseph Shippen developed in a manner which psychologist Stanley Schacter of Columbia University, who has studied twentieth-century American families, claims is typical of their respective birth positions. See Stanley Schacter, "Birth Order and Sociometric Choice," *Journal of Abnormal and Social Psychology,* vol. 68, no. 4 (April 1964), 453–456. Cautious support for the contention that second children are less dependent than first children appears in Robert R. Sears, "Ordinal Position in the Family as a Psychological Variable," *American Sociological Review,* vol. 15, no. 3 (June 1950), 397–401.

8. Frederick B. Tolles, *Meeting House and Counting House: The Quaker Merchants of Colonial Philadelphia, 1682–1763* (New York, 1963), pp. 119–120, indicates that "the Society of Friends itself was a highly

endogamous group. The Yearly Meeting in 1694 issued an unequivocal warning against unions with non-Friends: 'Take heed of giving your Sons and Daughters (who are Believers, and Profess, and Confess the Truth) in Marriage with Unbelievers for that was forbidden in all Ages, and was one Main Cause that brought the Wrath of God upon Old Israel.' The first book of discipline (1704) contained a distinct advice against marrying out of meeting, and the Yearly Meeting of 1712 cleared up any doubt that might have remained by providing that Friends who wedded 'out of unity' should be admonished and advised to condemn their action in a public acknowledgment; if they remain obstinate, they were disowned."

9. Edward Shippen [II]'s Will, No. 24, 1714, Philadelphia Will Book D, pp. 19–20, Philadelphia Recorder of Wills; Charles P. Keith, *The Provincial Councillors of Pennsylvania who held office between 1733 and 1776* (Philadelphia, 1883), pp. 49–50.

10. Edward Shippen's Will, No. 24, 1714, Philadelphia Will Book D, p. 19, Philadelphia Recorder of Wills; Tripartie Deed, Francis Richardson and Thomas Murray to Edward Shippen, Jr., and Samuel Preston, 30 Seventh Month 1707, Shippen Family Papers, Box 16, LC.

11. Edward Shippen [II]'s Will, No. 24, 1714, Philadelphia Will Book D, pp. 19–20, Philadelphia Recorder of Wills. Thomas Balch (*Letters and Papers Relating to Pennsylvania,* vol. 1, p. xix) claims that the "Ssariana ffibby" name in the will is Ariana Frisby, wife of James Frisby of Sassafras River, Maryland. He notes that Francina Shippen was godmother to her sister's daughter, Francina Augustina Frisby.

12. Deed, Rowland Ellis, Jr., to Thomas Story, "late of Philadelphia, now of Great Britain, gentleman," 2 April 1715, Shippen Family Papers, Box 16, LC. All subsequent references to Story indicate that he resided in England.

13. An estimate of Shippen's status in Germantown may be obtained from an analysis of the earliest known list of landholders of Philadelphia County: Landholders of Philadelphia County, 1734, Historical Society of Pennsylvania. "Joseph Shippin" of Germantown is listed, although no indication of acreage follows his name. There is no evidence that Shippen ever parted with any of his one hundred acres, hence at least as late as 1734 Joseph Shippen was one of the largest landholders in Germantown. Of the sixty-one individuals listed, no one owned more than one hundred acres, and two-thirds of the property owners held fifty acres or less.

14. Survey return for Joseph Shippen, 6 Fifth Month 1706, Shippen Family Papers, Box 15, LC; *Pennsylvania Magazine of History and Biography,* V (1881), 252, VI (1882), 15; Edward Shippen's Will, No. 241, 1712, Philadelphia Will Book C, p. 303, Philadelphia Recorder of Wills. Edward

Shippen III, Joseph's son, provides the basis for the family tradition concerning the Hillam estate in Edward Shippen [III] to John White, Chester, 9 7bre 1741, Maria Dickinson Logan Papers, HSP.

15. An engraving of Joseph Shippen's country home appears in the Boies Penrose Pictorial Philadelphia Collection, vol. 32, HSP. In it the Shippen mansion is entitled "Ye Roebuck Inn," as Joseph Shippen referred to it in his will of 1741. Although it is possible that the house was as large as it is in the undated engraving, it seems architecturally possible that the building may have been only half as large when Shippen lived there and that it was enlarged later when it became an inn. This suggestion is admittedly entirely speculative; however, it does offer an explanation of why the Shippen country home was so large and even had two front doors. Although Henry H. Glassie (*Pattern in the Material Folk Culture of the Eastern United States* [Philadelphia, 1968], pp. 58–59) indicates that some mid-Atlantic farmhouses had two front doors, he fails to make clear how early and how frequently this feature appeared in America. His two examples are of buildings in Frederick County, Maryland and near Gettysburg, Pennsylvania. Though the brick house in Maryland was apparently built with two doors, Glassie describes the stone one in Pennsylvania as "basically two houses built end to end."

16. Harry M. and Margaret B. Tinkcom and Grant Miles Simon, *Historic Germantown from the Founding to the Early Part of the Nineteenth Century, A Survey of the German Township* (Philadelphia, 1955), p. 1; James T. Lemon, "Urbanization and the Development of Eighteenth-Century Southeastern Pennsylvania and Adjacent Delaware," *William and Mary Quarterly*, 3d ser., vol. XXIV, no. 4 (October 1967), 527, 541; Francis D. Pastorius, "Positive Information from America . . . 1684," in *Narratives of Early Pennsylvania, West New Jersey, and Delaware, 1630–1707*, ed. Albert C. Myers (New York, 1912), pp. 376, 386, 390, 399, 407, 433.

17. Joseph Shippen's genealogical entries in his Bible, quoted in Balch, *Letters relating to Pennsylvania*, vol. I, p. 11. Robert Shippen was vice-chancellor of Oxford in 1723.

18. Edward and Joseph Shippen to Honored Father, London, 24 Fifth Month 1700, Edward Shippen, Jr., Letterbook, 1700–1701, Etting Papers, Miscellaneous Manuscripts, vol. I, p. 36, HSP; Balch, *Letters relating to Pennsylvania*, vol. I, p. 11.

19. H. J. Habakkuk, "England," in *The European Nobility in the Eighteenth Century: Studies of the Nobilities of the major European states in the pre-Reform Era*, ed. Albert Goodwin (New York, 1967), pp. 13, 19. Habakkuk asserts that it was "extremely rare for a younger son of a peer to go into trade. . . . It was only among the gentry with large families that

trade was at all a common occupation for a younger son." In this regard the Shippens did not resemble the British peerage; certain other characteristics of the family, such as the fact that *all* the sons went into trade or business of some kind, seem to set them apart from the English gentry as well.

20. Joseph Shippen described himself as a "gentleman" in the following documents: Obligation, Joseph Shippen to Humphrey Morrey, 3 May 1721, Shippen Papers, Box 1, HSP; Deed, Joseph Shippen to William Shippen [II], 4 November 1738; Deed, Joseph Shippen to Edward [III], Joseph [II], and William [II] Shippen, 27 February 1740, Shippen Family Papers, Box 16, LC; Joseph Shippen to William Shippen [II], 13 September 1740, Shippen Family Papers, Box 3, LC.

21. *The European Nobility of the Eighteenth Century,* ed. Albert Goodwin, is useful for providing a comparative view of the status and influence of the aristocracies of England, France, Spain, Lombardy, Prussia, Austria, Hungary, Sweden, Poland, and Russia. It also facilitates comprehension of the degree to which the Shippen family resembled families of the European aristocracies.

22. Tolles, *Meeting House and Counting House,* pp. 230–238. Tolles indicates that although Quaker tribalism became particularly intense by mid-century when the Quakers conceived of themselves as a threatened minority, "the notion of being a 'peculiar people' had never been completely foreign to the Philadelphia Quaker mind." By 1702 the Quakers were already in a minority; by 1750 they represented about twenty-five percent of the population of Philadelphia, and the Quaker historian, Robert Proud (*The History of Pennsylvania in North America,* 2 vols., Philadelphia, 1797–1798, vol. II, p. 339) estimated that by 1770 the Quakers comprised only one-seventh of the total. Despite the relative decline, Quakers controlled much of Philadelphia and Pennsylvania life until the late 1750s. The end of that decade not only marked the end of a political era in Pennsylvania but also "the beginning of a thoroughgoing 'reformation' in the Society of Friends," in which they generally turned inward to cultivate "the inner plantation." Minutes of the Meeting of Friends at Germantown are not at the Arch Street Meeting House in Philadelphia, nor at the Friends Historical Library at Swarthmore College. Frederick Tolles (head of the Friends Historical Library) and Willman Spawn (who has the most thorough knowledge of the collections at the Arch Street Meeting House) and others who have extensive knowledge of Quaker sources believe that the records of the Germantown meeting were lost long ago.

23. Jordan, *Families,* vol. I, p. 101; Obligation, Joseph Shippen to Humphrey Morrey, 3 May 1721, Shippen Papers, Box 1, HSP.

24. Obligation, Joseph Shippen to Humphrey Morrey, 3 May 1721, Shippen Papers, Box 1, HSP.

25. Alexander Grant to Joseph Shippen, Salem, 30 9 br. 1721, Shippen Papers, vol. 15, p. 1, HSP.

26. Jerry Frost, "Quaker Families in Colonial America" (Ph.D. dissertation, University of Wisconsin, 1968), *passim.* Defiance of Quaker mores increased considerably after 1720. For example, Tolles, *Meeting House and Counting House,* p. 233, indicates that after 1720 the number of Friends disowned for marrying out of meeting rose markedly.

27. Edward Shippen [III] to Sally Plumley, Boston, 3 August 1725, Shippen, Balch Papers, vol. I, p. 9, HSP.

28. *Ibid.* During the eighteenth century, people commonly used the term "mother-in-law" or "son-in-law" to refer to people called "stepmother" or "stepson" in modern terminology.

29. Edward Shippen to Miss Plumley, Boston, 9 August 1725, in Balch, *Letters relating to Pennsylvania,* vol. I, pp. 66–69.

30. *Ibid.*

31. James Logan to William Penn, Jr., 12 August 1706, Penn-Logan book, compiled by Deborah Morris Logan, HSP; Esther Shippen's Will, No. 326, 1724, Philadelphia Will Book D, p. 407. The catalog for the Library Company of Philadelphia indicates that the inventory and appraisement of the estate of Esther Shippen, 1724, is in the Powel Family Papers, 1723–1853. A thorough search of that collection in July 1970 did not uncover any papers concerning Esther Shippen. Esther Shippen's will makes her dislike of Joseph Shippen obvious. She left the bulk of her estate to her son William Shippen; she divided two thousand acres in Pennsylvania and forty acres in Blockley township, Philadelphia County among Joseph's sons Edward III and Joseph II, and Edward II's daughter Margaret. Esther also made bequests to her sister-in-law Ann Wilcox and her cousin Sarah Warren. Although even a daughter of Esther Shippen's husband by a former wife received a bequest of £50, Joseph Shippen received nothing at all.

32. Lemon, "Urbanization and the Development of Eighteenth-Century Southeastern Pennsylvania and Adjacent Delaware," pp. 505–508, 541–542; Evarts B. Greene and Virginia D. Harrington, *American Population before the Federal Census of 1790* (New York, 1932), p. 114; Carl Bridenbaugh, *Cities in the Wilderness: The First Century of Urban Life in America, 1625–1742* (New York, 1964), pp. 143, 303.

33. Lemon, "Urbanization and the Development of Eighteenth-Century Southeastern Pennsylvania and Adjacent Delaware," p. 505.

34. Governor Fletcher to the Board of Trade, 1696, *Documents Relative to the Colonial History of the State of New York,* ed. E. B. O'Callaghan and Berthold Fernow (15 vols., Albany, 1856–1887), vol. IV, p. 159.

35. *Pennsylvania Gazette,* 18 Twelfth Month 1728.

36. Bridenbaugh (*Cities in Wilderness,* p. 175) believes that "the five years following 1715 saw a gradual recovery from this temporary [economic] setback, and by the end of the period [three decades following 1690] all five towns were facing a long era of peace and thriving trade." This generalization crumbles when applied to Philadelphia. Nash, *Quakers and Politics,* pp. 56–57, 320–321; Frederick Tolles, *James Logan and the Culture of Provincial America* (Boston, 1957), pp. 16–17, 24, 118–119; Lemon, "Urbanization and Development of Eighteenth-Century Southeastern Pennsylvania and Adjacent Delaware," pp. 505–506, 542; Arthur L. Jensen, *The Maritime Commerce of Colonial Philadelphia* (Madison, 1963), pp. 2–40.

37. Grantee Index, Philadelphia Recorder of Deeds; Receipt for ground rent, Joseph Shippen to Abraham Carlisle (Kerlyle), 15 June 1726, Shippen Papers, Balch Papers, vol. I, p. 10, HSP; John Daly and Allen Weinberg, *Genealogy of Philadelphia County Subdivisions* (Philadelphia, 1966), p. 56. Philadelphia was divided into wards in 1705, the boundaries of which did not change until 1785. The first division indicates population was densest in High Street, Chestnut, and Walnut wards (three city squares). In any case eight of the original ten wards were located between Walnut Street and Mulberry (Arch) Street. The area above Seventh Street was undivided and largely undeveloped until after the American Revolution.

38. Joseph Shippen's Will, No. 196, 1741, Philadelphia Will Book F, p. 219, Philadelphia Recorder of Wills; Notice of Public Vendue of a lot on Second Street, being part of the estate of Edward Shippen, deceased, to [Charles] Plumsted, 15 August 1730, Brayton Collection, Miscellaneous Manuscripts, 1683–1799, HSP. Some papers concerning the estate of Humphrey Morrey are scattered throughout the Shippen Papers, vol. 27, HSP.

39. Copy of Deed, Andrew Hamilton to Edward Shippen, 11 September 1734, Shippen Papers, vol. 15, p. 17, HSP; Deed, Andrew Hamilton to Edward Shippen [III], 1734, Society Miscellaneous Collection, under Andrew Hamilton, HSP; Perqeomink Mine account of dividends paid to Edward Shippen [III], 1734–1740, Shippen Papers, vol. 27, p. 110, HSP.

40. *American Weekly Mercury,* 19–26 June 1729.

41. Joseph Shippen to Edward Shippen [III], 15 July 1740, Balch, *Letters relating to Pennsylvania,* vol. I, p. 70.

42. Frequently, throughout their adult lives, Edward III and William II condemned luxury and idleness. Both praised the virtues of thrift, frugality, and strong religious convictions. They also made strenuous efforts to provide for the advancement of their children. In short, their actions often implied criticism of the role which their father had chosen in life. Edward III expressed the resentment succinctly when he confided to his son, "I have almost gone through the World & have gained a little experience by my own Mistakes and Blunders, having had no Friends to advise me, as your Brother and Sister have. . . . You are not able to conceive without great Consideration, the unspeakable Advantage of having such a Bosom friend, that always has & always will, make your happiness his Study." Edward Shippen [III] to Dear son [Edward Shippen IV], Lancaster, 20 March 1754, Shippen Papers, vol. 11, p. 4, HSP. The lives of Edward III and William II indicate both were highly motivated; in part this motivation is indirect evidence of their relationship with their father. Russell R. Dynes, Alfred C. Clarke, and Simon Dinitz ("Levels of Occupational Aspiration: Some Aspects of Family Experience as a Variable," *American Sociological Review,* vol. 21, no. 2 [April 1956], 212–215) find that unsatisfactory interpersonal relationships in the family were significantly related to high aspirational levels and satisfactory relationships were related to lower aspirational levels. Joseph Shippen II, who emulated his father by retiring to the country to become a gentleman, presumably had a better relationship with his father and was less ambitious than his brothers.

43. Notice of Public Vendue of lot on Second Street, being part of the estate of Edward Shippen, deceased, 15 August 1730, Brayton Collection, Miscellaneous Manuscripts, 1683–1799, HSP.

44. Jordan, *Families,* vol. I, pp. 101, 123–131; Christ Church, Marriages, 1709–1810, Collections of the Genealogical Society of Pennsylvania, vol. 179, p. 4063.

45. Tolles, *Logan,* pp. 13, 28, 77, 139.

46. *Dictionary of American Biography,* ed. Allen Johnson and Dumas Malone (22 vols., New York, 1928–1944), vol. IV, pp. 3–4; autobiographical sketch of James Logan in A. C. Myers, *Immigration of Irish Quakers into Pennsylvania, 1682–1750* (Swarthmore, 1902), pp. 238–240; Tolles, *Logan, passim.*

47. James Logan to J. S. Cardel, Stenton, 15 March 1731/32, Jonathan Dickinson Letterbook, 1698–1701/James Logan Letterbook, 1731–1732, 1741–1742, p. 43, Maria Dickinson Logan Collection, HSP.

48. James Logan to Sa[muel] Storke, Pennsylvania, 15 June 1732, Jonathan Dickinson Letterbook, 1698–1701/James Logan Letterbook, 1731–1732, 1741–1742, p. 67, Maria Dickinson Logan Collection, HSP.

49. Tolles, *Logan,* pp. 146–147; Power of Attorney, James Logan to Edward Shippen [III], Philadelphia, 24 June 1730, Logan Papers, vol. I, p. 95, HSP. A fuller account of the Logan-Shippen partnership will be given in chapter four.

50. Joseph Shippen [II] to Dear Brother [Edward Shippen III], South Carolina, 24 February 1727/28; Barbados, 20 May 1733; Joseph Shippen [II] to Brother Ned [Edward Shippen III], London, 3 February 1737/38, Shippen Papers, vol. I, pp. 17, 33, 41, HSP; Christ Church, Baptisms, 1709–1768, Collections of the Genealogical Society of Pennsylvania, vol. 102, p. 218.

51. James Thatcher, *American Medical Biography,* with a new Introduction and Bibliography by Whitfield J. Bell, Jr. (2 vols., New York, 1966), vol. II, pp. 80–82. Jordan, *Families,* vol. I, p. 101.

52. Indenture, Joseph Shippen to William Shippen, 13 September 1740, Shippen Family Papers, Box 3, LC.

53. Deed, Joseph Shippen to Edward, Joseph, and William Shippen, 27 February 1740, Shippen Family Papers, Box 16, LC.

54. *Ibid.*; Deed, Joseph Shippen to William Shippen, 4 November 1738, Shippen Family Papers, Box 16, LC; Philadelphia Deed Book G, vol. 2, pp. 486, 502, Philadelphia Recorder of Deeds; Indenture, Joseph Shippen to Edward Shippen, 1738, recorded in Indenture of Release, Edward Shippen [III] to Joseph Shippen [II], 1 August 1741, Shippen Family Papers, Box 15, LC.

55. Joseph Shippen's Will, No. 196, 1741, Philadelphia Will Book F, p. 219, Philadelphia Recorder of Wills.

CHAPTER IV

1. The influence of the order of arrival in the family upon the personality of an individual is a subject which several modern psychologists and sociologists have studied. Several scholars have recognized the oldest child's need to achieve. Studies of *American Men of Science, American Men of Letters,* Rhodes Scholars, *Who's Who,* and other groups of prominent individuals reveal a significant preponderance of firstborn sons. Of course other variables must be taken into account, as they are in: Bernard C. Rosen, "Family Structure and Achievement Motivation," *American Sociological Review,* vol. 26, no. 4 (August 1961), 574–585; Stanley Schacter, "Birth Order, Eminence and Higher Education," *American Sociological Review,* vol. 28, no. 5 (October 1963), 757–768 (see especially note four); and Robert R. Sears, "Ordinal Position in the Family as a Psychological Variable," *American Sociological Review,* vol. 15, no. 3 (June 1950), 397–

401; James Walter and Nick Stinnett, "Parent-Child Relationships: A Decade Review of Research," *Journal of Marriage and the Family*, vol. 33, no. 1 (February 1971), 91–95. Also provocative are James H. S. Bossard, *Parent and Child* (Philadelphia, 1953), and James H. S. Bossard and Eleanor S. Boll, *The Large Family System* (Philadelphia, 1956), which deal with patterns in authority, affection, and personality development. To a striking degree, the personalities of these Shippens resemble the general traits that these studies attribute to a child's position in a family's sequence of births.

2. Edward Shippen [III] to Sally Plumley, Boston, 9 August 1725, Shippen, Balch Papers, vol. 1, p. 9, HSP.

3. Coseh James Halsy to Cos. Shippens, Boston, 7 February 1726, Shippen Papers, vol. 1, p. 13, HSP.

4. Joseph Shippen [II] to Dear Brother [Edward Shippen III], S[outh] C[arolina], 24 February 1727/8, Shippen Papers, vol. 1, p. 17, HSP. Humphrey Murry [Morrey] and Edward Shippen [III], Account Book, 1728, Shippen Papers, vol. 1, p. 19, HSP.

5. Francis Richardson, Jr. to Coz. Edward Shippen [III], Kent upon Delaware, 4 July 1729, Three Lower Counties, 1655–1805, Am 423, p. 155, HSP.

6. Thomas Balch, *Letters and Papers relating to Pennsylvania* (5 vols., private printing, Philadelphia, 1855), vol. 1, p. 84.

7. Frederick B. Tolles, *James Logan and the Culture of Provincial America* (Boston, 1957), pp. 188, 195; James Logan to Edward Shippen [III], 3 September 1730; James Logan to E[dward] S[hippen III], 1730, Logan Papers, vol. 1, pp. 99, 100, 101, 104, HSP; J[ames] Logan to E[dward] Shippen [III], Philadelphia, 20 September 1733, 20 August 1731, 6 December 1731; James Logan to E[dward] S[hippen III], 8 April [1732], Logan Papers, vol. 2, pp. 43, 8, 13, 24, HSP. Numerous receipts from Edward Shippen III to various fur traders may be consulted in vol. 27 of the Shippen Papers at the Historical Society of Pennsylvania. At least four dozen missives from Logan to Shippen regarding their business enterprise appear in the first seventy pages of vol. 2 of the Logan Papers at the Historical Society of Pennsylvania.

8. James Logan to E[dward] S[hippen III], 3 September 1730, Logan Papers, vol. 1, p. 97, HSP.

9. *Ibid.*

10. James Logan to E[dward] S[hippen III], Stenton, 25 March 1731, 30 July 1731, 23 August 1731, Logan Papers, vol. 1, p. 110, vol. 2, pp. 6, 9, HSP; Edward Shippen [III], Accounts of Skins, 1731, Shippen Papers, vol. 27, p. 19, HSP; Edward Shippen, Account of Sales, 1731–1732, Shippen

Papers, vol. 1, p. 29, HSP; J[ames] L[ogan] to E[dward] S[hippen III], 19 July 1733, 12 July 1734, 3 September 1730, Logan Papers, vol. 2, pp. 42, 52, vol. 1, p. 97, HSP. Edward Shippen III's receipts to various traders and notes concerning goods allotted to them provide useful details about Logan and Shippen's enterprise; they are found in volume twenty-seven of the Shippen Papers at the Historical Society of Pennsylvania.

11. James Logan to E[dward] S[hippen III], 1730, Logan Papers, vol. 1, p. 100, HSP.

12. James Logan to Edward Shippen [III], Philadelphia, 3 September 1730, Logan Papers, vol. 1, p. 98, HSP.

13. James Logan to E[dward] S[hippen III], 1 March 1731, Logan Papers, vol. 1, p. 113, HSP.

14. J[ames] L[ogan] to E[dward Shippen III], 6 December 1731, Logan Papers, vol. 2, p. 13, HSP.

15. J[ames] L[ogan] to E[dward] Shippen [III], 27 December 1731, Logan Papers, vol. 2, p. 15, HSP.

16. J[ames] L[ogan] to E[dward] Shippen [III], 5 February 1731/32, Logan Papers, vol. 2, p. 19, HSP. J[ames] L[ogan] to E[dward] Shippen [III], 15 March 1731/32, 23 April 1732, 8 June 1732, 2 February 1733/4, Logan Papers, vol. 2, pp. 23, 24, 26, 51, HSP.

17. J[ames] L[ogan] to E[dward] Shippen [III], 14 February 1731/2, 24 April 1732, 2 July 1732, 3 July 1733, 7 July 1733, Logan Papers, vol. 2, pp. 20, 25, 19, 39, 40, HSP.

18. *Pennsylvania Magazine of History and Biography*, XXIV (1900), 22, L (1926), 23–28; Deed, Andrew Hamilton to Edward Shippen [III], 1734, Society Miscellaneous Collection, under Andrew Hamilton, HSP; Copy of Deed, Andrew Hamilton to Edward Shippen [III], 1734, Shippen Papers, vol. 15, p. 17, HSP.

19. James Logan to E[dward] S[hippen III], Stenton, 4 December 1730/31, Logan Papers, vol. 1, p. 106, HSP. Esther Shippen's Will, No. 326, 1724, Philadelphia Will Book D, p. 407; William Shippen's Will, No. 174, 1730, Philadelphia Will Book E, p. 144, Philadelphia Recorder of Wills, Philadelphia City Hall Annex.

20. Edward Shippen [III] to John White, Chester, 9 7bre 1741, Maria Dickinson Logan Papers, HSP.

21. Edward Shippen's Will, No. 241, 1712, Philadelphia Will Book C, p. 303; Edward Shippen [II]'s Will, No. 24, 1714, Philadelphia Will Book D, p. 19; Inventory of the Estate of Edward Shippen [II], No. 24, 1714; Esther Shippen's Will, No. 326, 1724, Philadelphia Will Book D, p. 407; William Shippen's Will, No. 174, 1730, Philadelphia Will Book E, p. 144, Philadelphia Recorder of Wills, Philadelphia City Hall Annex.

22. Stephen Bordley to Charles Hynson, London, 23 December 1734, Stephen Bordley Letterbook, 1727–1735, p. 132, MHS.

23. James Logan to E[dward] S[hippen], Stenton, 4 December 1730/31, Logan Papers, vol. 1, p. 106, HSP.

24. Stephen Bordley to Charles Hynson, London, 21 January 1734/35, Stephen Bordley Letterbook, 1727–1735, pp. 141–142, MHS.

25. Stephen Bordley to [Vachel] Denton, London, 21 January 1734/35, Stephen Bordley Letterbook, 1727–1735, p. 145, MHS.

26. Stephen Bordley to Charles Hynson, London, 21 January 1734/35, Stephen Bordley Letterbook, 1727–1735, pp. 141–142, MHS.

27. Stephen Bordley to My Dear Bett [Elizabeth Bordley], London, 23 December 1734, Stephen Bordley to Mrs. Jenings, 23 December 1734, Stephen Bordley to W[illiam] Harris, 21 January 1734/35, Stephen Bordley Letterbook, 1727–1735, pp. 129–130, 131, 144, MHS. For a contemporary criticism of what appeared the common practice of undertaking marriage for mercenary reasons and thereby considering interest more than passion, see *Reflections on Courtship and Marriage*, Philadelphia, 1746. Carl Van Doren, *Benjamin Franklin* (New York, 1964), pp. 152–153, attributes the anonymous pamphlet to Franklin. The editor, Leonard Labaree, of the *Papers of Benjamin Franklin*, vol. 3, p. 74, denies the ascription. No evidence is offered to demonstrate Franklin wrote the piece and in his judgment the pamphlet's style is not Franklin's.

28. Stephen Bordley to M[atthias] H[arris], 22 May 1740, Stephen Bordley Letterbook, 1738–1740, p. 67, MHS; Stephen Bordley to Richard Ford, 18 September 1742, Stephen Bordley Letterbook, 1740–1747, p. 48, MHS.

29. William Blair to Cozn Shippen, Boston, 17 August 1734, Joseph Shippen Papers, No. 1577, LC.

30. Esther Shippen's Will, No. 326, 1724, Philadelphia Will Book D, p. 407, Philadelphia Recorder of Wills, Philadelphia City Hall Annex.

31. Joseph Shippen [II] to Dear Brother [Edward Shippen III], Barbados, 20 March 1733, Shippen Papers, vol. 1, p. 33, HSP.

32. Joseph Harrison, Will, No. 387, 1734, Philadelphia Will Book E, p. 310, Philadelphia Recorder of Wills, Philadelphia City Hall Annex. Joseph Harrison, Inventory of Estate, No. 387, 1734, Philadelphia Recorder of Wills, Philadelphia City Hall Annex. *American Weekly Mercury*, 5 September 1734.

33. James Thatcher, *American Medical Biography*, ed. Whitfield J. Bell, Jr. (2 vols., New York, 1967), vol. 2, pp. 80–82; George Whitefield to William Shippen [II], Boston, 14 October 1754, Watson's Annals Am 301, p. 300, HSP; William Shippen [II] to George Whitefield, Philadelphia, 11 September 1758, George Whitefield Papers, No. 47, LC; Betsy Copping

Corner, *William Shippen, Jr., Pioneer in American Medical Education* (Philadelphia, 1951), p. 58.

34. Carl Bridenbaugh, *Cities in Revolt* (New York, 1964), p. 5.

35. Edward Shippen [III], Account of Sales of Merchandise, 1742, Shippen Papers, vol. 27, p. 36, HSP.

36. Edward Shippen [III], Account of Sales of Merchandize, 20 February 1746, Shippen Papers, vol. 27, p. 39, HSP; Edward Shippen [III], An Account of Sales of Merchandise, June 1742, Shippen-Burd-Hubley Papers, HSP; Edward Shippen [III], Account of Sales of Merchandise, June 1742, Shippen Papers, transferred from Society Collection, HSP; Edward Shippen [III], Account of Sales of Merchandise, 29 October 1743, Shippen Papers, vol. 27, p. 81, HSP; Edward Shippen [III], Copy of Account of Samuel Storke and Son with Edward Shippen, 20 February 1746, Shippen-Burd-Hubley Papers, HSP.

37. Edward Shippen to ———, Philadelphia, 31 8ber 1744, Shippen Family Papers, vol. 15, LC.

38. Thomas Greenough to Edward Shippen [III], Boston, 8 May 1743, Shippen Papers, vol. 1, p. 63, HSP.

39. Tho[mas] Greenough to Edward Shippen [III], Boston, 25 August 1748, Shippen Papers, vol. 1, p. 77, HSP.

40. Joseph Shippen [II] to Brother Ned [Edward Shippen III], London, 3 February 1737/8, Shippen Papers, vol. 1, p. 41, HSP.

41. *Ibid.*

42. Joseph Shute to Edward Shippen [III], Charles Town, So[uth] Carolina, 1 February 1734/5, Joseph Shippen II's Account against Logan and Shippen, 26 November 1737, Shippen Family Papers, vol. 15, LC; *Pennsylvania Gazette,* 18 September 1740.

43. Samuel Storke & Son to Edward [III] and Joseph Shippen [II], London, 21 April 1745, Shippen Papers, HSP; Account of Sales from Joseph Shippen [II] to Edward Shippen [III], 20 February 1746, Shippen Family Papers, vol. 15, LC.

44. Deed, John Crutcher to Joseph Shippen [II], 1 June 1742, Shippen Family Papers, Box 16, LC.

45. Edward Shippen [III] to Joseph Shippen [II], 11 January 1752, Edward Shippen Letterbook, 1751–1752, Small Books, No. 10, Shippen Papers, HSP.

46. Edward Shippen [III] to Dear Brother [William Shippen II], 7 February 1752, Edward Shippen Letterbook, 1751–1752, Small Books, No. 10, Shippen Papers, HSP.

47. *Ibid.*

48. Deed, Edward Shippen [III] and William Shippen [II] to Joseph Shippen [II], 5 February 1752, Shippen Family Papers, Box 17, LC.

49. Because Joseph II's son, Joseph Shippen, was only eight years old at this time, the major expenses of his education were almost a decade in the future.

50. Edward Shippen [III] to Dear Mr. Burd [James Burd], Philadelphia, 8 November 1752, Shippen Papers, vol. 1, p. 143, HSP.

51. William Shippen II is described as "physician" or "practitioner of physick," for example, in Deed, Edward Shippen [III] to William Shippen [II], 13 January 1745, and Mortgage, Edward Shippen [III] et al. to Samuel Bonham and Thomas Hyam, 31 July 1745, Shippen Family Papers, vol. 15, LC.

52. William Mangridge, Alexander Hamilton et al. to Edward Shippen [III], Philadelphia, 14 March 1740/41, Shippen Papers, vol. 15, p. 37, HSP.

53. In 1771, the owners of the Perkiomen mine, who had continued to invest in the venture after Shippen refused, advertised that they would sell the holdings. They claimed Shippen had no right to any money derived from the sale. Although Edward III recounted that he and his father "both laid out a great deal of Money, & I, by his Commands, attended the Company many years and kept the accounts in which I had abundance of troubles," his claim did not hold up in court. Edward Shippen [III] to Edward Shippen, Jr. [IV], Lancaster, 20 August 1771, Shippen Papers, vol. 12, p. 6, HSP; Edward Shippen, Jr. [IV], to Edward Shippen [III], Philadelphia, 1 January 1772, Shippen Papers, Box 1, HSP.

54. Edward Shippen [III] to John White, Chester, 9 7bre 1741, Maria Dickinson Logan Papers, HSP.

55. *Ibid.* Although the ancestors beyond four generations survive only as names, and the Shippen family rise to eminence began in the late seventeenth century, it seems plausible that the Shippens of Philadelphia could have concocted any story they wished, for few would be in a position to challenge it. This sort of fabrication happened among some families, particularly in the nineteenth century. In chapter one of *James Logan,* Frederick Tolles demolishes one such myth which the Logan family adhered to throughout most of the nineteenth and part of the twentieth century.

56. H. J. Habakkuk, "England," in *The European Nobility in the Eighteenth Century,* ed. Albert Goodwin (New York, 1967), p. 2; Bernard Bailyn, "The Beekmans of New York: Trade, Politics, and Families," *William and Mary Quarterly,* 3d ser., vol. XIV, no. 4 (October 1956), 605, 607.

57. Edward Shippen [III] to John White, Chester, 9 7bre 1741, Maria

Dickinson Logan Papers, HSP. In this regard, because Edward III was willing to sell his interest in Hillam and Germantown Plantation, he sold an inherited lot in Germantown for £100 to his partner James Logan; see, Deed, Edward Shippen to James Logan, 1 January 1742/3, Ashmead Scrapbook, AM 009, p. 9, HSP.

58. As far as interest in the family's past or English kin were concerned, Edward III showed more interest than any other Shippen in the eighteenth century.

59. *Pennsylvania Gazette*, 14–21 June 1739; Tripartite Indenture of Partition between Edward Shippen [III], Joseph Shippen [II], and William Shippen [II], 10 March 1741/2, Shippen Family Papers, Box 16, LC; Deed of Partition, Mrs. Jekyll and Messrs. Shippen, 30 September 1743, Shippen Family Papers, Box 15, LC; Agreement of Division, Joseph Shippen [II], Edward Shippen [III] and William Shippen [II], 1744, Tripartite Indenture, Edward Shippen [III], Joseph Shippen [II], and William Shippen [II], 28 October 1745, Shippen Family Papers, Box 16, LC.

60. Deed, Israel Pemberton and Anthony Morris, executors and trustees, to Edward Shippen [III], 31 July 1745; Deed, Edward Shippen [III] to William Shippen [II], 13 January 1745, Shippen Family Papers, Box 16, LC; Copy of Deed, Conrad Waltecker to Edward Shippen [III], 11 March 1746, Shippen Papers, vol. 15, p. 65, HSP; Receipts for ground rents, Mary Annis to Edward Shippen [III], 1742–1750 and 1754–1766, Maria Dickinson Logan Papers, HSP; Patent, John, Thomas, and Richard Penn to Edward Shippen [III], 29 April 1741, Shippen Family Papers, Box 16, LC.

61. Thomas McKee to Edward Shippen [III], Pesetown, 4 July 1744, Northern, Interior, and Western Counties, p. 9, HSP; Deed, William and Matthew Rogers to Edward Shippen [III], 29 September 1741; Lease of tracts of land in Lancaster County, Edward Shippen [III] to Richard Peters, 30 November 1745, Peters Papers, vol. 1, pp. 65, 67, vol. 2, p. 47, HSP; Deed, Josh Steer to James Logan and Edward Shippen [III], 5 October 1739, Shippen Family Papers, vol. 15, LC; John Budd to William Allen and Edward Shippen [III], 19 June 1749, Claude W. Unger Collection, HSP.

62. Henry Steer to Shippen & Lawrence, Lisbon, 30 8ber 1749, Shippen Family Papers, vol. 15, LC.

63. Edward Shippen [III] to Edward Shippen, Jr. [IV], Philadelphia, 18 September 1749, Miscellaneous Manuscripts Collection, APS. Bond, Edward Shippen [III] and Thomas Lawrence, Jr., to Thomas Lawrence, 26 January 1746/47, Provincial Delegates, vol. 5, p. 54, HSP; Bond, Hugh

Crawford to Edward Shippen [III] and Thomas Lawrence, Jr., 13 October 1747; Bond, Hugh Crawford to Edward Shippen [III] and Thomas Lawrence, Jr., 4 June 1747; Bond, John Owen and David Thondrick to Edward Shippen [III] and Thomas Lawrence [Jr.], 30 October 1746; Bond, John Owens to Edward Shippen [III] and Thomas Lawrence, Jr., 15 June 1747; Bond, John Owen to Edward Shippen and Thomas Lawrence, Jr., 17 August 1748, Shippen Papers, vol. 15, p. 77, HSP; Bond, James and John Lawrey to Edward Shippen [III] and Thomas Lawrence, Jr., 6 August 1748; Account, Thomas McKee to Shippen and Lawrence, 1740, Shippen Papers, vol. 15, pp. 17, 73, 63, 69, 77, 75; vol. 1, p. 97, HSP; Statement relative to Indian trade transacted by Hockley, Trent, and Croghan with Shippen and Lawrence, 24 November 1748, Cadwalader Collection, Trent and Croghan Papers, HSP.

64. Deed, Septimus Robinson, sheriff, to William Shippen [II], 26 July 1740; Deed, Susanna Fairman and Benjamin Field to William Shippen [II], 20 October 1741; Deed, Susanna Fairman to William Shippen [II], 20 October 1741; Deed, Thomas Leech and Jacob Leech to William Shippen [II], 18 October 1748; Deed, Samuel Hastings to William Shippen [II], 15 April 1741; Deed, Samuel Hastings to William Shippen [II], 5 April 1745, Shippen Family Papers, Box 16, LC.

65. Deed, Edward Shippen [III] to William Shippen [II], 1 July 1741; Deed, Edward [III] and Mary Shippen to William Shippen [II], 15 March 1747; Deed, Joseph Shippen [II] to William Shippen [II], 28 December 1748; Deed, Jehu Claypoole to William Shippen [II], 30 December 1743; Deed, Elizabeth Broom et al. to William Shippen [II], 28 September 1745; Deed, Elizabeth Broom et al. to William Shippen [II], 9 August 1748, Shippen Family Papers, Box 16, LC.

66. Charles S. Boyer, *Early Forges and Furnaces in New Jersey* (Philadelphia, 1931, reprinted 1963), pp. 149–150; Post Card of Shippen Manor, Oxford, New Jersey, Shippen Family Papers, Box 20, LC. A fuller account of the Shippen's iron works appears in chapter seven.

67. The proprietor's favors are realized more fully later. Already, however, the Shippens could benefit from the services which their grandfather, Edward Shippen I, had performed for William Penn. Edward Shippen III could also gain from his close connection with James Logan, the provincial secretary and Penn's most trusted friend in the colony.

68. *Minutes of the Common Council of the City of Philadelphia, 1704–1776* (Philadelphia, 1847).

69. Norman S. Cohen, "William Allen: Chief Justice of Pennsylvania, 1704–1780" (Ph.D. dissertation, University of California, 1966), pp. 5–6,

92, 96, 103–104, 107, 111; Charles P. Keith, *The Provincial Councillors of Pennsylvania Who Held Office between 1733 and 1776* (Philadelphia, 1883), pp. 6–13, 120–130.

70. *Minutes of the Common Council of the City of Philadelphia, 1704–1776,* indicate that forty members of the corporation were present in 1744 when Edward Shippen III was elected mayor. Twelve of the voters were related to Shippen or his kinsmen. They were Nathaniel Allen, William Allen, Joshua Emlen, Andrew Hamilton, James Hamilton, Anthony Morris, Jr., Joseph Morris, Samuel Powel, Jr., Edward Shippen III, Joseph Shippen II, William Till, and Charles Willing. The way in which these men were related may be grasped by consulting the schematic representation of the Shippen family kinship network which appears in the appendix.

71. John F. Watson, *Annals of Philadelphia* (3 vols., Philadelphia, 1887), vol. 1, p. 210.

72. Here and elsewhere the eighteenth-century Shippens contradict what Peter Laslett, *The World We Have Lost* (New York, 1965), p. 99, regards as "a law which seems to obtain for the whole pre-industrial world, that once a man reached the marriage age he would tend to go on getting married whenever he found himself without a wife." The Shippens are not unique, for exceptions to Laslett's law are rather abundant when one surveys numerous families in colonial Philadelphia. By implication John Demos, "Families in Colonial Bristol, Rhode Island: An Exercise in Historical Demography," *William and Mary Quarterly,* 3d ser., XXV, no. 1 (January 1968), 40, raises similar objections. This suggests one of two things. Either Laslett misconstrues the preindustrial era, or significant changes in the family preceded the Industrial Revolution by at least several decades. The second alternative implies serious modification of Laslett's static and probably oversimplified pre-industrial era.

73. Edward Shippen [III] to James Logan, Philadelphia, 5 December 1747, Shippen Papers, vol. 10, p. 3, HSP.

74. *Ibid.*

75. Edward Shippen [III] to Dear Son [Joseph Shippen III], Philadelphia, 3 January 1750, Shippen, Balch Papers, vol. 1, p. 26, HSP.

76. Edward Shippen [III] to Joseph Shippen [III], Philadelphia, 4 January 1750, Shippen Papers, vol. 1, p. 83, HSP.

77. Edward Shippen [III] to Dear Son [Joseph Shippen III], Philadelphia, 3 January 1750, Shippen, Balch Papers, vol. 1, p. 26, HSP.

78. *Ibid.*

79. Joseph Shippen, Jr. [III] to Dear & Loving Mammy [Mrs. Edward Shippen III], Newark, 18 January 1750, Shippen, Balch Papers, vol. 1, p. 27, HSP.

80. The Robert Feke portrait of Mary (Gray) Shippen is in the possession of the Newark Museum, Newark, New Jersey. The portrait of Joseph Shippen III by Feke was destroyed by fire in 1923; it is reproduced in A. C. Myers, *Hannah Logan's Courtship* (Philadelphia, 1904), p. 266, and in Henry Wilder Foote, *Robert Feke* (Cambridge, Mass., 1930), facing p. 188. Another reproduction of it is located at the Historical Society of Pennsylvania. Account of Edward Shippen [III] with Richard Singleton, 16 May 1747; James Silvery to Edward Shippen [III], 18 June 1747, Shippen Family Papers, vol. 15, LC.

81. Edward Shippen [III] to Dear Son [Joseph Shippen III], Philadelphia, 3 January 1750, Shippen, Balch Papers, vol. 1, p. 26, HSP.

82. Edward Shippen [III] to Joseph Shippen [III], Philadelphia, 5 March 1750, Shippen Papers, APS.

83. Although Edward Shippen III moved to Lancaster around 1752, according to the minutes of the Common Council of Philadelphia, he continued his political career in Philadelphia. As an alderman he attended meetings as late as 1762. Notice of Lancaster County Court of Quarter Sessions of Peace, 7 February 1737, Shippen Papers, vol. 2, p. 46, HSP; *Pennsylvania Archives,* ed. John Linn and William H. Egle (19 vols., Harrisburg, 1874–1893), 2d ser., vol. IX, pp. 773–775; *Pennsylvania Archives,* ed. William Henry Egle (26 vols., Harrisburg, 1894–1899), 3d ser., vol. IX, pp. 16–19.

CHAPTER V

1. The sole exception thus far uncovered appears in Sarah [Shippen] Burd to James Burd, 12 October 1749, Burd-Shippen-Hubley Papers, HSP, in which she informs her husband that she has weaned little Salley at age seven months. The reason for this was that she was pregnant.

2. Demographic information on the Shippens appears in tabular form in the appendix. The Shippens are typical of most colonial families in the sense that demographic information about them roughly coincides with the findings of John Demos in "Families in Colonial Bristol, Rhode Island: An Exercise in Historical Demography," *William and Mary Quarterly,* 3d ser., vol. XXV, no. 1 (January 1968), 40; Philip J. Greven, Jr.'s *Four Generations: Population, Land, and Family in Colonial Andover, Massachusetts* (Ithaca, 1970), pp. 34, 119, 121, 207, 209; and the general trends which quantified studies of the colonial population seem to be uncovering. Because the Shippens were richer than most colonists, they married at a somewhat younger age than the average for all colonists. That the rich married earlier than the poor or "middling" orders of eighteenth-century

society is confirmed by T. H. Hollingsworth's "A Demographic Study of British Ducal Families," in *Population in History, Essays in Historical Demography*, ed. D. V. Glass and D. E. C. Eversley (Chicago, 1965), p. 377. No such compilation yet exists for the colonies, but John Waters's *The Otis Family in Provincial and Revolutionary Massachusetts* (Chapel Hill, 1968), p. viii, for example, finds the younger marriages and larger families "the prerogative of the wealthy."

3. Paul Henry Mussen and John Janeway Conger, *Child Development and Personality* (New York, 1956), pp. 136–169.

4. Edward Shippen [III] to ———, Philadelphia, 31 8ber 1744, Shippen Family Papers, vol. 15, LC. C. E. A. Bedwell, "American Middle Templars," *American Historical Review*, vol. XXV, no. 4 (July 1920), 683.

5. Edward Shippen, Jr. [IV] to Joseph Shippen, Jr. [III], London, 25 February 1748, Balch Papers, vol. 1, p. 13, HSP.

6. Mary Shippen to Dear Cousin, 20 October 1748, Shippen Papers, vol. 1, p. 91a, HSP.

7. Sarah Burd to Edward Shippen [IV], Philadelphia, 24 October 1749; Edward Shippen, Jr. [IV] to Joseph Shippen, Jr. [III], London, 9 October 1749, Balch Papers, vol. 1, pp. 25, 24, HSP.

8. Edward Shippen [IV] to Edward Shippen [III], London, 23 January 1749, Balch Papers, vol. 1, p. 20, HSP.

9. Edward Shippen, Jr. [IV] to Brother Jemmy [James Burd], London, 1 August 1749, Shippen Papers, vol. 1, p. 93, HSP.

10. Edward Shippen [III] to Edward Shippen, Jr. [IV], Philadelphia, 16 September 1749, Miscellaneous Manuscripts Collection, APS.

11. Edward Shippen [IV] to Joseph Shippen [III], London, 2 August 1749, Balch Papers, vol. 1, p. 21, HSP.

12. Joseph Shippen, Jr. [III] to Edward Shippen [III], Newark, 12 May 1750, Shippen Papers, vol. 10, p. 11, HSP.

13. Joseph Shippen, Jr. [III] to Edward Shippen [III], Newark, November 1750, Shippen Papers, vol. 10, p. 17, HSP; Edward Shippen [III] to Thomas Penn, Philadelphia, 21 March 1752, Penn Papers, Official Correspondence, vol. 5, p. 231, HSP; Joseph Shippen, Jr. to Dear Brother [Edward Shippen IV], June 1752, Joseph Shippen, Jr., Letterbook, 1752, Small Books, Shippen Papers, HSP.

14. Thomas Penn to James Hamilton, London, 13 July 1752, Thomas Penn Correspondence, APS.

15. *Minutes of the Common Council of the City of Philadelphia, 1704–1776* (Philadelphia, 1847); Edward Shippen, Esq. [IV]'s Certificate of shipment of goods in good order, Philadelphia, 28 November 1754, Shippen Family Papers, vol. 15, LC; in Edward Shippen [III] to Mon cher fils

Joseph Shippen [III], Philadelphia, 4 Xbre 1751, Shippen Papers, vol. 1, p. 125, HSP after Edward "votre frère le Judge de la Cour de L'admisanté," he added that at present it was a position without profit.

16. Edward Shippen, Jr. [IV] to Edward Shippen [III], Philadelphia, 8 June 1753, Shippen Papers, vol. 1, p. 127, HSP. In general scholars have asserted that romantic love was a consequence of the impact of the Industrial Revolution upon the traditional family. William Josiah Goode's *World Revolution and Family Patterns* (New York, 1963), chap. 1, Frank F. Furstenburg, Jr.'s "Industrialization and the American Family: A Look Backward," *American Sociological Review*, vol. 31, no. 3 (June 1966), 326–337, and Herman R. Lantz, Margaret Britton, Raymond Schmitt, and Eloise Snyder's "Pre-Industrial Patterns in the Colonial Family in America: A Content Analysis of Colonial Magazines," in *Courtship and Marriage in Contemporary America: An Anthology*, ed. Arthur Kline and Morris Medley (printed for the confidential use of students at Indiana State University, n.d.) find evidence of romantic love before industrialization. Abundant evidence indicates that romantic love existed in the Shippen family during the fourth and fifth generations.

17. Edward Shippen, Jr. [IV] to Edward Shippen [III], Philadelphia, 14 September 1752, Shippen Papers, vol. 10, p. 41, HSP.

18. *Ibid.*

19. William Allen to Edward Shippen [III], 25 July 1753, Balch Papers, vol. 1, p. 34, HSP.

20. *Ibid.*

21. Edward Shippen, Jr. [IV] to Edward Shippen [III], Philadelphia, 24 September 1752, Shippen Papers, vol. 10, p. 41, HSP.

22. William Allen to Edward Shippen [III], 25 July 1753, Balch Papers, vol. 1, p. 34, HSP.

23. *Ibid.*

24. Bernard Bailyn, *Education in the Forming of American Society: Needs and Opportunities for Study* (New York, 1960), pp. 24–25; Demos, "Families in Colonial Bristol, Rhode Island," *passim*; Peter Laslett, *The World We Have Lost: England before the Industrial Age* (New York, 1965), pp. 4, 11–12, 21.

25. This letter of advice appears in Edward Shippen [III] to Dear Son [Edward Shippen IV], Lancaster, 20 March 1754, Shippen Papers, vol. 11, p. 4, HSP.

26. The kinship bonds of the Shippens with the Allens, Francises, Willings, and others may be readily grasped by consulting Appendix B.

27. Edward Shippen [III] to Dear Son [Edward Shippen IV], Lancaster, 20 March 1754, Shippen Papers, vol. 11, p. 4, HSP.

28. Joseph Shippen, Jr. [III] to Edward Shippen [III], 24 April 1750, Shippen Papers, vol. 10, p. 9, HSP.

29. *Minutes of the Common Council of the City of Philadelphia,* 31 July 1750.

30. Thomas Penn to James Hamilton, London, 12 February 1749, Thomas Penn Correspondence, APS.

31. *Ibid.* John L. Steward, "Historical Sketch of the University," in *Benjamin Franklin and the University of Pennsylvania,* ed. Francis Newton Thorpe (Washington, 1893), p. 216; Horace Mather Lippincott and Thornton Oakley, *Philadelphia* (Philadelphia, 1926), p. 202; Benjamin Franklin, *Proposals Relating to the Education of Youth in Pennsylvania,* in *Papers of Benjamin Franklin,* ed. Leonard Labaree (New Haven, 1961), vol. 3, pp. 395–421; Edward Potts Cheyney and Ellis Paxson Oberholtzer, *University of Pennsylvania: Its History, Influence, Equipment, and Characteristics, with Biographical Sketches and Portraits of Founders, Benefactors, Officers, and Alumni* (2 vols., Boston, 1901–1902), vol. 1, pp. 43–66.

32. Constance M. Greiff, Mary W. Gibbons, and Elizabeth G. C. Menzies, *Princeton Architecture* (Princeton, 1967), pp. 23, 43–44; Cheyney and Oberholtzer, *University of Pennsylvania,* vol. 1, p. 256; Charles P. Keith, *The Provincial Councillors of Pennsylvania who held office between 1733 and 1776, and Those Earlier Councillors who were some time Chief Magistrates of the Province, and their Descendants* (Philadelphia, 1883), p. 53.

33. A decade later the entire enrollment was about sixty or seventy students according to William Shippen [II] to George Whitfield, 11 September 1758, George Whitfield Papers, LC.

34. John Cunningham, *Newark* (Newark, 1966), pp. 58–59. See also Cunningham's chapter 7, "College Town," in *Newark.*

35. Edward Shippen [III], Esq. Account, 1749, Shippen Family Papers, vol. 15, LC.

36. For example see Joseph Shippen, Jr. [III] to Edward Shippen [III], 2 March 1750; Joseph Shippen, Jr. [III] to Edward Shippen [III], Newark, 14 September 1751, Shippen Papers, vol. 10, pp. 7, 29, HSP; Joseph Shippen, Jr. [III] to Edward Shippen [III], Newark, 2 March 1752; Joseph Shippen, Small Book, Shippen Papers, HSP; Joseph Shippen, Jr. [III] to Edward Shippen [III], Newark, 18 August 1752, Shippen Papers, vol. 10, p. 37, HSP.

37. Abundant family correspondence survives in the Shippen Papers at the Historical Society of Pennsylvania and the American Philosophical Society. See especially Letters of Edward Shippen [III] to Joseph Shippen [III], 1750–1778, Joseph Shippen [III]'s Letterbook, 26 January 1763–15

April 1773, and Edward Shippen [III]'s Letterbooks, 10 vols., 24 September 1754–4 May 1781, at the American Philosophical Society.

38. Joseph Shippen, Jr. [III] to Edward Shippen [III], Newark, 24 April 1750, Shippen Papers, vol. 10, p. 9, HSP.

39. Joseph Shippen, Jr. [III] to [a college friend], 3 February 1752, Joseph Shippen, Jr. [III]'s Letterbook while at Newark, 1752, Small Books, No. 2, Shippen Papers, HSP.

40. Joseph Shippen, Jr. [III] to John Fleming, Newark, 27 June 1750, Shippen Papers, vol. 10, p. 15, HSP.

41. Joseph Shippen, Jr. [III] to Edward Shippen [III], Newark, 19 April 1750; Joseph Shippen, Jr. [III] to Edward Shippen [III], Newark, 30 March 1751; Joseph Shippen, Jr. [III] to Edward Shippen [III], Newark, 30 May 1751; Joseph Shippen, Jr. [III] to Edward Shippen [III], Newark, 3 February [1752?], Shippen Papers, vol. 10, pp. 7, 19, 23, 31, HSP.

42. There are indications that, though diligent in all his studies, Joseph had a practical bend of mind that questioned the value of much "School Knowledge" which he might "never have occasion to use." Edward Shippen [III] to Joseph Shippen, Jr. [III], Philadelphia, 13 June 1751, Balch Papers, vol. 1, p. 32, HSP.

43. Joseph Shippen, Jr. [III] to Edward Shippen [III], Newark, 3 February 1752, Shippen Papers, vol. 10, p. 31, HSP.

44. Joseph Shippen, Jr. [III] to Edward Shippen [III], New Rotchelle [*sic*], 18 August 1752, Shippen Papers, vol. 10, p. 37, HSP.

45. Joseph Shippen [III] to Mon tres cher & honoré Père [Edward Shippen III], 13 February 1750, Shippen Papers, transferred from Society Collection, HSP; Edward Shippen [III] to Joseph Shippen [III], 15 August 1751; Joseph Shippen, Jr. [III] to Edward Shippen [III], Newark, 3 August 1752, Shippen Papers, vol. 1, p. 141; vol. 10, p. 35, HSP. There are numerous Edward Shippen III to Mons. Joseph Shippen Le Jeune [III] at Nouvelle Ark letters in French in volume one of the Shippen Papers at the Historical Society of Pennsylvania; for example, see: 16 April 1750, 22 9bre 1750, 13 December 1750, 17 May 1750, 20 Xbre 1750. Joseph Shippen III's letters in French to his father appear in volume ten of the Shippen Papers; for example, see: 22 July 1751, 13 May 1751, and 9 January 1751.

46. Edward Shippen [III] to My Dear Son [Joseph Shippen III], Philadelphia, 28 May 1752, Edward Shippen Letterbook, APS.

47. Joseph Shippen, Jr. [III] to Edward Shippen [III], Newark, 21 December 1750, Shippen Papers, vol. 10, p. 21, HSP.

48. Edward Shippen [III] to Joseph Shippen [III], Philadelphia, 13

June 1751, Balch Papers, vol. 1, p. 32, HSP. Joseph Shippen, Jr. [III] to Edward Shippen [III], Newark, 23 May 1752, Shippen Papers, vol. 10, p. 35, HSP.

49. Joseph Shippen, Jr. [III] to Edward Shippen [III], Newark, 26 June 1750, Shippen Papers, vol. 10, p. 13, HSP.

50. Edward Shippen [IV] to Joseph Shippen [III], London, 3 May 1750, Balch Papers, vol. 1, p. 29, HSP; Edward Shippen [III] to Joseph Shippen [III], Philadelphia, 9 May 1752; Edward Shippen [III] to Joseph Shippen [III], Philadelphia, 10 August 1750; Joseph Shippen, Jr. [III] to Edward Shippen [III], Newark, 9 April 1751; Joseph Shippen, Jr. [III] to Edward Shippen [III], Newark, 21 December 1750, Shippen Papers, vol. 1, pp. 141, 107; vol. 10, pp. 19, 21, HSP.

51. Joseph Shippen, Jr. [III] to Edward Shippen [III], Newark, 26 June 1750, Shippen Papers, vol. 10, p. 13, HSP.

52. Joseph Shippen, Jr. [III] to Edward Shippen [III], Newark, 18 December 1752, Shippen Papers, Box 1, HSP.

53. Joseph Shippen, Jr. [III] to Edward Shippen [III], Newark, 20 August 1753, Shippen Papers, vol. 10, p. 39, HSP.

54. Edward Shippen [III] to Joseph Shippen, Jr. [III], 7 May 1752, Shippen Papers, vol. 1, p. 137, HSP.

55. Edward Shippen [III] to Dear Son [Edward Shippen IV], Lancaster, 20 March 1754, Shippen Papers, vol. 11, p. 4, HSP.

56. Edward Shippen [III] to Dear Son [Edward Shippen IV], Philadelphia, 8 March 1754; Edward Shippen [III] to My Dear Son [Edward Shippen IV], Lancaster, 20 March 1754; Edward Shippen [III] to Dear Son [Joseph Shippen III], Lancaster, 12 April 1754, Shippen Papers, vol. 11, pp. 3, 4; vol. 1, p. 159, HSP.

57. Study of children in the United States, England, Italy, and Mexico indicates that parental dominance adversely affects a desire to achieve and to make scholastic progress. Even when variables such as birthplace, religion, social class were controlled, parental dominance retained its effects. See Glen H. Elder, Jr., "Family Structure and Educational Attainment: A Cross-National Analysis," *American Sociological Review*, vol. 30, no. 1 (February 1965), 81–96.

58. Joseph Shippen, Jr. [III] to Cousin William Shippen, Jr. [III], 17 May 1755, Joseph Shippen, Jr., Letterbook, Small Books, No. 3, Shippen Papers, HSP.

59. For additional information about Lancaster, its social structure and leadership, see Jerome Herman Wood, Jr.'s "Conestoga Crossroads: The Rise of Lancaster, Pennsylvania, 1730–1789" (Ph.D. dissertation, Brown University, 1969).

60. Edward Shippen, Jr. [IV] to Edward Shippen [III], Philadelphia, 18 February 1756, Balch Papers, vol. 1, p. 44, HSP; Edward Shippen [III] to Dear Cousin [William Allen], Lancaster, 4 July 1755; Joseph Shippen, Jr. [III] to Edward Shippen [III], Lancaster, 16 July 1755, Shippen Papers, vol. 1, pp. 207, 211, HSP; *Papers of Benjamin Franklin,* ed. Labaree, vol. 5, p. 195; Norman Sonny Cohen, "William Allen: Chief Justice of Pennsylvania, 1704–1780" (Ph.D. dissertation, University of California, Berkeley, 1966), pp. 200–202; *Colonial Records* (16 vols., Philadelphia, 1838–1853), vol. III, pp. 8, 304, 394, 409, 410, 427.

61. Edward Shippen, Jr. [IV] to Edward Shippen [III], Philadelphia, 18 February 1756, Balch Papers, vol. 1, p. 44, HSP.

62. Edward Shippen, Jr. [IV] to Edward Shippen [III], Philadelphia, 18 February 1756, in Thomas Balch, *Letters and Papers relating to Pennsylvania* (5 vols., private printing, Philadelphia, 1855), pp. 51–52.

63. Joseph Shippen [III], Plan of a Fort, Lancaster, 26 January 1756, Shippen Papers, transferred from Society Collection, HSP; Joseph Shippen, Jr. [III] to Governor Robert H. Morris, Lancaster, 19 April 1756, Stauffer Collection, vol. 30, p. 2336, HSP; Edward Shippen [III] to James Burd, Lancaster, 22 April 1756, Shippen Papers, vol. 2, p. 53, HSP.

64. Edward Shippen [III] to James Burd, Lancaster, 22 April 1756, Shippen Papers, vol. 2, p. 53, HSP.

65. Pedigree of the family of Edward Shippen of Lancaster, Taken from his own account, Shippen Family, Genealogy, Society Collection, HSP; Lily L. Nixon, *James Burd: Frontier Defender, 1726–1793* (Philadelphia, 1941), pp. 1–20. Some papers concerning the Burd estate in Scotland survive in the Papers of Edward Burd, Society Collection, HSP.

66. Edward Shippen, Esq., Account, 1749, Shippen Family Papers, vol. 15, LC; Sarah Burd to James Burd at Georgetown, Maryland, Philadelphia, 12 October 1749, Burd-Shippen-Hubley Papers, HSP; [James Burd], merchant, Account Book, 1750–1756, APS; Edward Shippen [III] to Joseph Shippen, Jr. [III], Philadelphia, 18 July 1751, Shippen Papers, vol. 1, p. 115, HSP; *Pennsylvania Gazette,* 7 February 1748/9, 18 May 1749, 22 June 1749, 10 August 1749.

67. William Harlee to James Burd, Philadelphia, 26 October 1750, Shippen Papers, vol. 1, p. 95, HSP.

68. An Account of Coaches, Landaus, Charriots, and Four Wheel Chairs, 1761, Proud Miscellaneous Manuscripts, Box 2, No. 71, HSP; Balch, *Letters relating to Pennsylvania,* vol. III, p. 6.

69. Joseph Shippen, Jr. [III] to ——, 15 January 1752, Small Books, Shippen Papers, HSP. It was not uncommon in eighteenth-century Philadelphia for seemingly prosperous merchants to go bankrupt, nor was the

258   Notes to Pages 94–95

Shippens' response to cushion the shock and protect the unfortunate individual rare. For quick access to numerous financial failings, see the Minutes of the Philadelphia Monthly Meeting. William Griffitts and Joseph Pemberton are among the prominent failures who come readily to mind. In 1760 a shocked Benjamin Franklin wrote his wife, "I am extremely concerned with you at the Misfortune of our Friend Mr. Griffitts. How could it possibly happen?" Although the Society of Friends disowned Griffitts, his family connections served him well. Griffitts's brother was a provincial councillor who married the daughter of the wealthy and politically powerful Isaac Norris. He also had family connections with the Powels, Morrises, and Fishbournes. The family and friends petitioned the Pennsylvania Assembly and saved Griffitts from the worst consequences of his failure. (See *Papers of Benjamin Franklin,* ed. Labaree, vol. 8, p. 328; *Pennsylvania Genealogical Magazine,* vol. XXII (1961), 13; *Colonial Records,* vol. VIII, pp. 666–667. Joseph Pemberton was the son of Israel Pemberton, Jr., "King of the Quakers"; details of his bankruptcy appear in the minutes of the Monthly Meeting and deeds by which Pemberton conveyed all his property to several members of the Society of Friends who then attempted to settle with his creditors. Theodore Thayer, *Israel Pemberton: King of the Quakers* (Philadelphia, 1943), p. 196, and Judy DiStephano, "A Concept of Family in Colonial America: The Pembertons of Pennsylvania" (Ph.D. dissertation, Ohio State University, 1970), give the details of the action of the embarrassed family. The role of the Quaker father as being responsible for his son and attempting to assist him is similar to Shippen's.

70. Edward Shippen [III] to Dear Son [Edward Shippen IV], Lancaster, 20 March 1754, Shippen Papers, vol. 11, p. 4, HSP.

71. According to Edward Shippen [III] to Mon cher fils Joseph Shippen [III], at Newark, Philadelphia, 8 January 1752, Shippen Papers, vol. 1, p. 119, HSP, "Monsr Walter Stirling (L'ssoc ——— Monsieur Burd) vient d'arriver de Londres & ils ont requlé [requis] leurs Comptes & le dernier est in dette au Premier la somme de £1,110 Sterling & Mons[ieu]r Sterling lui donne neuf ans pour lui payer quelque tems sans intèrêt." In Joseph Shippen, Jr., to Edward Shippen, 15 January 1752, Joseph Shippen, Jr., Letterbook, Small Books, No. 3, Shippen Papers, HSP, Joseph Shippen III admitted the terms were generous, but could not conceive of how Burd could do it even then.

72. Edward Shippen [III] to James Burd, Lancaster, 21 June 1760, Shippen Papers, vol. 5, p. 55, HSP.

73. Edward Shippen [III] to Mon cher fils Joseph Shippen [III], Philadelphia, 25 April 1751, Shippen Papers, vol. 1, p. 137, HSP.

74. Edward Shippen [III] to Mr. Burd, Philadelphia, 12 December 1752, Edward Shippen Letterbook, APS.

75. Edward Shippen [III] to Dear Children [the Burds], Philadelphia, 1 May 1752; Edward Shippen [III] to Dear Children [the Burds], Philadelphia, 22 May 1752; Edward Shippen [III] to Mr. Burd, Philadelphia, 30 July 1752, Edward Shippen Letterbook, APS.

76. Edward Shippen [III] to Dear Children [the Burds], Lancaster, 24 September 1753, *Letters relating to Pennsylvania,* p. 23.

77. James Burd to Edward Shippen [III], Shippensburg, 1 October 1752, 29 December 1752, Burd Papers, HSP; William McIlvaine to James Burd, merchant, Philadelphia, 26 May 1753; Joseph Shippen, Jr. [III] to Dear Brother [James Burd], Lancaster, 2 April 1754; James Burd to ———, Shippensburg, 11 March 1755, Shippen Papers, vol. 1, pp. 151, 157, 173, HSP.

78. Edward Shippen [III] to Dear Son [Edward Shippen IV], Carlisle, 10 January 1756, Shippen Papers, vol. 11, p. 7, HSP.

79. *Ibid.*

80. James Burd to Edward Shippen [III], Shippensburg, 24 August 1755, Shippen Papers, vol. 2, p. 3, HSP.

81. Edward Shippen [III] to Mr. Burd, 8 July 1755, Shippen Papers, vol. 1, p. 215, HSP.

82. Robert Thompson, George Ross, and Joseph Shippen, Jr. [III] to Governor Robert H. Morris, Lancaster, 1 November 1755, Dreer Collection, New Series in Boxes, under Ross, HSP.

83. Report of Benjamin Chew, Alexander Stedman, William West, and Edward Shippen [III] to Governor and Council, 21 April 1756, Penn Manuscripts, Assembly and Provincial Council of Pennsylvania, Large Folio, p. 82, HSP.

84. Edward Shippen [III] to James Burd, Lancaster, 7 August 1755, Shippen Papers, vol. 2, p. 1, HSP.

85. James Burd to Edward Shippen [III], Shippensburg, 27 April 1755; James Burd to My Dear Love [Sarah Burd], From the Wood, 15 May 1755, HSP; Edward Shippen [III] to James Burd, Lancaster, 28 August 1755, Shippen Papers, vol. 1, pp. 179, 183, vol. 2, p. 1, HSP. For additional information about the road-building activities, etc., of Burd and Shippen, see relevant years in volumes one and two of the Shippen Papers at the Historical Society of Pennsylvania.

86. Joseph Shippen, Jr. [III] to Edward Shippen [III], Camp at Harris', 15 May 1756; Joseph Shippen, Jr. [III] to Edward Shippen [III], 17 May 1756, Shippen Papers, vol. 2, pp. 55, 57, HSP; Edward Shippen [III] to Dear Son [Joseph Shippen III], Lancaster, 14 August 1756, Dreer Collection, vol. 20, Mayors of Philadelphia, HSP; Edward Shippen [III] to Dear Son [Joseph Shippen III], Lancaster, 1 August 1756, Shippen Papers, vol. 2, p. 61, HSP. Abundant correspondence between Edward Shippen III and his sons Joseph Shippen III and James Burd can be found in volume two

of the Shippen Papers at the Historical Society of Pennsylvania. For details on the life of James Burd at Fort Augusta, his care of the fort and store, military affairs, etc., see James Burd Letterbook, 1756–1758, Shippen Papers, HSP. Volumes two through four of the Shippen Papers at the Historical Society of Pennsylvania contain abundant letters about the war.

87. Edward Shippen, Jr. [IV] to Edward Shippen [III], Philadelphia, 19 August 1756, Shippen Papers, vol. 2, p. 65, HSP.

88. Edward Shippen, Jr. [IV] to Edward Shippen [III], Philadelphia, 19 August 1756, Shippen Papers, vol. 2, p. 65, HSP. Although Neddy saw implications for his own career, this does not imply Neddy acted solely out of his own personal motives. At the beginning of the summer he informed Burd that "your friends are anxious for your welfare and promotion, I am desired by some to inform you that the Royal American Regiment now raising in Pennsylvania now has vacancies; your friends think they could easily get you a lieutenancy if you wish it, this only as the first step toward promotion." These thoughts were expressed in Edward Shippen, Jr. [IV] to James Burd, Philadelphia, 29 June 1756, Shippen Papers, vol. 2, p. 47, HSP.

89. Edward Shippen [III] to My Dear Capt. Shippen, Lancaster, 27 October 1756, Shippen Papers, vol. 2, p. 77, HSP.

90. That Edward III encouraged his son's making decisions for himself rather than continuing his excessive dependence upon his father's opinions gains substantiation in Edward Shippen [III] to Joseph Shippen, Jr. [III], Lancaster, 9 May 1757, Shippen Papers, vol. 2, p. 173, HSP. In it Edward III urged, "When I write my Sentiments to you both, you are to use them only as hints, for it is impossible I can always be right and therefore you will I hope take your own measures when ever you cannot agree with me." Edward Shippen [III] to James Burd, Lancaster, 9 August 1756; Edward Shippen [III] to Dear Son [Joseph Shippen III], Harris's, 13 7br 1756; James Burd to Edward Shippen [III], Ft. Augusta, 4 September 1756; Edward Shippen [III] to James Burd, Lancaster, 17 August 1756, Shippen Papers, vol. 2, pp. 65, 71, 61, HSP.

91. Joseph Shippen, Jr. [III] to Edward Shippen [III], Ft. Augusta, 23 April 1757; Joseph Shippen, Jr. [III] to James Burd, Lancaster, 19 May 1757; Joseph Shippen, Jr. [III] to James Burd, Lancaster, 16 June 1757; James Burd's account of the character of the Officers of the Augusta Regiment, 1757, Shippen Papers, vol. 2, pp. 161, 177, 211; vol. 3, p. 111, HSP.

92. Edward Shippen [III] to James Burd, Lancaster, 2 May 1758, Shippen Papers, vol. 3, p. 161, HSP.

93. Joseph Shippen, Jr. [III] to James Burd, Germantown, 30 April, 1758; Joseph Shippen, Jr. [III] to Edward Shippen [III], Philadelphia, 5

May 1758; Joseph Shippen, Jr. [III] to Lt. Col. James Burd, Philadelphia, 12 May 1758, Shippen Papers, vol. 3, pp. 159, 163, 149, HSP; Joseph Shippen [III]'s Commission as Lieutenant-Colonel, 31 May 1758, Commissions, HSP.

94. Joseph Shippen [III] to James Burd, Fort Bedford, 4 December 1759, Shippen Papers, vol. 4, p. 217, HSP.

95. Joseph Shippen [III] to James Burd, Fort Bedford, 6 January 1760, Shippen Papers, vol. 5, p. 1, HSP. Edward Shippen to Thomas Penn, Lancaster, 20 November 1759; Joseph Shippen [III] to Edward Shippen, Camp 6 miles west of Guest's Plantation, 18 September 1759, Shippen Papers, vol. 4, pp. 211, 149, HSP.

96. Joseph Shippen [III] to James Burd, Fort Bedford, 21 January 1760, Shippen Papers, vol. 5, p. 7, HSP.

97. Edward Shippen [IV] to Edward Shippen [III], Philadelphia, 14 December 1758, Balch Papers, vol. 1, p. 67, HSP.

98. Joseph Shippen, Jr. [III] to Edward Shippen [III], Fort Bedford, 6 January 1760, Shippen Papers, Box 1, HSP.

99. James Burd to Edward Shippen [III], Ft. Pitt, 15 July 1760, Shippen Papers, vol. 5, p. 65, HSP.

100. Sarah Burd to James Burd, Lancaster, 9 February 1760, Burd-Shippen-Hubley Papers, HSP.

101. E[dward Shippen III], Lancaster, 19 July 1760, Shippen Papers, vol. 5, p. 74, HSP.

102. Joseph Shippen, Jr. [III] to Col. James Burd, Philadelphia, 21 February 1763, Shippen Papers, vol. 6, p. 5, HSP. Edward Shippen [IV] to Edward Shippen [III], Philadelphia, 22 December 1759, Balch Papers, vol. 1, p. 78, HSP; Edward Shippen [III] to James Burd, Lancaster, 3 October 1761; Commission, Lt. Governor James Hamilton to James Burd, Esq., 16 March 1761, Edward Shippen, Jr. [IV] to Col. James Burd, Philadelphia, 12 March 1761; Edward Shippen [III] to Col. James Burd, Lancaster, 21 March 1761; Joseph Shippen, Jr. [III] to Col. James Burd, Philadelphia, 9 September 1762; Joseph Shippen, Jr. [III] to James Burd, Philadelphia, 24 September 1762, Shippen Papers, vol. 5, pp. 165, 131, 133, 207, 217, HSP.

103. Joseph Shippen, Jr. [III] to James Burd, Philadelphia, 7 July 1763, Shippen Papers, vol. 6, p. 37, HSP.

104. Edward Shippen [III] to James Burd, Lancaster, 21 July 1763, Shippen Papers, vol. 6, p. 45, HSP.

105. Joseph Shippen, Jr. [III] to James Burd, Philadelphia, 3 January 1764, Shippen Papers, vol. 6, p. 73, HSP.

106. Sarah Burd to James Burd, Lancaster, 27 November 1762, Burd-

Shippen-Hubley Papers, HSP; Joseph Shippen, Jr. [III] to James Burd, Lancaster, 14 June 1763; Edward Shippen [III] to James Burd, Lancaster, 15 July 1763; James Burd to Joseph Shippen, Jr. [III], Ft. Augusta, 19 January 1763, Shippen Papers, vol. 6, pp. 23, 35, 81, HSP.

107. James Burd to Edward Shippen [III], Lancaster, 20 August 1764, Burd-Shippen-Hubley Papers, folder 38, HSP.

108. Edward Shippen, Jr. [IV] to Joseph Shippen [III], Philadelphia, 19 February 1760; Edward Shippen [IV] to Joseph Shippen [III], Philadelphia, 21 February 1760; Joseph Shippen [III] to Edward Shippen [III], Philadelphia, 4 March 1760, Shippen, Balch Papers, vol. 1, pp. 93, 94, 96, HSP; Joseph Shippen [III] to Edward Shippen [III], Philadelphia, 22 March 1760, Shippen Papers, Box 1, folder presented by Mrs. Thomas Balch, HSP; Edward Shippen, Jr. [IV] to ———, Philadelphia, 5 April 1760, Joseph Shippen Papers, No. 1601, LC.

109. Edward Shippen [IV] to Joseph Shippen [III], Philadelphia, 21 February 1760, Shippen, Balch Papers, vol. 1, p. 94, HSP. Cousin Thomas Willing, for example, thought Joseph III would "sink Money at this time" if he went to England, and urged him to wait until "the Shock that the Trade must receive by a sudden peace is over." In the interim, he offered to be "concerned as you think proper" in a spring voyage to Quebec. Although Edward IV recommended it as a means to pass the summer "to good advantage," Joseph III preferred Cousin Allen's recommendation of Leghorn.

110. Edward Shippen [IV] to Joseph Shippen [III], Philadelphia, 21 February 1760, Shippen, Balch Papers, vol. 1, p. 94, HSP.

111. William Allen to David Barclay & Sons, Philadelphia, 20 July 1760, William Allen Letterbook, HSP.

112. Edward Shippen [IV] to Edward Shippen [III], Philadelphia, 26 March 1760, Shippen, Balch Papers, vol. 1, p. 97, HSP.

113. Joseph Shippen, Jr. [III] to Edward Shippen [III], Gibraltar, 16 May 1760, Shippen, Balch Papers, vol. 1, p. 103, HSP.

114. Joseph Shippen [III] to Edward Shippen [III], Gibraltar, 11 May 1760, Shippen Papers, vol. 5, p. 37, HSP. Edward Shippen, Jr. [IV] to Edward Shippen [III], Philadelphia, Shippen, Balch Papers, vol. 1, p. 100, HSP.

115. Joseph Shippen, Jr. [III] to Edward Shippen [III], Leghorn, 4 July 1760, Shippen, Balch Papers, vol. 1, p. 103, HSP.

116. Joseph Shippen, Jr. [III] to Edward Shippen, Jr. [IV], Leghorn, 14 July 1760, Joseph Shippen Letterbook, HSP. Joseph Shippen, Jr. [III] to Edward Shippen [III], Gibraltar, 16 May 1760, Shippen, Balch Papers, vol. 1, p. 103, HSP; Joseph Shippen, Jr. [III] to Dear Brother [Edward

Shippen IV], Leghorn, 4 July 1760, Shippen Papers, vol. 11, p. 22, HSP; Joseph Shippen, Jr. [III] to Edward Shippen [III], Leghorn, 14 July 1760; Edward Shippen, Jr. [IV] to Edward Shippen [III], Philadelphia, 17 September 1760, Shippen, Balch Papers, vol. 1, pp. 114, 118, HSP.

117. Joseph Shippen, Jr. [III] to Edward Shippen [III], Leghorn, 13 July 1760, Shippen, Balch Papers, vol. 1, p. 114, HSP.

118. Edward Shippen, Jr. [IV] to Edward Shippen [III], 27 November 1760, Shippen, Balch Papers, vol. 1, p. 121, HSP. Joseph Shippen [III] to Sir, Leghorn, 13 July 1760, Shippen Papers, vol. 15, p. 139, HSP.

119. Joseph Shippen Jr. [III] to Edward Shippen [III], Leghorn, 13 July 1760, Shippen, Balch Papers, vol. 1, p. 114, HSP.

120. Joseph Shippen [III] to Edward Shippen [III], London, 21 January 1761, Shippen Papers, vol. 10, p. 67, HSP.

121. Joseph Shippen, Jr. [III] to Dear Brother [Edward Shippen IV], London, 29 January 1761, Joseph Shippen, Jr. Letterbook, Shippen Papers, HSP. Ordre de Monsieur le Ministre J. G. Catt, Le Soussigné Ministre de Sa Majesté Britannique auprés du Loüable Corps Helvètique, Berne, 5 Decembre 1760, Shippen Papers, vol. 15, p. 143, HSP. Joseph Shippen [III] to Daniel Crispin, Naples, 3 October 1760, Shippen Papers, Box 1, Joseph Shippen, folder 12, HSP.

122. Joseph Shippen [III] to Edward Shippen [III], London, 21 January 1761, Shippen Papers, vol. 10, p. 67, HSP.

123. Joseph Shippen, Jr. [III] to Edward Shippen, Jr. [IV], London, 11 April 1761, Joseph Shippen Letterbook, Shippen Papers, HSP.

124. T[homas] P[enn] to [Joseph] Shippen [III], London, 10 September 1762, Thomas Penn Letterbook, HSP.

125. Keith, *Provincial Councillors,* p. 78, erroneously claims that Shippen's income from the office was only £11, and that this is why the self-sacrificing public servant petitioned the General Assembly for a raise in 1772 (Joseph Shippen, Jr. [III], Petition, to the Hon. House of Representatives of the Province of Pennsylvania in General Assembly, n.d., Shippen Papers, Box 1, HSP); *Pennsylvania Archives,* eighth series, ed. Gertrude MacKinney and Charles F. Hoban (8 vols., Harrisburg, 1931–1935), vol. VIII, p. 6855. According to Joseph III's letter to his father (Joseph Shippen to Dear Sir, 19 March 1762, Shippen Papers, vol. 11, p. 41, HSP), Joseph III's housekeeper, Nancy Saunders, received £13 per year.

126. Robert Rutherford to Joseph Shippen, Jr. [III], Esq., Leghorn, 21 May 1762, Shippen Papers, vol. 5, p. 191, HSP. *Pennsylvania Gazette,* 3 December 1761; *Pennsylvania Archives,* 3d ser., ed. William Henry Egle and George Edward Reed (30 vols., Harrisburg, 1894–1899), vol. IX, p. 335; *Pennsylvania Archives,* 8th ser., ed. MacKinney and Hoban, vol. VII,

pp. 5668, 5788, 5937, 6060, 6199, 6265, 6284, 6445, 6561, vol. VIII, pp. 6722, 6855, 6857, 7021, 7145, 7299, 7587; Joseph Shippen [III], Secretary of Pennsylvania, Account Book, 1768–1775, Shippen Papers, HSP; Proprietary Tax List, Philadelphia City and County, 1769, Genealogical Society of Pennsylvania. (The 1769 tax list is inaccurately reproduced in Pennsylvania Archives, 3d ser., ed. Egle, vol. XIV, pp. 1–220.)

127. John Morgan to Joseph Shippen [III], Naples, 12 May 1764, Shippen, Balch Papers, vol. 1, p. 127, HSP.

128. *Pennsylvania Gazette,* 6 October 1768.

129. Edward Burd to Edward Shippen [III], Philadelphia, 15 December 1768, Burd-Shippen-Hubley Papers, HSP.

130. Christ Church, Marriages, 1709–1810, Genealogical Society of Pennsylvania, Proceedings, vol. 179, p. 4342. Joseph Shippen to Dear Hon^r Sir, Philadelphia, 19 March 1762, Shippen Papers, vol. 11, p. 41, HSP.

CHAPTER VI

1. The fullest sketch of William Shippen III is Betsy Copping Corner's *William Shippen, Jr.: Pioneer in American Medical Education* (Philadelphia, 1951). Briefer accounts appear in James Thatcher's, *American Medical Biography,* ed. Whitfield J. Bell, Jr. (2 vols., New York, 1967), vol. 2, pp. 82–88; Edward Potts Cheyney and Ellis Paxson Oberholtzer, *University of Pennsylvania: Its History, Influence, Equipment, and Characteristics, with Biographical Sketches and Portraits of Founders, Benefactors, Officers, and Alumni* (2 vols., Boston, 1901–1902), vol. 1, p. 285; *Dictionary of American Biography,* ed. Allen Johnson and Dumas Malone (22 vols., New York, 1928–1944), vol. IX, pp. 117–118.

2. H. J. Habakkuk, "England," in *The European Nobility in the Eighteenth Century: Studies of the Nobilities of the Major European States in the Pre-Reform Era,* ed. Albert Goodwin (New York, 1967), p. 16.

3. Edward Shippen, Jr. [IV] to Edward Shippen [III], Philadelphia, 22 December 1757, Shippen Papers, vol. 3, p. 191, HSP.

4. *Ibid.*

5. T[homas] P[enn] to J[oseph] S[hippen II], London, 20 October 1758, Thomas Penn Letterbook, vol. 6, p. 1, HSP.

6. Edward Shippen, Jr. [IV] to Edward Shippen [III], Philadelphia, 19 September 1760, Shippen Papers, vol. 5, p. 99, HSP; T[homas] P[enn] to Joseph Shippen [II], London, 21 June 1760; T[homas] P[enn] to Joseph Shippen [II], London, 9 October 1761, Thomas Penn Papers, vol. 6, p. 273; vol. 7, p. 80, HSP.

7. Edward Shippen, Jr. [IV] to Edward Shippen [III], Philadelphia,

29 September 1760, Shippen Papers, vol. 5, p. 99, HSP. Edward IV goes on to describe the means and character of his cousin's intended mate.

8. Edward Shippen [IV] to Edward Shippen [III], Philadelphia, 3 December 1760, Shippen, Balch Papers, vol. 1, p. 122, HSP.

9. Christ Church, Marriages 1709–1810, Genealogical Society of Pennsylvania, Collections, vol. 179, p. 4277. Although no details survive concerning Catherine Shippen's dowry, comments about her contemporaries of roughly the same social standing give a sense of what transpired. For example, the 1753 marriage negotiations of her cousin Edward Shippen IV appear in chapter five. In 1768, Cousin Joseph Shippen III writes about "our Cousin Jemmy's [*sic*] Allen's forming a close Alliance with Mr. John Lawrence's only Daughter. The Match is absolutely fixed, and highly approved by the Families on both sides; and the two Fathers have settled the preliminaries to the Satisfaction of both. It is expected to be finished in three weeks or less." (Joseph Shippen, Jr. [III] to Edward Shippen [III], Philadelphia, 9 February 1768, Joseph Shippen Papers, No. 1656, LC.) His father responded to the information about this natural course of events by saying, "We think the Match . . . is very Suitable; especially as all ye nearest concerned are pleased with it. It was certainly well judged in the young Gentleman's father to get Preliminarys settled. I suppose the young Ladies Father must give the House where Mr. Frank lives with her at least." (Edward Shippen [III] to Joseph Shippen [III], Lancaster, 22 February 1768, Shippen Papers, vol. 10, p. 79, HSP.) Although material considerations almost always played a considerable role in marriages among the elite, other influences had a role. For example, in 1765 Edward Shippen IV informed his father that "I have reason to believe that the eldest daughter of a good Friend of ours is addressed by two powerful Rivals; The considerable Rank of one with his Education is like to prevail over the independent [fortune] of £2500 (sterling) p[er] an[num] of the other, who is a Carolina Gentleman." (Edward Shippen, Jr. [IV] to Hon^d Sir [Edward Shippen III], Philadelphia, 22 May 1765, Shippen Papers, vol. 11, p. 66, HSP.) Joseph Shippen [IV], University of Pennsylvania Biographical Catalog of Graduates, University of Pennsylvania Archives.

10. Both William Shippen and Joseph IV died at age twenty-three, and John, at age thirty. Only Joseph Shippen III, single until age thirty-six, may have given serious thought to bachelorhood as an alternative. This pattern takes on significance when one contrasts the Shippens with families in Europe. J. Hajnal's "European Marriage Patterns in Perspective" (in *Population in History, Essays in Historical Demography,* ed. D. V. Glass and D. E. C. Eversley [Chicago, 1965], pp. 101–143) discusses the "European pattern" which existed from 1740–1940, and may have begun even

before 1740. He finds that some children, especially younger ones, usually never married because of the amount of emphasis placed on the eldest son. Similarly, daughters usually married in their mid-twenties and younger sons at about age twenty-eight, twenty-nine, and frequently older than that. Also useful in this regard is T. H. Hollingsworth's "A Demographic study of the British Ducal Families," in *Population in History,* ed. Glass and Eversley, pp. 354–379.

11. *Minutes of the Common Council of Philadelphia, 1702–1776* (Philadelphia, 1847). Christ Church, Marriages 1709–1810, Collections of the Genealogical Society of Pennsylvania, vol. 179, p. 4330.

12. Edward Shippen [III] to James Burd, Lancaster, 2 April 1774, Shippen Papers, vol. 7, p. 87, HSP.

13. James Burd to Edward Shippen [III], Tinian, 9 April 1774, Shippen Papers, vol. 10, p. 173, HSP.

14. Joseph Shippen [II] to Edward Shippen [III], Philadelphia, 25 June 1775, Shippen Papers, vol. 7, p. 123, HSP. Christ Church, Marriages, 1709–1810, Collections of the Genealogical Society of Pennsylvania, vol. 179, p. 4390. Edward Shippen III's interest in his niece's welfare is evident in the comfort he tried to provide when she went to visit him "to recover her Spirits. She lately had the misfortune to bury her Little Daughter." Joseph Shippen II's letter of 25 June 1775 also indicates that the death of children brought about serious emotional strains; the reason for mentioning this is that historical attitudes toward death are not well established. Although death, at least within the Shippen family, was more common than in twentieth-century families, it still brought about similar emotional reactions.

15. *American Weekly Mercury,* 5 September 1734.

16. *Pennsylvania Gazette,* 31 March 1737. The interpretation offered here differs somewhat with that of Betsy Copping Corner's *William Shippen, Jr.,* p. 5 which claims Shippen's "mind and character was shaped by exceptionally favorable circumstances of birth, rearing and formal education." The observation seems more applicable to the other branches of the Shippen family insofar as benefits of birth are concerned. Only after extensive professional training could Shippen then draw on the distinction of the family name. Certainly the circumstances of the William II branch of the Shippen family were more favorable than most, but not exceptional in comparison to the primary branch of the Shippen family or to many other Philadelphia families of greater consequence. For additional information concerning the kind of education Shippen probably received at Samuel Finley's boarding school see Corner, *William Shippen, Jr.,* pp. 5–6;

Whitfield J. Bell, Jr.'s *John Morgan: Continental Doctor* (Philadelphia, 1965), pp. 24–25, 154; and *The Autobiography of Benjamin Rush,* ed. George W. Corner (Princeton, 1948), pp. 28–32, 38, 39. Finley (1715–1766) was a Presbyterian minister born in Ireland; he migrated to the colonies in 1734, studied with the Tennents, and became an itinerant preacher of the Great Awakening. Alan Heimert and Perry Miller in *The Great Awakening: Documents Illustrating the Crisis and Its Consequences* (New York, 1967), pp. 152–163, describe him as probably "the most aggressive of the prorevivalists." See also William B. Sprague, *Annals of the American Pulpit* (9 vols., New York, 1857–1869), vol. 3, pp. 96–101, and Archibald Alexander, *Biographical Sketches of the Founder, and Principal Alumni of the Log College* (Princeton, 1845), pp. 302–317.

17. Joseph Shippen, Jr. [III] to Edward Shippen [III], Newark, 30 March 1751, Shippen Papers, vol. 10, p. 19, HSP.

18. Joseph Shippen, Jr. [III] to Edward Shippen, Newark, 21 December 1750; Joseph Shippen, Jr. [III] to Edward Shippen [III], Newark, 9 April 1751, Shippen Papers, vol. 10, pp. 21, 19, HSP. The cordiality of the cousins may be inferred from some of their activities and correspondence; for example, see Joseph Shippen [III] to William Shippen, Jr. [III], Lancaster, 5 August 1754, 9 September 1754, 13 June 1755, Joseph Shippen, Jr. [III] Letterbook, Small Books No. 3, Shippen Papers, HSP.

19. Ezra Stiles, Diary, 25 September 1754, Massachusetts Historical Society *Proceedings,* series 2, vol. VII (1891–1892), 340.

20. Quoted in Corner, *William Shippen, Jr.,* p. 6.

21. Joseph Shippen, Jr. [III] to William Shippen, Jr. [III], Lancaster, 9 September 1754, Joseph Shippen, Jr., Letterbook, Small Books No. 3, Shippen Papers, HSP.

22. Cheyney and Oberholtzer, *University of Pennsylvania,* vol. 1, p. 256; George W. Norris, *The Early History of Medicine in Philadelphia* (Philadelphia, 1886), *passim*; Richard Harrison Shryock, *Medicine and Society in America, 1660–1860* (New York, 1960), pp. 1–43. Eighteen William Shippen II deeds from the period 1755 to 1774 are found in Box 17 of the Shippen Family Papers at the Library of Congress. Of them only two (one dated 25 November 1761 and the other dated 20 August 1765) identify Shippen as a chemist; about ninety percent indicate his occupation as "practitioner of physick."

23. Deed, Jacob Bankson to William Shippen [II], 10 October 1750; Deed, Joseph Shippen [II] to William Shippen [II], 18 February 1754; Deed, William Pearson to William Shippen [II], 6 November 1756; Deed, William Bradford to William Shippen [II], 25 November 1761; Deed, John

Wikoff to William Shippen [II], 10 March 1762; Deed, Edward Shippen [III] to William Shippen [II], 30 April 1765; Deed, Joseph Shippen [II] to William Shippen [II], 10 January 1767; Deed, William Stennard to William Shippen [II], 10 August 1768; Deed, Edward Shippen, Jr. [IV] to William Shippen [II], 14 December 1770, Shippen Family Papers, Box 17, LC.

24. William Shippen [II] to Edward Shippen [III], 2 September 1757, Shippen Papers, vol. 3, p. 33, HSP.

25. Evidence suggesting that Edward Shippen III gave financial assistance to his nephew William III will appear later in this chapter. Here it seems worth noting that in William Shippen, Jr. [III] to Edward Shippen [III], London, 10 March 1759, Shippen Papers, vol. 4, p. 9, HSP, the young man assures his uncle, "Your instructing Lessons upon ye frugal use of Time & money, are always in my mind & influence my conduct much."

26. William Shippen [II] to George Whitefield, Philadelphia, 11 September 1758, George Whitefield Papers, No. 47, LC.

27. William Shippen [II] to Edward Shippen [III], Philadelphia, 1 September 1758, Shippen Papers, vol. 3, p. 197, HSP.

28. *Ibid.*

29. William Shippen, Jr. [III] to Edward Shippen [III], London, 10 March 1759, Shippen Papers, vol. 4, p. 9, HSP.

30. William Shippen, Jr. [III], Journal, 4 August 1759, in Corner, *William Shippen, Jr.,* p. 14.

31. William Shippen, Jr. [III] to Edward Shippen [III], London, 10 March 1759, Shippen Papers, vol. 4, p. 9, HSP.

32. William Shippen III's London journal, 19 July 1759 to 22 January 1760, is reproduced with valuable editorial notes in Corner, *William Shippen, Jr.,* pp. 11–49.

33. William Shippen III, Journal, *passim,* Corner, *William Shippen,* pp. 11–34.

34. *Ibid.,* 31 July 1759, pp. 13–14.

35. *Ibid.,* 13 August 1759, p. 16.

36. *Ibid.,* 27 August 1759, p. 19. For a fuller treatment of Shippen's medical activities in London, see Corner, *William Shippen, Jr.* pp. 50–57, 65–73, 86–95.

37. By this time the people of London had come to accept the practice of dissecting human bodies; when Shippen carried the practice to the provinces, violent opposition confronted him.

38. Quoted in Corner, *William Shippen, Jr.,* p. 67.

39. Corner, *William Shippen, Jr.,* p. 69.

40. *Ibid.,* p. 80. Because Shippen's medical training abroad was very

similar to that of his rival John Morgan, chapters three and four of Bell's *John Morgan* are useful for additional details.

41. Whitfield J. Bell, Jr., "Some American Students of . . . Dr. William Cullen of Edinburgh, 1755–1766," American Philosophical Society, *Proceedings*, vol. XCIV (1950), 275–281. Thatcher, *American Medical Biography*, vol. 2, p. 83, exaggerates when he claims that William Shippen III "devoted all his leisure to the study of comparative anatomy."

42. William Shippen III, Journal, 26 September 1759, Corner, *William Shippen, Jr.*, p. 24.

43. In 1761 when the college sought a new president, trustee William Shippen II indicated his preference for "any Polite genteel Popular Gentleman" of "real piety & Godliness" to several candidates of learning, grace, and poise who in his mind lacked true religious conviction. He even vowed "I would rather have the awkward stammering [Samuel] Finley whom we know to be honest and who has all the Essential Qualifications of a Pres[id]ent—than the finest Orator in England without them." (William Shippen [II] to Edward Shippen [III], Philadelphia, 10 April 1761, Shippen Papers, vol. 5, p. 137, HSP.)

44. Thatcher, *American Medical Biography*, vol. 2, p. 81.

45. Edward Shippen [III] to Edward Shippen, Jr. [IV], Lancaster, 20 March 1754, Shippen Papers, vol. 11, p. 4, HSP.

46. William Shippen [II] to George Whitefield, Philadelphia, 11 September 1758, George Whitefield Papers, No. 47, LC.

47. William Shippen [II] to Edward Shippen [III], Philadelphia, 1 September 1758, Shippen Papers, vol. 3, p. 197, HSP.

48. William Shippen [II] to George Whitefield, Philadelphia, 11 September 1758, George Whitefield Papers, No. 47, LC.

49. William Shippen, Jr. [III] to Edward Shippen [III], London, 10 March 1759, Shippen Papers, vol. 4, p. 9, HSP.

50. *Ibid.*

51. For a useful and vivid comparison of interests, compare Shippen's journal with that kept by George Whitefield or William Steward, his traveling companion.

52. Thanksgiving Day was Thursday, November 29, 1759. According to Corner, *William Shippen, Jr.*, p. 46, on this day, by order of King George II, "sermons were preached in all the churches and prayers of gratitude were offered for a harvest of victories."

53. William Shippen III's Journal, 22 July 1759, Corner, *William Shippen, Jr.*, p. 11.

54. William Shippen III's Journal, 12 August, 4 November 1759, Corner, *William Shippen, Jr.*, pp. 16, 28. The customary aspect of attending

church is specific in the following entries in William Shippen III's journal: July 29, September 16, 23, November 4, 18, December 2, 1759, Corner, *William Shippen, Jr.,* pp. 13, 23, 24, 28 29, 30.

55. William Shippen III, Journal, 16 September 1759, Corner, *William Shippen, Jr.,* p. 23.

56. *Ibid.,* 5 August 1759, p. 14.

57. *Ibid.,* 16 September 1759, 20 January 1760, pp. 23, 24.

58. That medicine came first is evident throughout the journal. Specific entries which demonstrate this most clearly are Sunday, October 7 and 14, 1759, when Shippen dissected all day and evidently failed to attend church or record any thoughts about religion. On October 17, November 20, and December 21, 1759, he saw only half a play because he attended Hunter's lectures on anatomy earlier in the evening. On November 15, 1759, Shippen even passed up an opportunity to see David Garrick in deference to a medical lecture.

59. Corner, *William Shippen, Jr.,* William Shippen III, Journal, 27 July 1759, pp. 12–13.

60. *Ibid.,* 18 August 1759, p. 17.

61. *Ibid.,* 23 August 1759, pp. 18–19.

62. *Ibid.,* 5 September 1759, p. 21.

63. *Ibid.,* 18 December 1759, p. 31.

64. *Ibid.,* 10 September 1759, p. 22.

65. *Ibid.,* 13 September, 9 November 1759, pp. 22, 28.

66. *Ibid.,* 4 September 1759, p. 21.

67. *Ibid.,* 21 September 1759, p. 24.

68. *Ibid.,* 23 August 1759, p. 18. Corner provides an annotated list of the plays which Shippen saw, *William Shippen, Jr.,* pp. 75–77.

69. For example, see Thatcher's description of William Shippen III's character, in *American Medical Biographies,* vol. 2, p. 84: "His person was graceful, his manners polished, his conversation various, and the tones of his voice singularly sweet and conciliatory. In his intercourse with society he was gay without levity, and dignified without haughtiness or austerity." Even caustic Jacob Rush, who referred to Shippen as "the Cassius of Philadelphia," indicates that in public William Shippen III showed little of the enthusiasm of his father. In Jacob Rush to Benjamin Rush, London, 24 January 1774, Manuscript Correspondence of Benjamin Rush, vol. 34, p. 44, Library Company of Philadelphia, Rush writes: "I have long thought that Dr. Shippen extremely resembles in some Parts of his Character the infamous Cassius. . . . Like him he is, as Sir Richd Steele says of Cassius, quick to receive an Injury, slow to discover his Distaste. His Temper never flies into his Face, but descends to his Heart, and there

rankles into Malice, Envy, and Revenge. It was impossible to throw Cassius into a Passion. The calm Villain was too much the Master of himself ever to be seized with a Transport of honest Indignation. Our modern Cassius like him too cannot be taken off his Guard. There is no such Thing as ruffling his serene and equal Spirit."

The idea that a new order was emerging will be developed in chapters eight and nine. At this time it is appropriate to mention only that Bernard Bailyn in *Ideological Origins of the American Revolution* (Cambridge, Mass., 1967) points out that the colonists were very much aware of the growth of luxury, wickedness, and degeneration which pamphleteers derided. Gordon Wood suggests in "Rhetoric and Reality in the American Revolution," *William and Mary Quarterly*, 3d ser., vol. XXIII, no. 1 (January 1966), 3–32, that many colonists perceived the same tendencies in the colonies as well and that this explains the frenzy and irrationality of even fairly moderate revolutionaries such as John Adams, George Washington, and others. Wood suggests that the social and political conditions of the colonies made English Radical Whig thought most relevant to the revolutionary pamphleteers.

70. Benjamin Franklin recommended William Shippen III to Cullen as "the Son of a particular Friend of mine in Philadelphia, and bears himself the Character of an ingenious sober and discreet young Man, which persuades me that any Countenance you may show him will not be misplac'd." (B[enjamin] Franklin to Dr. [William] Cullen, 17 September 1760, Franklin Papers, APS.)

71. Shippen's dissertation was published in 1761. Benjamin Franklin's copy at the American Philosophical Society is found in translation in Corner, *William Shippen, Jr.*, pp. 127–146.

72. William Shippen [III] of Pennsylvania, *De Placentae cum Utero nexu* (Edinburgh, 1761), title page quoted in Corner, *William Shippen, Jr.*, p. 129.

73. John Morgan to Joseph Shippen, Jr. [III], London, 12 October 1761, Shippen Papers, vol. 5, p. 167, HSP.

74. Thatcher, *American Medical Biography*, vol. 2, p. 84. About twenty-five years after the trip to France, William Shippen III recalled that he had stayed about three months at the Hôtel de Londres in Rue Honoré. William Shippen [III] to Thomas Lee Shippen, 17 —— 1787, Shippen Family Papers, Box 5, LC.

75. Corner, *William Shippen, Jr.*, p. 96; Ethel Armes (ed.), *Nancy Shippen, Her Journal Book: The International Romance of a Young Lady of Fashion of Colonial Philadelphia with Letters to her and about her* (New York, 1968), pp. 24, 50–51.

76. About a decade later Ebenezer Hazard, gentleman, another graduate of Finley's academy, contrasted London with Philadelphia; to him Bristol and Edinburgh were more like home. In London, Hazard was struck by the corrupt manner of the people; "Luxury Extravagance & Vice of almost every kind prevail in a very great degree." After describing the hospitable, kind, industrious, and moral people of Scotland, he concluded that "compared with *London, Edinburgh* is *Heaven*." Ebenezer Hazard, Journal, "Reflections after return from Europe," n.d. [1771], vol. 2, Hazard Family Papers, HSP.

77. Corner, *William Shippen, Jr.*, p. 97, describes the family neighborhood, but she errs when she says Uncle Charles Willing greeted the young couple, for Willing died in 1754; also, Willing's daughter Mary, who married William Byrd of Westover, moved to Virginia, rather than staying in Philadelphia.

78. William Shippen III, Journal, 19 July, 27 August, 29, 30 December 1759, 1, 5, 18, 20 January 1760, Corner, *William Shippen Jr.*, pp. 11, 19, 32–34; *Pennsylvania Gazette,* 31 January 1765. Family visits were a duty when one lived near one's relatives and also when one passed through the area to which one's kin had removed. This is evident in the Shippen correspondence. For example, when Joseph Shippen III ventured to London in 1761, he corresponded with "Cousin Billey Shippen in Scotland." He "desired him to pay a visit to Colo[nel] Burds [Joseph III's "brother's"] Father's Family at Ormiston." William III agreed to do so and also hoped to meet his cousin in London later that year. (Joseph Shippen, Jr. [III] to Edward Shippen, Sr. [III], London, 8 May 1761, Joseph Shippen, Jr., Letterbook, Shippen Papers, HSP.)

79. John Fothergill to James Pemberton, London, July 1762, quoted in Thomas G. Morton and Frank Woodbury, *History of the Pennsylvania Hospital from its Foundation to* A.D. *1770* (Philadelphia, 1897), p. 357 and Corner, *William Shippen, Jr.*, pp. 98–99.

80. *Pennsylvania Gazette,* 11 November 1762. Thatcher, *American Medical Biography*, vol. 2, p. 85, considers Shippen's November 16, 1762, introductory lecture at the State House to a large gathering and subsequent lectures on anatomy to about twelve students "the origin of our medical school." Corner, *William Shippen, Jr.*, p. 100, says ten students attended the first series of lectures which she postulates were given in a converted carriage house or newly erected and unpretentious quarters on grounds owned by Shippen's father. Although after 1765 William Shippen III claimed that these lectures were the origins of the first medical school in the colonies, recent scholarly opinions award that honor to the more ambitious undertaking brought about by John Morgan in 1765.

81. *Pennsylvania Gazette,* 11 January 1770; Wardens of Philadelphia, Minutes, 1 July 1772, Independence Hall National Park Service; Corner, *William Shippen, Jr.,* pp. 96–105.

82. Quoted in Corner, *William Shippen, Jr.,* p. 99.

83. Shippen described his course in the *Pennsylvania Gazette,* 31 January 1765. Although the description is printed in Corner, *William Shippen, Jr.,* pp. 103–104, its relevance to a study of the family merits repetition. Shippen wrote: "Dr. Shippen, Jr., having been lately called to the assistance of a number of women in the country, in difficult labours, most of which was made so by the unskillful old women about them, the poor women having suffered extremely, and their innocent little ones being entirely destroyed, whose lives might have been easily saved by proper management, and being informed of several desperate cases in the different neighborhoods which had proved fatal to the mothers as to the infants and were attended with the most painful circumstances too dismal to be related, he thought it his duty immediately to begin his intended courses in Midwifery, and has prepared a proper apparatus for that purpose, in order to instruct those women who have virtue enough to own their ignorance and apply for instructions, as well as those young gentlemen now engaged in the study of that useful and necessary branch of surgery who are taking pains to qualify themselves to practice in different parts of the country with safety and advantage to their fellow citizens."

He continues, explaining that: "A course will consist of about twenty lectures in which he will treat of that part of anatomy which is necessary to understand that branch—explain all cases of Midwifery—natural, difficult and preternatural—and give directions how to treat them with safety to the mother and child; describe the diseases incident to women and children in the month, and direct to proper remedies; will take occasion during the course to explain and apply those curious anatomical plates and casts of the gravid uterus at the Hospital and conclude the whole with necessary cautions against the dangerous and cruel use of instruments. In order to make this course more perfect, convenient lodging is provided for the accommodation of a few poor women who otherwise might suffer for want of the common necessities on those occasions, to be under the care of a sober, honest matron, well acquainted with lying-in women, employed by the Doctor for that purpose. . . . The Doctor may be spoke with at his house in Front Street every morning between the hours of six and nine, or at his office in Laetitia Court every evening."

84. The commendation, from Provost William Smith, is quoted in Bell, *Morgan,* p. 29.

85. Samuel Powel to Samuel Morris, 2 September 1763, Robert C. Moon,

The Morris Family of Philadelphia (5 vols., Philadelphia, 1898–1909), vol. 2, p. 469, quoted in Bell, *Morgan*, p. 75.

86. Whitfield J. Bell, Jr.'s *John Morgan: Continental Doctor*, is an excellent full-length study of Shippen's rival. James T. Flexner presents a short glowing sketch in *Doctors on Horseback: Pioneers of American Medicine* (New York, 1944), pp. 3–46. Bell deals with the continuing Morgan-Shippen feud in far more depth than one can in a study of the Shippen family.

87. *Pennsylvania Gazette*, 9 May 1765; Bell, *Morgan*, p. 117; Corner, *William Shippen, Jr.*, p. 107.

88. Bell, *Morgan*, p. 125.

89. *Ibid.*, pp. 100–150; Corner, *William Shippen, Jr.*, pp. 106–110.

90. One of the many examples of this bickering is referred to in Jacob Rush to Benjamin Rush, London, 24 January 1774, Manuscript Correspondence of Benjamin Rush, vol. 34, p. 44, Library Company of Philadelphia, in which Jacob Rush writes to his brother,

"I am sorry that Dr. Shippen has kept any Students from attending your Lectures. At the same Time, I am not at all sorry that you are at Variance with him. Better, infinitely better is it to be at eternal Variance with a Man of his cool Malice and Treachery, than to have any Connection with him . . . since you are come to a Rupture with him, suffer me to put you upon your Guard agt letting rash or imprudent Expressions escape from you."

91. Bell, *Morgan*, pp. 137–138; *Pennsylvania Gazette*, 18 September 1766, 20 September 1770. It seems necessary to mention in regard to the Shippen-Morgan rivalry that there were limits upon the powers available to Shippen through his family connections. For example, Cousin William Allen, as both the third- and fourth-generation Shippens referred to the chief justice, recommended Morgan's medical society to the proprietor.

92. William Shippen [II] to Edward Shippen [III], Philadelphia, 9 August 1770, Miscellaneous Manuscripts Collection, APS. The Latin phrase, roughly translated, means: "Nothing is so difficult that it cannot be overcome by cleverness."

93. Thomas H. Montgomery, *A History of the University of Pennsylvania from Its Foundation to* A.D. *1770: Including Biographical Sketches of the Trustees, Faculty, the First Alumni, and Others* (Philadelphia, 1900), p. 550; Charles R. Hildeburn, "Descendants of Dr. William Shippen," in *Nancy Shippen, Her Journal Book*, ed. Armes, pp. 314–316. John T. Cunningham, *Newark* (Newark, 1966), p. 60, reproduces a letter purporting to show that John Shippen was at the College of New Jersey in 1752. Shippen was only twelve years old at the time; the style and content

of the letter are those of an older individual. Very likely John's older brother, William III, was the author of the "tart letter" discussing the marriage of President Burr to the twenty-one-year-old daughter of Jonathan Edwards.

94. Bell, *Morgan,* p. 157.

95. Edward Shippen [III] to James Burd, Lancaster, 6 December 1770, Shippen Papers, vol. 7, p. 25, HSP.

96. *Ibid.*

97. William Shippen [II] to Edward Shippen [III], Philadelphia, 8 March 1756, Thomas Balch, *Letters and Papers relating to Pennsylvania* (5 vols., private printing, Philadelphia, 1855), p. 52.

98. William Shippen [II] to Edward Shippen [III], 2 September 1757, Shippen Papers, vol. 3, p. 33, HSP.

99. Joseph W. Shippen to Messrs. Standley & Fulton and Thomas Fayerweather, New Providence, 18 September 1760; Joseph W. Shippen to Thomas Fayerweather, Philadelphia, 4 August 1761, Shippen Papers, vol. 5, pp. 95, 153b, HSP; William Shippen [II] to Thomas Fayerweather, Philadelphia, 5 May 1754, Gratz Collection, American Physicians, Case 7, Box 33, HSP.

100. An entry in the Daybook of Dr. William Shippen [II], 1763–1776, Shippen Family Papers, Box 27, LC, indicates that Joseph W. Shippen was at the Oxford Furnace in 1770. The Daybook has no pagination.

101. Shippen's entry into the manufacturing of iron and subsequent expansion of his interest in it contradicts the thesis of Charles S. Boyer's *Early Forges and Furnaces in New Jersey* (Philadelphia, 1963) which mentions them.

102. Grant of Royal License to William Shippen [II], 23 April 1755, Shippen Family Papers, Box 17, LC. An abstract of Shippen's commission is printed in the Genealogical Society of Pennsylvania, *Publications,* X (1929), 53. Boyer, *Forges and Furnaces in New Jersey,* pp. 149–159.

103. Articles of agreement, Jonathan Robeson and Joseph Shippen [II] and William Shippen [II], 3 April 1759, Wharton Papers, Box 1757–1759, HSP; (Shippen) Accounts, 1759–1765, Daybook of Dr. William Shippen [II], 1763–1776, Shippen Family Papers, Box 27, LC; William Shippen [II] to Edward Shippen [III], Philadelphia, 8 December 1755; William Shippen [II] to Edward Shippen [III], 2 June 1757, Shippen Papers, vol. 2, pp. 11, 195, HSP; Edward Shippen [IV] to Edward Shippen [III], Philadelphia, 4 December 1759, Shippen, Balch Papers, vol. 1, p. 75, HSP.

104. William Shippen [II]'s Will, probated 10 November 1801, Philadelphia Register of Wills, Philadelphia City Hall; Letter of Administration, Estate of Joseph W. Shippen, 28 October 1795, *New Jersey Archives,* series 1, vol. XXXVII (Jersey City, 1942), p. 317. Joseph W. Shippen's marriage

eluded the careful genealogist Charles Hildeburn who compiled the useful family tree for the publication of the Nancy Shippen journal in 1936. Upon publication of the journal, a descendant of Joseph W. Shippen, who had gained membership in the Society of Colonial Wars in New York, rectified the error. (Frank B. Warner, Sr., to Dr. Lloyd P. Shippen, Niagra Falls, New York, 20 March 1936, Shippen Family Papers, Box 30, LC.)

105. William Shippen III, Journal, 19 August 1759, Corner, *William Shippen, Jr.*, p. 17.

106. William Shippen [II] to Edward Shippen [III], 2 September 1757; William Shippen [II] to Dear Brother [Edward Shippen III], Philadelphia, 11 April 1756, Shippen Papers, vol. 3, p. 33; vol. 2, p. 43, HSP.

107. Hildeburn, "Descendants of William Shippen [III]," in Armes, ed., *Nancy Shippen Journal*.

108. Heimert and Miller, *The Great Awakening*, pp. 127–128.

109. Edward Burd to Sally Burd, Philadelphia, 17 November 1767, Shippen, Balch Papers, vol. 2, p. 5, HSP.

110. William Shippen [II] to Thomas Fayerweather, Philadelphia, 20 March 1770, Dreer Collection, Members of Old Congress, HSP.

111. William Shippen to Thomas Fayerweather [1772], Dreer Collection, Physicians and Chemists, vol. 4, p. 152, HSP.

112. Thatcher's Military Journal, 23 July 1780, quoted in the *Pennsylvania Magazine of History and Biography*, vol. XV (1891), 70.

113. *Pennsylvania Magazine of History and Biography*, vol. VIII (1884), 113, vol. XV (1891), 463–464, vol. LXXIII (1949), 431; Keith, *Provincial Councillors*, pp. 139–140.

CHAPTER VII

1. The influence of previous grandfathers was more impersonal and consisted largely of legacies. This occurred because Edward Shippen and Joseph Shippen died before their grandchildren attained their majority. When the former died, his eldest grandchild (Edward III) was only nine years old; when the latter died, his oldest grandchild (Edward IV) was twelve. Edward III, for example, retained almost no recollections of his grandfather at all. If Edward IV had any, they are not recorded. For comments on intergenerational relationships in modern families, see James Walter and Nick Stinnett, "Parent-Child Relationships: A Decade Review of Research," *Journal of Marriage and the Family*, vol. 33, no. 1 (February 1971), 99.

2. Edward Shippen [III] to Dear Children [The Burds], Lancaster, 24 July 1753, Shippen Papers, vol. 1, p. 149, HSP, is but one of numerous

references to the young Burds as "the Ducky Children." In a letter to James Burd (2 April 1754), Joseph Shippen III closes with love to his sister Sarah "& (to use the phrase of our good Daddy) the little ducky Children."

3. Edward Shippen [III] to Mr. [James] Burd, Philadelphia, 16 November 1752, Edward Shippen Letterbook, APS; Edward Shippen [III] to James Burd, Lancaster, 16 June 1757, in Thomas Balch, *Papers and Letters relating to Pennsylvania* (5 vols., private printing, Philadelphia, 1855), vol. 1, p. 84; Edward Shippen [III] to Capt. [Joseph] Shippen [III], Lancaster, 6 March 1758; Sarah Burd to Dear Mr. [James] Burd, Lancaster, October 1758, Shippen Papers, vol. 10, p. 65; vol. 11, p. 12, HSP.

4. Edward Shippen [III] to James Burd, Lancaster, 29 July 1758, Shippen Papers, vol. 3, p. 185, HSP.

5. Sarah Burd to James Burd, Lancaster, 11 October 1756, Burd-Shippen-Hubley Papers, HSP. The experience of the Burd family from about 1756–1764 makes the myopia of Daniel P. Moynihan's "The Negro Family: The Case for National Action" (in L. Rainwater and W. L. Yancey, *The Moynihan Report and the Politics of Controversy* (Boston, 1967), readily apparent. It seems pertinent to observe that similarities between the Burds' experience and that of modern lower-class families in London exist. For details of the analogy, see Michael Young and Peter Willmott, *Family and Kinship in East London* (Baltimore, 1962).

6. Sarah Burd to James Burd, Lancaster, 17 September 1759, Shippen, Balch Papers, vol. 1, p. 71, HSP.

7. Sarah Burd to "My D[ear] Mr. Burd, Lancaster, 12 August 1760; Sarah Burd to [James Burd], Lancaster, 30 August [1760 or 1761]; Sarah Burd to [James Burd], Lancaster, 17 July 1761, Shippen Papers, vol. 11, pp. 25, 34, 33, HSP; Sarah Burd to James Burd, Lancaster, 4 January 1763, Burd-Shippen-Hubley Papers, HSP.

8. Joseph Shippen [III] to James Burd, Lancaster, 31 May 1757, Shippen Papers, vol. 2, p. 191, HSP. "In a thriving Condition" and in "that Situation" are among several eighteenth-century phrases which refer to pregnancy.

9. Sarah Burd to James Burd, Lancaster, 23 July 1759, Shippen Papers, vol. 4, p. 97, HSP.

10. Edward Shippen [III] to James Burd, Lancaster, 13 August 1759, Shippen Papers, vol. 4, p. 115, HSP.

11. Edward Shippen [III] to James Burd, Lancaster, 15 7bre 1759, Shippen Papers, vol. 4, p. 147, HSP.

12. Sarah Burd to "My Dear Mr. Burd," Lancaster, 12 May 1759, Shippen Papers, vol. 11, p. 14, HSP.

13. Sarah Burd to "My Dear Mr. B[urd]," Lancaster, 14 August 1759, Shippen Papers, vol. 11, p. 15, HSP.

14. Sarah Burd to "My D[ear] Mr. B[urd]," Lancaster, 18 September 1760, Shippen Papers, vol. 11, p. 27, HSP.

15. Edward Shippen [III] to James Burd, Lancaster, 21 June 1760, Shippen Papers, vol. 5, p. 55, HSP.

16. James Burd to Edward Shippen [III], Carlisle, 12 June 1760, Shippen Papers, vol. 5, p. 53, HSP.

17. Edward Shippen [III] to James Burd, Lancaster, 21 June 1760, Shippen Papers, vol. 5, p. 55, HSP.

18. Edward Shippen, Jr. [IV] to Edward Shippen [III], Philadelphia, 30 June 1760, Shippen, Balch Papers, vol. 1, p. 109, HSP.

19. Edward Shippen, Jr. [IV] to Edward Shippen [III], Philadelphia, 27 November 1760, Shippen, Balch Papers, vol. 1, p. 121, HSP.

20. Edward Shippen [IV] to Edward Shippen [III], Philadelphia, 18 December 1760, Shippen, Balch Papers, vol. 1, p. 123, HSP. Joseph Shippen, Jr. [III] to Edward Shippen [III], Philadelphia, 5 April 1762, Burd-Shippen-Hubley Papers, HSP.

21. James Burd to ———, Fort Augusta, 10 January 1764, Shippen Papers, vol. 6, p. 77, HSP.

22. *Ibid.* Sarah Burd to [James Burd], Lancaster, 8 July 1763; Edward Shippen [IV] to Edward Shippen [III], 14 July [1763], quoted in Edward Shippen [III] to James Burd, Lancaster, 15 July 1763, Shippen Papers, vol. 11, p. 54; vol. 6, p. 35, HSP.

23. Sarah Burd to James Burd, Lancaster, 19 November 1763, Shippen Papers, vol. 11, p. 59, HSP.

24. Sarah Burd to James Burd, Lancaster, 4 October 1763, Peale Papers, Mills Collection, APS; Sarah Burd to James Burd, Lancaster, 4 November 1763, Shippen Papers, vol. 11, p. 58, HSP.

25. Edward Shippen [III] to James Burd, Lancaster, 7 January 1764, Shippen Papers, vol. 6, p. 75, HSP.

26. James Burd to Edward Shippen [III], Fort Augusta, 19 January 1764, Shippen Papers, vol. 6, p. 81, HSP.

27. *Ibid.*

28. Sarah Burd to James Burd, Lancaster, 3 March 1764, Shippen Papers, vol. 11, p. 62, HSP. Sarah Burd to James Burd, Lancaster, 10 January 1764; Sarah Burd to James Burd, Lancaster, 26 January 1764; Edward Shippen [III] to James Burd, Lancaster, 25 January 1764; Edward Shippen [III] to James Burd, Lancaster, 13 February 1764, Shippen Papers, vol. 11, pp. 60, 61; vol. 6, pp. 83, 87, HSP.

29. James Burd to Edward Burd, Lancaster, 20 August 1764, Burd-Shippen-Hubley Papers, folder 38, HSP.

30. Edward Shippen [III] to James Burd, Lancaster, 3 September 1757, Shippen Papers, vol. 3, p. 35, HSP.

31. James Burd to Edward Shippen [III], Fort Augusta, 23 April 1757, Shippen Papers, vol. 2, p. 159, HSP.

32. James Burd to Edward Burd, Lancaster, 20 August 1764, Burd-Shippen-Hubley Papers, folder 38, HSP.

33. *Ibid.*

34. *Ibid.* John Burd to [Sarah Burd], Kingston, Jamaica, 10 March 1756, Peale Papers, Mills Collection, APS; Edward Shippen [IV] to Edward Shippen [III], Philadelphia, 8 January 1758, Shippen Papers, Box 1, HSP; Edward Shippen to James Burd, Lancaster, 4 July 1758; Edward Burd to James Burd, Ormistown [Scotland], 4 November 1762, Shippen Papers, vol. 3, p. 179; vol. 5, p. 223, HSP.

35. James Burd to Edward Shippen [III], Tinian, 28 October 1771, folder 38, Burd-Shippen-Hubley Papers, HSP. Papers regarding the estate of Edward Burd of Ormiston, Scotland, 1765, in Papers of Edward Burd, Society Collection, HSP; James Burd to Jasper Yeates, Tinian, 30 December 1769, Burd Papers, HSP.

36. Edward Shippen, Jr. [IV] to Edward Shippen [III], Philadelphia, 12 March 1766, Shippen Papers, vol. 11, p. 73, HSP.

37. *Ibid.* The "spur" took the following form: "I suppose all the time you remain at Lancaster you must be diminishing your Capital, which, not being very large, ought not to be intrenched upon, more than is absolutely necessary." (Edward Shippen [III] to James Burd, Philadelphia, 7 April 1766, Shippen Papers, vol. 6, p. 143, HSP.)

38. Edward Shippen, Jr. [IV] to Edward Shippen [III], Philadelphia, 12 March 1766, Shippen Papers, vol. 11, p. 73, HSP.

39. Edward Shippen, Jr. [IV] to Edward Shippen [III], Philadelphia, 16 April 1766, Shippen Papers, vol. 11, p. 76, HSP.

40. Edward Shippen, Jr. [IV] to Edward Shippen [III], Philadelphia, 12 March 1766, Shippen Papers, vol. 11, p. 73, HSP. Edward Shippen to Mr. Grojean, Lancaster, 9 May 1766, Society Collection under Burd, HSP; Joseph Shippen, Jr. [III] to Edward Shippen [IV], Philadelphia, 21 May 1766, Shippen Papers, Box 1, folder presented by Mrs. Thomas Balch, HSP.

41. Edward Shippen III informed Burd, "The Colonel expresses his Satisfaction on the Compliment you paid him of naming the child after him." (Edward Shippen [III] to James Burd, Lancaster, 22 February 1768, Shippen Papers, vol. 6, p. 199, HSP.)

42. James Burd to Edward Shippen [III], Tinian, 4 February 1769, Shippen Papers, vol. 11, p. 94, HSP.

43. Edward Shippen [III] to James Burd, Lancaster, 3 September 1771, Shippen Papers, vol. 7, p. 43, HSP. Joseph Shippen, Jr. [III] to James

Burd, Philadelphia, 2 March 1767, Shippen Papers, vol. 6, p. 173, HSP; Bond, James Burd and John Annis, 30 April 1767, Shippen, Balch Papers, vol. 2, p. 4, HSP; Edward Shippen [III] to James Burd, Lancaster, 19 August 1768; Edward Shippen [III] to James Burd, Lancaster, 15 September 1768; James Burd to Edward Shippen [III], Tinian, 9 October 1768; James Burd to Edward Shippen [III], Tinian, 12 Xber 1768, Shippen Papers, vol. 6, pp. 209, 211; vol. 11, pp. 84, 87, HSP; James Burd to Edward Shippen [III], Tinian, 6 November 1768, Burd-Shippen-Hubley Papers, HSP; Edward Shippen, Jr. [IV] to James Burd, Philadelphia, 25 June 1769; Sarah Burd to James Burd, Tinian, 12 May 1770, Drawing of James Burd's land, Shippen Papers, vol. 7, p. 9; vol. 11, p. 122; vol. 4, p. 251, HSP.

44. Edward Shippen [III] to James Burd, Lancaster, 21 June 1760, Shippen Papers, vol. 5, p. 55, HSP.

45. Edward Shippen [III] to James Burd, Lancaster, 20 July 1771, Shippen Papers, vol. 7, p. 41, HSP.

46. *Ibid.* Edward Shippen to James Read, Lancaster, 15 December 1771, Shippen Papers, vol. 7, p. 57, HSP.

47. Edward Shippen [III] to James Burd, Lancaster, 25 October 1762, Shippen Papers, vol. 5, p. 223, HSP.

48. Edward Shippen [III] to James Burd, Lancaster, 4 January [1764], Shippen Papers, vol. 6, p. 75, HSP.

49. *Ibid.*

50. James Burd to Edward Shippen [III], Fort Augusta, 19 January 1764, Shippen Papers, vol. 6, p. 81, HSP. James Read to Edward Shippen, 24 July 1757; Edward Shippen [III] to James Burd, Lancaster, 25 September 1762, Shippen Papers, vol. 3, p. 11; vol. 5, p. 219, HSP. Edward Shippen III's interest in the formal education of his grandchildren continued almost until his death. For example, in 1771, he indicated an interest in editing a book for the study of the French language, and in 1778 sent a hand-written copy of "A Theme of the Verbs Simple & Compound of the Four Conjugations divided into Alphabetical order, by Edward Shippen in Lancaster, 1768" with the inscription "Edward Shippen Esqr, Gift to Jemmy & Josey Burd, Lancaster, 27 January 1778." Directions accompanying it indicated that those grandchildren should read two pages a day to their older brother Neddy Burd before they went to school. In 1778, Shippen also criticized the present mode of rushing students through various Latin books. He went on to explain in detail how he would instruct students, were he a schoolmaster. His school would start at six in the morning and not end until five in the evening; most importantly, "The master ought to begin and end ye School with prayer and sometime make

the pupils do so in their Turns." "A Theme of the Verbs Simple & Compound of the Four Conjugations, divided into Alphabetical order, by Edward Shippen in Lancaster, 1768," Shippen Papers, Small Books, HSP; Edward Shippen [III] to James Read, Lancaster, 15 December 1771; Edward Shippen [III] to James Burd, Lancaster, 27 January 1778; James Burd to Edward Shippen [III], Tinian, 31 July 1776, Shippen Papers, vol. 7, p. 57; vol. 8, p. 27; vol. 12, p. 43, HSP; James Burd to Edward Shippen [III], 19 August 1776, Burd-Shippen-Hubley Papers, HSP.

51. Indenture, Edward Burd to Edward Shippen, Jr. [IV], Philadelphia, 22 August 1765, Burd-Shippen-Hubley Papers, HSP; Edward Shippen, Jr. [IV] to Edward Shippen [III], Philadelphia, 14 June 1765, Shippen Papers, vol. 11, p. 68, HSP.

52. Edward Shippen, Jr. [IV] to Edward Shippen [III], Philadelphia, 11 June 1760, Shippen Papers, vol. 5, p. 53, HSP.

53. Edward Burd to Sally Burd, Philadelphia, 17 November 1767, Shippen, Balch Papers, vol. 2, p. 5, HSP.

54. Edward Burd to Sally Burd [his sister], Philadelphia, 16 October 1766, Burd Papers, HSP. J. Bennett Nolan, *Neddie Burd's Reading Letters, An Epic of the Early Berks Bar* (Reading, Pa., 1927), p. 24; Receipt, Edward Shippen, Jr. [IV] to Joseph Shippen, Jr. [III], 28 September 1767, Shippen Papers, vol. 6, p. 189, HSP.

55. Edward Burd, Notes on Law, 1760–1769, Shippen Papers, HSP; Bill, Paul Fooks to Edward Burd, September 1767; Edward Burd to James Burd, Philadelphia, 5 March 1768; Edward Burd to Edward Shippen [III], Philadelphia, 9 December 1760, Shippen Papers, vol. 6, pp. 189, 201; vol. 11, p. 86, HSP.

56. Edward Burd to Sally Burd, Philadelphia, 17 November 1767, Shippen, Balch Papers, vol. 2, p. 5, HSP.

57. Edward Burd to James Burd, 6 March 1767, quoted in Nolan, *Neddie Burd*, p. 27.

58. Edward Shippen, Jr. [IV] to Edward Shippen [III], Philadelphia, 12 September 1764, Shippen Papers, vol. 11, p. 63, HSP.

59. Edward Shippen, Jr. [IV] to Edward Shippen [III], Philadelphia, 20 September 1764, Shippen Papers, vol. 11, p. 64, HSP.

60. Edward Potts Cheyney and Ellis Paxson Oberholtzer, *University of Pennsylvania: Its History, Influence, Equipment, and Characteristics, with Biographical Sketches and Portraits of Founders, Benefactors, Officers, and Alumni* (2 vols., Boston, 1901–1902), vol. II, pp. 137–138.

61. *Ibid.*

62. Jasper Yeates to James Burd, Lancaster, 11 December 1767, Shippen Papers, vol. 6, p. 193, HSP.

63. *Ibid.*

64. Edward Burd to Dear Sister [Sally (Burd) Yeates], Philadelphia, 28 December 1767, Burd Papers, HSP.

65. Four years later when Sarah's younger sister married, her brother seemed reluctant to ask his grandfather Shippen for money, because "I know that you must have been at a good deal of Expense about Sister Molly." (Edward Burd to Edward Shippen [III], Philadelphia, 30 November 1771, Nolan, *Neddie Burd*, p. 29.) There is no reason to suspect that Edward Shippen III did not do the same for Salley Burd.

66. James Read to Edward Shippen, 22 November 1771, Shippen Papers, vol. 7, p. 51, HSP.

67. Edward Shippen [III] to James Burd, Lancaster, 12 October 1771, Shippen Papers, vol. 7, p. 45, HSP.

68. Edward Burd to James Burd, Philadelphia, 3 February 1767[?], Nolan, *Neddie Burd*, p. 25.

69. James Read to Edward Shippen [III], R[eading], 20 November 1771, Shippen Papers, vol. 7, p. 49, HSP.

70. Edward Burd to Edward Shippen [III], Philadelphia, 21 December 1771, Nolan, *Neddie Burd*, p. 25. James Burd to Edward Shippen, Tinian, 21 November 1771, folder 38, Burd-Shippen-Hubley Papers, HSP; Edward Shippen [III] to James Burd, Lancaster, 19 November 1771, Shippen Papers, vol. 7, p. 49, HSP.

71. Joseph Shippen, Jr. [III] to Edward Shippen [III], Philadelphia, 11 December 1771, Shippen and Swift, Balch Collection, HSP.

72. Mary S. Grubb to Dear & Honoured Madam [Sarah (Shippen) Burd], Hopewell Forge, 9 August 1772, Burd-Shippen-Hubley Papers, HSP. James Burd to Edward Shippen [III], Tinian, 19 December 1771, folder 38, Burd-Shippen-Hubley Papers, HSP; Sarah Burd to Sally [Yeates], Tinian, 18 December 1771; Mary Shippen' to Mrs. [Sarah] Burd, Lancaster, 18 April 1772; Sarah Burd to Sally Yeates, Tinian, 22 April 1772, Shippen Papers, vol. 12, pp. 7, 8, HSP.

73. Edward Shippen [III] to James Burd, Lancaster, 15 July 1772, Shippen Papers, vol. 7, p. 59, HSP.

74. Sarah Burd to James Burd, Hopewell Forge, 26 August 1772, Sarah Burd to James Burd, Hopewell Forge, 31 August 1772, Burd-Shippen-Hubley Papers, HSP.

75. Sarah Burd to Sally [Yeates], November 1773, Shippen Papers, vol. 12, p. 16, HSP.

76. Jasper Yeates to James Burd, Lancaster, 28 February 1774, Shippen Papers, vol. 7, p. 81, HSP.

77. *Ibid.* Sarah Burd to James Burd, Hopewell Forge, 7 February 1774, Burd-Shippen-Hubley Papers, HSP; Sarah Yeates to Dear & Honoured Madam [Mary Shippen], Hopewell Forge, 7 February 1774, Shippen Papers, vol. 12, p. 20, HSP. In general scholars have asserted that romantic love, emotional reactions to death, permissive child-rearing practices, and other "modern" characteristics were a consequence of the impact of the Industrial Revolution upon the traditional family. For example, Peter Laslett *(The World We Have Lost: England before the Industrial Revolution,* New York, 1965, pp. 95, 96, 120) speaks for many when he claims that "the emotional pattern of that [pre-industrial] society has vanished for ever, and people may then have had quite a different attitude to sudden death, orphanage, widowhood and living with step-parents. . . . The society of the pre-industrial world was inured to bereavement and the shortness of life. . . . [There existed] an attitude toward death which cannot easily be shared in the twentieth century." William Josiah Goode's *World Revolution and Family Patterns* (New York, 1963, chap. 1) raises doubts about the conventional wisdom. In general the Shippens' attitudes after about 1750 tend to contradict Laslett and support Goode.

78. Joseph Shippen, Jr. [III] to Edward Shippen [III], Shippen and Swift, Balch Collection, HSP.

79. John Demos, "Families in Colonial Bristol, Rhode Island: An Exercise in Historical Demography," *William and Mary Quarterly,* 3d ser., vol. XXV, no. 1 (January 1968), 40, 55; D. V. Glass and D. E. C. Eversley, eds., *Population in History: Essays in Historical Demography* (Chicago, 1965), pp. 88–90, 106–110, 113–116, 121, 364–365, 374–378, 454–456, 615; Philip J. Greven, Jr., "Family Structure in Seventeenth-Century Andover, Massachusetts," *William and Mary Quarterly,* 3d ser., vol. XXIII, no. 2 (April 1966), 241–242.

80. *Ibid.*

81. Sarah Burd to Edward Shippen [III], Tinian, 31 October 1773; Edward Shippen [III] to James Burd, Lancaster, 3 November 1773, Shippen Papers, vol. 10, p. 165; vol. 7, p. 73, HSP.

82. Edward Burd to Edward Shippen [III], Philadelphia, 23 July 1768; Edward Burd to Edward Shippen [III], Philadelphia, 11 August 1768, Shippen Papers, vol. 11, pp. 80, 81, HSP; Edward Burd to Edward Shippen [III], Philadelphia, 25 April 1769, Yeates-Burd Collection Box 2, folder 1, HSP; Nolan, *Neddie Burd,* p. 22; Edward Shippen [III] to Joseph Shippen [III], Lancaster, 15 October 1770, Society Collection under Burd, HSP.

83. Edward Burd to James Burd, 6 March 1767, Nolan, *Neddie Burd,* p. 27. Joseph Shippen III tried to sell Burd's house at Northampton for £300

or rent it for £20 per year. He failed to do either. (Joseph Shippen, Jr. [III] to James Burd, Philadelphia, 4 August 1766, Shippen Papers, vol. 6, p. 157, HSP.)

84. Edward Shippen, Jr. [IV] to Edward Shippen [III], Philadelphia, 24 August 1771, Shippen, Balch Collection, vol. 2, p. 11, HSP.

85. James Burd to Edward Shippen [III], Tinian, 5 September 1771, Burd-Shippen-Hubley Papers, HSP.

86. *Ibid.*

87. Edward Burd to Edward Shippen [III], Philadelphia, 30 November 1771, Burd-Shippen-Hubley Papers, HSP.

88. *Ibid.*

89. James Burd to Edward Shippen [III], Tinian, 16 January 1772, Burd-Shippen-Hubley Papers, HSP. Lemon, "Urbanization and the Development of Eighteenth-Century Southeastern Pennsylvania and Adjacent Delaware," *William and Mary Quarterly,* 3d ser., vol. XXIV, no. 4 (October 1967), 519, 536, 541; Nolan, *Neddie Burd,* p. 29.

90. Neddy Burd's request for the suit graphically illustrates his dependence upon the generosity of the Shippens. He explained to his grandfather that he requested a new suit, because "my white Cloathes are too thin for even the present weather & my brown Homespun is very threadbare and make me appear a little shabby—If I had a good Suit to wear on Sundays & other proper times I could wear my brown Homespun in common & save my new Cloathes so that they might be as good as new when I settle." (Edward Burd to Edward Shippen [III], Philadelphia, 30 November 1771, Burd-Shippen-Hubley Papers, HSP.) Neddy's mother also made him some new shirts for the occasion. (James Burd to Edward Shippen [III], Tinian, 6 June 1771, Burd-Shippen-Hubley Papers, HSP.)

91. Edward Burd to Edward Shippen [III], Reading, 18 May 1772, Shippen Papers, vol. 7, p. 59, HSP.

92. Neddy Burd to Edward Shippen [III], Reading, 19 November 1772, Shippen Papers, vol. 10, p. 147, HSP.

93. Edward Shippen, Jr. [IV] to Edward Burd, 28 May 1774, Society Collection under Burd, HSP.

94. James Burd to Edward Shippen, Tinian, 27 November 1773, Shippen Papers, vol. 10, p. 167, HSP.

95. James Read to Edward Shippen, Reading, 27 August 1774, Nolan, *Neddie Burd,* p. 33.

96. Edward Burd to Edward Shippen [III], Reading, 16 November 1774, Shippen Papers, vol. 7, p. 105, HSP.

97. *Ibid.*

98. James Read to Edward Shippen [III], Reading, 16 November 1774,

Shippen Papers, vol. 7, p. 105, HSP. There are many examples of nepotism in Pennsylvania politics during the first seven and a half decades of the eighteenth century. The quickest way to perceive it is to analyze the membership of the Common Council of Philadelphia, a closed corporation in which only members voted for the election of new councilmen. Without even mentioning kinship relationship such as brothers-in-law, cousins, uncles, nephews, and the like, we find the following instructive. Between 1704 and 1775 six Shippens, six Allens, four Morrises, and four Redmans sat in the council. During the same period, ten families had three councilmen, and eighteen families had two councilmen. Nepotism will be dealt with in chapters eight and nine. The analysis of the membership of the Common Council is based upon my compilation taken from the minutes.

99. A random selection of twenty-one other Philadelphians who married in the second half of the eighteenth century reveals seventeen married once, two married twice, and one married three times.

100. Edward Shippen [IV] to Edward Shippen [III], Philadelphia, 14 December 1758, Shippen, Balch Papers, vol. 1, p. 67, HSP. The bells in the city rang to celebrate the British conquest of Fort Duquesne; however, Edward IV noted the appropriateness of their tolling to his personal joys.

101. Edward Shippen, Jr. [IV] to Edward Shippen [III], Philadelphia, 17 July 1769, Shippen Papers, vol. 7, p. 15, HSP.

102. Edward Shippen [III] to Joseph Shippen [III], Lancaster, 6 September 1770, Shippen Papers, vol. 10, p. 107, HSP.

103. Edward Shippen, Jr. [IV] to Edward Shippen [III], Philadelphia, 11 June 1760, Shippen Papers, vol. 5, p. 53, HSP. Edward Shippen [III] to James Burd, Lancaster, 23 August 1757, Shippen Papers, vol. 3, p. 31, HSP; Edward Shippen [IV] to Edward Shippen [III], Philadelphia, 25 August 1757, Shippen, Balch Papers, vol. 1, p. 52, HSP; Edward Shippen [III] to Joseph Shippen [III], Lancaster, 24 February 1758, Shippen Papers, vol. 4, p. 5, HSP.

104. Joseph Shippen [III] to Edward Shippen [III], Philadelphia, 7 June 1770, Shippen Papers, vol. 10, p. 103, HSP.

105. Knowledge of birth control measures definitely existed in the fifth generation of Shippens. Margaret (Shippen) Arnold wrote to her sister Elizabeth (Shippen) Burd, "It gives me great pleasure to hear of your prudent resolution of not increasing your family; as I can never do better than to follow your example, I have determined upon the same plan; and when our Sisters have had five or six, we will likewise recommend it to them." (M[argaret] A[rnold] to Miss [sic] Burd, 30 [June 1780s or 1790s], Shippen, Balch Papers, vol. 2, p. 20, HSP.) Approximately two-year

intervals between childbirths suggests breast-feeding by the mother. See Albert Sharman, *Reproductive Physiology of the Post Partum Period* (Edinburgh, 1966), p. 86, and Christopher Tietze, "Lactation," in *Manual of Contraceptive Practice*, ed. Mary S. Calderone (Baltimore, 1964), pp. 230–231.

106. Joseph Shippen, Jr. [III] to Edward Shippen [III], Philadelphia, 11 December 1771, Shippen and Swift, Balch Collection, HSP. Carl Bridenbaugh, *Cities in Revolt: Urban Life in America, 1743–1776* (New York, 1964), p. 149, claims that the upper ranks of society, like their English counterparts, turned their children over to wet nurses. He gives no evidence that this practice became prevalent; all evidence about the Shippens indicates they nursed their infants.

107. Joseph Shippen, Jr., to Hon. John Penn, Esq., Philadelphia, 15 March 1773, Joseph Shippen Papers, No. 1723, LC.

108. *Ibid.* The death of Joseph III's and Jenny's eleven-month-old son Charles had similar effects. Joseph Shippen, Jr. [III] to Edward Shippen [III], Philadelphia, 10 August 1775, Shippen Papers, Box 1, HSP.

109. Joseph Shippen, Jr. [III] to Hon. John Penn, Philadelphia, 20 May 1773, Joseph Shippen Papers, No. 1727, LC.

110. *Ibid.*

111. Edward Shippen [III] to James Burd, Lancaster, 15 July 1769, Shippen Papers, vol. 7, p. 11, HSP.

112. Joseph Shippen [III] to Edward Shippen [III], Philadelphia, 1 November 1771, Shippen Papers, vol. 10, p. 127, HSP.

113. Edward Shippen [III] to Joseph Shippen, Jr. [III], Lancaster, 27 September 1774, Shippen Papers, Box 1, folder presented by Mrs. Thomas Balch, HSP.

114. Among several references to Dr. William Shippen II caring for the Edward III branch, the following are representative. In Edward Shippen [III] to Lt. Col. [Joseph] Shippen [III], Lancaster, 26 September 1759, Shippen Papers, vol. 4, p. 155, Edward III writes that the doctor had been caring for Edward IV's children for eleven days. Sometimes medical service was paid for by legal favors, for example, Edward Shippen, Jr. [IV]'s Account with William Shippen [II], 1752–1765, Joseph Shippen Papers, LC, which included inoculation of Edward IV's child and a Negro boy was settled this way; "My attendance on your Family I set against your advice to me in Law matters." This was not always the case, for example, at the bottom of a bill, William Shippen [II] and Son to Joseph Shippen, Jr. [III], Shippen Papers, vol. 6, p. 159, HSP, William III adds, "Dr. Cous— If you can cleverly spare so much money now, you will particularly oblige Dr. Cous your's affect.ly."

115. Joseph Shippen [III] to Jenny Shippen, Lancaster, 23 July 1769, Shippen Papers, Box 1, Joseph Shippen folder, HSP.

116. Edward Shippen [III] to Edward Shippen, Jr. [IV], Lancaster, 15 April 1775, Shippen Papers, vol. 12, p. 32, HSP.

117. Sarah Shippen to Honoured Madam, Philadelphia, 8 July 1766, manuscript affixed in Balch, *Letters relating to Pennsylvania,* vol. 1, p. 130. Joseph Shippen, Jr. [III] to Edward Shippen [III], Philadelphia, 7 April 1770; Joseph Shippen [III] to Edward Shippen [III], Philadelphia, 2 February 1771; Edward Shippen, Jr. [IV] to Edward Shippen [III], Philadelphia, April 1761; Edward Shippen [IV] to Edward Shippen [III], Philadelphia, 8 April 1762; Joseph Shippen [III] to Edward Shippen [III], Philadelphia, 20 May 1770, Shippen Papers, vol. 10, pp. 97, 113; vol. 11, p. 30, 43; vol. 10, p. 101, HSP; Elizabeth Shippen to Mary Shippen, Philadelphia, 9 July 1766, Shippen Papers, transferred from the Society Collection, HSP; Elizabeth Shippen to My Dear Cousen, Philadelphia, 23 December 1763, Burd Papers, HSP.

CHAPTER VIII

1. Pennsylvania politics and the coming of the Revolution receive intensive investigation in several significant studies. See William S. Hanna's *Benjamin Franklin and Pennsylvania Politics* (Stanford, 1964), James H. Hutson's *Pennsylvania Politics 1746–1770: The Movement for Royal Government and its Consequences* (Princeton, 1972), and Benjamin H. Newcomb's *Franklin and Galloway: A Political Partnership* (New Haven, 1972). Theodore Thayer's *Pennsylvania Politics and the Growth of Democracy, 1740–1776* (Harrisburg, 1953) is useful if read in conjunction with the above works.

2. Hutson's *Pennsylvania Politics* provides the most detailed account of the movement for royal government. Hanna, Newcomb, and Thayer are also helpful.

3. Quoted in Hutson, *Pennsylvania Politics,* p. 124.

4. *Ibid.,* p. 134.

5. Hanna views the proprietor in a favorable light and finds the Assembly often petty, unprincipled, and tyrannical. He also maintains that no matter the label—Quaker, Proprietary, legislature, or executive—the men who dominated the government and politics from 1750 to 1775 were very much alike. All were preoccupied with immediate concerns and power rather than principles. By contrast Newcomb holds a very favorable view of Franklin and Galloway. He maintains principles motivated the partners in their fight with an oppressive and inept Proprietary government.

Thayer, like many before him, supports a similar view. Hutson finds the degree of personal motivation unclear; he believes that Franklin acted as much in the public interest and with a desire to end tyranny as he did for personal reasons.

6. Newcomb, *Franklin and Galloway*, p. 80.

7. Edward Shippen, Jr. [IV] to Edward Shippen [III], Philadelphia, 17 October 1765, Shippen Papers, vol. 11, p. 70, HSP.

8. Edward Shippen [III] to Joseph Shippen [III], Lancaster, Christmas, 1765, Thomas Balch, *Letters and Papers relating to Pennsylvania* (5 vols., private printing, Philadelphia, 1855), vol. 1, p. 212.

9. Edward Shippen, Jr. [IV] to Edward Shippen [III], Philadelphia, 10 September 1765, Shippen Papers, vol. 11, p. 69, HSP.

10. Joseph Shippen, Jr. [III] to Edward Shippen, Jr. [IV], 9 November 1765; Joseph Shippen, Jr. [III] to James Burd, Philadelphia, 24 March 1766; Sarah Burd to James Burd, Lancaster, 28 March 1766; Edward Shippen [IV] to Joseph Shippen [III], Philadelphia, 16 April 1766, Shippen Papers, vol. 6, pp. 133, 14, 143; vol. 11, p. 75, HSP.

11. William Allen to John Penn (Penn Manuscripts, Official Correspondence, vol. 10, p. 158), quoted in Thayer, *Pennsylvania Politics*, p. 143.

12. Edward Shippen [III] to James Read, Lancaster, 4 July 1768, Shippen Papers, vol. 6, p. 209, HSP. *Pennsylvania Gazette*, 4 August 1768; *Pennsylvania Chronicle*, 18 July 1768.

13. William Allen to David and John Barclay, Philadelphia, 7 November 1769, William Allen Letterbook, p. 195, HSP.

14. Joseph Shippen, Jr. [III] to Edward Shippen [III], Philadelphia, 14 July 1770, Shippen and Swift, Balch Collection, HSP.

15. *Pennsylvania Journal*, 5 July 1770.

16. Joseph Shippen [III] to Edward Burd, Philadelphia, 3 October 1775, Society Small Collection, Edward Burd, HSP.

17. There were almost one hundred subscribers.

18. Edward Shippen [III] to James Burd, Lancaster, 28 June 1774, Shippen Papers, vol. 7, p. 91, HSP.

19. *Pennsylvania Archives*, second series, John P. Linn and William Henry Egle, eds. (19 vols., Harrisburg, 1874–1893), vol. XIII, p. 276; Subscription of Lancaster Co[unty] to Relief of the Distresses of the poor Inhabitants of the Town of Boston [1775], Lancaster County, 1772–1816, HSP.

20. James Burd to Edward Shippen [III], Tinian, 8 August 1774, Shippen Papers, vol. 7, p. 95, HSP. In this regard it seems important to indicate that both Edward Shippen III and James Burd owned slaves. Shippen later contemplated freeing his, but in December 1775 Burd described Lord

Dunsmore's proclamation offering freedom to Negroes and servants who deserted their masters and joined the royal forces to help suppress the rebellion as "a piece of Villany beyond Expression." James Burd to Edward Shippen [III], Tinian, 21 December 1775, Shippen Papers, vol. 7, p. 143, HSP.

21. *Ibid.*

22. Minutes of Committee of Paxton, 14 June 1775, Shippen Papers, vol. 7, p. 119; Lily Lee Nixon, *James Burd: Frontier Defender, 1726–1793* (Philadelphia, 1941), pp. 152–154.

23. Edward Shippen [III] to James Burd, Lancaster, 27 December 1774, Shippen Papers, vol. 7, p. 109, HSP.

24. Edward Shippen [III] to James Burd, Lancaster, 10 February 1775, Shippen Papers, vol. 10, p. 187, HSP.

25. James Burd to Edward Shippen [III], Tinian, 31 Xbre 1774; Edward Shippen [III] to Joseph Shippen [III], Lancaster, 20 August 1774, Shippen Papers, vol. 7, p. 109; vol. 10, p. 177, HSP; Edward Shippen [III] to Dear Son, Lancaster, 21 November 1774, Shippen, Balch Papers, vol. 2, p. 22, HSP. Many letters from Edward Shippen III in late 1774 in volume seven of the Shippen Papers at the Historical Society of Pennsylvania indicate concern lest a civil war be provoked in Boston, and also contain hard words for the British ministry.

26. Edward Shippen [III] to James Burd, Lancaster, 28 August 1774, Shippen Papers, vol. 7, p. 133, HSP.

27. Jasper Yeates to James Burd, Lancaster, 22 September 1775, Shippen Papers, vol. 7, p. 135, HSP.

28. James Burd to Brig. Gen. Thomas Mifflin, Tinian, 27 December 1776, Shippen Papers, vol. 7, p. 217, HSP. James Burd to Edward Shippen [III], Tinian, 23 July 1774; J[ames] B[urd] to Christian King and James Bortus and Ensign Godfried Croutchman, Tinian, 24 August 1775; Daniel Roberdeau, Certificate, Amboy, 12 September 1776, Shippen Papers, vol. 10, p. 175; vol. 7, pp. 131, 209, HSP. James Burd's activities during the Revolution are dealt with in Nixon's *James Burd,* chapters ten through thirteen.

29. Edward Burd to Edward Shippen [III], Prospect Hill, 3 October 1775, Shippen Papers, vol. 7, p. 137, HSP.

30. Joseph Shippen [III] to Edward Burd, Philadelphia, 3 October 1775, Society Small Collection, Edward Burd, HSP.

31. Edward Burd to Edward Shippen [III], Prospect Hill, 3 October 1775, Shippen Papers, vol. 7, p. 137, HSP.

32. Edward Shippen, Jr. [IV] to Edward Shippen [III], Philadelphia, 30 June 1775, Shippen Papers, vol. 12, p. 35, HSP.

33. Jasper Yeates to James Burd, Lancaster, 11 July 1775, Shippen Papers, vol. 7, p. 125, HSP.

34. *Ibid.*

35. Many things indicate that the Shippens bore no ill will toward Neddy Burd for bearing arms against British troops at Boston. For example, soon after Neddy Burd returned to Philadelphia his Uncle Edward Shippen IV wrote "[I] request you will take care of such actions of mine on the Docket as require anything to be done in them, & that you will draw the necessary Indictments and carry on the prosecutions for the Crown in my stead." Edward Shippen, Jr. [IV] to Edward Burd, Reading, 13 November 1775, Society Collection under Burd, HSP.

36. Edward Shippen [IV] to Edward Shippen [III], 31 May 1776, quoted in Edward Shippen [III] to James Burd, Lancaster, 6 June 1776, Shippen Papers, vol. 7, p. 183, HSP.

37. Joseph Shippen, Jr. [III] to Edward Shippen [III], Philadelphia, 18 November 1775, Provincial Delegates, vol. 4, p. 22, HSP.

38. *Ibid.* Joseph III's brother Edward IV's thoughts had been similar, for in January 1776 he lamented, "The Repulse of our Troops met with at Quebec, with the Death of Montgomery and the loss of Arnold['s] Men, give us little reason to expect a Reduction of Canada this winter." Edward Shippen, Jr. [IV] to Edward Shippen [III], Philadelphia, 19 January 1776, Shippen Papers, vol. 7, p. 190, HSP.

39. Edward Shippen [III] to James Burd, 10 July 1775; Edward Shippen [III] to Joseph Shippen [III], Lancaster, 14 July 1775, Shippen Papers, vol. 7, p. 125; vol. 10, p. 193, HSP. Edward Hand to Jasper Yeates, Camp on Prospect Hill, 20 August 1775, Edward Hand Correspondence, vol. 3, p. 4, LC.

40. Joseph Shippen, Jr. [III] to Edward Shippen [III], Philadelphia, 15 January 1776, Shippen Papers, vol. 7, p. 149, HSP.

41. *Ibid.*

42. Edward Shippen [III] to Dear Son, Lancaster, 19 January 1776, Shippen Papers, vol. 10, p. 197, HSP.

43. Joseph Shippen, Jr. [III] to Edward Shippen [III], Philadelphia, 29 February 1776, Shippen Papers, vol. 12, p. 123, HSP.

44. *Ibid.*

45. Joseph Shippen, Jr. [III] to Edward Shippen [III], Philadelphia, 12 March 1776, Shippen Papers, vol. 7, p. 157, HSP. Both Edward Shippen III and Jasper Yeates who opposed independence refused to run for the new seats. Thayer (*Pennsylvania Politics,* p. 159) calls Jasper Yeates a zealous Whig, yet when Yeates described politics in Lancaster County, Edward Shippen IV replied to him that he understood "the hard Necessity you

were under of disguising your Sentiments at a critical Conjuncture. While the Stream runs so rapidly there is no stemming it." Edward Shippen, Jr. [IV] to Jasper Yeates, 5 June 1776, Dreer Collection, Edward Shippen, HSP. In this regard Thayer's *Pennsylvania Politics* successfully refutes the simplistic democratic West versus the aristocratic East interpretation which forms a major thesis of Charles H. Lincoln's *The Revolutionary Movement in Pennsylvania, 1760–1776* (Philadelphia, 1901). Lincoln, one of the earliest proponents of the "internal revolution" concept, remains a very useful commentator.

46. Edward Shippen, Jr. [IV] to Jasper Yeates, Philadelphia, 11 March 1776, Shippen Papers, vol. 7, p. 156, HSP.

47. Joseph Shippen, Jr. [III] to Edward Shippen [III], Country House near Germantown, 11 May 1776, Joseph Shippen Papers, Nos. 1753–1754, LC.

48. *Ibid.*

49. Edward Shippen, Jr. [IV] to Jasper Yeates, 5 June 1776, Dreer Collection, Edward Shippen, HSP.

50. Joseph Shippen, Jr. [III] to Edward Shippen [III], 3 April 1776, Shippen Papers, vol. 7, p. 163, HSP.

51. William Shippen [II] to Edward Shippen [III], 27 July 1776, Shippen Papers, vol. 12, p. 41, HSP.

52. Bernard Bailyn touched off a very productive flow of insightful studies with the introduction to *The Pamphlets of the American Revolution, 1750–1766* (Cambridge, 1965) and elaboration of those ideas in *The Ideological Origins of the American Revolution* (Cambridge, 1967). In a particularly provocative and insightful essay, "Rhetoric and Reality in the American Revolution," in the *William and Mary Quarterly* (3d ser., vol. XXIII, no. 1 [January 1966], 3–32), Gordon Wood suggests that a significant connection between social reality and ideas existed. In *The Creation of the American Republic, 1776–1787* (Chapel Hill, 1969) Wood greatly amplifies his case. An understanding of the Shippen family and the way they and other families functioned in colonial Pennsylvania tends to corroborate Wood's thesis.

53. Wood, "Rhetoric and Reality," p. 31.

54. Andrew Burnaby, *Travels through the Middle Settlements in North-America. In the Years 1759 and 1760. With Observations upon the State of the Colonies* (2d ed., Ithaca, 1960), p. 56.

55. Carl Bridenbaugh, *Cities in Revolt: Urban Life in America, 1743–1776* (New York, 1964), p. 211.

56. *Ibid.*, p. 143.

57. *Ibid.*, p. 145.

58. The Eighteen Penny Provincial Tax List, 1772, Philadelphia City Hall Annex, indicates that 82 residents of Philadelphia owned country seats; 22 were merchants, 13 "Esquires," 9 gentlemen, 5 doctors, 4 widows, 3 shopkeepers, 2 innkeepers, and the rest belonged to men who claimed to be artisans. The seats varied in assessment from £4 to £200. Fifteen were valued between £4 and £9; 19 between £10 and £19; 14 between £20 and £25. Only ten were valued at £50 or more. Cousin William Allen's was valued at £60, John MacPherson's (which later became part of Peggy Shippen's dowry), at £70. Only two were rated at more than £70. Mary Master's country seat in West Northern Liberties was because it included 200 acres; Abel James's was valued at £200 because it contained 330 acres.

59. Bridenbaugh, *Cities in Revolt,* pp. 146, 340–342, 371; Frederick B. Tolles, *Meeting House and Counting House: The Quaker Merchants of Colonial Philadelphia, 1682–1763* (New York, 1963), pp. 130–131; *Pennsylvania Magazine of History and Biography,* XCV (1971), 351–362; J. Thomas Scharf and Thompson Westcott, *History of Philadelphia, 1609–1884* (3 vols., Philadelphia, 1884), vol. II, pp. 880–881; An Account of Coaches, Landaus, Chariots, and Four Wheel Chairs, 1761, Proud Miscellaneous Manuscripts, Box 2, No. 71, HSP. Tolles *(Meeting House and Counting House,* p. 131) quotes the following mid-eighteenth-century verse:

> Judge Allen drove a coach and four Of handsome dappled grays,
> Shippens, Penns, Pembertons, and Morrises,
> Powels, Cadwaladers, and Norrises
> Drove only pairs of blacks and bays.

Edward Shippen [III] to Edward Shippen, Jr. [IV], Lancaster, 17 April 1775; Edward Shippen, Jr. [IV] to Edward Shippen [III], Philadelphia, 20 April 1775, Shippen Papers, vol. 12, p. 31; vol. 7, p. 113, HSP; Joseph Shippen, Jr. [III] to Edward Shippen [III], Philadelphia, 24 June 1760, Shippen, Balch Papers, vol. 2, p. 7, HSP.

60. In a Memorandum of a Lease, Joseph Shippen, Jr. [III] to David Sproat, 8 January 1771, Shippen Papers, vol. 7, p. 35, HSP, Joseph III described himself as "gentleman"; Edward Shippen [IV] described himself as "gentleman" in his will of 26 June 1776, Shippen, Balch Papers, vol. 1, p. 84, HSP. Of the Shippens alive and living in Philadelphia in the 1770s only William II possibly stands as an exception to the tendency to conceive of oneself as a gentleman.

61. Louis Hartz, *The Liberal Tradition in America* (New York, 1955), pp. 52–53, claims a "psychic split . . . has always tormented the American 'aristocracy' " and that "the 'aristocrats' . . . were frustrated." This may

have been true in general, but does not seem appropriate to the Shippens in particular. Certainly they relied upon capitalistic endeavors such as collecting rents on their properties, yet that also characterized European aristocracies. Furthermore, Edward III, Edward IV, and Joseph III as well as some of their kinsmen, relied very heavily upon income from their public offices. Gordon Wood (*Creation of the American Republic,* p. 88) is probably correct when he confirms Hartz's generalization for revolutionary Pennsylvania, yet the Shippens again seem something of an exception. Although their position varied over time, when the founder of the family entered the province in the 1690s, his mercantile fortune was reputed to be £10,000 sterling, and he was certainly one of the wealthiest men in the colony. None of his descendants except in the William II line could ever have fitted the sneering remark that only a generation ago their family consisted of "leather apron men." Instead, the third- and fourth-generation Shippens of the Edward III branch (the officeholding branch) could and did point to the fact that a kinsman by the name of William Shippen served in Parliament.

62. Receipt "To 1 Years dressing his Hair 3 times every Week £6.0.0 To a Shaving Box of Soap £0.3.0 Gaspero Polumbo" to Edward Shippen, Jr. [IV], 28 November 1769, Edward Shippen, Jr. [IV] Papers, APS. Although many engaged in "luxurious" life styles described themselves by occupation such as their public office, esquire, merchant, and so forth, in the Eighteen Penny Provincial Tax, 1772, at Philadelphia City Hall, thirty-two residents of Philadelphia called themselves gentlemen. This number had jumped extraordinarily since 1769 when only one gentleman was listed. The uproar over the Townshend Acts and the general tendency toward greater simplicity explains the difference. When mentioning gentlemen, we must point out that one's position in a statistically divided tax list produces many peculiar errors. A number of gentlemen, for example, would be economically in the lower ranks of society because their wealth was not in a taxable form. And beyond a matter of money, Turbot Francis, gentleman, whose estate was valued at £12, not only enjoyed greater material possessions than an artisan assessed at the same amount, but his family connections to the Shippens and other families of political and social consequence made his chances for upward mobility much greater than most other people.

63. Quoted in Bridenbaugh, *Cities in Revolt,* p. 318. Aside from Edward Shippen IV's admonition to Neddy Burd for his gambling, the following note by Joseph Shippen III seems in character with the tendency Coates describes. "I am sorry to inform you that Mr. Jo Pemberton (Son of Israel) is certainly broke for a large Sum, viz. £30,000. . . . This extraor-

dinary Event is attributed entirely to high *Gaming,* which he has been in the practice of several Years and keeping low company." Joseph Shippen [III] to Edward Shippen [III], 18 November 1775, Provincial Delegates, vol. 4, p. 22, HSP.

64. Quoted in Bridenbaugh, *Cities in Revolt,* p. 315. When Governor James Hamilton announced the act outlawing lotteries, he explained that lotteries "tend to the manifest Corruption of Youth, and the Ruin and Impoverishment of many poor Families; . . . prove introductive of Vice, Idleness, Immorality, injurious to Trade, Commerce and Industry, and against the Common Good, Welfare and Peace of this Province." *Pennsylvania Gazette,* 4 March 1762.

65. Benjamin Rush to Ebenezer Hazard, Philadelphia, 2 August 1764, *Letters of Benjamin Rush,* ed. L. H. Butterfield (2 vols., Princeton, 1951), vol. 1, p. 7.

66. John Alford to Edward Shippen [III], Charlestown, 1 September 1760, Shippen Papers, vol. 5, p. 89, HSP. Wood, *Creation of the Republic,* pp. 91–124; Bridenbaugh, *Cities in Revolt,* pp. 154, 314–315, 321, 344, 348, 361, 363, Bridenbaugh's account of the five colonial towns between 1743 and 1776 indicates that these trends were perceived in New York, Charlestown, Boston, and Newport as well. Much of this criticism of luxury, vice, and corruption continues during and after the American Revolution. By then it seems very much like the Jeremiads which Perry Miller (*Errand into the Wilderness,* [New York, 1964], pp. 8–9) suggests appear to anthropologists as a means of relieving guilt over changing conditions as one accommodates oneself to a new social situation.

67. James Burd to Edward Shippen [III], Tinian, 4 Xbre 1774, Shippen Papers, vol. 7, p. 107, HSP.

68. Wood, "Rhetoric and Reality," pp. 26–27.

69. William Shippen [II] to Edward Shippen [III], 27 July 1776, Shippen Papers, vol. 12, p. 41, HSP.

70. *Pennsylvania Evening Post,* 30 April 1776. Lincoln, *Revolutionary Movement in Pennsylvania,* p. 94.

71. Pennsylvania with its Shippens, Allens, and their kinsmen seems typical of this in terms of the way they functioned in politics and exercised control. For example, Charles Carroll of Maryland feared that "all power might center in *one family*" and government office "like a precious jewel will be handed down from *father* to *son.*" (Quoted in Wood, *Creation of the Republic,* p. 79.) In 1765, John Adams sized up the situation as follows: "Has not his Honour the Lieutenant Governor discovered to the People in innumerable Instances, a very ambitious and avaricious Disposition? Has he not grasped four of the most important offices in the

Province into his own Hands? Has not his Brother in Law Oliver another of the greatest Places in Government? Is not a Brother of the Secretary, a Judge of the Superiour Court, Has not that Brother a son in the House? Has not the secretary a son in the House, who is also a Judge in one of the Counties? Did not that son marry the Daughter of another of the Judges of the Superior Court? Has not the Lieutenant Governor a Brother, a Judge of the Pleas in Boston? and a Namesake and near Relation who is another Judge? Has not the Lieutenant Governor a near Relation who is Register of his own Court of Probate, and Deputy Secretary? Has he not another near Relation who is Clerk of the House of Representatives? Is not this amazing ascendancy of one Family, Foundation sufficient on which to erect a Tyranny?" John Adams, Diary, 15 August 1765, *Diary and Autobiography of John Adams,* ed. L. H. Butterfield (4 vols., Cambridge, 1961), vol. 1, p. 260.

72. Although Edward Shippen III moved to Lancaster in 1752, he continued as an active aldermen in Philadelphia for at least another decade.

73. Comments about the Common Council are based upon analysis of its membership taken from its minutes and knowledge of kinship networks derived from numerous sources.

74. Charles P. Keith, *The Provincial Councillors of Pennsylvania who held office between 1733 and 1776* . . . (Philadelphia, 1883), pp. 53–89, 120–154; Edward Potts Cheyney and Ellis Paxson Oberholtzer, *University of Pennsylvania: Its History, Influence, Equipment, and Characteristics, with Biographical Sketches and Portraits of Founders, Benefactors, Officers, and Alumni* (2 vols., Boston, 1901–1902), vol. 1, pp. 247, 248, 255, 256, 272, 274, 285, 286, 304; vol. 2, pp. 4, 5, 137; *Pennsylvania Archives,* 1st ser., ed. Samuel Hazard (12 vols., Harrisburg, 1838–1860), vol. IX, pp. 600, 601; *Pennsylvania Archives,* 2d ser., ed. John P. Linn and William H. Egle (19 vols., Harrisburg, 1874–1893), vol. IX, p. 625; *Pennsylvania Archives,* 8th ser., ed. Gertrude MacKinney and Charles F. Hoban (8 vols., Harrisburg, 1931–1935), vol. VIII, p. 7194; Norman S. Cohen, "William Allen: Chief Justice of Pennsylvania, 1704–1780" (Ph.D. dissertation, University of California, Berkeley, 1966), pp. 306–309; William Denny to Edward Shippen [IV], 30 June 1757, Stauffer Collection, vol. 4, p. 375, HSP; *Pennsylvania Gazette,* 3 January 1771; Joseph Shippen, Jr. [III] to Edmund Physick, 4 November 1769, Dreer Collection, 4C Officers Serving in America before the American Revolution, HSP.

75. Aside from numerous specific examples used elsewhere, Joseph Shippen [III] to Edward Shippen [III], Philadelphia, 11 January 1771, Shippen Papers, vol. 10, p. 111, HSP, describes things well. He indicates that his brother and cousin Andrew Allen were just appointed to the Gov-

ernor's Council. His father had hinted something respecting Joseph Shippen III and his cousin John Allen; although Joseph III expected no new position, he thought that as soon as his Cousin John settled in town that he and Cousin Jemmy Allen will have preference over any others upon the first vacancies.

76. Commission, Edward Shippen, Jr. [IV] to James Tilghman, 29 July 1767, Shippen Papers, vol. 6, p. 186, HSP. When Edward Shippen IV wrote his will of 1776, he appointed James Tilghman as one of his executors. (Edward Shippen, Jr. [IV]'s Will, 26 June 1776, Shippen, Balch Papers, vol. 1, p. 84.) Cheyney and Oberholtzer, *University of Pennsylvania*, vol. 1, pp. 286–289, indicate that James Tilghman (1716–1793), who married Anne Francis, became secretary of the Land Office in 1765, member of the Provincial Council in 1767, and member of the Common Council in 1764. He held all those offices plus the one Shippen appointed him to until the Revolution.

77. Edward Shippen [III] to James Burd, Lancaster, 3 November 1773, Shippen Papers, vol. 7, p. 73, HSP; Edward Shippen, Jr. [IV] to Jasper Yeates, Philadelphia, 9 May 1776, Shippen, Balch Papers, vol. 2, p. 28, HSP. The evidence for family connections obtaining offices has already been presented.

78. Gordon Wood (*Creation of the Republic,* p. 143) finds at the heart of Whig philosophy a desire to destroy "the most insidious and powerful weapon of eighteenth-century despotism—the power of appointment. Nothing impressed the radical Whig mind more than the subtle means by which modern societies were enslaved by their rulers." His evidence leads to a conclusion that these feelings existed toward activities in the colonies as well as those in England.

79. The consensus school or interpretation of the American Revolution as a movement to conserve the past dominated the writings of the 1950s and early 1960s. Two of its most distinguished proponents present the basic arguments in brief form; they are Bernard Bailyn whose "Political Experience and Enlightenment Ideas in Eighteenth-Century America," appeared in the *American Historical Review*, vol. LXVII (January 1962), 339–351, and Edmund Morgan who wrote a survey *The Birth of the Republic, 1763–1789* (Chicago, 1956). Wood's brief treatment of "The Pennsylvania Revolution" (*Creation of the Republic,* pp. 83–90) characterizes it as a real revolution. Although Charles Lincoln reached the same conclusion in *The Revolutionary Movement in Pennsylvania* almost seventy years earlier, the evaluations differ in important regards.

80. Constitution of Pennsylvania, 1776, preamble, quoted in Thayer, *Pennsylvania Politics,* p. 211. The Constitution of Pennsylvania of 1776,

which is located in the Public Records Division of the Pennsylvania Historical and Museum Commission, is reprinted in its entirety in Thayer, *Pennsylvania Politics*, pp. 211–227.

81. In 1756 Edward Shippen IV ran for a seat in the Assembly. His father explains that he introduced Edward IV and Alexander Stedman to important politicians of Lancaster County "as agreeable to Cous Allen & ye other gentlemen in Philadelphia." (Edward Shippen [III] to [Joseph Shippen III], John Harris's, 13 7bre 1756, Shippen Papers, vol. 2, p. 71, HSP.) Edward IV described his attitude toward that elected office as follows: "For my part I am not anxious to be in the House, A Seat there would give me much Trouble and take up a great deal of my Time and yield no Advantage to my Family, whose Good I am bound first to consult. . . . However as our Friends thought it was necessary I should stand for Lancaster I gave my Consent." (Edward Shippen, Jr. [IV] to Edward Shippen [III], Philadelphia, 19 September 1756, Shippen Papers, Box 1, Edward Shippen folder, HSP.) Other families viewed seats in the General Assembly differently, and it seems almost inconceivable that the attempt to limit terms to four years in seven did not refer to such people as Isaac Norris, Thomas Leech, Joseph Fox, John Kearsley, John Kinsey, Israel Pemberton, and Edward Warner who served eighteen to thirty years almost without interruption.

82. Pennsylvania Constitution, 1776, Rights 6, 7, Sections 6, 7, 8, 30, 32, in Thayer, *Pennsylvania Politics*, pp. 213, 215–216, 223.

83. Pennsylvania Constitution, 1776, Section 19, in Thayer, *Pennsylvania Politics*, pp. 219–220.

84. Pennsylvania Constitution, 1776, Section 23, in Thayer, *Pennsylvania Politics*, p. 221. Pennsylvania Constitution, 1776, Sections 11, 19, 23, in Thayer, *Pennsylvania Politics*, pp. 217, 219, 221. The Shippens and Allens are not the only ones against whom these provisions are directed. For example, Benjamin Chew (1722–1810) held the following offices before the war: attorney general of Pennsylvania (1755–1769), member of the Provincial Council (1755–1775), register general of Pennsylvania (1765), chief justice of Pennsylvania (1774–1776), and recorder of Philadelphia (1755–1774). Richard Peters (1704–1776) was secretary of the Land Office, secretary of the province, and principal agent and commissioner of property for a quarter of a century after he arrived in the colony in the 1730s. Cheyney and Oberholtzer, *University of Pennsylvania*, vol. 1, pp. 272, 254.

85. Pennsylvania Constitution, 1776, Right 14, in Thayer, *Pennsylvania Politics*, p. 214.

86. *Ibid.*, Section 45, in Thayer, *Pennsylvania Politics*, p. 226. Comments of some radicals even after 1776 indicate the intensity of their concern.

For example, in the summer of 1777, Benjamin Rush believed, "A peace at this time would be the greatest curse that could befall us. I hope the war will last until it introduces among us the same temperance in pleasure, the same modesty in dress, the same justice in business, and the same veneration for the name of the Deity which distinguished our ancestors." (B. Rush to John Adams, Morristown, 8 August 1777, *Letters of Benjamin Rush*, ed. Butterfield, vol. 1, pp. 152–153.) Several months later William Shippen II exclaimed, "The People seem all infatuated [and] are running Mad into Luxury & extravagance of every kind. Whigs as well as Tories." (William Shippen [II] to Edward Shippen [III], Philadelphia, 10 January 1778, Shippen Papers, vol. 8, p. 27, HSP.) *Pennsylvania Gazette*, 31 March, 19 May 1779.

87. The following incidents indicate some of the reasons why people resented the Shippens; the second example appears entirely unethical. Edward III, James Burd, Curtis Grubb (a brother of Burd's son-in-law), and their associates used their influence to block the creation of a new county in 1773 which they felt would adversely affect "Mr. Hamilton's town of Lancaster." Burd was certain that in the Governor's Council Hamilton, the Shippen brothers, Tilghman, and Andrew Allen would do likewise. All those men were kinsmen. (James Burd to Edward Shippen [III], Tinian, 11 September 1773, Shippen, Balch Papers, vol. 2, p. 18, HSP; Edward Shippen [III] to Joseph [III] and Edward [IV] Shippen, Lancaster, 17 September 1773, Shippen Papers, vol. 10, p. 161, HSP.) In Edward Shippen, Jr. [IV] to Joseph Shippen, Jr. [III], Lancaster, 7 May 1769, Shippen, Balch Papers, vol. 2, p. 6, HSP, Edward IV suggests that surveyors of their lands on the Chillisquakey work carefully and that "a hint of a Gratuity in case they should please us, together with the Opinion they may have of your being able hereafter to oblige them on account of your connection with the Governor, will be the most likely means of our Succeeding." Between about 1750 and 1775 the Shippen family connections almost always protected any member's hold on his office. For example, when Edward Shippen III sued Penn's agent, Richard Hockley, Edward Shippen IV informed his father, "the Propr[ietor] I dont doubt . . . harbours some little Resentment against you . . . but I am persuaded he will never order Mr. Hamilton to supercede you, on acco[un]t of your Connections with Mr. Ham[ilto]n & Mr. Allen who I'm sure he would not wish to offend."

88. For a perceptive analysis of Philadelphia as a "private city," see Sam Bass Warner, Jr., *The Private City, Philadelphia in Three Periods of Its Growth* (Philadelphia, 1968), especially pages twenty-one and twenty-three, and more generally chapters one and two. According to Warner, the

essence of privatism "lay in its concentration upon the individual and the individual's search for wealth . . . socially, privatism meant that the individual should see his first loyalty as his immediate family, and that a community should be a union of such money-making, accumulating families."

89. Many general accounts of Loyalists and other works on the period consider the Shippens as examples. Aside from popular works, scholarly studies frequently refer to Edward Shippen IV and certain other Shippens as "Tories," meaning they wished to extend prerogative powers of the king. For example, see Lorenzo Sabine, *Biographical Sketches of Loyalists of the American Revolution, with an Historical Essay,* with new introduction by Ralph Adams Brown (2 vols., Port Washington, New York, 1966), vol. 2, pp. 297–300; Wallace Brown, *The King's Friends: The Composition and Motives of the American Loyalist Claimants* (Providence, 1965), p. 136; Wallace Brown, *The Good Americans, The Loyalists in the American Revolution* (New York, 1969), p. 234.

90. Edward Shippen [III] to Joseph Shippen [III], Lancaster, 13 July 1776, Shippen Papers, Box 1, folder presented by Mrs. Thomas Balch, HSP. At the same time, Edward continued to oppose the idea of independence.

91. This should come as no great surprise, though American historians have always ignored the possibility in preference to more dramatic explanations. Sir Lewis Namier's studies of political leaders of eighteenth-century England concludes that parochial, personal, and often petty considerations (not broad perspectives and lofty ideologies) motivated members of Parliament. Without denegrading the importance of ideology to many colonists during the same period, we find that to a large degree the Shippens appear quite similar. Regardless of the role ideology played in causing the Revolution, the Shippens seem quite typical of the inhabitants of Philadelphia in their response to it after 1776, if one accepts Sam Bass Warner's evaluation: "The divisions among Philadelphia's citizens reflected personal attitudes toward the revolutionary governments established in Pennsylvania and toward the Continental Congress" (Warner, *Private City,* p. 23). For example, Edward Shippen IV opposed the revolutionary Provincial Convention because he believed that it would establish "a form of Government not very favourable to Liberty." He continued, "Surely they [the people of Lancaster] would not be willing to give up all our Charter privileges at one stroke; many of our people here who even sigh for an Independence are averse to the measure now proposed, as tending to deprive us of some valuable Rights, without an Assurance of a Substitute." (Edward Shippen, Jr. [IV] to Jasper Yeates, Philadelphia, 23 May 1776, Shippen, Balch Collection, vol. 2, p. 29, HSP.) The concept of a private city becomes

especially useful in explaining why Edward Burd, who was wounded and captured by the British after the Declaration of Independence, visited his uncles the Shippens on the way to the front and why he remained on cordial terms with them.

92. Joseph Shippen, Jr. [III] to Edward Shippen [III], Philadelphia, 3 July 1776, Shippen Papers, vol. 12, p. 125, HSP.

93. Although Wallace Brown (*The Good Americans: The Loyalists in the American Revolution* [New York, 1969], pp. 233–234) considers Edward Shippen part of the Loyalist (or possibly Tory) contingent, a closer appraisal of the lawyer suggests that he was not a member of that small minority. If Pennsylvania was "the stronghold of moderates, neutralists, and pacifists," as Brown claims, then Edward Shippen IV and indeed most of the Shippens were typical in their response.

94. Edward Shippen, Jr. [IV] to Joseph Shippen [III], Amwell, 23 June 1776, Shippen, Balch Papers, vol. 2, p. 30, HSP.

95. Edward Burd to James Burd, 28 July 1776, Shippen Papers, vol. 7, p. 195, HSP.

96. James Burd to Edward Shippen [III], Tinian, 25 July 1776, Shippen Papers, vol. 7, p. 193, HSP.

97. Joseph Shippen, Jr. [III] to Edward Shippen, Jr. [IV], Northern Liberties, 19 July 1776, Shippen Papers, vol. 12, p. 40, HSP.

98. Joseph Shippen, Jr. [III] to Jasper Yeates, Philadelphia, 3 July 1776, Shippen, Balch Papers, vol. 2, p. 31, HSP.

99. *Ibid.*

100. Edward Shippen, Jr. [IV] to Joseph Shippen [III], Amwell, 23 June 1776, Shippen, Balch Papers, vol. 2, p. 30, HSP.

101. *Ibid.*

102. Joseph Shippen, Jr. [III] to Edward Shippen, Jr. [IV], Northern Liberties, 19 July 1776, Shippen Papers, vol. 12, p. 40, HSP.

103. Thomas Balch, who knew some of the fifth-generation Shippens and tended to sympathize with them, wrongly asserts that Joseph Shippen III moved to Kennett Square about 1773 because of his expensive family and ill health. To support this he quotes a letter indicating Joseph III was ill in March 1777. The Shippen Papers however make it abundantly clear that Joseph III's move occurred in September 1776 and that the Revolution lay at the heart of his reason. Likewise, S. A. Davies's statement that "the only reason why he [Joseph Shippen III] did not enter the revolutionary army was feeble health" is totally unfounded. (S. A. Davies, *Princeton College in the Eighteenth Century* [New York, 1872], pp. 25–26.)

104. Joseph Shippen, Jr. [III] to Edward Shippen, Jr. [IV], Northern Liberties, 19 July 1776, Shippen Papers, vol. 12, p. 40, HSP.

105. Edward Burd to James Burd, tavern within 4 miles of Brunswick, 28 July 1776, Shippen Papers, vol. 7, p. 195, HSP.

106. Edward Shippen, 3d [V] to Edward Shippen [III], Philadelphia, 11 March 1777, Shippen, Balch Papers, vol. 2, p. 36, HSP.

107. Joseph Shippen, Jr. [III] to Edward Shippen, Jr. [IV], Kennett Square, 2 September 1777, Shippen Papers, vol. 12, p. 81, HSP.

108. *Ibid.*

109. Orders of Council re Joseph Shippen, Jr. [III], 4 August 1777, Shippen Papers, vol. 10, p. 205, HSP.

110. Joseph Shippen, Jr. [III] to Timothy Matlack, Kennett Square, Chester Co., 20 April 1780, Shippen Papers, vol. 8, p. 69, HSP.

111. Joseph Shippen [III] to Jasper Yeates, Kennett Square, 17 March 1778, Shippen, Balch Papers, vol. 2, p. 39, HSP.

112. Joseph Shippen, Jr. [III] to Jasper Yeates, Kennett Square, 27 January 1778, Shippen, Balch Papers, vol. 2, p. 37, HSP; Edward Shippen [III] to James Burd, Lancaster, 24 February 1779; James Burd to Edward Shippen [III], Tinian, 5 April 1779; Joseph Shippen, Jr. [III] to Dear Nephew [Edward Burd], Kennett Square, 25 September 1780; Joseph Shippen, Jr. [III] to Edward Burd, Kennett Square, 13 August 1780, Shippen Papers, vol. 8, p. 47; vol. 12, pp. 90, 98; vol. 11, p. 95, HSP.

113. Edward III called Lord North "that Great Murderer," because "a Butcher is too Christian an epithet." Edward Shippen [III] to Joseph Shippen [III], Lancaster, 2 July 1775, Shippen Papers, Box 1, folder presented by Mrs. Thomas Balch, HSP.

114. Edward Shippen [III] to James Burd, Lancaster, 7 November 1776, Shippen Papers, vol. 7, p. 211, HSP.

115. *Ibid.*

116. Edward Shippen [III] to James Burd, Lancaster, 14 November 1776, Shippen Papers, vol. 7, p. 213, HSP. James Burd to Edward Shippen [III], Tinian, 23 October 1776, Shippen Papers, vol. 12, p. 59, HSP; James Burd to Edward Shippen [III], Tinian, 13 November 1776, Peale Papers, Mills Collection, APS; James Burd to Edward Shippen, Tinian, 20 November 1776; Edward Shippen [III] to James Burd, Lancaster, 30 December 1776, Shippen Papers, vol. 12, p. 61; vol. 7, p. 215, HSP.

117. Edward Shippen, Jr. [IV] to Edward Shippen [III], Philadelphia, 11 March 1777, Shippen Papers, Box 1, Edward Shippen folder, HSP.

118. Postscript, 16 March 1777, to Edward Shippen, Jr. [IV] to Edward Shippen [III], Philadelphia, 11 March 1777, Shippen Papers, Box 1, Edward Shippen folder, HSP. James Burd to Edward Shippen [III], Tinian, 14 May 1777, Shippen Papers, vol. 12, p. 78, HSP.

119. Edward Shippen [III] to Joseph Shippen [III], Lancaster, 6 May

1777, Shippen Papers, vol. 10, p. 203, HSP. Edward III did not even own his own house at Lancaster. This however is characteristic of many Shippens, for example, Edward III rented his "great house" in Philadelphia to his son Edward IV; Edward IV rented a house to his brother Joseph III; in 1778 Jasper Yeates bought the house in which his grandfather Edward Shippen III lived and allowed him to continue there until death.

120. Edward Shippen, Jr. [IV] to Edward Shippen [III], Philadelphia, 6 April 1770, Shippen, Balch Papers, vol. 2, p. 8, HSP.

121. Joseph Shippen [III] to Edward Shippen [III], Philadelphia, 28 April 1770, Shippen Papers, vol. 10, p. 101, HSP.

122. Edward Shippen [III] to Dear Son, Lancaster, 9 September 1775, Shippen Papers, vol. 12, p. 36, HSP.

123. Edward Shippen III and his son Edward IV also gave legal advice to William Allen on how to draft a will so as to avoid confiscation of parts of his estates which ordinarily would have been the consequence of his son Andrew Allen's treason against the revolutionary government.

124. Edward Shippen, Jr. [IV] to Edward Shippen [III], Philadelphia, 11 March 1777, Shippen Papers, Box 1, Edward Shippen folder, HSP; Edward Shippen [III] to Edward Shippen, Jr. [IV], Lancaster, 12 August 1777; William Shippen [II] to Edward Shippen [III], 21 September 1776; Edward Shippen, Jr. [IV] to Edward Shippen [III], 29 July 1777, Shippen Papers, vol. 12, p. 80; vol. 10, p. 201; vol. 8, p. 13, HSP.

125. Edward Shippen, Jr. [IV] to Edward Shippen [III], Philadelphia, 5 October 1778, Shippen Papers, vol. 8, p. 41, HSP.

126. Edward Shippen [III] to James Burd, Lancaster, 28 September 1778; Edward Shippen [III] to Francis Campbell and Mathew Henderson, Lancaster, 23 October 1779; Edward Shippen [III] to Francis Campbell and Mathew Henderson, Lancaster, 12 October 1780; Edward Shippen [III] to Samuel Tate, Lancaster, 15 November 1780, Shippen Papers, vol. 8, p. 39; vol. 16, p. 17; vol. 6, p. 43, HSP.

127. Edward Shippen [III] to Joseph Shippen [III], Lancaster, October 1778, Shippen Papers, Box 1, folder presented by Mrs. Thomas Balch, HSP.

128. Edward Shippen [III] to James Burd, Lancaster, 17 July 1778, Shippen Papers, vol. 8, p. 35, HSP.

129. T[imoth]y Matlack to Edward Shippen [III], Philadelphia, 8 April 1779, Joseph Shippen Papers, Nos. 1762–1763, LC. James Burd to Edward Shippen [III], Tinian, 4 September 1778, Shippen Papers, vol. 12, p. 82, HSP.

130. James Burd to Edward Shippen [III], Tinian, 4 December 1776, Shippen Papers, vol. 12, p. 65, HSP.

131. Edward Shippen [III] to James Burd, Lancaster, 9 January 1777, Shippen Papers, vol. 8, p. 1, HSP.

132. James Burd to Edward Shippen [III], Tinian, 7 March 1777, Shippen Papers, vol. 12, p. 76, HSP.

133. James Burd to Edward Shippen [III], Tinian, 4 September 1778; J[asper] Yeates to James Burd, Lancaster, 19 February 1779; J[asper] Yeates to James Burd, Lancaster, 11 June 1789, Shippen Papers, vol. 12, p. 82; vol. 8, pp. 45, 71, HSP.

134. Edward Shippen, Jr. [IV] to Joseph Shippen [III], Philadelphia, 13 November 1776; Edward Shippen [IV] to Edward Shippen [III], 31 December 1776, Shippen Papers, Box 1, HSP.

135. Edward Shippen, Jr. [IV] to Edward Shippen [III], Philadelphia, 18 January 1777, Shippen, Balch Papers, vol. 2, p. 35, HSP.

136. *Ibid.*

137. Edward Shippen 3d [V] to Edward Shippen [III], Philadelphia, 11 March 1777, Shippen, Balch Papers, vol. 2, p. 36, HSP.

138. Edward Shippen, Jr. [IV] to Edward Shippen [III], Philadelphia, 18 January 1777, Shippen, Balch Papers, vol. 2, p. 35, HSP. In this letter Edward IV refers to Washington's forces as "our troops."

139. Elizabeth Shippen to Mrs. Yeates, The Cottage, 5 June 1777, Shippen Papers, transferred from the Society Collection, HSP.

140. Edward Shippen, Jr. [IV] to Edward Shippen [III], Falls of Schuylkill, 12 July 1777, Shippen Papers, vol. 8, p. 13, HSP.

141. Elizabeth Shippen to Mrs. Yeates, The Cottage, 20 August 1777, Stauffer Collection, vol. 17, p. 1232, HSP.

142. Edward Shippen, Jr. [IV] to Edward Shippen [III], Philadelphia, 21 December 1778, Shippen, Balch Papers, vol. 2, p. 43, HSP.

143. Edward Burd to James Burd, Sunbury, 1 November 1775, Shippen Papers, vol. 7, p. 139, HSP.

144. Edward Burd to James Burd, Reading, 15 March 1776; Edward Burd to James Burd, Reading, 22 December 1775, Shippen Papers, vol. 7, pp. 161, 145, HSP.

145. *Ibid.*

146. Edward Burd to James Burd, Reading, 6 July 1776, Shippen Papers, vol. 7, p. 183, HSP.

147. Edward Burd to James Burd, Reading, 6 July 1776, Shippen Papers, vol. 7, p. 185, HSP.

148. *Ibid.*

149. [William Shippen II] to Edward Shippen [III], 5 September 1776; James Burd to Edward Shippen [III], Tinian, 11 September 1776, Shippen Papers, vol. 12, pp. 38, 50, HSP; Edward Shippen [III] to Jasper Yeates, Lancaster, 13 September 1776, Yeates Papers, Correspondence 1762–1780, HSP; Edward Burd to James Burd, Philadelphia, 12 December 1776, Shippen Papers, vol. 7, p. 213, HSP.

150. Elizabeth Tilghman to Elizabeth Shippen Burd, Chester Town, 29 January 1778 [1779], Shippen, Balch Papers, vol. 2, p. 38, HSP.

151. In *Crisis of the Aristocracy, 1558–1641* (Oxford, 1965), Lawrence Stone indicates the English Civil War in the seventeenth century destroyed family ties and pruned family trees. The marriage of Major Edward Burd to Elizabeth Shippen is characteristic of the Shippen family during the American Revolution in the sense that it provided a concrete example of a general tendency. The Revolution did not destroy family ties, neither did it prune the family tree. Edward Burd to Edward Shippen [III], Reading, 22 August 1778; Sarah Burd to Edward Burd, Tinian, 25 September 1778; Edward Burd to James Burd, Philadelphia, 8 September 1778; Edward Shippen to James Burd, Philadelphia, 12 March 1779, Shippen Papers, vol. 12, pp. 87, 89; vol. 8, pp. 37, 49, HSP.

152. Edward Shippen, Jr. [IV] to Edward Shippen [III], Philadelphia, 21 December 1778, Shippen, Balch Papers, vol. 2, p. 43, HSP.

153. Edward Shippen, Jr. [IV] to Edward Shippen [III], Falls of Skuylkil [*sic*], 28 June 1780, Shippen Papers, Box 1, Edward Shippen folder, HSP.

154. *Ibid.*

155. Edward Shippen, Jr. [IV] to Edward Shippen [III], Philadelphia, 3 July 1778, Shippen Papers, Box 1, Edward Shippen folder, HSP; Edward Shippen, Jr. [IV] to Jasper Yeates, Philadelphia, 10 March 1781, Stauffer Collection, vol. 8, p. 924, HSP.

156. James T. Flexner's *The Traitor and the Spy: Benedict Arnold and John Andre* (New York, 1953) and Willard M. Wallace's *Traitorous Hero: The Life and Fortunes of Benedict Arnold* (New York, 1954) are recent accounts of Benedict Arnold.

157. Edward Shippen [III] to James Burd, Lancaster, 2 January 1779, Shippen Papers, vol. 8, p. 43, HSP. Thomas Balch reflects nineteenth-century values and wishful thinking on the part of Peggy Shippen's kinsmen and descendants when he says Peggy's father never liked Arnold because the general was not a gentleman, his birth and early education were low, and that his peddling and smuggling trade neither improved his manners or morals. Balch, *Letters relating to Pennsylvania*, vol. 1, p. 160.

158. Balch repeats family traditions that "to the great distress of her family, she [Peggy] returned his [Arnold's] love." Because her dowry was important, this misconstrues the situation; manuscripts indicate approval by the family. Balch, *Papers relating to Pennsylvania*, vol. 1, p. 160. Wallace repeats Balch with no additional evidence; in fact his claim that the Shippens "were none too eager" to see the marriage take place, and that they "did not wish the courtship hastened," seems a perverse interpre-

tation of the course of events. Peggy Shippen probably met Arnold during the summer of 1778 (definitely by September) and married the following April; at most she knew him only nine months before the marriage took place. (Wallace, *Traitorous Hero,* pp. 170–174.) Aside from Edward Shippen IV's own comments, the following manuscripts indicate approval of the marriage by Peggy Shippen's kinsmen: Elizabeth Tilghman to Elizabeth Shippen Burd, Chester Town, 29 January 1778 [1779], Shippen, Balch Papers, vol. 2, p. 38, HSP; E[lizabeth] Tilghman to Mrs. Eliza Burd, Chester Town, 14 April 1779, Shippen and Swift, Balch Collection, HSP; A. Coxe to Sarah Shippen Burd [*sic* Elizabeth Shippen Burd], Sunbury, Sunday Evening [1779], Burd-Shippen-Hubley Papers, HSP; Edward Burd to Jasper Yeates, 3 January 1779, in J. Bennett Nolan, *Neddie Burd's Reading Letters, An Epic of Early Berks Bar* (Reading, Pa., 1927), p. 93; *Pennsylvania Evening Post,* 23 April 1779.

159. A typical example of the unsubstantiated romantic view is Charles Burr Todd's *The Real Benedict Arnold* (New York, 1903). In chapter three he gives the following account. Peggy Shippen was "a Tory when Arnold married her; she always remained a Tory at heart; her family and friends were sympathizers with the British cause." "She was the most potent factor" in causing his defection, and the arguments she used "we can readily imagine." He claims Peggy Shippen Arnold and John Andre conspired treason and then she brought her husband into the plot in September 1780. More recent and reliable accounts indicate Arnold himself engaged in treason in May 1779. Aside from innuendoes, the only support Todd has is a confession "which has all the ear-marks of truth," because Aaron Burr and his wife who divulged it "were the soul of honor." In chapter seventeen of Isaac N. Arnold's *The Life of Benedict Arnold; His Patriotism and His Treason* (Chicago, 1897) the author destroys the reliability of *The Memoirs of Aaron Burr* by Matthew L. Davis (the only evidence which is not circumstantial which Todd used) when he writes "Some time after their [the Arnold's] marriage—how long we are not told —Mrs. Burr repeated the conversation to her husband, and Burr, some time within the half-century following, repeated the conversation to Davis. It is hearsay evidence, three times removed, and repeated with years of interval between the repetitions. As such, it is worthless, independent of the notorious character of Burr."

160. Willard's *Traitorous Hero* agrees with Carl Van Doren's *Secret History of the American Revolution* (New York, 1941), which claims that Peggy knew of the treason and participated in it, but that it cannot be determined whether or not she influenced Arnold to become a traitor. Van Doren indicates that the decision was primarily Arnold's. The use of

Peggy's letters to Major Andre was the device used to send messages. Arnold used invisible ink and wrote between the lines. It seems at least plausible that Peggy did not know about this, and certainly after the plot was discovered and the Arnolds applied to the British government for rewards for the general's services, the possibility that Peggy's role was distorted so as to increase emoluments cannot be discarded as wholly unlikely. An examination of the Sir Henry Clinton Papers, William Howe Papers, Miscellaneous Manuscripts, and other pertinent collections at the William L. Clements Library revealed no new evidence to substantiate charges against Peggy Shippen Arnold.

161. Edward Burd to James Burd, Lancaster, 10 November 1780, Shippen Papers, vol. 8, p. 79, HSP.

162. Edward Hand to Jasper Yeates, Infantry Camp, 3 October 1780, Hand Correspondence, Force transcripts, vol. 3, p. 34, LC.

163. Edward Shippen, Jr. [IV] to Jasper Yeates, Cottage, 1 November 1780, James Burd to Edward Burd, Tinian, 20 November [1780], Shippen, Balch Papers, vol. 2, pp. 47, 15, HSP.

164. Edward Burd to James Burd, Lancaster, 10 November 1780, Shippen Papers, vol. 8, p. 79, HSP.

165. *Ibid.*

166. Edward Shippen [III] to James Burd, Lancaster, 9 November 1777, Shippen Papers, vol. 8, p. 5, HSP; Jane Shippen to Joseph Shippen [III], Philadelphia, 25 March 1775; Joseph Shippen [III] to Edward Shippen [III], Philadelphia, 20 April 1775, Shippen Papers, Box 1, HSP. Even the account books of William Shippen II and III indicate the cordiality which continued among the Shippens, for example, entries in Account Book of Dr. William Shippen, 1775–1793, Shippen Family Papers, Box 28, LC, include: Edward Shippen, Esq. [IV] over £25 between 1785 and 1787, Charles Willing, £116 from 1785–1787, Joseph Shippen [III], £38 from 1775–1776 (twenty-six entries in seven months), and Thomas Willing, £41 between 1775 and 1776. Entries in William Shippen Account Book, 1775–1793, Shippen Family Papers, Box 3, LC, include mention of Thomas Willing, Charles Willing, and Edward Burd. Both books mention officials of the prewar, revolutionary, and postwar governments; aside from those mentioned above are George Washington, Thomas Jefferson, Tench Francis, Edmund Randolph, Robert S. Jones, Joseph B. McKean, John Hancock, Governor Penn, General Knox, Charles Thomson, and various others.

167. William Shippen [II] to Edward Shippen [III], 2 7br 1776, Shippen Papers, vol. 12, p. 46, HSP.

168. William Shippen [II] to Jasper Yeates, Philadelphia, 21 October 1775, Shippen Papers, transferred from the Society Collection, HSP;

William Shippen [II] to Edward Shippen [III], 4 January 1777, Shippen, Balch Papers, vol. 2, p. 33, HSP; Bond, Joseph Shippen [II], yeoman, to General Loan Office of Pennsylvania, 6 July 1774, Shippen Papers, vol. 7, p. 95, HSP; Mortgage, Joseph Shippen [II] to Elizabeth Harmar, 23 February 1776, Shippen Papers, Box 15, LC; Cheyney and Oberholtzer, *University of Pennsylvania*, vol. 1, p. 257.

169. Wood, *Creation of the Republic*, p. 87, confuses William Shippen II and his son William Shippen III. The radical thoughts belong to William Shippen II. Thomas Lee Shippen was the son of William Shippen III.

170. John Morgan, Memorial to the Continental Congress, 30 July 1777, quoted in Whitfield Jenks Bell, Jr., *John Morgan: Continental Doctor* (Philadelphia, 1965), p. 218.

171. For more extensive coverage of the Morgan-Shippen feud during the War for Independence and a discussion of the medical department, see Bell, *Morgan*, pp. 178–239.

172. John Morgan, *A Vindication of His Public Character in the Station of Director-General* (Boston, 1777), p. xxv.

173. William Shippen, Jr. [III] to George Washington, Newark, 19 October 1776, Gratz Collection, American Physicians, Case 7, Box 33, HSP; *Pennsylvania Gazette*, 17 July 1776; *Pennsylvania Evening Post*, 11, 17 January 1776; *Pennsylvania Magazine* (July 1776), p. 344; *Pennsylvania Gazette*, 17 July 1776.

174. B[enjamin] Rush to John Adams, Reading, 21 October 1777, *Letters of Benjamin Rush*, ed. Butterfield, vol. 1, p. 161.

175. B[enjamin] Rush to John Adams, Trenton, 1 October 1777, *Letters of Benjamin Rush*, ed. Butterfield, vol. 1, pp. 155–156. Chapter thirteen of Bell's *Morgan* handles Rush's role in more detail. On one occasion, with savage humor Rush suggested that the way to win the war was to "lead them [the enemy] through any of the villages in Lancaster county where we have a hospital, and I will ensure you that in 6 weeks there shall not be a man of them alive or fit for duty." (Quoted in Bell, *Morgan*, p. 225.) The following manuscripts provide details of the complaints against William Shippen III: Benjamin Rush to My dear Julia [Rush], Yorktown, 12 January 1778; Benjamin Rush to ———, Lancaster, 1 February 1778; Benjamin Rush to John Adams, Philadelphia, 12 February 1812, Manuscript Correspondence of Benjamin Rush, vol. 29, pp. 120C, 120B, 136, Library Company of Philadelphia; Photostats, Benjamin Rush to ———, 13 December 1777, 25 January, 30 January, 9 March, 20 April 1778, Society Miscellaneous Collection under Rush, HSP; Photostats, John Morgan to Sam[uel] Huntington, 25 October, 22 November,

20 December 1779, 28 March 1780, Society Miscellaneous Collection under Morgan, HSP.

176. Benj[amin] Rush to ―――― [1778–1780?], Manuscript Correspondence of Benjamin Rush, vol. 29, p. 119, Library Company of Philadelphia.

177. The charges were:

"First—Fraud, in selling Hospital stores as your own property, & in making use of Continental Waggons for the Transportation of the same.

"Second—Speculating in, & selling Hospital stores, whilst the sick were perishing for the want of them; accompanied with Peculation, and Adulteration of Hospital Wines at Bethlehem.

"Third—Keeping no regular Books & Accounts with proper Checks and Vouchers for the Expenditure of public Moneys & Hospital stores: And neglecting and refusing to pay just & reasonable Hospital Accounts and misusing the persons who applied for settlement.

"Fourth—Neglect of Hospital duty, from which many of the sick suffered in a shameful and shocking Manner, and making false Reports to the President of the Congress of the state of the Hospital & of the sick.

"Fifth—Scandalous and infamous Practices such as are unbecoming the Character of an Officer & Gentleman, in aspersing, and calumniating the Reputation and Conduct of your Superior Officers to Members of Congress in order to vilify, degrade and supplant them."

Quoted in Whitfield J. Bell, Jr. "The Court Martial of Dr. William Shippen, Jr., 1780," *Journal of the History of Medicine and Allied Sciences,* XIX, no. 3 [1964], 227–228.)

178. Whitfield J. Bell, Jr., reconstructed the court-martial in "The Court Martial of Dr. William Shippen, Jr., 1780," *ibid.,* pp. 218–238. He covers the court-martial and events leading up to it in greater detail in chapters eleven, twelve, and thirteen of *John Morgan.*

179. *Pennsylvania Packet,* 25 November 1780.

180. Edward Hand was the brother-in-law of Jasper Yeates who was Edward Shippen III's grandson. Edward Shippen III and his brother William II were close friends, and Edward III had contributed to the education of William III. As the court-martial began, Yeates received a letter from "Your affectionate kinsman" Hand, saying "Doctor Shippen's trial goes slowly." Several other times that summer he corresponded with Yeates on the same subject. (Edward Hand to Jasper Yeates, Morris Town, 29 March 1780; Edward Hand to Jasper Yeates, 5 June 1780, Edward Hand Correspondence, Force Transcripts, vol. 3, pp. 26, 27, 29, LC). Hand closed a letter in August 1780 saying, "My respects to Mr. Shippen, Miss Patty etc., and am Dr. Yeates your affectionate Kinsman." (Edward Hand to Jasper Yeates, camp near Toppan, 19 August 1780, Edward Hand

Correspondence, Force Transcripts, vol. 3, p. 32, LC.) Lest this indictment be pushed beyond legitimate limits, it seems fair to acknowledge that Hand erupted with righteous indignation a few months later upon the discovery of the treason of Benedict Arnold; at that time he wrote, "Pardon, My Dear Sir, My warmth, which the respect I once bore the man on account of his connexion with a worthy family cannot restrain." (Edward Hand to Jasper Yeates, Infantry Camp, 3 October 1780, Hand Correspondence, Force Transcripts, vol. 3, p. 34, LC.) Of course Arnold's treason seemed to all contemporaries far worse than Shippen's misconduct in the Medical Department; Arnold had only married into the Shippen family a few years earlier and was despised by the Shippens for his treason.

181. Quoted in Bell, *Morgan*, p. 235.

182. Ethel Armes (ed., *Nancy Shippen, Her Journal Book: The International Romance of a Young Lady of Fashion of Colonial Philadelphia with Letters to Her and about Her* [New York, 1968], p. 110) attributes certain characteristics of an ideal gentleman to William Shippen III when she writes that his service in the war was "so largely gratuitous." William Shippen III informed Washington that he had been useful in qualifying young gentlemen for Continental hospitals and the army as well as private life after he left "public service." William Shippen, Jr. [III] to George Washington, Philadelphia, 29 April 1781, Gratz, American Physicians, Case 7, Box 33, HSP.

183. William Shippen III's relationship with his children can be readily grasped by reading the journal of Ann (Shippen) Livingston at the Library of Congress (edited by Ethel Armes as *Nancy Shippen, Her Journal Book*) and the journal and voluminous correspondence between William Shippen III and his son Thomas Lee Shippen while the latter was in England and New York during the 1780s. These manuscripts are also located in the Shippen Papers at the Library of Congress.

184. Armes, *Nancy Shippen, Her Journal Book*, pp. 95–111. The letters which Armes reproduces are found in the Shippen Papers at the Library of Congress.

185. Joseph Shippen [III] to Edward Shippen [III], Philadelphia, 24 February 1770; Joseph Shippen [III] to Edward Shippen [III], Philadelphia, 22 June 1770; Joseph Shippen [III] to Edward Shippen [III], Philadelphia, 22 December 1770; Joseph Shippen [III] to Edward Shippen [III], Philadelphia, 1 July 1771, Shippen Papers, vol. 10, pp. 95, 105, 111, 121, HSP; Joseph Shippen, Jr. [III] to Edward Shippen [III], Philadelphia, 30 July 1771, Shippen and Swift, Balch Collection, HSP; Edward Shippen [III] to Richard Penn, Lancaster, 11 January 1772, Shippen, Balch Papers, vol. 2, p. 13, HSP; James Burd to Edward Shippen [III],

Tinian, 23 April 1773, Shippen Papers, vol. 10, p. 157, HSP; Edward Shippen [IV] to J[asper] Yeates, Philadelphia, 19 September 1775, Shippen, Balch Papers, vol. 2, p. 26, HSP; William Shippen [II] to Edward Shippen [III], 10 April 1775, Shippen Papers, vol. 7, p. 111, HSP; William Shippen [II] to Dear Brother [Edward Shippen III], 6 May 1775, Miscellaneous Manuscripts Collection, APS.

186. J[asper] Yeates to Edward Burd, Lancaster, 4 November 1777, Shippen Papers, vol. 12, p. 83, HSP.

187. Edward Shippen [III] to James Burd, Lancaster, 14 May 1778, Shippen Papers, vol. 8, p. 31, HSP. Edward Burd to James Burd, Lancaster, 26 May 1777; Edward Shippen [III] to Joseph Shippen [III], Lancaster, 2 June 1777; Edward Shippen [III] to James Burd, Lancaster, 8 August 1777, Shippen Papers, vol. 8, p. 11; vol. 10, p. 205; vol. 8, p. 13, HSP; Sarah Burd to Dear & Honored Madam [Mary (Gray) Shippen], Tinian, 16 November 1777, Stauffer Collection, vol. 17, p. 1232, HSP; William Shippen [II] to Edward Shippen [III], Philadelphia, 10 January 1778, Shippen Papers, vol. 8, p. 27, HSP; Edward Shippen [III] to James Burd, Lancaster, 30 June 1778, Shippen Papers, vol. 8, pp. 27, 33, HSP.

188. Edward Shippen [III] to James Burd, Lancaster, 26 December 1778, Shippen Papers, vol. 8, p. 43, HSP.

189. Sarah Burd to Edward Shippen [III], Tinian, 15 August 1778, Burd-Shippen-Hubley Papers, HSP; Edward Shippen, Jr. [IV] to Edward Shippen [III], Philadelphia, 31 August 1780, Shippen Papers, Box 1, Edward Shippen folder, HSP; Edward Burd to James Burd, Lancaster, 10 November 1790; Edward Shippen [III] to Mr. & Mrs. Burd, Lancaster, 15 February 1780; Edward Shippen [III] to Mathew Henderson, Lancaster, 22 August 1780, Shippen Papers, vol. 8, pp. 79, 67; vol. 16, p. 39, HSP; Edward Shippen [IV] to Edward Shippen [III], Philadelphia, 26 September 1780, Shippen Papers, Box 1, HSP; James Read to Edward Shippen [III], 17 October 1780, Shippen Papers, vol. 8, p. 77, HSP.

190. James Burd to Edward Shippen [III], Tinian, 7 April 1781, Shippen Papers, vol. 12, p. 106, HSP.

191. J[asper] Yeates to James Burd, Lancaster, 10 April 1781, Shippen Papers, vol. 8, p. 85, HSP.

192. Sarah Burd to Edward Shippen [III], Tinian, 3 March 1781, Shippen Papers, vol. 12, p. 104, HSP; Edward Hand to Jasper Yeates, Camp near Dobbs Ferry, 17 July 1781, Hand Correspondence, Force Transcripts, vol. 3, pp. 36–37, LC; Joseph Shippen, Jr. [III] to Edward Burd, Kennett Square, 28 August 1781; Sarah Burd to James Burd, [Lancaster], 18 September 1781, Shippen Papers, vol. 12, pp. 110, 111, HSP.

193. J[asper] Yeates to Edward Burd, Lancaster, 24 September 1781, Shippen Papers, vol. 11, p. 112, HSP.

194. Sarah Burd to James Burd, Lancaster, 25 September 1781, Burd-Shippen-Hubley Papers, HSP.

195. Joseph Shippen, Jr. [III] to Edward Burd, Kennett Square, 12 October 1781, Shippen Papers, vol. 11, p. 113, HSP.

CHAPTER IX

1. This statement refers to the colonial branch of the Shippen family. No evidence suggests that the Shippens in America were in contact with or knew much about the activities of the Shippens in England after about the third decade of the eighteenth century. Peggy Shippen Arnold and Joseph W. Shippen are the only colonial Shippens who had left Pennsylvania by the end of the War for Independence.

2. In an overview of the Shippen family after the death of Edward Shippen III in 1781, the continued use of the designation of "the Edward III branch," "the Joseph II branch," and the "William II branch" is most sensible for an analysis of the family's activities with reference to the colonial period. Modification in time would make other conceptualizations more precise, yet the introduction of a new series of names would precipitate confusion.

3. Docket, "My Brother Edw. Shippen Esq's Acco[un]t with me from 26 July 1729 [*sic*] as taken from his Books, & settled with me at Plumley the 4th June 1802; when he paid me the Balance of £222.6.11, Shippen-Burd-Hubley Papers, HSP; Edward Shippen [IV] to Joseph Shippen [III], Philadelphia, 29 June 1793, Shippen Papers, vol. 8, p. 179, HSP; Edward Shippen [IV]'s Account with Joseph Shippen [III], settled 28 July 1798; Edward Shippen [IV]'s Account with Joseph Shippen [III], settled 12 June 1799, Shippen-Burd-Hubley Papers, HSP.

4. Joseph Shippen [III] to Edward Burd, Lancaster, 1 March 1784, Lancaster, 3 July 1784; Joseph Shippen [III] to Peter Conrad, Lancaster, 16 August 1784; Joseph Shippen [III] to Edward Burd, Lancaster, 19 August 1784; Edward Burd to Joseph Shippen [III], Philadelphia, 7 September 1784; Joseph Shippen [III] to Edward Burd, Lancaster, 11 September 1784; Lease, Joseph Shippen, Jr. [III] to Frederick Wilbert, 3 December 1784; Joseph Shippen [III] to Edward Burd, Lancaster, 27 December 1784; Edward Burd to Joseph Shippen [III], Philadelphia, 10 December 1784; Joseph Shippen [III] to Edward Burd, Lancaster, 12 July 1785, Shippen Papers, vol. 13, pp. 5, 17; vol. 16, p. 121; vol. 13, p. 21; vol. 8, p. 113; vol.

13, p. 25; vol. 16, p. 141; vol. 13, p. 43; vol. 8, p. 115; vol. 13, p. 51, HSP; William Shippen [II?] to Joseph Shippen [III], Germantown, 25 July 1785, Miscellaneous Manuscripts Collection, APS; Edward Burd to Joseph Shippen [III], Philadelphia, 2 November 1786, Shippen Papers, vol. 8, p. 139, HSP; Edward Shippen [IV] to Joseph Shippen [III], Philadelphia, 22 December 1790, Shippen Papers, vol. 8, p. 171; HSP; Power of Attorney, Joseph Shippen [III] to Edward Burd, 1792; Edward Shippen [IV] to Jasper Yeates, Philadelphia, 28 February 1784, Hampton L. Carson Collection, HSP; Edward Shippen [IV] to Joseph Shippen [III], Philadelphia, 12 June 1782, William Allen Letterbook, Shippen Letters, HSP; Edward Shippen [IV] to Samuel Breck, 16 June 1794, Breck Manuscripts, folder 101, Library Company of Philadelphia; examples of Edward Shippen IV letters to Joseph Shippen III on the subject of land in Philadelphia are found in the Shippen Papers, vol. 8, pp. 101, 103, 105, 109, 115, 119, 123, 163.

5. Joseph Shippen [III] to Edward Shippen [IV], Lancaster, 18 May 1789, Shippen Papers, Box 1, HSP.

6. Edward Shippen [IV] to Joseph Shippen [III], 17 June 1782, William Allen Letterbook, Shippen Letters, HSP; Edward Shippen [IV] to Joseph Shippen, Jr. [III], Philadelphia, 24 April 1783; Edward Shippen [IV] to Joseph Shippen [III], Philadelphia, 13 June 1783, Shippen Papers, vol. 8, pp. 91, 92, HSP; Daniel Duncan to Joseph Shippen [III], Shippensburg, 11 April 1785, Shippen-Burd-Hubley Papers, HSP; List of Debts due from sundry People at Shippensburg for lands and arreas of rents, 16 May 1785, Shippen Papers, vol. 29, p. 127, HSP; Edward Shippen, Jr. [IV] to Joseph Shippen [III], Philadelphia, 15 June 1786, Lamberton Scotch-Irish Collection, vol. 2, p. 89, HSP; James Lowrey to Edward Shippen [IV], Shippensburg, 17 July 1789; Mathew Henderson to Joseph Shippen [III], Shippensburg, 21 July 1789, Shippen-Burd-Hubley Papers, HSP.

7. Edward Shippen [IV] to Joseph Shippen [III], Philadelphia, 29 October 1788, Shippen Papers, vol. 8, p. 159, HSP. "Circumstances of the times" included Connecticut claims of northern Pennsylvania, John Nicholson's impeachment just as he was about to purchase a huge tract, a lack of hard money, and the slight demand for land in the 1780s.

8. Edward Shippen [IV] to Joseph Shippen [III], Philadelphia, 26 March 1796, Shippen Papers, vol. 8, p. 189, HSP.

9. Deed, Edward Shippen [IV] and Joseph Shippen [III], Gentlemen, to John Reynolds, 1 June 1782, Shippen Papers, vol. 16, p. 59, HSP; Edward Shippen [IV] to Joseph Shippen [III], Philadelphia, 25 June 1787; Edward Shippen [IV] to Joseph Shippen, Jr. [III], Philadelphia, 2 April 1790, Northern, Interior, and Western Counties, pp. 101, 123, HSP;

Lease, Edward [IV] and Joseph [III] Shippen to Sarah Henry, 27 May 1793, Shippen-Burd-Hubley Papers, HSP; Edward Shippen [IV] to Joseph Shippen [III], Philadelphia, 19 September 1789, Shippen Papers, Box 1, HSP; Joseph Shippen [III] to Edward Burd, Lancaster, 20 October 1786, Shippen Papers, vol. 13, p. 98, HSP; Joseph Shippen [III] to Dear Brother [Edward Shippen IV], Lancaster, 3 November 1788, Shippen Papers, Box 1, HSP; Joseph Shippen [III] to Dear Bro[the]r [Edward Shippen IV], Plumley, 20 May 1797, Shippen-Burd-Hubley Papers, HSP; Receipt for taxes on Edward [IV] and Joseph [III] Shippen tracts in Bedford County for 1791–1797, 1 February 1799, Shippen Papers, transferred from the Society Collection, HSP; Joseph Shippen [III], Account of land in Plumb township, Allegheny County, 28 June 1809, Dreer Collection, under Robert Hall, HSP; Deed, James Ash to Edward Burd and Sarah Lea and Executors of Joseph Shippen [III] of 11 tracts of land on Chest Creek, 2 March 1810, Society Collection, Papers of Edward Burd, HSP. Other references to Edward IV and Joseph III land transactions are found in Shippen Papers, vol. 8, pp. 93, 97, 107, 113, 147, 181, 183, 187, 191, HSP; and Shippen, Balch Papers, vol. 2, pp. 53, 55, 56, 62, 68, 70, 72, 74, 75, HSP.

10. Edward Shippen [IV] to Joseph Shippen [III], Philadelphia, 30 December 1792, Shippen Papers, vol. 8, p. 177, HSP.

11. Joseph Shippen, Jr. [III] to Edward Burd, Lancaster, 29 December 1783, Shippen Papers, Box 1, HSP. Joseph Shippen, Jr. [III] to Edward Shippen [IV], Kennett Square, 6 March 1782; Joseph Shippen, Jr. [III] to James Burd, Lancaster, 15 November 1783, Shippen Papers, vol. 12, p. 114; vol. 8, p. 95, HSP. See a description of Joseph III's farm in the *Pennsylvania Gazette,* 16 July 1783, and the Shippen Papers, vol. 10, p. 209, HSP.

12. Edward Shippen, Jr. [V] to Joseph Shippen, Jr., Esq. [III], Philadelphia, 16 June 1784, Shippen Papers, vol. 8, p. 107, HSP.

13. *Ibid.*

14. Deed, Edward Shippen [IV] and Joseph Shippen [III], Gentlemen, to John Reynolds, 1 June 1782, Shippen Papers, vol. 16, p. 59, HSP.

15. Edward Burd to Joseph Shippen, Jr. [III], Philadelphia, 10 December 1784, Shippen Papers, vol. 8, p. 115, HSP; Bond, Edward Shippen [V] merchant of Philadelphia to William Fitch, Esq., of the Parish of Marybond in Middlesex County, England, 24 July 1785, Shippen Papers, transferred from the Society Collection, HSP.

16. Edward Shippen [IV] to Joseph Shippen [III], Philadelphia, 2 October 1785, Shippen Papers, vol. 8, p. 127, HSP.

17. Shippen and Funck, Announcement of New Store in Lancaster, 1 May 1786, Shippen Papers, vol. 10, p. 127, HSP.

18. John Penn to Joseph Shippen, Jr. [III], Esq., Philadelphia, 7 January 1786, Dreer Collection, under Penn, in boxes, HSP. Joseph Shippen, Jr. [III] to Edward Shippen, Jr. [IV], Lancaster, 26 February 1787, Shippen Papers, vol. 8, p. 143, HSP; Docket of Lease of house in King Street, Lancaster, James Bickham to Joseph Shippen, Jr. [III], 15 March 1788, Miscellaneous Papers 1772–1816, Petition for Lebanon-Lancaster County, p. 131, HSP; George Patterson to James Burd, Juniata, 2 April 1788, Shippen Papers, vol. 8, p. 153, HSP.

19. Mary (Shippen) McIlvaine was Joseph III's niece, his brother Edward IV's third oldest daughter.

20. Joseph Shippen [III] to Edward Burd, Lancaster, 2 February 1789, Shippen Papers, vol. 13, p. 131, HSP.

21. Edward Shippen [IV] to Joseph Shippen [III], Philadelphia, 3 July 1788, Bucks County Miscellaneous Papers, 1682–1850, p. 145, HSP; Joseph Shippen [III] to Dear Brother [Edward Shippen IV], Lancaster, 1 September 1788; Joseph Shippen [III] to Dear Brother [Edward Shippen IV], Lancaster, 7 February 1789; Joseph Shippen [III] to Edward Shippen [IV], Lancaster, 21 March 1789; Joseph Shippen [III] to Edward Shippen [IV], Westtown, 26 March 1790, Shippen Papers, Box 1, HSP; Edward Shippen [IV] to Joseph Shippen [III], Philadelphia, 17 July 1788, Shippen Papers, vol. 8, p. 155, HSP; Edward Shippen [IV] to Joseph Shippen [III], Philadelphia 4 September 1788, Bucks County Miscellaneous Papers, 1682–1850, p. 147, HSP; Edward Shippen [IV] to Joseph Shippen [III], Philadelphia, 26 September 1788, Shippen Papers, vol. 8, p. 157, HSP.

22. Mary Shippen to Molly Yeates, Westtown, 11 October 1790, Shippen and Swift, Balch Papers, HSP.

23. Mary Shippen to Dear Cousin [Molly Yeates], Westtown, 15 April 1790, Shippen and Swift, Balch Papers, HSP.

24. Mary Shippen to Mrs. Joseph Shippen [III], Chestertown, 22 July 1790, Shippen Papers, Box 1, HSP.

25. Mary Shippen to Mrs. J. Shippen [III], Chestertown, 1 August 1790; Mary Shippen to My dear mama [Mrs. Joseph Shippen III] Chestertown, 1 August 1790, Shippen and Swift, Balch Papers, HSP; Mary Shippen to [Molly Yeates], Westtown, 17 October 1790, Shippen Papers, Box 1, HSP.

26. Mary Shippen to My dear Cousin, Philadelphia, 18 January 1792, Shippen and Swift, Balch Papers, HSP.

27. Mary Shippen to Miss Yeates, 22 January 1791, Shippen and Swift, Balch Papers, HSP.

28. Mary Shippen to My dear Cousin, Philadelphia, 18 January 1792, Shippen and Swift, Balch Papers, HSP.

29. Edward Shippen [IV] to Joseph Shippen, Jr. [III], Philadelphia, 31 December 1791, Shippen, Balch Papers, vol. 2, p. 69, HSP.

30. J[oseph] Shippen [III] to Mary Shippen, Philadelphia, Westtown, 12 February 1792; Mary Shippen to Mrs. J[oseph] Shippen [III], 3 March 1792; M[ary Shippen] to Mrs. [Joseph] Shippen [III], Philadelphia, 6 December 1792; Elizabeth Bordley to Miss Shippen, 22 December 1793; Mary Shippen to Mrs. Joseph Shippen [III], Philadelphia, 28 November [1790–1793], Shippen and Swift, Balch Papers, HSP; Invitation to Philadelphia Assembly to Miss P[olly] Shippen, Shippen, Balch Papers, vol. 1, p. 7, HSP.

31. In addition to Joseph III's economic problems stemming from his loss of office in the Revolution, and problems with land and other business transactions, he sired four children during the 1780s; the children survived, hence during that decade he had to support seven offspring; his family was about half that size during his affluent decade before the Revolution.

32. Edward Shippen [IV], Cashbook, 1782–1806, Am 13720, HSP. Aside from the ambitious nature which always characterized Edward IV, an additional pressure to regain stature for himself was his responsibility to the Shippen family's symbolic estate. By now about eight decades of tradition made it imperative that he succeed. For a fuller treatment of "symbolic estates" and their influences, see chapter five of Bernard Farber's *Kinship and Class: A Midwestern Study* (New York, 1971).

33. One thing which enabled Joseph III to continue his conception of himself as a gentlemen was the Shippen family history in Pennsylvania, or its symbolic estate. In *Kinship and Class* (pp. 100–101), Farber explains that "old families who base their legitimation on family history can maintain their position without a large financial or property base."

34. Edward Shippen [IV] to Joseph Shippen [III], Philadelphia, 27 February 1782, Shippen Papers, Box 1, HSP.

35. Edward Shippen [IV] to Joseph Shippen [III], Philadelphia, 10 April 1782, Shippen Papers, Box 1, HSP.

36. Edward Shippen [IV] to Jasper Yeates, Philadelphia, 6 July 1782, Shippen, Balch Papers, vol. 2, p. 51, HSP.

37. *Ibid.*

38. Edward Shippen [IV], Cashbook, 1782–1806, AM 13720, HSP. Edward Shippen [IV] to Joseph Shippen [III], Philadelphia, 4 March 1792, Shippen Papers, vol. 8, p. 175, HSP; Power of Attorney, William Hamilton

to Edward Shippen [IV], Gratz Collection, Pennsylvania Series, Provincial Conference, Case 1, Box 16, HSP; Jasper Yeates to Edward Shippen [IV], Lancaster, 13 July 1782, Shippen, Balch Papers, vol. 2, p. 51, HSP.

39. J[asper] Yeates to Edward Burd, York, 28 January 1795, Burd-Shippen-Hubley Papers, HSP. Yeates explained his disapproval of the "low bred Dutch Girl" a bit further; she was "without even Money or Friends, his [James Burd, Jr.] associating with the meaner Part of the Community must after some Time debase his Mind & have the most pernicious Effect on his Morals." For some additional details on the family's attempts to coerce James Burd, Jr., see: Jasper Yeates to Edward Burd, Lancaster, 27 June 1790; Jasper Yeates to Edward Burd, 5 September 1790; Jasper Yeates to Edward Burd, Lancaster, 21 February 1791, Shippen Papers, vol. 13, pp. 181, 187, 207, HSP. James Burd to Edward Burd, Tinian, 31 January 1783, Shippen Papers, vol. 12, p. 117, HSP; James Burd to Edward Burd, Tinian, 16 August 1784, Burd-Shippen-Hubley Papers, HSP. Although the Burds approved their daughter Jane's marriage to George Patterson, the new "loving and dutiful son" lacked much formal education and polish. For example, his letters bristle with errors in spelling and grammar, such as "on our rode to this place wee met the millar . . . thare is grate many Jersey people to Juniata wanting land." (George Patterson to James Burd, Juniata, 27 November 1783, Shippen Papers, vol. 8, p. 97, HSP.)

40. Certificate of appointment of Joseph Shippen [III] of Chester County to Judgeship of Court of Common Pleas, Chester County, 17 August 1791, Shippen Papers, Box 1, HSP; Commission of John Shippen [Joseph III's son] as Notary Public in Chester County, 22 April 1795, Commissions, Stille Case, HSP; Papers of the Estate of James Burd, 1793–1810, Burd Papers, HSP.

41. Edward Shippen [IV] to Joseph Shippen [III], Philadelphia, 2 October 1785, Shippen Papers, vol. 8, p. 127, HSP.

42. *Pennsylvania Archives*, 3d. ser., ed. William Henry Egle (26 vols., Harrisburg, 1894–1897), vol. X, pp. 587–588; *Pennsylvania Archives*, 2d. ser., eds. John P. Linn and William H. Egle (19 vols., Harrisburg, 1874–1893), vol. 3, pp. 717, 718, 724.

43. Edward Shippen to the President and Supreme Executive Council, Philadelphia, 20 November 1786, Shippen Papers, vol. 8, p. 141, HSP.

44. Moses Levy to George Read, Philadelphia, 22 September 1789, Read Manuscripts, p. 39, HSP.

45. *Ibid.*

46. Edward Shippen [IV] to Jasper Yeates, Philadelphia, 23 February 1791, Am 284, Chief Justices of the Supreme Court of Pennsylvania, p. 17a.

47. After the Revolution, several candidates for state and local offices analyzed a rival for a particular office in terms of family interest. An example of this continuing influence at work appears in J. Hubley to Edward Burd, Philadelphia, 18 August 1789, Shippen Papers, vol. 13, p. 155, HSP. Jacob Hubley applied for the office of recorder and register of Berks County; he urged his brother-in-law, the prothonotary of the Supreme Court of Pennsylvania, to come at once to Chester County to help obtain the job.

48. Edward Shippen [IV] to Joseph Shippen [III], Philadelphia, 7 March 1784, Shippen Papers, vol. 8, p. 103, HSP.

49. *Ibid.*

50. Deed, Joseph Shippen [II] to William Shippen [II], 10 July 1788, Shippen Family Papers, Box 18, LC.

51. Deed, Joseph [II] and Mary Shippen to William Shippen [II], 5 February 1784; Joseph Cowperthwait, Esq., High Sheriff, to William Shippen [II], 1 November 1787, Shippen Family Papers, Box 20, 17, LC; *Pennsylvania Magazine of History and Biography*, vol. VI (1893), 15; Edward Shippen [IV] to Joseph Shippen [III], Philadelphia, 2 August 1795, Shippen Papers, vol. 8, p. 185, HSP; Deed, Edward Shippen [IV], Joseph Shippen [III] and his wife Jenny to William Shippen [II], 26 May 1800, Shippen Family Papers, Box 18, LC.

52. This can be true of the extended family for many reasons. For example, in *Kinship and Class* (p. 6) Farber points out, "At higher socio-economic levels, kinship sustains social differentiation in society, whereas among lower class populations, it keeps a lumpenproletariat within the social system," yet impedes upward social mobility for members of a lower class extended family.

53. Ann Home (Shippen) Livingston, Diary, 10 May 1783, Shippen Family Papers, vol. 2, LC.

54. Ann Home (Shippen) Livingston, Diary, 18 April 1783, Shippen Family Papers, vol. 2, LC.

55. *Ibid.*

56. Ann Home (Shippen) Livingston, Diary, 15 May 1783, Shippen Family Papers, vol. 2, LC.

57. Ann Home (Shippen) Livingston, Diary, 16 May 1783, Shippen Family Papers, vol. 2, LC.

58. Ann Home (Shippen) Livingston, Diary, 19 May 1783, Shippen Family Papers, vol. 2, LC.

59. Ann Home (Shippen) Livingston, Diary, 5 June 1783, Shippen Family Papers, vol. 2, LC. Ann Home (Shippen) Livingston, Diary, 27 April, 17 May 1783, Shippen Family Papers, vol. 2, LC.

60. Ann Home (Shippen) Livingston, Diary, 10 January 1784, Shippen Family Papers, vol. 2, LC. Ann's diary reveals many incidents which helped her sustain the view that her father was indeed indulgent. For example, on March 7, 1784, when William III angrily refused to let his daughter borrow the chariot, she burst into tears; later that evening he said "as much as he cou'd say to make up with his spoilt daughter." When Bushrod Washington asked Ann to a party at Mt. Peace, her father refused to let her go because of the weather. In her diary Ann records (7 April 1784), "I was fool enough to cry & refuse to eat my dinner, but Papa made up with me in the afternoon—& said I shou'd go tomorrow."

61. Ann Home (Shippen) Livingston, Diary, 24 February 1784, Shippen Family Papers, vol. 2, LC. Thomas Lee Shippen to William Shippen, Jr. [III], 5 February 1784, Shippen Family Papers, vol. 5, LC.

62. Ann Home (Shippen) Livingston, Diary, 24 February 1784, Shippen Family Papers, vol. 2, LC.

63. Ann Home (Shippen) Livingston, Diary, 18 April 1784, Shippen Family Papers, vol. 2, LC.

64. Ann Home (Shippen) Livingston, Diary, 9 May 1784, Shippen Family Papers, vol. 2, LC.

65. *Ibid.*

66. Ann Home (Shippen) Livingston, Diary, 7 September 1784, Shippen Family Papers, vol. 2, LC. Ann Home (Shippen) Livingston, Diary, 1 May 1784, Shippen Family Papers, vol. 2, LC.

67. Ann Home (Shippen) Livingston, Diary, 5 October 1784, Shippen Family Papers, vol. 2, LC.

68. Ann Home (Shippen) Livingston, Diary, 24 February 1785, Shippen Family Papers, vol. 2, LC.

69. Arthur Lee to Ann (Shippen) Livingston, 9 May 1788, Shippen Family Papers, vol. 4, LC. Ann Home (Shippen) Livingston, Diary, 5 March 1785, Shippen Family Papers, vol. 2, LC; Henry B. Livingston to Mrs. Ann H. Livingston, 17 May 1785, Shippen Family Papers, vol. 4, LC; Ann Home Livingston to Sir [Henry B. Livingston], 30 June 1787, Ann Home Livingston Letterbook, 1786–1787, Box 4, LC.

70. Ann Home Livingston to Henry B. Livingston, Philadelphia, 7 February, 7 March 1789; Ann Home Livingston to Mrs. [Harriet] Livingston, 10 February 1789; Ann Home Livingston Letterbook, 1788–1789, Shippen Family Papers, Box 4, LC; Arthur Lee to Nancy (Shippen) Livingston, New York, 21 March 1789; Margaret Livingston to Mrs. Livingston at Dr. Shippen's in Philadelphia, 29 March 1789, 9 February 1785, 30 November1793, 24 February 1797, Shippen Family Papers, Box 4, LC.

71. A note copied from the tombstone at "Woodlands," Shippen Family Papers, Box 20, LC, reads: "Here lie the remains of Ann Hume [*sic*] Livingston daughter of Dr. William Shippen, who died August 23, 1841—in the 78th year of her age." "The remains of Miss Margaret Beekman Livingston daughter of Henry Beekman and Ann Hume Livingston, died July 1, 1864—in the 82nd year of her age." Ethel Armes (*Nancy Shippen, Her Journal Book,* p. 299) quotes contemporary letters which indicate that although Margaret Beekman Livingston left Clermont Manor to live with her mother in Philadelphia, the large bequest of her grandmother was not forfeited.

72. Thomas Lee Shippen to Edward Burd, London, 23 December 1787, Burd-Shippen-Hubley Papers, HSP. Thomas Lee Shippen signed the letter "your devoted friend & kinsman"; he was Burd's father-in-law's nephew.

73. Ethel Armes, ed., *Nancy Shippen, Her Journal Book,* p. 95; Richard Henry Lee to William Shippen [III], Chantilly [Virginia], 7 January 1783, Feinstone Collection, APS; Thomas Lee Shippen to Nancy (Shippen) Livingston, Williamsburg, 26 February 1784, Shippen Papers, Box 6, LC; Arthur Lee to Thomas Lee Shippen, Annapolis, 6 April 1784, Shippen Family Papers, Box 3, LC; Richard Henry Lee to Thomas Lee Shippen, Trenton, 10 November 1784, Shippen Family Papers, Box 3, LC.

74. Th[omas] Jefferson to Thomas Lee Shippen, Paris, 15 October 1785, Shippen Family Papers, Box 3, LC.

75. Thomas Lee Shippen to My very dear Mamma, Inner Temple, 30 September 1786, Shippen Family Papers, Box 6, LC.

76. Thomas Lee Shippen to William Shippen, Jr. [III], London, 18 August 1786, Shippen Family Papers, Box 6, LC. Jefferson also gave Shippen useful legal information: for example, see Thomas Lee Shippen, "The Crown Law Common Plac'd," 1 January 1786, No. 745, Maryland Historical Society, which includes seven pages in Shippen's hand on "Remarks on the Chancery Jurisdiction etc by Th[omas] Jefferson" which were "copied from Mr. Jefferson's manuscript." Th[omas] Jefferson to W. Shippen [III], Paris, 8 May 1786, Shippen Family Papers, Box 3, LC; Thomas Lee Shippen to William Shippen, Jr. [III], London, 24 August 1786, Shippen Family Papers, Box 6, LC. Many Americans, including Pennsylvanians and Philadelphians feared the evil influences of Europe and England. For example, when Charles Thomson, secretary of the Continental Congress, introduced his kinsman Isaac Norris (son of "our ancient and worthy friend Charles Norris") to Benjamin Franklin in Paris, he noted that from the young man's letters England "has no charms for him." (C[harles] T[homson] to Doctr B. Franklin, 26 April 1783, Papers of

Charles Thomson, vol. 1, no. 7712, LC.) Thomson later informed Jefferson, "The people of Europe and America seem to be pursuing different amusements; while the former are diverting themselves with bubbles of air and quarreling with one another for toys & rattles, the latter are employed in the encrease of their species & providing the means of subsistence." He admitted however that "the people [in America] are not yet sufficiently impressed with a sense of what they owe to their national character." (Charles Thomson to Thomas Jefferson, New York, 6 April 1786, Charles Thomson Papers, vol. 2, no. 7833, LC.)

77. Thomas Lee Shippen to Arthur Lee, 30 [September 1786], Shippen Family Papers, Box 7, LC.

78. Thomas Lee Shippen to William Shippen, Jr. [III], Bath, 29 December 1786, Shippen Family Papers, Box 6, LC.

79. Thomas Lee Shippen to William Shippen, Jr. [III], Temple, 2 February 1787, Shippen Family Papers, Box 6, LC. In this connotation, it seems necessary to remark that one of the first things Thomas Lee Shippen did upon his return to Philadelphia was to have his family coat of arms engraved. (Thomas Lee Shippen, Accountbook of Family Expenses, 13 February 1793, Shippen Family Papers, Box 1, LC.) This hardly reflects his rhetorical flourishes condemning "distinctions not founded in nature." As far as virtue and vice were concerned, this virtuous American gentleman jumped into bed for sensuous delight with young English women on several different occasions; Thomas Lee Shippen describes these escapades in his journal (Shippen Family Papers, Box 1, LC.)

80. A[rthur] Lee to Thomas Lee Shippen [1787], Shippen Family Papers, Box 3, LC. The italics in the quotation were mine; the full quotation reads: "The Science of Government is no trifling matter. It requires education, & experience . . . it requires the leisure which independent fortune gives, & the elevation of mind which birth & rank impart. Without these you might as well attempt to make fine China out of common earth, as Statesmen & Politicians out of men, born, bred, & busied in the sordid occurrences of common life." In another letter probably written in 1787 (Shippen Family Papers, Box 3, LC) Arthur Lee suggested that his nephew become a British subject "which is almost as respectable as that of an american citizen," and practice law at Westminster, where the connections the young lawyer had made would enable him to become chief justice of the King's Bench or Lord High Chancellor. This was the course of action Lee had contemplated for himself before the Revolution. Lee was disgusted with the effects of the Revolution which had not produced a better society; he observed, "The same unprincipled pursuit of private speculations—the same sacrifice of the public honor & interests to the selfish

objects of Individuals . . . the most baneful of all luxuries, the luxury of the commonpeople, who are more extravagant than any people in the world of the same rank—all these conspire the dessolution of governm[en]t, the corruption of manners, the insecurity of property & the distruction of national faith, character & confidence." (A[rthur] L[ee] to Thomas Lee Shippen, 2 May 1787, Shippen Family Papers, Box 3, LC.)

81. The court-martial of William Shippen III for charges of speculating with hospital stores during the War for Independence was dealt with at length in chapter eight. A brief reminder appeared in *The Philadelphiad: or, New Pictures of the City; Interspersed with a Candid Review and Display of Some First-Rate Modern Characters of both Sexes* . . . (2 vols., Philadelphia, 1784), vol. 1, p. 52:

> Whene'er your horse is troubled with the gout,
> Apply to S—— he can drive it out;
> Give him but cash he'll turn the old to young,
> For S—— can do wonders *with his tongue*;
>   * * *
> Poor luckless soldiers too can tell *with grief*
> His skillful aid, and social kind relief;
> If *stores* could speak "they could a tale unfold
> Would scare e'en fraud and make his blood run cold.

82. Thomas Lee Shippen, Journal, 1 April 1787; Thomas Lee Shippen to William Shippen [III], Inner Temple, 5 June 1787, Shippen Family Papers, Box 1, 6, LC.

83. William Shippen [III] to Thomas Lee Shippen, 17———1787, Shippen Family Papers, Box 5, LC.

84. William Shippen [III] to Thomas Lee Shippen, Philadelphia, 7 May 1787, Shippen Family Papers, Box 5, LC.

85. *Ibid.*

86. William Shippen [III] to Thomas Lee Shippen, Philadelphia, 26 April 1788, Shippen Family Papers, Box 5, LC.

87. William Shippen [III] to Thomas Lee Shippen, Philadelphia, 3 May 1788, Shippen Family Papers, Box 5, LC.

88. Thomas Lee Shippen to William Shippen [III], Geneva, 25 September 1788, Shippen Family Papers, Box 6, LC.

89. Thomas Lee Shippen, Journal, 2 October 1788, Shippen Family Papers, Box 1, LC.

90. Thomas Lee Shippen to William Shippen [III], London, 22 November 1788, Shippen Family Papers, Box 6, LC. William Shippen [III] to Thomas Lee Shippen, Philadelphia, 21 February 1788, Shippen Family

Papers, Box 5, LC; Gordon S. Wood, *Creation of the American Republic 1776–1787* (Chapel Hill, 1969), pp. 46–47.

91. Thomas Lee Shippen to William Shippen [III], London, 2 March 1789, Shippen Family Papers, Box 6, LC.

92. William Shippen [III] to Thomas Lee Shippen, 20 May 1787, Shippen Family Papers, Box 5, LC.

93. Thomas Lee Shippen to [Elizabeth Carter (Farley) Bannister], Chatham, 12 November 1790, Shippen Family Papers, Box 6, LC.

94. Alice Shippen to Mrs. Bannister, Philadelphia, 13 February 1791; William Shippen Jr. [III] to [Elizabeth Carter Bannister], Philadelphia, 14 February 1791, Shippen Family Papers, Box 8, LC; Thomas Lee Shippen, Book of Account of Family Expenses begun 1 June 1791, Shippen Family Papers, Box 1, LC.

95. Thomas Lee Shippen to Nancy Shippen Livingston, New York, 28 July 1793, Shippen Family Papers, Box 6, LC.

96. Thomas Lee Shippen describes himself as "Gentleman" in James Hardie's *The Philadelphia Directory and Register* (2d. ed., Philadelphia, 1794.)

97. William Shippen, Jr. [III] to Benjamin Rush, 11 October 1793, Manuscript Correspondence of Benjamin Rush, vol. 36, p. 93, Library Company of Philadelphia.

98. Benj Rush to Ashton Alexander, Philadelphia, 21 December 1795 [*sic* 1798], *Letters of Benjamin Rush,* ed. Lyman Butterfield (2 vols., Princeton, 1948), vol. 2, p. 766.

99. Benjamin Rush, Epitaph of Thomas Lee Shippen [1798], Manuscript Correspondence of Benjamin Rush, vol. 39, p. 115, Library Company of Philadelphia.

100. A[lice] Shippen to Mrs. E[lizabeth] C[arter] Shippen at Mrs. Dunbars, Williamsburg, Virginia, [Philadelphia], 14 January 1799, Shippen Family Papers, Box 8, LC. There are several more letters from Alice Shippen to her son's widow in Box 8, Shippen Family Papers, LC.

101. Numerous deeds regarding the property of William Shippen II are found in the Shippen Family Papers, Boxes 7 and 8, LC. William II rented several properties. After his death, William Shippen III and Samuel and Susanna (Shippen) Blair partitioned the Germantown properties; deeds of partition are found in the same place. Also of value is William Shippen [II]'s Will, written 30 July 1783, in the Shippen Papers, vol. 10, p. 219, HSP; it is recorded in Philadelphia by the Register of Wills. *Wistar's Eulogium on William Shippen, M.D., delivered before the College of Physicians of Philadelphia, March 1809,* (in *American Medical Biography,* ed. Whitfield J. Bell, Jr. [2 vols., New York, 1967], vol. 2, pp. 82–

88) is the major source of James Thatcher's sketch of William Shippen, Jr. [III]. Benjamin Rush, C[aspar] Wistar, James Woodhouse, Benjamin Smith Barton, Philip Syng, J. S. Dorsey (by order of the Medical Professors), Respect to memory of Dr. Shippen, University of Pennsylvania, 22 July 1808, Manuscript Correspondence of Benjamin Rush, vol. 39, pp. 116–117, Library Company of Philadelphia.

Appendix A

Vital Statistics of Five Generations

The following compilation is based on numerous sources, such as church records, wills, family Bibles, family histories, genealogies, collected biographies, and the like.

This list includes those who bore the Shippen name and their off-spring; women born into the Shippen family, who changed their names when they married, are included with their children. (For example, Anne [Shippen] Willing, Sarah [Shippen] Burd, and their children.)

The date of marriage appears next to the woman's name; in those instances where the woman married more than once, the date refers to the time when she married a Shippen.

The number of children usually follows the father's name, for the children used his surname. If a man married more than once, the total number of children he had is listed after his name; the number he had by each wife is listed after her name.

Brackets around a number indicate some degree of uncertainty. A figure followed by a plus sign (for example, 32+) is the lowest possible estimate. A dash indicates that the category does not apply. With the exceptions implicit in the above explanations, blank spaces indicate information unknown.

GENERATION IN AMERICA	LIFESPAN			MARRIAGE			Years Widow(er)	CHILDREN				Age at Father's Death
	Dates	Years	Times	Date	Age	Length		No. Born	No. Mature	No. Marry	Age Bore Last Child	
F I R S T												
EDWARD I	1639–1712	74	3		32,50,67		1,1	11	4	3		42
Elizabeth Lybrand	–1688		1	1671		17	—	8	3	3	—	
Rebekah (Howard) Richardson	–1705		2	1689		16	1	1	0	0		
Francis Richardson	–1688											
Esther (Wilcox) James	–1724		2	1706		6	?,12	2	1	0		
Philip James												
S E C O N D												
FRANCIS	1672–1673	1	—	—	—	—	—	—	—	—	—	—
EDWARD	1674–1674	1	—	—	—	—	—	—	—	—	—	—
WILLIAM	1675–1676	1	—	—	—	—	—	—	—	1	—	—
EDWARD II	1678–1714	36	1	c.1705–10	c.27–33		—	[2]	1	1	—	34
Francina Vanderheyden		70	2									
Col. Hynson												
JOSEPH I	1679–1741	62	2	1703	24,42	13	5	7	4	4		33
Abigail Grosse	–1716		1				—	7	4	4	—	
Rose (Budd) McWilliams	1680–		3	1721	?,41		—	0	0	0		
Charles Plumley												
John McWilliams												
MARY	1681–1688	7	—	—	—	—	—	—	—	—	—	—
ANN	1684–1712	28	1	1706	22	6	—	[0]	0	0	—	28

Name	Years	Age												
Thomas Story	1662–1742	80	1	—	44	—	30	—	—	—	—	—	—	—
ELIZABETH	1691–1692	1	—	—	—	—	—	—	—	—	—	—	—	—
JOHN	1707–1707	1	—	—	—	—	—	—	0	0	0	—	—	4
WILLIAM I	1708–1731	23	0	—	—	—	—	—	—	—	—	—	—	—
THIRD														
❖ (Issue of Edward II and Francina [Vanderheyden])														
MARGARET	–1762 c.60		1	1734	—	—	20	—	[3]	3	[2]	—	—	minor
John Jekyll	–1742		1	—	—	—	—	—	—	—	—	—	—	—
❖ (Issue of Joseph I and Abigail [Grosse])														
EDWARD III	1703–1781	78	2	—	22,44	8	12,3	20	[3]	7	3	3	—	38
Sarah Plumley	1706–1735	29	1	1725	19	10	—	—	7	7	3	3	—	28
Mary (Gray) Nowland	1706–1778	72	2	1747	?,41	31	–2*	—	0	0	0	0	—	—
John Nowland	–1750													
ELIZABETH	1705–1714	9	—	—	—	—	—	—	—	—	—	—	—	—
JOSEPH II	1706–1793	87	1	—	—	—	—	—	9	9	6	5	—	35
Mary Kearney														
WILLIAM	1708–1716	8	—	—	—	—	—	—	—	—	—	—	—	—
ANNE	1710–1791	81	1	1730	20	24	37	—	11	11	10	8	43	31
Charles Willing	1710–1754	44	1	—	20	—	—	—	—	—	—	—	—	—
WILLIAM II	1712–1801	89	1	1735	23	39	27	—	[4+]	11	4	3	—	29
Susannah Harrison	1711–1774	64	1	—	24	—	—	—	—	—	—	—	[32]	—
ELIZABETH	1714–1714	1	—	—	—	—	—	—	—	—	—	—	—	—
FOURTH														
❖ (Issue of Margaret [Shippen] and John Jekyll)														
John Jekyll			1	1766										
—— Webb														

*In this instance it means minus two years. Although presumed dead, her first husband was still alive when she married Edward III.

327

GENERATION IN AMERICA	LIFESPAN			MARRIAGE				CHILDREN				
	Dates	Years	Times	Date	Age	Length	Years Widow(er)	No. Born	No. Mature	No. Marry	Age Bore Last Child	Age at Father's Death
Francina Jekyll				1758								
William Hicks	1735–1772	37	[1]		23	[14]						
Arianna Margaretta Jekyll	1741–1812	71	1	1763	22	43	6		4	[2]	[32?]	1
James Chalmers	c.1727–1806	c.79	1		c.36							
❖ (Issue of Edward III and Sarah [Plumley])												
ELIZABETH	1726–1726	1	—	—	—	—	—	—	—	—	—	—
JOSEPH	1727–1727	1	—	—	—	—	—	—	—	—	—	—
twins												
WILLIAM	1727–1727	1	—	—	—	—	—	—	—	—	—	—
EDWARD IV	1729–1806	77	1	1753	24	41	12	8	6	5	—	52
Margaret Francis	1735–1794	59	1		18						[33?]	
SARAH	1731–1784	53	1	1748	17	36	9	11	8	7	41	50
James Burd	1726–1793	67	1		22							
JOSEPH III	1732–1810	78	1	1768	36	32	9	10	7	5	—	49
Jane Galloway	1745–1801	56	1		23						48	
ROSE	1734–1734	1	—	—	—	—	—	—	—	—	—	—
❖ (Issue of Joseph II and Mary [Kearney])												
CATHERINE	1737–[1739]	3	—	—	—	—	—	—	—	—	—	—
MARGARET	1739–1740	1	—	—	—	—	—	—	—	—	—	—
CATHERINE	1740–1812	72	[1]	1760	20	1	[51]	[0]	—	—	—	53
Richard Wallin	–1761		—		—	—						
MARY	1741–1742	1	—	—	—	—	—	—	—	—	—	—

Name	Dates	Age	M	Marr.	Age							
JOSEPH IV	1743–1766	23	0	—	—	—	—	0	0	0	—	—
MARY	1745–		1	1767	30	—						
John Peel		?										
ABIGAIL	1746–		1	1767	21							
Edward Spence		?										
ANN	1749–		1	1774	25	[18]						
Robert Strettel Jones	1745–1792	47	1		29		7	3	3	2		
MARGARET	1751–		1	1780	29							
John Adams												
❖ (Issue of Anne [Shippen] and Charles Willing)												
Thomas Willing	1731–1821	90	1	1763	32	18	40	13	10	10	—	23
Anne McCall	1745–1781	36	1		18		—				35	
Anne Willing	1733–1812	79	1	1762	29	38	12	7	5	4	44	21
Tench Francis, Jr.	1730–1800	70	1		32		—				—	
Dorothy Willing	1735–1782	47	1	by 1750	by 15	32+	—	[3]	3	3	26+	19
Walter Stirling	1718–1786	68	1		by 32		4	[2]	2	2	—	
Charles Willing	1738–1788	50	1	1760	22	28	—				37	16
Eliz. Hannah Carrington	1740–1795	55	1	1761	20		19				35+	
Mary Willing	1740–1814	74	1		21	16	37	10	8	7		14
William Byrd, III	1729–1777	48	1	1769	32	24	—				33	12
Elizabeth Willing	1742–1830	88	1		27		37	2	0	0	—	
Samuel Powel	1739–1793	54	1		30		—	2	0	0	—	9
Richard Willing	1745–1798	53	1	1775	21			?				
Margaret Kortwright												
Abigail Willing	1747–1791	44	0	—	—	—	—	0	0	0	—	7
Joseph Willing	1749–1750	1	—	—	—	—	—	—	—	—	—	—
James Willing	1751–1801	50	0	—	—	—	—	0	0	0	—	3
Margaret Willing	1753–1816	63	1		22	37	4	6	4	3	33	1
Robert Hare	1752–1812	60	1		23		—				—	
❖ (Issue of William and Susannah [Harrison])												
WILLIAM III	1736–1808	72	1		26	39	7	8	2	2		65

GENERATION IN AMERICA	LIFESPAN			MARRIAGE				CHILDREN				
	Dates	Years	Times	Date	Age	Length	Years Widow(er)	No. Born	No. Mature	No. Marry	Age Bore Last Child	Age at Father's Death
Alice Lee	1736–1801	65	1	1762	26		—				48	—
JOSEPH W.	1737–1795	58	1					9				
Martha Axford				—			[c.14+]			0		
JOHN	1740–1770	30	0					0	0	0	—	—
SUSANNA	1743–1821	78	1	1767	24	51	3	5	3–5	3	34	58
Samuel Blair	1741–1818	77	1		26							
F I F T H ❖ (Issue of Edward IV and Margaret [Francis])												
ELIZABETH	1754–1828	74	1	1778	24	50		[2]	1	1	32	52
SARAH	1756–1831	75	1	1787	29	6	38	[5]	5	2	33	50
Thomas Lea	1757–1793	36	1		28	–						
MARY	1757–		1	1785	28	7+					44+	?
William McIlvaine			3									
EDWARD V	1758–1809	51	1	1785	27	24		8	8	3	36	48
Eliz. Juliana Footman	1762–1848	86	1		23		39					
MARGARET	1760–1804	44	1	1779	19	22	3	7	5	4	34	—
Benedict Arnold	1741–1801	60	2		26,38							
JOHN FRANCIS	1762–1763	1	—	—								—
JAMES	1766–1769	3	—	—								—
JAMES	fl.1776–1784		?									

❖ [Issue of Sarah [Shippen] and James Burd)

Sarah Burd	1749–1829	80	1	1767	18	50	12	10	5	3	37	44
Jasper Yeates	1745–1817	72	1		22			4	3	2		42
Edward Burd	1751–1833	82	1		27		5					
ELIZABETH SHIPPEN	(see issue of Edward IV and Margaret [Francis] Shippen)											
Mary Shippen Burd	1753–1774	21	1	1771	18	3	14	2	2	2	21	40
Peter Grubb	1740–1786	46	1		31							
Allen Burd	1754–1764	10										
Jane Burd	1757–		1	1783	26	14+		9	6	5	40	36
George Patterson	1762–1814	52	1		21							
Anne Burd	1759–1760	1										
Margaret Burd	1761–		1	1786	25	18+		8	5	3	c.43	32
Jacob Hubley	1757–				29							
Elizabeth Burd	1762–1763	1										
James Burd	1765–							[3]	3	2		28
Elizabeth Baker												
Joseph Burd	1768–		2									
Catherine Cochran												
Harriet Bailey												
Elizabeth Burd	1772–		0									

❖ (Issue of Joseph III and Jane [Galloway])

ROBERT	1769–1840	71	1	1791	22	43	6	13	12	7		41
Pricilla Thompson	1771–1834	63	1		20						43	
SARAH	1770–1773	3	1									
JOHN	1771–1805	34	1	1789	18			[1]	1	0		
Abigail C. Reynolds												
MARY	1773–1809	36	1	1793	26	16		11	6	5	35	
Samuel Swift	1771–1847	76	1		28	38						
CHARLES	1774–1775	1										
ANNE	1775–1776	1										
ELIZABETH	1780–1801	21	0					0	0	0		

GENERATION IN AMERICA	LIFESPAN			MARRIAGE				CHILDREN				
	Dates	Years	Times	Date	Age	Length	Years Widow(er)	No. Born	No. Mature	No. Marry	Age Bore Last Child	Age at Father's Death
MARGARET	1782–1876	94	0	—	—			0	0	0	—	—
JOSEPH GALLOWAY	1783–1857	74	1	1814	31	43	—	[4]			—	27
Anna Maria Buckley	1790–1865	75	1		24		8					
HENRY C.	1788–1839	51	1	1817	29	[c.15+]		10	10	7		22
Eliz. Wallis Evans	1798–		1		19						—	
❖ (Issue of William II and Alice [Lee])												
ANN HOME	1763–1841	78	1	1781	18	(separated within months)					19	45
Henry Beekman Livingston	1750–1831	81			31			1	1		—	
THOMAS LEE	1765–1798	33	1	1791	26	7			1	0		
Eliz. Carter (Farley)					31			[2]		1	—	
Bannister	1774–1826	52	3		?,17,?		—					
❖ (Issue of Susanna [Shippen] and Samuel Blair)												
Francis Van Hook Blair	–1848		1	1816					[0]			
Charles Pierce												
Susan Shippen Blair	1771–1843	73	1	1792	21	11						47
Isaac Roberdeau												
William Shippen Blair			[0]									
Abigail Philips Blair			[0]									
Samuel Blair	1777–1859	82	1	1802	25	11	46	7	2	2		41
Esther Smith	–1813											

Appendix B

The Shippen Family Kinship Network: A Schematic Presentation

The following reconstitution of the kinship network is based upon numerous sources, such as church records, wills, deeds, family Bibles, family histories, genealogies, collected biographies, and the like.

Because of the limitations of space and also in order to avoid confusion, children who died before attaining age twenty-one are omitted. Sixth and subsequent generations in America are also deleted. Some distant kinsmen, who receive no mention by the Shippens, are eliminated to preserve clarity.

Marriages are indicated by "-m-"; the date of the marriage appears above that symbol. For example:

'71
EDWARD I-m-Elizabeth Lybrand
(1639–1712)   (–1688)

means Edward Shippen I married Elizabeth Lybrand in 1671. (Whether dates refer to the seventeenth, or eighteenth, or nineteenth centuries can be readily ascertained by consulting the birth and death dates of the parties involved.)

In order to present the kinship network in a manageable form, a division into sections B-1 through B-5 becomes necessary. The branches are linked; cross references (such as "see B-2" or "see B-3") facilitate concurrent use of several charts.

B-1.   Five Generations Who Bore The Shippen Name (and Spouses)

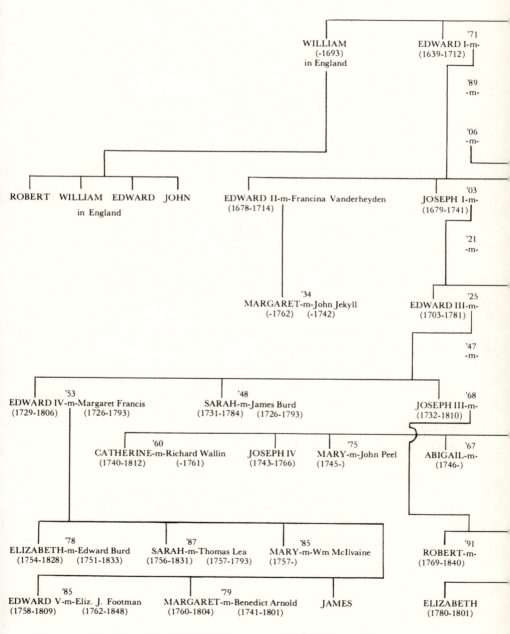

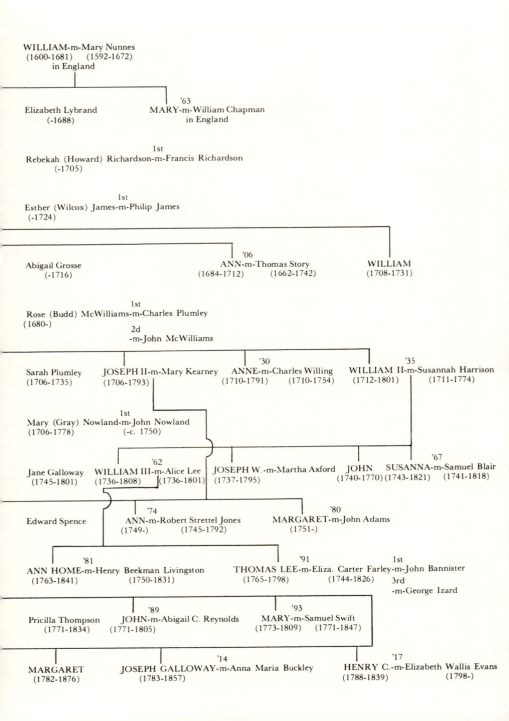

WILLIAM-m-Mary Nunnes
(1600-1681)   (1592-1672)
  in England

Elizabeth Lybrand   '63
  (-1688)   MARY-m-William Chapman
                          in England

                  1st
Rebekah (Howard) Richardson-m-Francis Richardson
        (-1705)

            1st
Esther (Wilcox) James-m-Philip James
    (-1724)

Abigail Grosse   '06
  (-1716)   ANN-m-Thomas Story   WILLIAM
                (1684-1712)   (1662-1742)   (1708-1731)

              1st
Rose (Budd) McWilliams-m-Charles Plumley
(1680-)
                      2d
                  -m-John McWilliams

Sarah Plumley   JOSEPH II-m-Mary Kearney   '30   '35
(1706-1735)   (1706-1793)   ANNE-m-Charles Willing   WILLIAM II-m-Susannah Harrison
                          (1710-1791) (1710-1754)   (1712-1801)   (1711-1774)

              1st
Mary (Gray) Nowland-m-John Nowland
(1706-1778)   (-c. 1750)

                      '62   '67
Jane Galloway WILLIAM III-m-Alice Lee   JOSEPH W.-m-Martha Axford JOHN   SUSANNA-m-Samuel Blair
(1745-1801)   (1736-1808) (1736-1801) (1737-1795)   (1740-1770)(1743-1821)   (1741-1818)

                      '74   '80
Edward Spence   ANN-m-Robert Strettel Jones   MARGARET-m-John Adams
                (1749-)   (1745-1792)   (1751-)

        '81   '91   1st
ANN HOME-m-Henry Beekman Livingston   THOMAS LEE-m-Eliza. Carter Farley-m-John Bannister
(1763-1841)   (1750-1831)   (1765-1798)   (1744-1826)   3rd
                                                        -m-George Izard

                      '89   '93
Pricilla Thompson JOHN-m-Abigail C. Reynolds   MARY-m-Samuel Swift
(1771-1834)   (1771-1805)   (1773-1809)   (1771-1847)

                          '14   '17
MARGARET   JOSEPH GALLOWAY-m-Anna Maria Buckley   HENRY C.-m-Elizabeth Wallis Evans
(1782-1876)   (1783-1857)   (1788-1839)   (1798-)

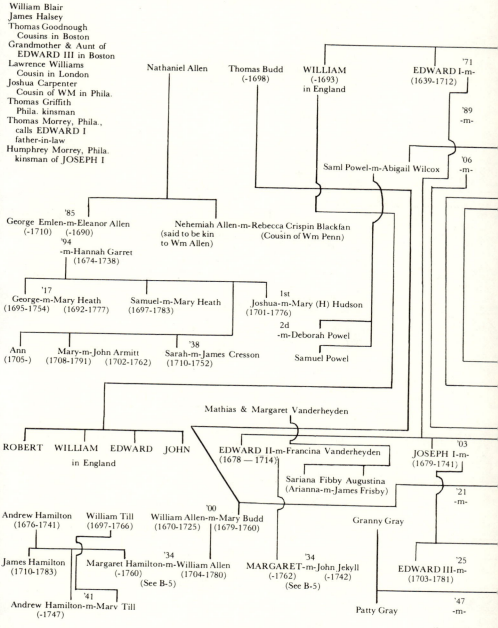

William Blair
James Halsey
Thomas Goodnough
    Cousins in Boston
Grandmother & Aunt of
    EDWARD III in Boston
Lawrence Williams
    Cousin in London
Joshua Carpenter
    Cousin of WM in Phila.
Thomas Griffith
    Phila. kinsman
Thomas Morrey, Phila.,
    calls EDWARD I
    father-in-law
Humphrey Morrey, Phila.
    kinsman of JOSEPH I

Nathaniel Allen

Thomas Budd
(-1698)

WILLIAM
(-1693)
in England

'71
EDWARD I-m-
(1639-1712)

'89
-m-

'06
-m-
Saml Powel-m-Abigail Wilcox

'85
George Emlen-m-Eleanor Allen
(-1710)   (-1690)
'94
-m-Hannah Garret
(1674-1738)

Nehemiah Allen-m-Rebecca Crispin Blackfan
(said to be kin   (Cousin of Wm Penn)
to Wm Allen)

'17
George-m-Mary Heath
(1695-1754)   (1692-1777)

Samuel-m-Mary Heath
(1697-1783)

1st
Joshua-m-Mary (H) Hudson
(1701-1776)
2d
-m-Deborah Powel

Ann
(1705-)

Mary-m-John Armitt
(1708-1791) (1702-1762)

'38
Sarah-m-James Cresson
(1710-1752)

Samuel Powel

Mathias & Margaret Vanderheyden

ROBERT   WILLIAM   EDWARD   JOHN
               in England

EDWARD II-m-Francina Vanderheyden
(1678 — 1714)

'03
JOSEPH I-m-
(1679-1741)

Sariana Fibby Augustina
(Arianna-m-James Frisby)

'21
-m-

Andrew Hamilton
(1676-1741)

William Till
(1697-1766)

'00
William Allen-m-Mary Budd
(1670-1725) (1679-1760)

Granny Gray

James Hamilton
(1710-1783)

'34
Margaret Hamilton-m-William Allen
(-1760)   (1704-1780)
        (See B-5)

'34
MARGARET-m-John Jekyll
(-1762)   (-1742)
    (See B-5)

'25
EDWARD III-m-
(1703-1781)

'41
Andrew Hamilton-m-Mary Till
(-1747)

'47
Patty Gray   -m-

(See B-3)

*Significant kinsmen whose precise lineage was not
determined are listed in upper left quadrant.

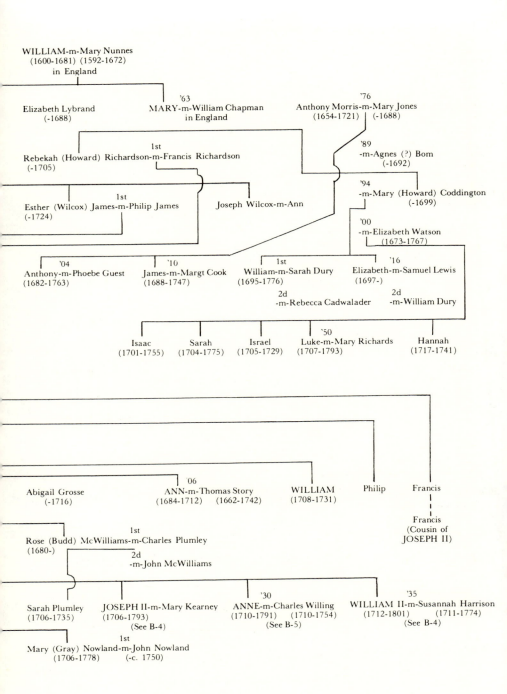

WILLIAM-m-Mary Nunnes
(1600-1681) (1592-1672)
in England

Elizabeth Lybrand
(-1688)

'63
MARY-m-William Chapman
in England

'76
Anthony Morris-m-Mary Jones
(1654-1721) (-1688)

1st
Rebekah (Howard) Richardson-m-Francis Richardson
(-1705)

'89
-m-Agnes (?) Bom
(-1692)

'94
-m-Mary (Howard) Coddington
(-1699)

Esther (Wilcox) James-m-Philip James   1st
(-1724)

Joseph Wilcox-m-Ann

'00
-m-Elizabeth Watson
(1673-1767)

'04
Anthony-m-Phoebe Guest
(1682-1763)

'10
James-m-Margt Cook
(1688-1747)

1st
William-m-Sarah Dury
(1695-1776)

'16
Elizabeth-m-Samuel Lewis
(1697-)

2d
-m-Rebecca Cadwalader

2d
-m-William Dury

Isaac
(1701-1755)

Sarah
(1704-1775)

Israel
(1705-1729)

'50
Luke-m-Mary Richards
(1707-1793)

Hannah
(1717-1741)

Abigail Grosse
(-1716)

'06
ANN-m-Thomas Story
(1684-1712)   (1662-1742)

WILLIAM
(1708-1731)

Philip

Francis

Francis
(Cousin of
JOSEPH II)

1st
Rose (Budd) McWilliams-m-Charles Plumley
(1680-)

2d
-m-John McWilliams

Sarah Plumley
(1706-1735)

JOSEPH II-m-Mary Kearney
(1706-1793)
(See B-4)

'30
ANNE-m-Charles Willing
(1710-1791)   (1710-1754)
(See B-5)

'35
WILLIAM II-m-Susannah Harrison
(1712-1801)   (1711-1774)
(See B-4)

1st
Mary (Gray) Nowland-m-John Nowland
(1706-1778)   (-c. 1750)

B-3. The Edward III Branch*

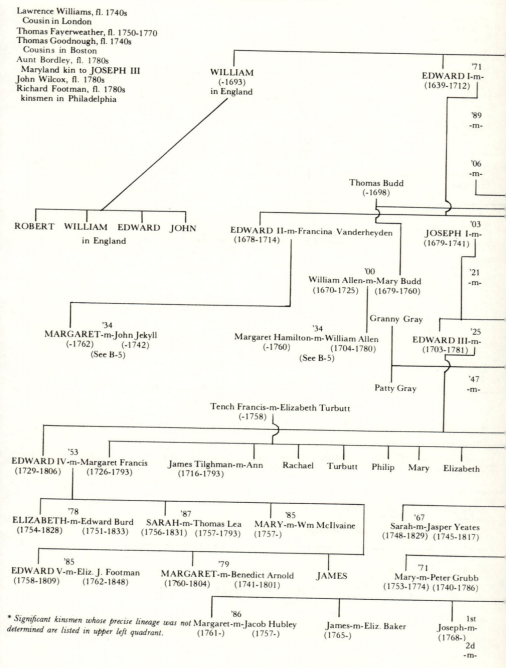

Lawrence Williams, fl. 1740s
  Cousin in London
Thomas Fayerweather, fl. 1750-1770
Thomas Goodnough, fl. 1740s
  Cousins in Boston
Aunt Bordley, fl. 1780s
  Maryland kin to JOSEPH III
John Wilcox, fl. 1780s
Richard Footman, fl. 1780s
  kinsmen in Philadelphia

WILLIAM
(-1693)
in England

'71
EDWARD I-m-
(1639-1712)

'89
-m-

'06
-m-

Thomas Budd
(-1698)

ROBERT   WILLIAM   EDWARD   JOHN
in England

EDWARD II-m-Francina Vanderheyden
(1678-1714)

'03
JOSEPH I-m-
(1679-1741)

'00
William Allen-m-Mary Budd
(1670-1725)   (1679-1760)

'21
-m-

Granny Gray

'34
MARGARET-m-John Jekyll
(-1762)   (-1742)
(See B-5)

'34
Margaret Hamilton-m-William Allen
(-1760)   (1704-1780)
(See B-5)

'25
EDWARD III-m-
(1703-1781)

Patty Gray

'47
-m-

Tench Francis-m-Elizabeth Turbutt
(-1758)

'53
EDWARD IV-m-Margaret Francis
(1729-1806)   (1726-1793)

James Tilghman-m-Ann   Rachael   Turbutt   Philip   Mary   Elizabeth
(1716-1793)

'78
ELIZABETH-m-Edward Burd
(1754-1828)   (1751-1833)

'87
SARAH-m-Thomas Lea
(1756-1831)   (1757-1793)

'85
MARY-m-Wm McIlvaine
(1757-)

'67
Sarah-m-Jasper Yeates
(1748-1829) (1745-1817)

'85
EDWARD V-m-Eliz. J. Footman
(1758-1809)   (1762-1848)

'79
MARGARET-m-Benedict Arnold
(1760-1804)   (1741-1801)

JAMES

'71
Mary-m-Peter Grubb
(1753-1774) (1740-1786)

*Significant kinsmen whose precise lineage was not
determined are listed in upper left quadrant.

'86
Margaret-m-Jacob Hubley
(1761-)   (1757-)

James-m-Eliz. Baker
(1765-)

1st
Joseph-m-
(1768-)
2d
-m-

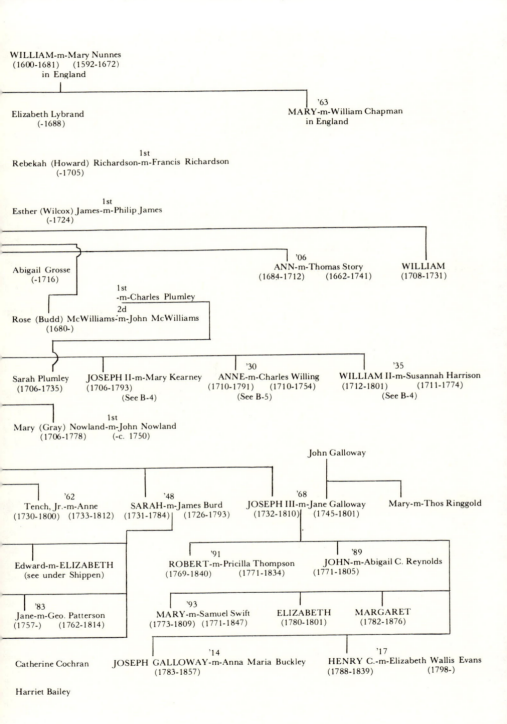

WILLIAM-m-Mary Nunnes
(1600-1681) (1592-1672)
in England

Elizabeth Lybrand
(-1688)

'63
MARY-m-William Chapman
in England

1st
Rebekah (Howard) Richardson-m-Francis Richardson
(-1705)

1st
Esther (Wilcox) James-m-Philip James
(-1724)

Abigail Grosse
(-1716)

'06
ANN-m-Thomas Story
(1684-1712) (1662-1741)

WILLIAM
(1708-1731)

1st
-m-Charles Plumley
2d
Rose (Budd) McWilliams-m-John McWilliams
(1680-)

Sarah Plumley
(1706-1735)

JOSEPH II-m-Mary Kearney
(1706-1793)
(See B-4)

'30
ANNE-m-Charles Willing
(1710-1791) (1710-1754)
(See B-5)

'35
WILLIAM II-m-Susannah Harrison
(1712-1801) (1711-1774)
(See B-4)

1st
Mary (Gray) Nowland-m-John Nowland
(1706-1778) (-c. 1750)

John Galloway

'62
Tench, Jr.-m-Anne
(1730-1800) (1733-1812)

'48
SARAH-m-James Burd
(1731-1784) (1726-1793)

'68
JOSEPH III-m-Jane Galloway
(1732-1810) (1745-1801)

Mary-m-Thos Ringgold

Edward-m-ELIZABETH
(see under Shippen)

'91
ROBERT-m-Pricilla Thompson
(1769-1840) (1771-1834)

'89
JOHN-m-Abigail C. Reynolds
(1771-1805)

'83
Jane-m-Geo. Patterson
(1757-) (1762-1814)

'93
MARY-m-Samuel Swift
(1773-1809) (1771-1847)

ELIZABETH
(1780-1801)

MARGARET
(1782-1876)

Catherine Cochran

'14
JOSEPH GALLOWAY-m-Anna Maria Buckley
(1783-1857)

'17
HENRY C.-m-Elizabeth Wallis Evans
(1788-1839) (1798-)

Harriet Bailey

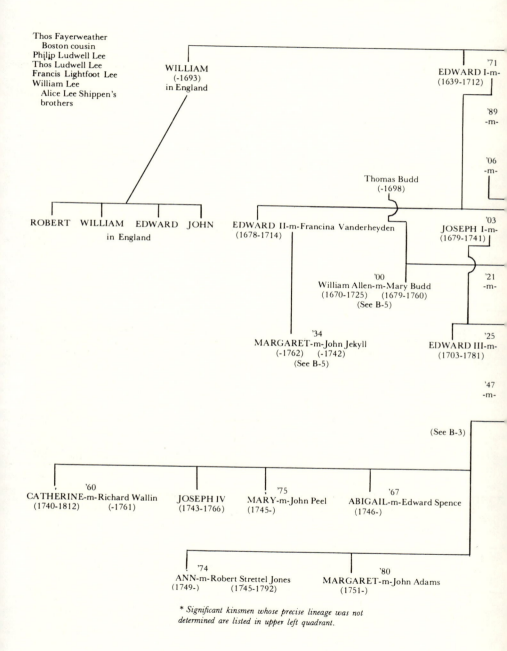

Thos Fayerweather
Boston cousin
Philip Ludwell Lee
Thos Ludwell Lee
Francis Lightfoot Lee
William Lee
    Alice Lee Shippen's
    brothers

WILLIAM
(-1693)
in England

'71
EDWARD I-m-
(1639-1712)

'89
-m-

'06
-m-

Thomas Budd
(-1698)

ROBERT   WILLIAM   EDWARD   JOHN
         in England

EDWARD II-m-Francina Vanderheyden
(1678-1714)

'03
JOSEPH I-m-
(1679-1741)

'00
William Allen-m-Mary Budd
(1670-1725)   (1679-1760)
        (See B-5)

'21
-m-

'34
MARGARET-m-John Jekyll
(-1762)   (-1742)
    (See B-5)

'25
EDWARD III-m-
(1703-1781)

'47
-m-

(See B-3)

'60
CATHERINE-m-Richard Wallin
(1740-1812)   (-1761)

JOSEPH IV
(1743-1766)

'75
MARY-m-John Peel
(1745-)

'67
ABIGAIL-m-Edward Spence
(1746-)

'74
ANN-m-Robert Strettel Jones
(1749-)   (1745-1792)

'80
MARGARET-m-John Adams
(1751-)

* Significant kinsmen whose precise lineage was not
determined are listed in upper left quadrant.

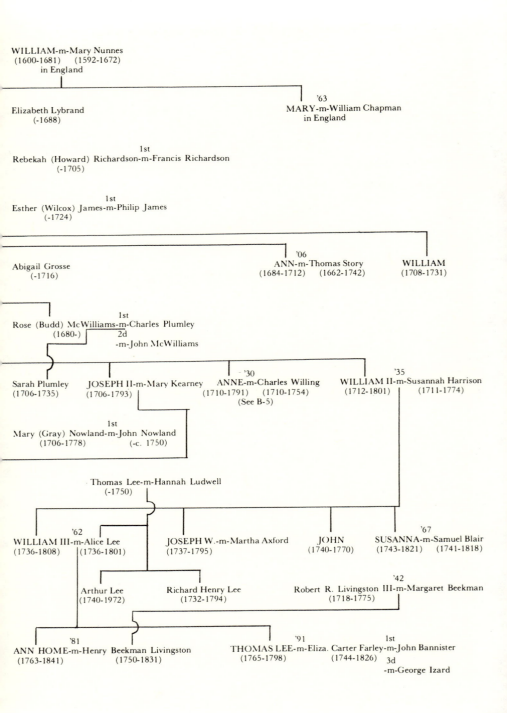

WILLIAM-m-Mary Nunnes
(1600-1681)   (1592-1672)
in England

Elizabeth Lybrand
(-1688)

'63
MARY-m-William Chapman
in England

1st
Rebekah (Howard) Richardson-m-Francis Richardson
(-1705)

1st
Esther (Wilcox) James-m-Philip James
(-1724)

Abigail Grosse
(-1716)

'06
ANN-m-Thomas Story
(1684-1712)   (1662-1742)

WILLIAM
(1708-1731)

1st
Rose (Budd) McWilliams-m-Charles Plumley
(1680-)   2d
                    -m-John McWilliams

Sarah Plumley
(1706-1735)

JOSEPH II-m-Mary Kearney
(1706-1793)

- '30
ANNE-m-Charles Willing
(1710-1791)   (1710-1754)
(See B-5)

'35
WILLIAM II-m-Susannah Harrison
(1712-1801)   (1711-1774)

1st
Mary (Gray) Nowland-m-John Nowland
(1706-1778)   (-c. 1750)

Thomas Lee-m-Hannah Ludwell
(-1750)

'62
WILLIAM III-m-Alice Lee
(1736-1808)   (1736-1801)

JOSEPH W.-m-Martha Axford
(1737-1795)

JOHN
(1740-1770)

'67
SUSANNA-m-Samuel Blair
(1743-1821)   (1741-1818)

Arthur Lee
(1740-1972)

Richard Henry Lee
(1732-1794)

'42
Robert R. Livingston III-m-Margaret Beekman
(1718-1775)

'81
ANN HOME-m-Henry Beekman Livingston
(1763-1841)   (1750-1831)

'91
THOMAS LEE-m-Eliza. Carter Farley-m-John Bannister
(1765-1798)   (1744-1826)   3d
                              -m-George Izard

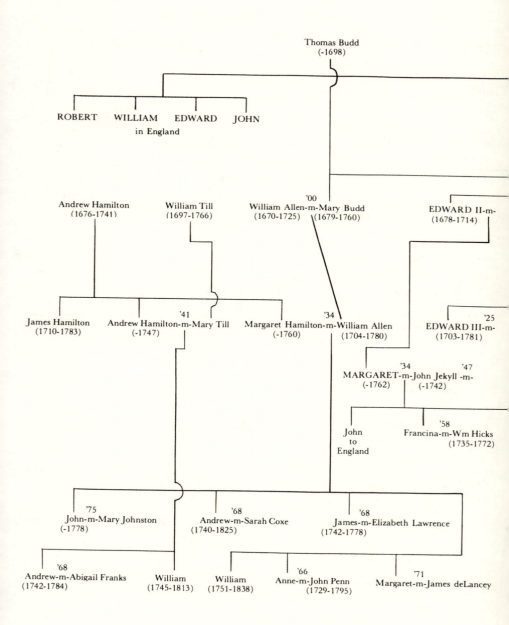

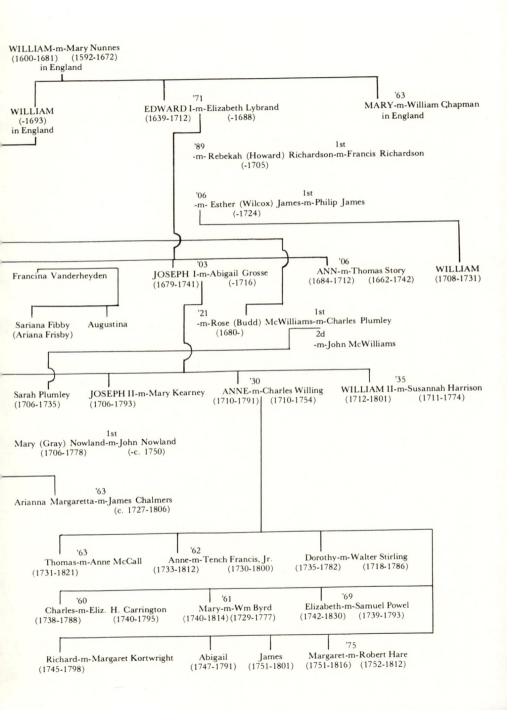

WILLIAM-m-Mary Nunnes
(1600-1681)   (1592-1672)
in England

WILLIAM
(-1693)
in England

'71
EDWARD I-m-Elizabeth Lybrand
(1639-1712)   (-1688)

'63
MARY-m-William Chapman
in England

'89   1st
-m- Rebekah (Howard) Richardson-m-Francis Richardson
(-1705)

'06   1st
-m- Esther (Wilcox) James-m-Philip James
(-1724)

Francina Vanderheyden

'03
JOSEPH I-m-Abigail Grosse
(1679-1741)   (-1716)

'06
ANN-m-Thomas Story
(1684-1712)   (1662-1742)

WILLIAM
(1708-1731)

Sariana Fibby   Augustina
(Ariana Frisby)

'21
-m-Rose (Budd) McWilliams-m-Charles Plumley
(1680-)

1st

2d
-m-John McWilliams

Sarah Plumley
(1706-1735)

JOSEPH II-m-Mary Kearney
(1706-1793)

'30
ANNE-m-Charles Willing
(1710-1791)   (1710-1754)

'35
WILLIAM II-m-Susannah Harrison
(1712-1801)   (1711-1774)

1st
Mary (Gray) Nowland-m-John Nowland
(1706-1778)   (-c. 1750)

'63
Arianna Margaretta-m-James Chalmers
(c. 1727-1806)

'63
Thomas-m-Anne McCall
(1731-1821)

'62
Anne-m-Tench Francis, Jr.
(1733-1812)   (1730-1800)

Dorothy-m-Walter Stirling
(1735-1782)   (1718-1786)

'60
Charles-m-Eliz. H. Carrington
(1738-1788)   (1740-1795)

'61
Mary-m-Wm Byrd
(1740-1814)(1729-1777)

'69
Elizabeth-m-Samuel Powel
(1742-1830)   (1739-1793)

Richard-m-Margaret Kortwright
(1745-1798)

Abigail
(1747-1791)

James
(1751-1801)

'75
Margaret-m-Robert Hare
(1751-1816)   (1752-1812)

Bibliography

A. PRIMARY SOURCES

MANUSCRIPTS

American Philosophical Society
American Philosophical Society. Archives, 1768–1965. 112 boxes.
American Philosophical Society. Miscellaneous Manuscript Collection.
Burd, James (?). Account Book, 1750–1756.
Burd-Shippen Papers, 1742–1788. 6 boxes, 3 vols.
Feinstone Collection.
Franklin, Benjamin. Papers.
Hall, David. Letterbook, 1764–1767.
Horsfield, Timothy. Papers, 1733–1771. 2 vols.
Hutchinson, James. Papers, 1771–1928.
Peale Papers. Mills Collection.
Penn, Thomas. Correspondence, 1747–1771. 1 vol.
Shippen, Edward. Letters and Papers, 1727–1789. 3 boxes.
Shippen, Edward, Jr. Papers. 19 pieces.
Shippen, Joseph. Wastebook, 1749–1750. 1 vol.
Shippen, Joseph, Jr. Letterbook, 1763–1773. 1 vol.
Shippen, William, Jr. Journal, 1759–1760. 1 vol.
Shippen, William, Jr. Recipe Book, 1789–1791. 1 vol.
Smyth, Frederick. Papers, 1756–1816. 56 pieces.

Arch Street Meeting House
Philadelphia Monthly Meeting. Book of Marriages.
Philadelphia Monthly Meeting. Minutes.
Philadelphia Monthly Meeting. Miscellaneous Papers of the Monthly Meeting.
Women's Monthly Meeting of Philadelphia. Minutes.

Friends Historical Library

Hinshaw, William Wade. Card Index of American Quaker Genealogy.

Genealogical Society of Pennsylvania

Genealogical Society of Pennsylvania. Collections.
Proprietary Tax List. Philadelphia City and Philadelphia County, 1769. (Xerox Copy.)

Historical Society of Pennsylvania

An Account of Coaches, Landaus, Chariots, and Four Wheel Chairs, 1761. Proud Miscellaneous Manuscript, Box 2, No. 71.
Allen, William. Letterbook.
Ashmead Scrapbook.
Bradford Collection. Unbound Correspondence.
Brayton Collection. Miscellaneous Manuscripts.
Bucks County. Miscellaneous Papers, 1682–1850.
Burd Papers.
Burd-Shippen-Hubley Collection. 1 box.
Cadwalader Collection. Trent and Croghan Papers.
Carson, Hampton L. Collection.
Chester County. Papers.
Chief Justices of the Supreme Court of Pennsylvania.
Commissions. Stille Case.
Deeds.
Dickinson, Jonathan/James Logan Letterbook.
Dreer Collection. Old Congress.
Dreer Collection. Physicians and Chemists.
Fallon Scrapbook.
Gratz Collection. American Physicians.
Gratz Collection. European Miscellaneous.
Gratz Collection. Old Congress.
Gratz Collection. Pennsylvania Series Provincial Conference.
Irvine Papers.
Lamberton Scotch-Irish Manuscripts.
Lancaster County, 1724–72, 1772–1816. 2 vols.
Landholders of Philadelphia County, 1734.
Lawrence, Martha Morris. Collection.
List of Philadelphia City and County Taxables, 1760. Proud Miscellaneous Manuscript, Box 2, No. 71.
Logan, Maria Dickinson Papers.
Logan Papers.

McKean Papers.

Marriage Certificates.

Miscellaneous Papers, 1772–1816. Petitions for Lebanon-Lancaster County.

Northern, Interior, and Western Counties.

Ohio Company. Etting Manuscripts.

Pemberton Papers in Etting Collection.

Penn, Thomas. Letterbooks.

Penn Accounts.

Penn Manuscripts. Assembly and Provincial Court of Pennsylvania. Large folio.

Penn Manuscripts. Granville Penn Book.

Penn Papers.

Penn Papers. Official Correspondence.

Pennsylvania. Records of the Prison Society. 18 vols.

Pennsylvania Miscellaneous Papers. Penn and Baltimore, Penn Family.

Peters Papers.

Petitions and Memorials.

Philadelphia County, Miscellaneous Papers of.

Potts, Jonathan. Papers.

Proud, Robert. Miscellaneous Manuscripts.

Provincial Delegates.

Read, James, Papers of.

Richardson, Francis. Letterbook, 1681–1688.

Shippen, Edward. Cashbook, 1782–1806.

Shippen, Edward, Jr., Docket of, 1779–1780.

Shippen, Balch Papers. 2 vols.

Shippen Papers. 33 vols. 11 boxes and other vols.

Shippen Papers. T. Balch Collection. 5 vols.

Shippen Papers. Transferred from the Society Collection.

Shippen and Swift. Balch Papers. 1 vol.

Shippen-Burd-Hubley Papers. 1 box.

Society Collection.

Society Small Collection.

Stauffer, David. Collection.

Stauffer Collection. Mayors.

Taylor Papers. Chester County Surveys, 1701–1740.

Taylor Papers, 1723–1750.

Tax Lists. Philadelphia County, 1693.

Tax List of Freeholders of the City of Philadelphia, 1756.

Three Lower Counties, 1655–1805.

Unger, Claude W. Collection.

Westcott, Thompson. Officers of Pennsylvania and Philadelphia, 1682–1885. 2 vols.
Wharton Papers.
Yeates Papers.
Yeates-Burd Collection.

Lancaster County Court House
Lancaster County Court House. Probate Records.

Library Company of Philadelphia
McAllister Manuscripts.
Powel Family Papers, 1723–1853.
Ramsay Letters.
Rush, Benjamin. Manuscript Correspondence of Benjamin Rush.

Library of Congress
Hand, Edward. Correspondence. Force Transcripts. 4 vols.
Independence Hall. National Park Service. Wardens of Philadelphia, Minutes.
Shippen, Edward and Joseph. Correspondence, 1727–1783(5?). 1 vol.
Shippen, Joseph. Papers, 1727–1783. 1 vol.
Shippen Family Papers. 28 vols.
Thomson, Charles. Papers, 1765–1845. 3 vols.
Whitefield, George. Papers.

Maryland Historical Society
Bordley, Stephen. Letterbooks.
Gillmore Papers.
Shippen, Thomas Lee. "The Crown Law Common Plac'd," 1786.
Tilghman, James. Papers.
Vertical File.

Pennsylvania Land Record Office, Harrisburg, Pennsylvania
Patent Book.

Philadelphia City Hall Annex
Philadelphia. Probate Records.

Philadelphia City Hall Archives
Deed Books.
Carriage Tax Register, 1790–1794.

Philadelphia Carriage Tax Lists.
Philadelphia City Hall Archives. Eighteen Penny Provincial Tax, 1772.
Philadelphia Tax Lists.

William L. Clements Library, Ann Arbor, Michigan

Clinton, Sir Henry. Papers.
Gage, Thomas. Papers.
Howe, William. Papers.
Miscellaneous Manuscripts.

PRINTED MATERIAL

Adams, John. *Diary and Autobiography of John Adams.* Edited by Lyman
H. Butterfield. 4 vols. Cambridge, Mass., 1961.
American Weekly Mercury, 1719–1749.
Burnaby, Andrew. *Travels through the Middle Settlements in North-
America. In the Years 1759 and 1760. With Observations upon the
State of the Colonies.* 2d ed. Ithaca, 1960.
Effective Supply Tax, City of Philadelphia, 1779. *Pennsylvania Archives.*
Edited by William Henry Egle. 3d ser., vol. XIV (Harrisburg, 1891),
pp. 470–561.
Effective Supply Tax, County of Philadelphia, 1779. *Pennsylvania Archives.*
Edited by William Henry Egle. 3d ser., vol. XIV (Harrisburg, 1891),
pp. 564–743.
Franklin, Benjamin. *Papers of Benjamin Franklin.* Vols. 1–14 edited by
Leonard W. Labaree, et al, vols. 15 on edited by William B. Willcox,
et al. New Haven, 1959–.
Minutes of the Provincial Council of Pennsylvania, 1683–1776. 16 vols.
Philadelphia, 1838–1853.
Morgan, John. *A Vindication of his Public Character in the Station of
Director-General.* Boston, 1777.
Pennsylvania Archives. Edited by Samuel Hazard. 1st ser., 12 vols., Harris-
burg, 1838–1860.
Pennsylvania Archives. Edited by John B. Linn and William Henry Egle.
2d ser., 19 vols. Harrisburg, 1874–1890.
Pennsylvania Archives. Edited by William Henry Egle and George Edward
Reed. 3d ser., 30 vols. Harrisburg, 1894–1899.
Pennsylvania Archives. Edited by Gertrude MacKinney and Charles F.
Holsan. 8th ser., 8 vols. Harrisburg, 1931–1935.
Pennsylvania Archives. Edited by Samuel Hazard, et al. 9th ser., 138 vols.
Harrisburg and Philadelphia, 1852–1949.

Pennsylvania Evening Post, 1775–1784.
Pennsylvania Gazette, 1728–1815.
Pennsylvania Journal, 1742–1793.
Pennsylvania Magazine; or American Monthly Museum. Philadelphia, 1775–1776.
Pennsylvania Packet, 1771–1790.
Philadelphia Common Council. *Minutes of the Common Council of the City of Philadelphia, 1704–1776.* Philadelphia, 1847.
The Philadelphia Directory. Francis White. Philadelphia, 1785.
The Philadelphia Directory and Register. James Hardie. 2d ed. Philadelphia, 1794.
Philadelphia Directory for 1796. Thomas Stephens. Philadelphia, 1796.
The Philadelphia Directory for 1797. Cornelius William Stafford. Philadelphia, 1797.
The Philadelphia Directory for 1798. Cornelius William Stafford. Philadelphia, 1798.
The Philadelphia Directory for 1800. Cornelius William Stafford. Philadelphia, 1800.
The Philadelphiad; or, New Pictures of the City; Interspersed with a Candid Review and Display of Some First-Rate Modern Characters of Both Sexes: Delineated in a Friendly and Satirical Manner, and Containing Sketches of the Materials that Distinguish the Following Places, Viz.: Court-House, Hospital for Lunatics, New Jail, Bell's Book Store, Theatre, State House and Bagnio Coffee-House. With Other Entertaining Anecdotes, Humorous, Moral and Sentimental. 2 vols. Philadelphia, 1784.
Proprietary Tax, City of Philadelphia, 1769. Edited by William Henry Egle. *Pennsylvania Archives.* 3d ser., vol. XIV (Harrisburg, 1897), pp. 150–220.
Proprietary Tax, County of Philadelphia, 1769. Edited by William Henry Egle. *Pennsylvania Archives.* 3d ser., vol. XIV (Harrisburg, 1897), pp. 1–147.
Record of Pennsylvania Marriages, prior to 1810. Vol. I, 1895, Clarence M. Busch, in *Pennsylvania Archives.* Edited by John B. Linn and William H. Egle. 2d ser. Harrisburg, 1896.
Rush, Benjamin. *The Autobiography of Benjamin Rush, His "Travels through Life" together with his Commonplace Book for 1789–1813.* Edited by George W. Corner. Princeton, 1948.
———. *Letters of Benjamin Rush.* Edited by Lyman H. Butterfield. 2 vols. Princeton, 1951.
Smith, John. *Hannah Logan's Courtship; A True Narrative, the Wooing*

of the Daughter of James Logan, Colonial Governor of Pennsylvania, and Divers other Matters, As Related in the Diary of her Lover, the Honorable John Smith, Assemblyman of Pennsylvania and King's Councillor of New Jersey, 1736–1752.* Edited by Albert Cook Myers. Philadelphia, 1902.

Stiles, Ezra. Diary. Massachusetts Historical Society. *Proceedings.* 2d ser., vol. VII (1891–1892).

Story, Thomas. *A Journal of the Life of Thomas Story, Containing an Account of his Remarkable Convincement of, and Embracing the Principles of Truth, as held by the People Called Quakers. And also of His Travels and Labours in the Service of the Gospel, with Many Other occurrences and Observations.* Newcastle upon Tyne, 1747.

Suffolk County Massachusetts. *Suffolk Deeds.* 14 vols. Boston, 1880–1906.

"Taxables in Chestnut, Middle, and South Wards Philadelphia: 1754." *Pennsylvania Genealogical Magazine.* Annotated by Hannah Roach. Vol. XXI (1959), 159–196.

"Taxables in Chestnut, Walnut, and Lower Delaware Wards, Philadelphia, 1767." *Pennsylvania Genealogical Magazine.* Vol. XXII (1962), 170–185.

"Taxables in the City of Philadelphia, 1756." *Pennsylvania Genealogical Magazine.* Annotated by Hannah Roach. Vol. XXII (1961), 3–41.

Thomas, Gabriel. *An Historical and Geographical Account of Pennsylvania; and of West New Jersey in America.* London, 1698.

United States Bureau of the Census. *Historical Statistics of the United States, Colonial Times to 1957.* Washington, 1960.

B. SECONDARY SOURCES

PUBLISHED MATERIAL

Adams, Brooks. *The Emancipation of Massachusetts: The Dream and the Reality.* Boston, 1962.

Alexander, Archibald. *Biographical Sketches of the Founder, and Principal Alumni of the Log College.* Princeton, 1845.

Appleton's Cyclopaedia of American Biography. Edited by James Grant Wilson and John Fiske. 6 vols. New York, 1894.

Armes, Ethel, ed. *Nancy Shippen, Her Journal Book: The International Romance of a Young Lady of Fashion of Colonial Philadelphia with Letters to Her and about Her.* New York, 1968.

Arnold, Isaac N. *The Life of Benedict Arnold: His Patriotism and His Treason.* Chicago, 1897.

Bailyn, Bernard. "The Beekmans of New York: Trade, Politics, and Families: A Review Article." *William and Mary Quarterly.* 3d ser., Vol. XIV, no. 4 (October 1957), 598–608.

———. *Education in the Forming of American Society: Needs and Opportunities for Study.* New York, 1960.

———. *Ideological Origins of the American Revolution.* Cambridge, Mass., 1967.

———. *The New England Merchants in the Seventeenth Century.* New York, 1964.

———. "Political Experience and Enlightenment Ideas in Eighteenth-Century America." *American Historical Review.* Vol. LXVII, no. 2 (January 1962), 339–351.

———, ed. *Pamphlets of the American Revolution, 1750–1765.* Cambridge, Massachusetts, 1965.

Bailyn, Bernard and Bailyn, Lotte. *Massachusetts Shipping, 1697–1714; A Statistical Study.* Cambridge, Mass., 1959.

Balch, Thomas Willing. "English Ancestors of the Shippen Family and Edward Shippen of Philadelphia." *Pennsylvania Magazine of History and Biography.* Vol. XXVIII (1904), 385–402.

———. *Letters and Papers relating to Pennsylvania.* 5 vols. Private printing. Philadelphia, 1855.

———. *The Philadelphia Assemblies.* Philadelphia, 1916.

Barker, Charles Arno. *The Background of the Revolution in Maryland.* New Haven, c. 1940. Reprinted in Archon Books, 1967.

Beath, Robert B. *Historical Catalogue of the St. Andrew's Society of Philadelphia, with Biographical Sketches of Deceased Members, 1749–1913.* Philadelphia, 1913.

Bedwell, C. E. A. "American Middle Templars." *American Historical Review.* Vol. XXV, no. 4 (July 1920), 680–688.

Bell, Whitfield J., Jr. "The Court Martial of Dr. William Shippen, Jr., 1780." *Journal of the History of Medicine and Allied Sciences.* Vol. XIX, no. 3 (July 1964), 218–238.

———. *John Morgan: Continental Doctor.* Philadelphia, 1965.

———. "Some American Students of 'That Shining Oracle of Physic,' Cullen of Edinburgh, 1755–1766." *Proceedings.* American Philosophical Society. Vol. XCIV (1950), 275–281.

Bossard, James H. S. *Parent and Child.* Philadelphia, 1953.

Bossard, James H. S. and Boll, Eleanor S. *The Large Family System.* Philadelphia, 1956.

Boyer, Charles S. *Early Forges and Furnaces in New Jersey.* Philadelphia, 1931. Reprinted 1963.

Bridenbaugh, Carl. *Cities in Revolt: Urban Life in America, 1743–1776.* New York, 1964.

————. *Cities in the Wilderness: The First Century of Urban Life in America, 1625–1742.* New York, 1964.

Bridenbaugh, Carl and Bridenbaugh, Jessica. *Rebels and Gentlemen: Philadelphia in the Age of Franklin.* New York, 1962.

Bronner, Edwin B. *William Penn's "Holy Experiment": The Founding of Pennsylvania, 1681–1701.* Philadelphia, 1962.

Bronson, William White and Hildeburn, Charles R. *The Inscriptions in St. Peter's Church Yard, Philadelphia.* Camden, 1879.

Brown, Wallace. *The Good Americans, The Loyalists in the American Revolution.* New York, 1969.

————. *The King's Friends: The Composition and Motives of the American Loyalist Claimants.* Providence, 1965.

Brunhouse, Robert Levere. *The Counter-Revolution in Pennsylvania, 1776–1790.* Philadelphia, 1942.

Calderone, Mary S. *Manual of Contraceptive Practice.* Baltimore, 1964.

Cappon, Lester J. "The Colonial Period Reexamined." *Research Opportunities in American Cultural History.* Edited by John Francis McDermott, Lexington, Ky., 1961, pp. 2–17.

Cheyney, Edward Potts. *History of the University of Pennsylvania, 1740–1940.* Philadelphia, 1940.

Cheyney, Edward Potts and Oberholtzer, Ellis Paxson. *University of Pennsylvania: Its History, Influence, Equipment, and Characteristics, with Biographical Sketches and Portraits of Founders, Benefactors, Officers, and Alumni.* 2 vols. Boston, 1901–1902.

Clark, Edward L. *A Record of the Inscriptions on the Tablets and Gravestones in the Burial-Grounds of Christ Church, Philadelphia.* Philadelphia, 1864.

Corner, Betsy Copping. *William Shippen, Jr., Pioneer in American Medical Education: A Biographical Essay.* Philadelphia, 1951.

Cousins, Frank and Riley, Phil M. *The Colonial Architecture of Philadelphia.* Boston, 1920.

Cunningham, John T. *Newark.* Newark, N.J., 1966.

Daly, John and Weinberg, Allen. *Genealogy of Philadelphia County Subdivisions.* Philadelphia, 1966.

Davies, S. A. *Princeton College in the Eighteenth Century.* New York, 1872.

Demos, John. "Families in Colonial Bristol, Rhode Island: An Exercise in Historical Demography." *William and Mary Quarterly.* 3d ser., Vol. XXV, no. 1 (January 1968), 40–57.

Dictionary of American Biography. Edited by Allen Johnson and Dumas Malone. 22 vols. New York, 1928–1944.

Dunn, Richard S. *Puritans and Yankees: The Winthrop Dynasty of New England, 1630–1717.* Princeton, 1962.

Dynes, Russell R.; Clarke, Alfred C.; and Dinitz, Simon. "Levels of Occupational Aspiration: Some Aspects of Family Experience as a Variable." *American Sociological Review.* Vol. 21, no. 2 (April 1956), 212–215.

Edwards, John N., ed. *The Family and Change.* New York, 1969.

Elder, Glen H., Jr. "Family Structure and Educational Attainment: A Cross-National Analysis." *American Sociological Review.* Vol. 30, no. 1 (February 1965), 81–96.

Elias, N. and Scotson, J. L. *The Established and the Outsiders: A Sociological Enquiry into Community Problems.* London, 1965.

Fairchild, Byron. *The Messrs. William Pepperrell: Merchants of Piscataqua.* Ithaca, 1954.

Farber, Bernard. *Kinship and Class: A Midwestern Study.* New York, 1971.

Finch, Mary E. *Wealth of Five Northamptonshire Families, 1540–1640.* Oxford, 1956.

Flexner, James Thomas. *Doctors on Horseback: Pioneers of American Medicine.* New York, 1944.

———. *The Traitor and the Spy; Benedict Arnold and John Andre.* New York, 1953.

Foote, Henry Wilder. *Robert Feke, Colonial Portrait Painter.* Cambridge, Mass., 1930.

Frost, Jerry William. *The Quaker Family in Colonial America: A Portrait of the Society of Friends.* New York, 1973.

Furstenberg, Frank F., Jr. "Industrialization and the American Family: A Backward Look." *American Sociological Review.* Vol. 31, no. 3 (June 1966), 326–337.

Genealogical Society of Pennsylvania. *Publications.* 16 vols. ————1946. This periodical is continued under the title *Pennsylvania Genealogical Magazine.*

Glass, D. V. and Eversley, D. E. C., eds. *Population in History: Essays in Historical Demography.* Chicago, 1965.

Glassie, Henry H. *Pattern in Material Folk Culture of the Eastern United States.* Philadelphia, 1968.

Goldwaite, Richard A. *Private Wealth in Renaissance Florence: A Study of Four Families.* Princeton, 1968.

Goode, William. *World Revolution and Family Patterns.* New York, 1963.

Goodman, Nathan G. *Benjamin Rush, Physician and Citizen, 1746–1813.* Philadelphia, 1934.

Goodwin, Albert, ed. *The European Nobility in the Eighteenth Century: Studies of the Nobilities of the Major European States in the Pre-Reform Era.* New York, 1967.

Gordon, Michael. Review of Richard Sennett's *Families against the City* (Cambridge, Mass., 1970), in *Journal of Marriage and the Family.* Vol. 33, no. 2 (May 1971), 391–392.

Greene, Evarts B. and Harrington, Virginia D. *American Population before the Federal Census of 1790.* New York, 1932.

Greenfield, Sidney. *English Rustics in Black Skin: A Study of modern forms in a pre-industrialized society.* New Haven, 1966.

Greiff, Constance M.; Gibbons, Mary W.; and Menzies, Elizabeth G. C. *Princeton Architecture: A Pictorial History of Town and Campus.* Princeton, 1967.

Greven, Philip J., Jr. "Family Structure in Seventeenth-Century Andover, Massachusetts." *William and Mary Quarterly.* 3d ser., Vol. XXIII, no. 2 (April 1966), 234–256.

———. *Four Generations: Population, Land, and Family in Colonial Andover, Massachusetts.* Ithaca, 1970.

Hajnal, J. "European Marriage Patterns in Perspective." *Population in History, Essays in Historical Demography.* Edited by D. V. Glass and D. E. C. Eversley. Chicago, 1965.

Handlin, Oscar. *The Uprooted: The Epic Story of the Great Migration That Made the American People.* New York, 1951.

Hanna, William S. *Benjamin Franklin and Pennsylvania Politics.* Stanford, 1964.

Hartz, Louis. *The Liberal Tradition in America.* New York, 1955.

Hawke, David. *In Midst of a Revolution.* Philadelphia, 1961.

Hazard, Samuel. *Annals of Pennsylvania from the Discovery of the Delaware . . . 1609–82.* Philadelphia, 1850.

———. *Register of Pennsylvania.* 16 vols. Philadelphia, 1834–1836.

Hedges, James B. *The Browns of Providence Plantations: Colonial Years.* Cambridge, Mass., 1952.

Heimert, Alan and Miller, Perry, eds. *The Great Awakening: Documents Illustrating the Crisis and Its Consequences.* New York, 1967.

Henretta, James A. "Economic Development and Social Structure in Colonial Boston." *William and Mary Quarterly.* 3d ser., Vol. XXII, no. 1 (January 1965), 75–92.

Hinshaw, William Wade, ed. *Encyclopedia of American Quaker Genealogy.* 3 vols. Ann Arbor, 1936–1944.

Hollingsworth, T. H. "A Demographic Study of British Ducal Families." *Population in History, Essays in Historical Demography.* Edited by D. V. Glass and D. E. C. Eversley. Chicago, 1965.

Hutson, James H. *Pennsylvania Politics 1746–1770: The Movement for Royal Government and Its Consequences*. Princeton, 1972.

Illick, Joseph Edward. *William Penn, the Politician: His Relations with the English Government*. Ithaca, 1965.

James, Sidney V. *A People among Peoples: Quaker Benevolence in Eighteenth-Century America*. Cambridge, Mass., 1963.

Jensen, Arthur L. *The Maritime Commerce of Colonial Philadelphia*. Madison, 1963.

Johnson, R. Winder. *The Ancestry of Rosalie Morris Johnson*. Privately printed. Philadelphia, 1905.

Jones, Rufus, assisted by Gummere, Amelia M. and Sharpless, Isaac. *The Quakers in the American Colonies*. New York, 1966.

Jordan, John W., ed. *Colonial Families of Philadelphia*. 2 vols. New York, 1911.

———. *Colonial and Revolutionary Families of Pennsylvania: Genealogical and Personal Memoirs*. 3 vols. New York, 1911.

Keith, Charles P. *Chronicles of Pennsylvania from the English Revolution to the Peace of Aix-la-Chapelle, 1688–1748*. 2 vols. c. 1917. Reprinted Freeport, N.Y., 1969.

———. *The Provincial Councillors of Pennsylvania Who Held Office between 1733 and 1776, and Those Earlier Councillors Who Were Some Time Chief Magistrates of the Province, and Their Descendants*. Philadelphia, 1883.

Kenney, Alice P. *The Gansevoorts of Albany: Dutch Patricians in the Upper Hudson Valley*. Syracuse, 1969.

Land, Aubrey C. *The Dulanys of Maryland: A Biographical Study of Daniel Dulany, the Elder (1685–1753) and Daniel Dulany, the Younger (1722–1797)*. Baltimore, 1955.

Lantz, Herman R.; Britton, Margaret; Schmitt, Raymond; and Snyder, Eloise. "Pre-Industrial Patterns in the Colonial Family in America: A Content Analysis of Colonial Magazines." *Courtship and Marriage in Contemporary America: An Anthology*. Edited by Arthur Kline and Morris Medley. Printed for confidential use of students at Indiana States University, n.d.

Laslett, Peter. *The World We Have Lost: England before the Industrial Age*. New York, 1965.

Lemisch, Jesse. "The American Revolution Seen from the Bottom Up." *Towards a New Past: Dissenting Essays in American History*. Edited by Barton J. Bernstein. (New York, 1969), pp. 3–45.

Lemon, James T. "Urbanization and the Development of Eighteenth-Century Southeastern Pennsylvania and Adjacent Delaware." *William and Mary Quarterly.* 3d ser., Vol. XXIX, no. 4 (October 1967), 501–542.

Lincoln, Charles H. *The Revolutionary Movement in Pennsylvania, 1760–1776.* Philadelphia, 1901.

Lippincott, Horace Mathier and Oakley, Thornton. *Philadelphia.* Philadelphia, 1926.

Lockridge, Kenneth A. *A New England Town: The First Hundred Years, Dedham, Massachusetts, 1636–1736.* New York, 1970.

McAlpin, Charles W. and Collins, Varnum Lansing. *General Catalogue of Princeton University, 1746–1906.* Princeton, 1908.

Magazine of American History. 1877–1893.

Main, Jackson Turner. *Social Structure of Revolutionary America.* Princeton, 1965.

Martin, John Hill. *Chester (and its vicinity), Delaware County, in Pennsylvania; with Genealogical Sketches of Some Old Families.* Philadelphia, 1877.

———. *Martin's Bench and Bar of Philadelphia, Together with other Lists of persons appointed to Administer the Laws in the City and County of Philadelphia, and the Province and Commonwealth of Pennsylvania.* Philadelphia, 1883.

Middleton, Arthur Pierce. *Tobacco Coast: A Maritime History of Chesapeake Bay in the Colonial Era.* Newport News, 1953.

Miller, Perry. *Errand into the Wilderness.* New York, 1964.

Montgomery, Morton Luther. *History of Bucks County in Pennsylvania.* Philadelphia, 1886.

———. *History of Reading, Pennsylvania and the Anniversary Proceedings of the Sesqui-Centennial, July 5–12, 1898.* Reading, Pa., 1898.

Montgomery, Thomas H. *A History of the University of Pennsylvania from Its Foundation to A.D. 1770; Including Biographical Sketches of the Trustees, Faculty, the First Alumni and Others.* Philadelphia, 1900.

Moon, Robert C. *The Morris Family of Philadelphia.* 5 vols. Philadelphia, 1898–1909.

Morgan, Edmund S. *The Birth of the Republic, 1763–1789.* Chicago, 1956.

———. *The Puritan Family: Religion and Domestic Relations in Seventeenth-Century New England.* Boston, 1944.

Morton, Thomas G., and Woodbury, Frank. *History of the Pennsylvania Hospital from Its Foundation to A.D. 1770.* Philadelphia, 1897.

———. *The History of the Pennsylvania Hospital, 1751–1895.* Philadelphia, 1895.

Moynihan, Daniel Patrick. "The Negro Family: The Case for National

Action," in L. Rainwater and W. L. Yancey, *The Moynihan Report and the Politics of Controversy*. Boston, 1967.

Mussen, Paul Henry and Conger, John Janeway. *Child Development and Personality*. New York, 1956.

Myers, Albert Cook. *Immigration of Irish Quakers into Pennsylvania, 1682–1750, with Their Early History in Ireland*. Swarthmore, 1902.

————, ed. *Narratives of Early Pennsylvania, West New Jersey, and Delaware, 1630–1707*. New York, 1912.

————. *Quaker Arrivals at Philadelphia, 1682–1750, Being a List of Certificates of Removal Received at Philadelphia Monthly Meeting of Friends*. Philadelphia, 1902.

Nash, Gary B. *Quakers and Politics, Pennsylvania, 1681–1726*. Princeton, 1968.

Newcomb, Benjamin H. *Franklin and Galloway: A Political Partnership*. New Haven, 1972.

Nixon, Lily Lee. *James Burd: Frontier Defender, 1726–1793*. Philadelphia, 1941.

Nolan, James Bennett. *Early Narratives of Berks County*. Reading, Pa., 1927.

————. *The Foundation of the Town of Reading in Pennsylvania*. Reading, Pa., 1929.

————. *Neddie Burd's Reading Letters, An Epic of the Early Berks Bar*. Reading, Pa., 1927.

Norris, George W. *The Early History of Medicine in Philadelphia*. Philadelphia, 1886.

O'Callaghan, E. B. and Fernow, Berthold, eds. *Documents Relative to the Colonial History of the State of New York*. 15 vols. Albany, 1856–1887.

Palmer, Robert R. *The Age of the Democratic Revolution: A Political History of Europe and America, 1760–1800*. 2 vols. Princeton, 1959–1964.

Pennsylvania Genealogical Magazine. Vols. XVI–, 1947–. This is a continuation of *Publications* of Genealogical Society of Pennsylvania.

Pennsylvania Magazine of History and Biography, 1877–.

Proud, Robert. *The History of Pennsylvania in North America* . . . 2 vols. Philadelphia, 1797–1798.

Rosen, Bernard C. "Family Structure and Achievement Motivation." *American Sociological Review*. Vol. 26, no. 4 (August 1961), 574–585.

Rosser, Colin and Harris, Christopher. *The Family and Social Change: A Study of Family and Kinship in a South Wales Town*. New York, 1965.

Rutman, Darrett B. *Winthrop's Boston: Portrait of a Puritan Town, 1630–1649*. Chapel Hill, 1965.

Sabine, Lorenzo. *Biographical Sketches of Loyalists of the American Revo-*

lution, with an Historical Essay, with new introduction by Ralph Adams Brown. Port Washington, N.Y., 1966.

Saveth, Edward. "The American Patrician Class: A Field for Research." *Kinship and Family Organization.* Edited by Bernard Farber. New York, 1966, pp. 257–268.

Schacter, Stanley. "Birth Order, Eminence and Higher Education." *American Sociological Review.* Vol. 28, no. 5 (October 1963), 757–768.

———. "Birth Order and Sociometric Choice." *Journal of Abnormal and Social Psychology.* Vol. 68, no. 4 (April 1964), 453–456.

Scharf, J. Thomas and Westcott, Thompson. *History of Philadelphia, 1609–1884.* 3 vols. Philadelphia, 1884.

Sears, Robert R. "Ordinal Position in the Family as a Psychological Variable." *American Sociological Review.* Vol. 15, no. 3 (June 1950), 397–401.

Selsam, J. Paul. *Pennsylvania Constitution of 1776.* Philadelphia, 1936.

Sharman, Albert. *Reproductive Physiology of the Post-Partum Period.* Edinburgh, 1966.

Shryock, Richard H. "Eighteenth Century Medicine in America." American Antiquarian Society. *Proceedings.* New ser., Vol. 59 (1949), 275–292.

———. *Medicine and Society in America, 1660–1860.* New York, 1960.

Sprague, William B. *Annals of the American Pulpit.* 9 vols. New York, 1857–1869.

Stone, Lawrence. *The Crisis of the Aristocracy, 1558–1641.* Abridged edition. New York, 1967.

Thatcher, James. *American Medical Biography.* Edited by Whitfield J. Bell, Jr. 2 vols. New York, 1967.

Thayer, Theodore. *Israel Pemberton: King of the Quakers.* Philadelphia, 1943.

———. *Pennsylvania Politics and the Growth of Democracy, 1740–1776.* Harrisburg, 1953.

Thorpe, Francis Newton, ed. *Benjamin Franklin and the University of Pennsylvania.* Washington, D.C., 1893.

Tinkcom, Harry M.; Tinkcom, Margaret B.; and Simon, Grant Miles. *Historic Germantown from the Founding to the Early Part of the Nineteenth Century, A Survey of the German Township.* Philadelphia, 1955.

Todd, Charles Burr. *The Real Benedict Arnold.* New York, 1903.

Tolles, Frederick. *James Logan and the Culture of Provincial America.* Boston, 1957.

———. *Meeting House and Counting House: The Quaker Merchants of Colonial Philadelphia, 1682–1763.* New York, 1963.

Van Doren, Carl. *Benjamin Franklin.* New York, 1964.

——. *Secret History of the American Revolution, an Account of the Conspiracies of Benedict Arnold and numerous others, drawn from the Secret Service Papers of the British Headquarters in North America, now for the first time examined and made Public*. New York, 1941.

Vann, Richard T. "Nurture and Conversion in the Early Quaker Family." *Journal of Marriage and the Family*. Vol. 31, no. 4 (November 1969), 639–643.

Walker, Lewis Burd. *The Burd Papers: Extracts from Chief Justice William Allen's Letterbook*. Pottsville, Pa., 1897.

Wallace, Willard M. *Traitorous Hero: The Life and Fortunes of Benedict Arnold*. New York, 1954.

Walter, James and Stinnett, Nick. "Parent-Child Relationships: A Decade Review of Research." *Journal of Marriage and the Family*. Vol. 33, no. 1 (February 1971) 70–111.

Warner, Sam Bass, Jr. *The Private City: Philadelphia in Three Periods of Its Growth*. Philadelphia, 1968.

Waters, John J., Jr. *The Otis Family in Provincial and Revolutionary Massachusetts*. Chapel Hill, 1968.

Watson, John F. *Annals of Philadelphia and Pennsylvania in the Olden Time*. 2 vols. Philadelphia, 1857.

Weinberg, Allen, comp. *Warrants and Surveys of the Province of Pennsylvania, 1759*. Philadelphia, 1965.

Wertenbaker, T[homas] J[efferson]. *Princeton, 1746–1896*. Princeton, 1946.

Westcott, Thompson. *The Historic Mansions and Buildings of Philadelphia with some notice of their owners and occupants*. Philadelphia, 1895.

White, Philip. *The Beekmans of New York in Politics and Commerce, 1647–1877*. New York, 1956.

Williams, William Morgan. *The Sociology of an English Village: Gosforth* Glencoe, Ill., 1956.

——. *A West Country Village, Ashworthy: Family, Kinship, and Land*. London, 1963.

Wood, Gordon S. *Creation of the American Republic, 1776–1787*. Chapel Hill, 1969.

——. "Rhetoric and Reality in the American Revolution." *William and Mary Quarterly*. 3d ser., Vol. XXIII, no. 1 (January 1966), 3–32.

Wrigley, E. A., ed. *An Introduction to English Historical Demography from the Sixteenth to the Nineteenth Century*. London, 1966.

Young, Michael and Willmott, Peter. *Family and Kinship in East London*. Baltimore, 1962.

Unpublished Material

Biographical Catalog. University Archives. University of Pennsylvania.
Cohen, Norman Sonny. "William Allen: Chief Justice of Pennsylvania, 1704–1780." Ph.D. dissertation, University of California, Berkeley, 1966.
DiStephano, Judy. "A Concept of Family in Colonial America: The Pembertons of Pennsylvania." Ph.D. dissertation, Ohio State University, 1970.
Frost, Jerry William. "The Quaker Family in Colonial America: A Social History of the Society of Friends." Ph.D. dissertation, University of Wisconsin, 1968.
Gordon, Patricia Joan. "The Livingston Family of New York, 1675–1860: Kinship and Class." Ph.D. dissertation, Columbia University, 1959.
Lemon, James T. "A Rural Geography of Southeastern Pennsylvania in the Eighteenth Century: The Contributions of Cultural Inheritance, Social Structure, Economic Conditions and Physical Resources." Ph.D. dissertation, University of Wisconsin, 1964.
Weidman, John W. "The Economic Development of Pennsylvania until 1723." Ph.D. dissertation, University of Wisconsin, 1935.
Wood, Jerome Herman, Jr. "Conestoga Crossroads: The Rise of Lancaster, Pennsylvania, 1730–1789." Ph.D. dissertation, Brown University, 1969.

Index

Academy of Philadelphia, 85
Adams, John, 294
Adams, Margaret (Shippen) , 108, 211
adoption, informal, 219
Alford, John, 170
Allen, Andrew, 165, 171, 172, 184, 199,
    216, 298, 302
Allen, Andrew, Jr., 184
Allen, James, 171, 199, 265, 296
Allen, John, 102–103, 170, 171, 172, 176,
    199, 296
Allen, Margaret, 145
Allen, William, 7, 69–71, 73, 79, 81, 83,
    92, 97, 99, 102–103, 105, 108–109, 112,
    132, 135, 140, 146, 157, 159–161, 167–
    174, 197, 199, 216–217, 274, 292, 302
Allen, William, Jr., 184
Allen family, 168, 173, 175, 199, 285
Allen-Hamilton-Shippen kinship net-
    work, 154–155
Ambo, 59
America, 320
American Revolution, 8, 167
Amwell, N.J., 165, 176
Andre, John, 185, 190, 306
annuities. *See* inheritance
apprenticeship, 29, 32–33, 45, 77, 113,
    125, 141, 143
aristocracies: American, English, Euro-
    pean, 7, 37–38, 49, 65, 83, 108, 174,
    216, 292–293
Arnold, Benedict, 186, 188–190, 304–306
Arnold, Margaret (Shippen) , 153, 185,
    189–190, 210, 223, 285, 292, 304–306,
    311

Axford, Martha. *See* Shippen, Martha
    (Axford)

bachelorhood, 265. *See also* marriage
Baily, Henry, 53
Bailyn, Bernard, 3, 4, 272, 292, 296
Barclay and Son, 109
Bartholomew's Fair, 120
Barton, Mr., 134
Beardsley, Alexander, 23
bequest. *See* inheritance
Biddle, Mr., 147
bigamy, 70–71
birth control, 150–151, 285
Black Betty (Black Bess) , 28
Blair, Samuel, 128–129, 322
Blair, Samuel, Jr., 129
Blair, Susanna (Shippen) , 111, 127–
    129, 322
Booth's Academy, 215
Bordley, Aunt, 205, 213
Bordley, Stephen, 57
Borough Fair, 120
Boston, 6, 10–12, 15, 161–162, 294
Boston Tea Party, 161
Boyd plantation, 136
breast feeding, 151, 286
bride, pregnant, 25. *See also* marriage,
    pregnancy
Bridenbaugh, Carl, 3
Bristol, England, 272
Brown, Wallace, 300
Bucks County, 17
Budd, Mary, 69
Budd, Rose. *See* Rose (Budd) Shippen